SELLING

THE PERSONAL FORCE IN MARKETING

SELLING
THE PERSONAL FORCE IN MARKETING

Donald W. Jackson, Jr.
Arizona State University

William H. Cunningham
University of Texas at Austin

Isabella C. M. Cunningham
University of Texas at Austin

WILEY

JOHN WILEY & SONS
New York   Chichester   Brisbane
Toronto   Singapore

Library of Congress Cataloging in Publication Data:

Jackson, Donald W., 1944 –
    Selling: the personal force in marketing / by Donald W. Jackson, Jr.,
William H. Cunningham, Isabella C. M. Cunningham.
    p.   cm.

    Includes index.
    ISBN 0-471-86400-5
    1. Selling.   I. Cunningham, William Hughes.   II. Cunningham,
Isabella C. M.   III. Title.
HF5438.25.J33 1988
658.8'5—dc19

Printed in the United States of America

10 9 8 7 6 5 4 3 2

Dedicated to W. J. E. CRISSY
Scholar, consultant, mentor, friend

Photo Credits

About
the Authors

DONALD W. JACKSON, Jr. is currently professor of marketing and director of the M.B.A. for Executives Program at Arizona State University. He serves on the editorial boards of the *Journal of Marketing, Journal of Personal Selling and Sales Management*, and *Advances in Distribution Research* and is a member of the American Marketing Association, Southern Marketing Association, and Academy of Marketing Sciences. He has written numerous articles for professional and refereed journals, and he serves as a consultant to many firms, trade associations, and governmental agencies. His B.A. degree was awarded by Albion College, and his M.B.A. and Ph.D. degree were earned at Michigan State University.

WILLIAM CUNNINGHAM is currently President of The University of Texas at Austin and holds the Regents Chair in Higher Education Leadership. Before becoming President, he served as Dean of the College of Business Administration and Graduate School of Business and taught marketing.

He has served as editor of the *Journal of Marketing* and on the editorial review board of the *Journal of Marketing Research*. He is currently a member of the American Marketing Association, Southern Marketing Association, Southwest Social Science Association, Decision Sciences Institute, and Association of Consumer Research. He has contributed numerous articles to professional and refereed journals, coauthored several other texts, and consulted with many organizations. He received his B.A., M.B.A., and Ph.D. degrees from Michigan State University.

ISABELLA CUNNINGHAM is currently Ernest A. Sharpe Centennial Professor in Communications and professor of advertising at The University of Texas at Austin. She serves on the editorial boards of the *Journal of Advertising, Journal of Advertising Research, Current Issues in Research in Advertising, European Journal of Marketing*, and *Social Science Quarterly*. At present she is a member of the American Marketing Association, Brazilian Bar Association, Southern Marketing Association, American Academy of Advertising, Southwest Marketing Association, American Advertising Federation, and The Austin Advertising Club. She has written numerous articles for professional and refereed journals, and she has coauthored several books. She has a J.D. and an M.B.A. in marketing from Brazilian universities, as well as an M.B.A. and a Ph.D. in marketing from Michigan State University.

Preface

In view of the quantity and diversity of books on selling, it seems appropriate to describe the kind of book this is. We claim no "seven secrets of sales success." In fact, we do not think they exist. This book is neither cookbook nor handbook; rather it is a conceptually oriented treatment in depth of the dynamics of the selling–buying process. We hold that selling in the firm can be understood only as an integral part of the total marketing effort. We see members of the sales force both as the firm's representatives in the competitive marketplace and as managers of a business, their sales territories.

The text complements the classroom instructor in forming a learning system. Selling has both knowledge and skill ingredients. Skills are acquired only through practice. For this reason we provide an application exercise and cases for each chapter in the book.

The book is organized into eighteen chapters. To assist those who have not had a previous marketing course, we begin by discussing selling and how it fits in the marketing effort of the firm. *Chapters 1 and 2*, The Modern Salesperson and Selling and the Marketing Effort, discuss the various dimensions of sales positions and the relation between selling and the other functions of a marketing department. In order to obtain insight into what a salesperson does, it is important to know about the company's total marketing effort.

The next three chapters deal with self-management for the salesperson. *Chapter 3*, Setting Objectives: The First Step in Self-management, *Chapter 4*, Territory Management Strategies, and *Chapter 5*, Developing Account and Call Strategies, cover aspects of self-management critical to sales success. These steps must be taken if salespeople are to be prepared to make sales calls.

Chapter 6, Understanding the Buyer as an Individual, makes it clear that today's salesperson must have a firm foundation in the behavioral sciences in order to work effectively with customers. It is important to understand fundamental ideas about human behavior in order to appreciate the buying–selling process.

In *Chapter 7*, Different Approaches to Selling, various approaches to selling are identified, and situations in which each is important are described. Various selling styles are also described.

Chapters 8 through 14 cover various aspects of the actual sales call. The Contact, Sending Messages, Supporting Your Message: Visual Aids and Demonstrations, Securing Feedback, Adjusting to the Prospect, Handling Objections, and Closing and Postsale Activities. The crux of selling takes place when salespeople and buyers are face to face. Each of the critical aspects of the sales call must be handled well if a sale is to be made.

Chapter 15, Different Types of Selling Situations, examines how the principles, methods, and techniques discussed in the previous portions of the text can be applied in different selling situations. Retail selling, industrial selling, and selling in the service sector are covered.

In this age of increased selling costs, the telephone is an important sales tool to cut costs, save time, and increase productivity. Various aspects of using the telephone are examined in depth in *Chapter 16,* Using the Telephone in Selling.

Chapter 17, Legal and Ethical Dimensions of Selling, examines various legal constraints and highlights ethical dilemmas with respect to salespeople and their relations with their company, competitors, customers, and company resources.

In *Chapter 18,* Career Management, various aspects of finding a first job in selling are explored, as are career opportunities in selling and sales management. Finally, various aspects of career planning and continued self-development are examined.

January 1988

DONALD W. JACKSON, JR.
WILLIAM H. CUNNINGHAM
ISABELLA C. M. CUNNINGHAM

Acknowledgments

Special acknowledgment and thanks go to W. J. E. Crissy, who contributed a major portion of the previous edition of this text. Many of his ideas and contributions have stood the test of time and continue to appear in the present text. Bill Crissy was a knower and a doer. His contributions to the thinking of the authors were major. In addition, he served as a role model of the consummate professional salesperson. Previous editions of the text were also influenced by Robert M. Kaplan and Harold C. Cash, who worked with Bill Crissy. We would also like to thank the following individuals who contributed a substantial amount of time and effort to the text. Lynn Winkleman, DeAnn Clem and Debbie Ward worked tirelessly on the production of the manuscript. In addition, Nelda Crowell provided us with editorial assistance during the early stages of the manuscript. Finally, we would like to thank the reviewers for their insights and suggestions. The reviewers for the text included Professor Duane Bachman, Central Missouri State University; Professor Robert Collins, Oregon State University; Professor B. J. Dunlap, Appalachian State University; Professor Myron J. Leonard, West Carolina State University; Professor Lynn Louderback, New Mexico State University; Professor H. Reed Muller, Salisbury State College; Professor Jim Null, Memphis State University; Professor Lloyd Ott, Weber State College; Professor Ed Simpson, Miami University; Professor A. J. Wedell, Colorado State University; and Professor Thomas R. Wotruba, San Diego State University. These individuals greatly enhanced the quality of the book, and we are grateful for their efforts.

D. W. J. Jr
W. H. C.
I. C. M. C.

A Message
for the Student

Your course in selling should be one of the most stimulating and exciting college classroom learning experiences. No aspect of business is more creative or challenging than selling. In our competitive enterprise system the customer is "king." Each business, through its marketing and sales effort, seeks to have its products chosen over those of the competition. The personal selling effort is often the key means of accomplishing this.

The study of selling is useful for a variety of reasons. First, if you are contemplating a rewarding career in sales work, this course is a prime step toward professional preparation. Second, if you are entering the broad field of marketing, the study of selling can be extremely useful in understanding the behavior of others. If you plan to enter the business world in any capacity, it is important to understand as much as possible about the selling–buying process. Effective selling is a critical factor in the very survival of every business. No firm can exist without customers, and only effective selling can create and keep customers.

Several study aids are provided at the end of each chapter, in the form of chapter summaries and problems. In addition, each chapter has an application exercise which relates your knowledge of selling to actual selling in the real world. These exercises are followed by cases, which enable you to use creative thinking and problem solving in selling situations. If you thrive on challenges, enjoy problem solving, have a yen for the new, and want to be "your own person," a selling career may be just right for you.

As a reader you should think of yourself as a new salesperson in your first selling position. The book is written in the second person so that you can actually apply these concepts to a selling position.

Contents

The Modern
Salesperson

After studying this chapter, you should be able to

1. Understand why it is important to study selling.
2. Differentiate between traditional and modern views of selling.
3. Identify the various roles of the modern salesperson.
4. Recognize some differences in various sales jobs.
5. Specify qualities of a successful salesperson.
6. Point out some trends in modern selling.

**THE MODERN
SALESPERSON**

Personal selling consists of finding people who require your product or service, studying their needs, presenting your offering in such a way that your potential customers are convinced of its benefit to them, answering any objections they may have, asking for a commitment to close, and following up to ensure that those who have bought from you are satisfied. Truly professional selling is a process that fosters the development of a mutually beneficial relationship in which buyer and seller alike both profit and benefit. This mutually beneficial arrangement leads to long-term relationships, repeat business, and favorable word-of-mouth communication with other customers or prospects.

The need for effective selling has become urgent for several reasons. First, deregulation has made many industries very sales conscious, especially banks and telephone companies, which are now facing increased competition. Second, the average cost of an industrial sales call is $205, so employers want every call to count.[1]

REASONS TO STUDY SELLING

There are two good reasons why you should study selling. First, regardless of what line of work you choose, there is a need to sell your ideas to others, and second, there are numerous career opportunities in selling.

Everyone Is a Part-time Salesperson

Whether or not you pursue a career in selling, the principles and ideas contained in this book should prove useful to you. No matter what career you pursue, you will have to sell your ideas to family or friends or to higher management, to investors or to employees. For example, each of the following activities involves selling ideas or concepts.

- A person asks the boss for a raise.
- A manager tries to convince the president of the company to institute a new training program.
- Parents try to persuade their children to stay away from drugs.
- A boy asks a girl for a date.
- A sales manager tries to persuade salespeople that they can win a sales contest.
- An inventor tries to get a loan from a banker.

There is an old business axiom, "Nothing happens until a sale is made"; this axiom is equally true in activities other than selling. For instance, even with the best ideas in the world, if you cannot convince others of their worth, you will not get the opportunity to implement them.

Thus, learning to determine the other person's needs, to ask questions, to listen, to overcome objections, and to close will help you be a better

[1]Jeremy Main, "How to Sell by Listening," *Fortune*, Vol. 111, No. 3 (February 4, 1985), p. 52.

communicator, even if you do not end up in sales. In the event that you do become a salesperson, there will be a wealth of opportunities to apply the concepts you will learn in this book.

Career Opportunities in Selling

A career in sales enables a person to make social contributions, to continue to grow, to gain financial rewards, and to have freedom from direct supervision. A sales career also brings opportunities for advancement.

A social contribution As a salesperson you have an opportunity to make a genuine contribution to society. Effective selling is the key to our private enterprise economy: sales representatives provide the transactions that enable business to flourish. The professional salesperson sees the need for mutual profit in the selling–buying relationship and hence provides benefits to individuals and organizations by helping them to buy profitably. If sales were not being made, business would be at a standstill. In a sense, you create jobs for other individuals who make and use the products you sell.

Continuing growth You also have an opportunity to learn about many facets of business. Your work is likely to involve you in helping each of your customers and prospects to solve a variety of problems. In the process, you inevitably add to your own business knowledge. Contrast this learning with work that is done completely within the confines of a company and often solely within a single department. You can also directly apply your new knowledge in making additional sales. For instance, a salesperson selling a telephone system to an industrial user would have to be knowledgeable about the client's communication needs, expansion possibilities, and financing capabilities; moreover, while examining the firm's needs for a telephone system, the salesperson might uncover a need for computer terminals to assist in handling information.

Success in selling depends heavily on your continually improving your skills in handling people. In turn, these same skills provide you with a special talent that is useful in all your interpersonal relationships. Skill in dealing with people has applications in your home, with your friends and acquaintances, and in such nonwork pursuits as community organizations and church groups. These useful skills give you a competitive edge wherever people are to be understood and influenced. No other occupational field provides so great an opportunity to meet such a wide variety of people in an intimate, personal, persuasive relationship.

Field selling also provides abundant variety. The unexpected is to be expected; no two days are alike. Even the same account varies from call to call. In sustaining favorable selling–buying relations, you face new problems to solve and new applications for your creativity. Many salespeople also enjoy the variety encountered in traveling through their territories.

Financial rewards In addition to the substantial nonmaterial rewards, selling also provides an opportunity to make a good living. Table 1.1 illustrates the rise in the average salesperson's total compensation—from $22,359 in 1979 to $32,481 in 1985. During the same period, the average senior salesperson's compensation increased to $41,403, and the average sales supervisor's compensation climbed to $48,863.

Related to this rise in financial expectations is the fact that many sales representatives are compensated in proportion to the results they achieve. Even when compensation is in the form of straight salary, raises are earned on the basis of personal performance. Incomes in sales—both initially and over time—are higher than in most other occupations.

It is interesting to note how sales representatives are paid. A study by *Sales and Marketing Management* Magazine (Table 1.2) found that only 17 percent of the nation's sales representatives are paid on a straight salary; 36 percent are paid on a salary-plus-bonus plan; 31 percent on a salary-plus-commission plan; and 9 percent on a salary-plus-commission, plus-bonus plan. In the salary-plus-bonus system, you receive additional compensation based on a more subjective evaluation than the commission arrangement. With a bonus system, your firm's management will examine such factors as how hard you work, how much new business you have created, and how you handle customer complaints. With the salary-plus-commission system, you are normally paid your commission strictly on the basis of how much you sell during a particular time period. Only 7 percent of the sales representatives surveyed were paid strictly on commission; here the salespeople are allowed to draw a specified amount against the commissions they earn for selling, so that they can "smooth out" their take-home pay.

TABLE 1.1
HOW SALESPEOPLE'S TOTAL COMPENSATION IS GROWING[a]

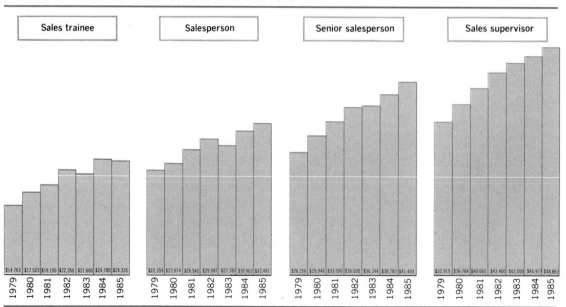

[a]This survey included account representatives and sales engineers, as well as retail, industrial products, nontechnical, and service salespeople.

SOURCE: Sales and Marketing Management, (February 17, 1986), p. 54.

A LOOK AT SOME TOP
SALES PERFORMERS

TOM OLDS

Tom Olds is both a C.P.A. and an M.B.A., and he makes between $50,000 and $100,000 a month selling wind turbines for ZOND in Southern California. The biggest challenge, he has found, is customer unfamiliarity with technical aspects of the equipment and its reliability. Olds believes that selling is really just helping people. "I could never sell something I didn't believe in 100 percent. If you don't feel this way, you'll never be able to talk to someone who might be worth $20 million or $30 million and not be overwhelmed by the difference between your position in life and his."

SHARON SNOWDEN

Sharon Snowden was the top salesperson for the biggest distributor of Sharp photocopiers in the United States, often taking home $7000 a month. She now sells word-processing systems for Lanier Business Products. After teaching school for several years, she finally decided that, "I wanted more freedom to set my own schedule, to grow and be rewarded based on performance rather than seniority." Her sales philosophy, she says, is that "I never sell price. I sell service, reliability, and the fact that our company is honest and sound . . . I love sales. It is the ultimate challenge."

BEN FELDMAN

Ben Feldman has sold nearly a billion dollars' worth of life insurance, mostly for New York Life, since 1960. His toughest sale, he says, was to the chief executive officer of a major corporation who insisted he was too busy to see any life insurance man. Feldman handed the secretary an envelope containing five $100 bills and asked for five minutes of the man's time. He got it and eventually sold him more than $50 million worth of life insurance. Asked about his greatest sale, Feldman, now 71, insists, "I don't know. I haven't made it yet."

DON POKORNI

Don Pokorni, a successful salesman of commercial and industrial real estate in Southern California, earns an annual income in the six figures. He explains his sales philosophy this way: "Most people in my field concentrate on listing properties or selling them. I work the other side of the street, concentrating on human relationships. I meet executives who might not have a current need; I get to know them, their business and their requirements very well. Then, when they have a need, I am the obvious choice to call, since I am able to fill their needs quickly and to their exact specifications. This approach takes more time, but it leads to the best deals and to the most lasting business relationships."

SOURCE: Donald J. Moine, "Going for the Gold in the Selling Game," *Psychology Today* (March 1984), pp. 36 – 44. Reprinted with permission from *Psychology Today* magazine. Copyright © 1984, by the American Psychological Association.

TABLE 1.2

TYPES OF COMPENSATION EARNED BY SALES PEOPLE

COMPENSATION TYPES	PERCENTAGE OF RESPONDENTS
Salary only	17.4
Draw against commission	6.5
Salary plus commission	30.7
Salary plus individual bonus	33.7
Salary plus group bonus	2.7
Salary plus commission and bonus	9.0
Total	100.0

SOURCE: "Survey of Selling Costs," *Sales and Marketing Management,* Vol. 136, No. 3, (February 7, 1986), p. 57. Bill Communications Corp.

Freedom from direct supervision Perhaps no other career affords the same opportunity to be independent of direct supervision as does a selling career. To a great extent, you are master of your own destiny. Many individuals do not like to be closely supervised, and many sales positions offer a unique opportunity to be as independent as possible, while still having the advantages of working for an organization. As an example, many sales representatives plan their own schedules. They may work irregular hours. They do not punch a time clock, and in fact they may go for several weeks without face-to-face contact with their superior. If you want to be your own boss, selling comes closer to giving you the independence you need than do most other positions within an organization.

Opportunities for advancement Sales positions also offer a good starting ground for many types of managerial positions. Most marketing management people have had sales experience; indeed, selling is the entry-level position for almost all marketing management or sales management positions. The knowledge of customers and their behavior gained from sales is invaluable. Sales jobs are usually characterized by clearly identifiable results, which makes it easy to identify high performers and groom them for management positions.

Many top-level managerial positions are also being filled by people with sales or marketing backgrounds. One study, for example, found that chief executive officers were more likely to come from marketing and sales backgrounds than any other discipline.[2]

Salespeople may also advance to more senior sales positions when they acquire more lucrative territories or advance to positions such as national accounts salesperson or headquarters salesperson.

[2]See "What Is the Fastest Track to the Executive Suite? Sales/Marketing," *Marketing News,* Vol. 17 (July 6, 1984), p. 7.

Differences Between Traditional and Modern Selling

The job of the modern salesperson is very different from selling jobs in the past. The differences between the traditional and modern approaches are shown in Table 1.3.

As shown in Table 1.3, the traditional approach was very salesperson-oriented; it tried to create needs in customers by talking at them. The goal was to make sales, and the approach was not very flexible. On the other hand, the modern view is that selling should be customer-oriented and the salesperson should try to discover customers' needs by discussing their situation with them. The goal of modern selling is to build long-term relationships and to create customers who will be involved in repeat business, as opposed to just generating sales. This approach is very flexible because it can adapt to the unique needs and situation of the customer.

Roles of the Modern Salesperson

As a modern salesperson, you must assume a number of roles if you are to be successful. Although their importance differs with various types of sales positions, these roles do illustrate the divergent aspects of selling.

Educator One of your key roles as a salesperson is to educate your customers about new products, services, processes, or approaches to doing business. In a complex, technical world such as ours, it is important to keep customers and prospects learning about changes that are taking place.[3] The better you are able to educate your customers about your firm's offerings, the more successful you will be as a salesperson.

Change agent Since new products, services, processes, or approaches reach your customers through you, you are acting as a change agent, seeing that

TABLE 1.3
TRADITIONAL SELLING VERSUS MODERN SELLING

TRADITIONAL SELLING	MODERN SELLING
Is salesperson-oriented	Is customer-oriented
Creates needs	Discovers needs
Talks at customers	Discusses with customer
Makes sales	Makes customers
Is inflexible	Is adaptable

SOURCE: Adapted from Anthony J. Alessandra and Phillip S. Wexler, *Non-Manipulative Selling* (New York, NY: Prentice Hall Press, 1975), p. 6.

[3]Stewart Henderson Britt, "Applying Learning Principles to Marketing," *MSU Business Topics*, Vol. 23, No. 2 (Spring 1975), pp. 5–12.

your firm's new products are introduced into your customer's business as smoothly as possible. The considerable research that has been done on change agents has revealed that a change agent's success is positively related to several factors: the person's efforts, the person's client orientation, the extent to which the change agent's program is compatible with the client's needs, the change agent's empathy with clients, and the change agent's similarity to clients.[4] Although these findings were not generated from sales situations, they do offer some insight into qualities of a successful salesperson.

Problem solver One of the key contributions of the modern salesperson is identifying and solving customer problems. As a problem solver you identify the prospect's needs, assist in listing possible solutions to these needs, work with the prospect to evaluate the advantages and disadvantages of each alternative, help select the best alternative, and thus help solve the customer's problem.

The problem-solving role was exhibited by a salesperson for a copier supplier. She found that one of her prospects did not have enough room in the office for the machine that best suited the prospect's needs. By having a special shelf built for her company's machine at her own expense, she solved the customer's space problem and made a sale she otherwise would not have made.

Innovator One trait that distinguishes outstanding salespeople is their knack for innovation. Success depends on seeking out new ways to do business and not being content with old approaches.[5] For example, Paul Johnson of Johnson Industrial Sales was able to improve the static shielding in a cable. As a

---

A MODERN PROFESSIONAL APPROACH TO SELLING

We don't create needs, but we make prospects aware of existing needs and enhance their desire to satisfy those needs. The transition from relating benefits to mutually agreed upon criteria to closing is smooth and natural. We perform a real and valuable service to our customers. We are proud to be professional salespeople.

SOURCE: Reprinted by permission of Gestetner Corporation.

---

[4]See Everett M. Rogers, *Diffusion of Innovations,* third edition (New York: Free Press, 1983), pp. 317–324.

[5]For a discussion of how to influence the adoption of an innovation, see Samuel Rabino, "Influencing the Adoption of an Innovation," *Industrial Marketing Management,* Vol. 12, No. 4 (October 1983), pp. 233–241.

A salesperson educating prospects.

producer of audio components, he suggested changing from a cotton filler (the material between the wire and the outer plastic jacket) to polyethylene. The results were less static crackling, fewer breakages in the customer's operation, easier availability, and reduced costs.[6]

Manager As a salesperson, you must manage your time and territory. You must set objectives, develop strategies, and evaluate your results—all management tasks. Because you do not have direct ongoing supervision while you are in the field, you must manage yourself. It is useful to think of your territory as a small business that must be managed like any other business. Given the high cost of selling and the rapidly changing environment, this territory management takes on increased importance.

Communicator Most people, if asked to identify the outstanding trait of salespeople, would probably respond that salespeople are talkers; they are able to express themselves well. Yet the modern view of selling encompasses a much broader communications task. As a salesperson, you must discover your customers' needs, which means asking the right questions, listening, and interpreting nonverbal communications. In addition, you must adjust your vocabulary and the content of your presentation, depending on the back-

[6]Somerby Dowst, "Complete Salesmanship: That's What Buyers Appreciate," *Purchasing*, Vol. 97, No. 4 (August 16, 1984), p. 60.

ground and interests of your audience. Thus, your communication role is much broader than merely being an effective talker.

Researcher Modern selling has many research-oriented components. In order to determine customers' needs or to qualify them as prospects, it is often necessary for you to do library research as well as to study the current position of the firm in question. Some firms actually conduct surveys of their customers' needs.[7] Finally, given your close contact with customers, you are in a unique position to conduct informal marketing research: eliciting customer reactions to new products, distribution, or promotions. This informal research is an important source of information for your company.

Informant When you have market information from your territory, it is important that you provide this information to your company.[8] An informed management can make appropriate adjustments in strategy. How, for instance, do product managers in the home office in New York find out that there is a competitor's test market in Peoria, Illinois? They find out through the sales force. Aladdan Synergestics, a producer of food service products and systems, even paid its salespeople for providing marketing intelligence.[9]

One study of salespeople collecting information revealed that the data often came in too late to be useful, were distorted, or were not sent back at all.[10] Another study found that only 14 percent of the sales force reported back about the introduction of a new competitive product.[11] You can provide valuable information to your firm if you report what goes on in your territory to them. At Warner Electric Brake and Clutch, one part of the salesperson's monthly report is a list of the three best potential-product ideas (either new products or product line extensions) heard about from customers.[12]

Forecaster An important role you can play is to forecast sales in your territory. You are in a unique position to know the specifics about how each customer in your territory will behave. You might know, for example, that one customer is planning on greatly expanding operations, whereas another is having labor problems and is facing a strike. This knowledge allows you to

---

[7]For a review of the use and role of the sales force as an extension of the marketing research function, see David Grace and Tom Pointon, "Marketing Research Through the Salesforce," *Industrial Marketing Management,* Vol. 9, No. 4 (Fall 1980), pp. 53–58.

[8]See, for example, Kenneth R. Evans and John L. Schlacter, "The Role of Sales Managers and Salespeople in a Marketing Information System," *Journal of Personal Selling and Sales Management,* Vol. 5, No. 2 (November 1985), pp. 49–58.

[9]Al Prillaman, "Aladdan Puts a Bounty on Marketing Intelligence," *Sales and Marketing Management,* Vol. 126, No. 5 (April 6, 1981), pp. 66–68.

[10]Gerald Albaum, "Horizontal Information Flow," *Journal of the Academy of Management,* Vol. 7, No. 1 (1964), pp. 21–33.

[11]See Dan H. Robertson, "Communication and Salesforce Feedback," *Journal of Business Communication,* Vol. 11 (1974), pp. 3–9.

[12]Tom Peters and Nancy Austin, *A Passion for Excellence* (New York: Random House, 1985), p. 26.

forecast developments in your territory. Many companies count on utilizing information from salespeople as one input to their sales forecast.

Modifier Because you see customers' reactions to products as well as how they actually use products, you may be able to suggest modifications in products that will make them more useful to your customers. Feedback from customers led one materials-handling salesperson to suggest a new line of shelving that was much narrower. The new line soon became one of the company's best sellers because it saved valuable space for customers. By the same token, on the basis of customers' reactions to your company's policies, you may be able to suggest changes in policies that would serve the customers' needs better.

Psychologist As a salesperson, you are dealing with people. Therefore, you must have an understanding of how people think, feel, and act.[13] This sensitivity and understanding of people is critical to sales success. Thus, a great deal of this book is dedicated to the psychology of selling. In addition to the many roles of the modern salesperson, there are also a number of dimensions that differentiate types of sales positions.

DIFFERENT TYPES OF SALES POSITIONS

In considering selling as a career, you will want to explore different types of sales positions. These can vary from retail selling to selling industrial equipment worth hundreds of thousands of dollars.

Classification of Sales Positions

There is no one classification that adequately describes all sales representatives or their activities. However, it is useful to examine various types of sales positions in order to see the diverse nature of opportunities in selling.

Route selling The primary job of route salespeople is delivering merchandise. Bread, heating oil, newspapers, and milk are examples of products sold in this manner. Although good service and a pleasant manner will increase sales, your selling responsibilities are of secondary importance and few new accounts will generally be obtained.

Retail selling Clerks in department stores, clothing stores, specialty shops, and appliance shops are retail salespeople. Most retail salespeople function mainly as order takers; however, many retailing careers start out with selling positions. In addition, a position as a clerk gives you an opportunity to distinguish yourself from other retail salespeople if you are knowledgeable, dependable, and customer-oriented. More information about retail selling is given in Chapter 15.

---

[13]See Sally Scanlon, "Every Salesperson a Psychologist," *Sales and Marketing Management,* Vol. 120, No. 2 (February 6, 1978), pp. 34–36.

The retail salesperson.

Inside order taking Examples of jobs in which orders are taken inside would be working in the parts department in an automobile dealership, or working for a steel service center taking orders for steel. If you accept a position as an inside salesperson, you typically do not leave your place of business, and customers have virtually made up their minds about what they want before they talk with you.[14] Often the inside salesperson's primary way of doing business is via the telephone. Although inside salespeople may offer suggestions at times regarding what other individuals have bought, they seldom try to convince the customer to upgrade the quality of merchandise asked for or to make additional purchases.

Trade selling In trade selling the salesperson works in the field and calls on individual retail stores. Products sold in this manner include food and household products. Many salespeople working for wholesalers could also be classified as trade salespeople. In this type of job, you would seldom attempt to sell anything to the customer that does not already appear on the shelf with the exception of new products, which you would introduce. However, you might get involved in setting up displays or rotating stocks or selling customers on cooperative advertising. You might also help train customer personnel

[14]For a discussion on the changing role of the inside salesperson, see Ben M. Enis, "Role Gap Narrows Between Inside and Outside Industrial Salespersons," *Marketing News,* Vol. 13 (April 4, 1980), p. 3; or James A. Narus and James C. Anderson, "Industrial Distributor Selling: The Roles of Outside and Inside Sales," *Industrial Marketing Management,* Vol. 15, No. 1 (February, 1986), pp. 55–62; or "48 Ways to Use Inside Sales," *Industrial Distribution,* Vol. 72, No. 5 (May 1982), pp. 101–105.

in how to use, sell, or care for your products. In this job, as in the job of the
delivery salesperson, you will be more successful if you have a pleasant personality, are dependable, and offer your customers good service.

Missionary selling Missionary salespeople are not expected to make a sale
but are expected to call on customers to build goodwill. In industrial selling,
these people are often called factory representatives. An example would be a
salesperson of a major rubber company, who calls on distributors' accounts.
Your function in such a position would be to try to build the confidence of
the accounts in the rubber company so that they will purchase rubber products through your distributor, to help the distributor with inventory control,
to provide technical assistance, and to help train distributor salespeople. As
a missionary salesperson, if you received an order, you would turn it over to
your distributor. Frequently, you and the representative of the local distributor
would make joint calls, visiting the distributors together. Another example of
a missionary salesperson would be a "detail person" who represents pharmaceutical companies and calls on doctors to try to get them to prescribe
certain drugs.

Technical selling In technical selling, the greatest emphasis is placed on
technical knowledge. The product to be sold may be used in manufacturing
or research departments of a company. Sometimes the person doing the selling is referred to as a sales engineer. Normally, you would have acquired a
substantial amount of technical training in addition to your college or university education. Products such as electronics would be sold by technical salespeople. Another example would be a materials-handling salesperson. If you
accepted this type of job, you would spend a great deal of time designing
systems that would solve the peculiar problems of your various customers.
Your technical knowledge would be vital to your success. More information
on industrial selling can be found in Chapter 15.

Selling of tangibles Sales representatives for copy machines, word proces-
sors, or office furniture are selling tangibles. These positions frequently have
a dual task. First, the salesperson must convince prospects that their present
merchandise does not serve their needs; then he or she must sell prospects
the particular product.

Selling of intangibles Insurance, financial services, advertising, and consulting are all intangibles. Selling them is the most difficult because the service
cannot be readily demonstrated or dramatized. If you took a job selling services, you would have to sell yourself and your company's reputation as well
as the service you want the prospect to buy. More can be found on selling
services in Chapter 15.

Additional Dimensions of the Sales Position
Although the classification given is useful, other factors also significantly affect the nature of the sales job. Among them are the types of accounts, types
of customers within accounts, types of products, size of order, degree of
problem solving, geographical areas, and nonselling duties.

Types of accounts Selling jobs vary according to the types of accounts being cultivated. At one extreme, you might call on households as buying units; at the other extreme, you might call on only large manufacturing establishments. Another way to look at types of accounts is according to their variation within a territory. Variablity of accounts is an important dimension on which to differentiate many selling jobs. One salesperson might be expected to call on small machine shops as well as large manufacturers, whereas another salesperson might have only one major customer. Selling jobs within the same company may vary greatly in this way. For example, in a large, dense market, considerable specialization of sales staff according to type of clientele is feasible, whereas in a smaller, widely dispersed market, a salesperson for the same firm may have to call on everyone who is a customer or prospective customer for any of the firm's products.

Some firms even go so far as to segment their sales territory by type of account. You may have precisely defined categories of customers and prospects to call on, and your territory may overlap geographically with several other territories. For instance, within a particular geographical area, a computer company may have one salesperson who specializes in financial institutions and one who specializes in retailers. As more technical knowledge is required to understand the uses of the firm's products, there is likely to be greater segmentation by the type of account in the market.

Types of customers within accounts Related to the dimension of variability of accounts is variability of people within the individual account. At one extreme, you might call on only the purchasing agent. At the other extreme, you might have to call on purchasing agents, operating personnel, research and development specialists, and other members of management in order to make sales.

One type of salesperson in industrial selling, the executive salesperson, sells products or services to executives. Examples of products sold in this manner are computers, consulting services, and employees' insurance programs. The products and services are usually not component parts or materials, but are more likely to be equipment or services. Executive salespeople call on executives such as controllers, personnel managers, or data-processing managers.

The range in level of sophistication of persons called on within accounts makes up another significant dimension. For example, as an industrial salesperson, you might well have to present products and service to people on the production line as well as to top executives. In contrast, as a salesperson for a clothing manufacturer, you might call on department and specialty store buyers who are relatively similar in their knowledge and sophistication. Customers might also vary significantly with respect to their formal education. If you were selling to a chemical firm, you might deal routinely with people who have doctorates, whereas if you were calling on building contractors, you might meet with very successful people who have little formal education.

Types of products Another factor that differentiates various sales jobs is types of products handled. Sales positions may differ with respect to the extent of the product line and the required service.

The extent of the product line is the number of different products you carry. For instance, if you worked for an electronics distributor, you might have 5000 catalog entries to handle, whereas if you worked for a soft drink bottler, you would have a relatively narrow line of soft drinks. This dimension would most likely be reflected in the structure of the field sales force of an individual firm. The company that has a diverse line of products often differentiates the selling jobs by major product groupings. The rationale for this differentation is that one salesperson cannot possibly understand all the products in sufficient depth to sell them effectively. The degree of product specialization is likely to be directly related to the extent and complexity of the technical knowledge required to understand and use the product and the size of the order generally received. Products ordered in small volume will typically be grouped together and might be sold by a manufacturer's representative (who represents the manufacturer and is paid a commission) or a distributor who stocks the product for resale.

Another aspect of the product is the ratio of service to product in the offering to be sold. The offering might include the product alone, with minimal service or you might have to provide considerable advice and service before the sale, in order to generate the business, and again after the sale as part of what has been purchased. Within the same industry, there may be considerable differences on this dimension. Competitor A may make service an important part of the selling job. Competitor B may have a separate field service organization, involving sales personnel only incidentally in a supportive capacity.

Size of order Considerable variation exists in the size of an order. If you sold only large machines to manufacturers, each transaction would involve thousands of dollars. For instance, one salesperson made only three sales of supercomputers in 1985 and yet probably earned over $250,000. In this company one of the supercomputers might cost up to $20 million.[15] On the other hand, if you sell certain supplies, an order may not exceed $100. This dimension, in turn, influences not only the time and investment in each account, but also the number of customers and prospects constituting a sales territory. The larger the transaction, the greater is your selling time and the fewer accounts you will be able to handle.

Degree of problem solving Sales jobs can be differentiated according to the degree of problem solving required in the use of the products and services. If you work for a computer firm, you might have to make a detailed analysis of likely uses of equipment in order to sell it. In contrast, if you work for a firm offering office supplies, you would seldom have to prove the usefulness of your products. In markets where problem solving is an important consideration, firms are likely to provide you with considerable technical assistance. However, you must still be sufficiently adept as a problem solver to define problems and know what talents within the company are needed to solve them.

---

[15]"Where Three Sales a Year Make You a Superstar," *Business Week,* No. 2933 (February 17, 1986), pp. 76–77.

Geographical areas Sales jobs vary dramatically in the size of the geographical areas covered. Some sales territories could be composed of several states, or, in the extreme, the entire country; other territories could be as small as several square blocks of a large city. The amount of travel and the number of sales calls that you can make will vary considerably, depending on the size of the geographical area of your territory.

Nonselling duties Selling jobs also vary in the number and complexity of their nonselling duties. One salesperson might be furnished with clerical and technical support so that more time can be devoted to making actual calls. Another salesperson, in addition to making calls, might have responsibility for collecting bills, doing preliminary design on proposals, participating in dealers' sales meetings, and helping retailers with displays.

QUALITIES OF A SUCCESSFUL SALESPERSON

Occupations in selling range from the retail sales clerk behind the counter to the industrial salesperson. Formal education requirements may range from a high school diploma to advanced degrees, depending on the technical nature of the product line and the sophistication of the customers. A wide range of individual differences in age, experience, education, and other factors is evident even among sales personnel of the same firm, and no set pattern of talents, traits, and motives necessarily spells success. However, despite this diversity, a number of traits seem to be characteristic of successful sales representatives.

Intelligence
In general, the more technical your product line and the more sophisticated your clients, the greater is your need for a high level of intelligence. Intelligence is needed to master information about your company's products and to cope with the problems of their use. In addition, you must be able to communicate with sophisticated decision makers. Special aptitudes may be needed, depending on both the nature of the products and the uses and applications associated with them. For example, selling construction equipment may require mechanical abilities, whereas selling interior decorating services may put a premium on artistic aptitude.

Knowledge
The amount and kind of education you need, like the level of intelligence, depends on the technical nature of the selling job and the level of sophistication of your customers and prospects. Any salesperson, of course, has to have knowledge beyond that obtained in school. In fact, in some selling fields such as investments, information is accumulating so rapidly that substantial time must be devoted each week merely to keeping up.

The knowledge needed for any selling job may be thought of as three-dimensional: general knowledge, business knowledge, and technical knowledge. The amount of *general knowledge* required is mainly related to the

BUYERS RATE SALESPEOPLE: HERE'S WHAT THEY LIKED

A sample of 300 purchasing managers was asked to identify the outstanding characteristics of the salesperson they liked best. These were the characteristics attributed to the outstanding salespeople.

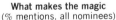

What makes the magic
(% mentions, all nominees)

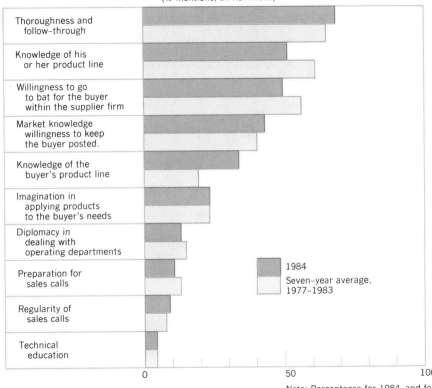

Note: Percentages for 1984, and for seven-year average, total 300 because respondents were asked to check three outstanding characteristics for their nominees.

SOURCE: Somerby Dowst, "Complete Salesmanship: That's What Buyers Appreciate," *Purchasing*, Vol. 97 (August 16, 1984), p. 62. Reprinted with permission from *Purchasing* magazine. Copyright © 1984, by Cahners Publishing Company.

background of your customers and prospects. It provides you with something in common with the prospect. The amount of *business knowledge* required is related to the nature of your accounts and the importance of the product line from the standpoint of the customers and prospects. For example, as an industrial salesperson handling heavy machinery that requires large capital investments, you would need more knowledge of finances and accounting than would someone selling business forms, for which financing is much less important. The *technical knowledge* required also varies according to the different marketing practices adopted by firms. It is not uncommon for a firm to follow up on an initial sales presentation with a team of engineers or trained technicians who demonstrate the product. Your job would be limited to knowing the factors that might make the product desirable for the client.

Verbal Skills

The ability to communicate verbally is universally required in all fields of selling. In no other occupational field is this ability as crucial to success. Your skill in verbal communication depends on having an adequate vocabulary, selecting the most effective ways of phrasing ideas, and developing voice qualities that enable your message to be conveyed with clarity, sincerity, and conviction.

Feedback Skills

In addition to verbal skills, you also need feedback skills to get information from customers and prospects. These consist of *questioning techniques* designed to get information from the prospect, *listening skills* that allow you to take this information in and process it, and the ability to *monitor* the *nonverbal communications* of the prospect. Most products and services today are bought for a variety of reasons, and identifying the prospect's motives and interests is critical.

Planning Skills

Planning is essential in all fields of selling. However, several factors influence the amount or level of planning needed and its importance to your success. First, the more decentralized the sales organization, the more important it is for you to be a good planner. As you are given increased authority to act on behalf of the company, greater care must be taken in planning actions and commitments. Second, the less supervision there is, the greater the need to be good at self-supervising and, consequently, the more important it is to be skillful in planning your own work. Third, the more complex the selling–buying relation, the more need there is for skillful planning. A higher level of planning skill is needed to determine the key decision makers in a large corporation than to influence an individual prospect or customer. Fourth, the more drawn out negotiations are likely to be, the greater is the need for planning. Thus, if you must conduct several calls to achieve a purchase, you should plan carefully to make each call count and each enhance the previous contacts. The wide scope of your planning encompasses the ways you will cover your territory and manage each account, your plans for specific calls, identifying the key decision makers to be influenced, and management of you time.

Personality

Several personality traits that are desirable in a salesperson are social sensitivity, flexibility, durability in relationships, empathy, drive, enthusiasm, and motivation.

Social sensitivity You must possess a considerable amount of social sensitivity—being "others-conscious," not "self-conscious." This is the ability to pick up small changes in other persons' reactions and to develop empathy with them.

Flexibility Just as important as social sensitivity is a capacity for flexibility or the ability to adjust to the other person. It would be useless for you to note changes in the other person's reactions and not be able to adjust effectively to them. This does not mean that you are putting on an act. The effective salesperson is flexible enough to adjust to a wide variety of reactions in the other person. But your behavior must not seem contrived or phoney.

Durability in relationships Since you must sustain personal relationships over time, it is important to be able to maintain long-term people relationships. Being dependable, following up, and being knowledgeable are all qualities that enable you to "wear well" with your customers.

Empathy Another key trait is empathy, that is, the ability actually to sense the feelings and thoughts of others and to relate to them. This ability to pick up feedback from others and to relate to them is very important, because it allows you to adjust and modify your strategy based on the buyers' reactions.[16]

Drive Another desirable personality trait is drive. As a salesperson you may have to keep long, irregular hours as well as almost daily adjusting to the frustration of refusals and unexpected competitive behavior. You must also face uncontrollable factors that upset your plans and still have sufficient physical and psychological energy to cope with challenges. You must be able to direct your energy toward worthwhile goals and to reset goals as the need occurs. Finally, you must have as much enthusiasm on the last call of the day as on the first call in the morning.

Enthusiasm Another quality of successful salespeople is enthusiasm. This quality generally shows up in three ways: in a general positive attitude, in enthusiasm toward your job, and in enthusiasm toward your products or services. If you have a generally positive attitude toward your life and the things that go on around you, this will transfer to your customers: enthusiasm is contagious.

Selling activities, particularly those conducted face to face, should have a high level of interest for you if you are to be effective. If selling is fun, you

[16]See, for example, Jeanne Greenberg and Herbert Greenberg, "The Personality of a Top Salesperson," *Nation's Business,* Vol. 71, No. 12 (December 1983), pp. 30–32.

can show enthusiasm for your job, which in turn will have a favorable influence on your customers or prospects.

Finally, you should also be enthusiastic toward your product line. If you are sold on your product line, it will be much easier for you to sell it to others.

Motivation As a salesperson, you will probably have a strong urge to achieve success and to score victories over the competition. Each of your accomplishments sets the stage for seeking new ones.

A salesperson works in an environment of change; therefore, you must find much of your personal security within yourself. If you are to be effective in your work, you have to see change as a challenge rather than a problem. You will have to view each unanticipated event or reaction as a chance to display your skill and your ability to cope with change.

SOME TRENDS IN SELLING

In this section several current trends in selling are discussed. These are not the only trends or are they characteristic of all selling, but they may give you a flavor of some changes that are taking place. These trends include greater numbers of women in selling, increased use of personal computers, greater use of the telephone, people-oriented training, a stress on building relationships, and reliance on a national accounts sales force.

Women in Selling

Until quite recently field selling jobs have been open only to men, but an increasing number of women are being employed for these jobs today.[17] For instance, in October 1982 there were 207,000 women employed as salespeople, selling commodities other than retail products; in October 1985 there were 252,000, for an increase of 22 percent.[18] Individual companies are also finding that they are hiring more women as salespeople. For example, Johnson and Johnson, a diversified marketer of medical and pharmaceutical supplies and consumer products, had 17.6 percent women on the sales force in 1978 and 31 percent in 1984.[19]

Many feel woman have an advantage in selling because their social nurturing seems to make them good with people.[20] A study of 3000 sales

---

[17]See, for example, Robert N. Carter and Milton R. Bryant, "Women as Industrial Sales Representatives," *Industrial Marketing Management,* Vol. 9, No. 1 (February 9, 1980), pp. 23–26; or Connie McClung Siegel, "The Risks and Rewards of a Sales Career," *Cosmopolitan,* Vol. 193, No. 3 (September 1982), pp. 138–147.

[18]*Employment and Earnings,* Bureau of Labor Statistics, U.S. Department of Labor, Vol. 32, No. 11 (November 1985), p. 28; and idem, Vol. 30, No. 11 (November 1983), p. 27.

[19]Rayna Skolnik, "A Woman's Place Is on the Sales Force," *Sales and Marketing Management,* Vol. 134, No. 3 (August 16, 1985), p. 34.

[20]Robert N. Carter and Milton R. Bryant, "Women as Industrial Sales Representatives," *Industrial Marketing Management,* Vol. 9, No. 1 (February 9, 1980), p. 26.

More women are entering careers as salespeople.

managers who were members of the Sales Executives Club of New York found that sales managers thought that women tended to follow through better than men, had a better attitude, and were superior to men in reliability.[21]

Use of Personal Computers

More than ever, salespeople are using personal computers. Some salespeople have them in the office, some at home, and some are taking them on the road. Portable computers, many no larger than a small briefcase, are being used for order tracking, inventory information, lead tracking, and electronic mail, and as a tickler file to aid in time management.[22]

The womenswear division of Wrangler found portable computers to be useful. With the help of computers, they developed an information system able to tell which of the companies' product lines was available for shipment.

---

[21]Howard Niles, "Sales Jobs Open Up for Women," *Dun's Review*, Vol. 11, No. 3 (March 1978), p. 86.

[22]Peter Finch, "How Computers Are Reshaping the Sales Process," *Business Marketing*, Vol. 70, No. 6 (June 1985), p. 110.

This knowledge kept customers from ordering merchandise that could not be delivered and kept salespeople from losing commissions.[23]

Other companies have personal computers available for all or some of their sales forces. American Hospital Supply, for instance, offers to sell to its salespeople a system that allows them to enter orders, keep files on customers, send out mass mailings, and research and prepare customer bids.[24]

Another company that has a computerized system for their salespeople is PPG. Figure 1.1 gives an example of the information that is available to their salespeople from the system.

One example of the types of programs that can accompany a personal computer is electronic mail. Salespeople can receive messages, enter orders, obtain information, and find out about order lead times. These programs can improve productivity and improve customer service.

For salespeople who spend a great deal of time on the telephone, there is a software progam called Exsell, which turns a computer into an integrated telemarketing workstation. It organizes customer and prospect data, prints labels, prints reports, and keeps records.[25] The point of all this is that salespeople are finding many uses for personal computers. As costs of hardware and software come down, as more software becomes available, and as personal computers become more portable, they will be more and more useful as aids to salespeople.

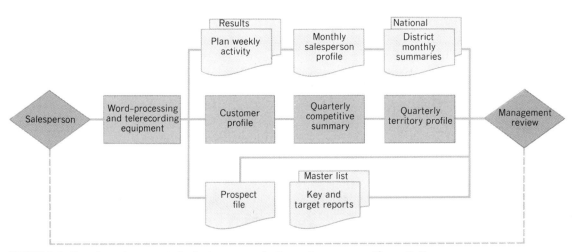

FIGURE 1.1 Flowchart of a computerized sales communication system. SOURCE: Thayer C. Taylor, "Paperless Call Reports Bring PPG More Data," *Sales and Marketing Management*, Vol. 132, No. 1 (December 5, 1983), p. 54.

[23]Thayer C. Taylor, "The Wrangler Lap-Top Experiment," *Sales and Marketing Management*, Vol. 134, No. 7 (May 13, 1985), pp. 54–56.

[24]Peter Finch, "How Computers Are Reshaping the Sales Process," *Business Marketing*, Vol. 70, No. 6 (June 1985), p. 116.

[25]Ibid. p. 118.

The telephone can increase a salesperson's productivity.

Use of Telephone

As sales costs soar, using the telephone to make appointments, call on small accounts, follow up, and fill in orders is increasingly important.[26] McGraw-Hill projects an eightfold increase in the number of telephone sales representatives between 1984 and 1990, primarily because of a higher level of consumer acceptance of doing business over the telephone.[27]

Although the telephone cannot replace face-to-face contact with customers it can be a useful way for the salesperson to prospect, make appointments, qualify leads, handle smaller accounts, follow up, handle small orders, and field complaints and inquiries. Using the telephone can increase productivity by saving travel time and by increasing the number of calls a salesperson can make. One salesperson for a firm selling sportswear to golf pro shops called each of the customers in his territory every Monday to fill in orders and set appointments for the rest of the week. It would have been impossible to call on each of these accounts personally every week, because his territory was an entire state; however, he could keep in touch by telephone.

New technologies such as the cellular phone also mean that travel time can be more productive. Salespeople can now make calls from their cars

[26]John I. Coppett and Roy Dale Voorhees, "Telemarketing: Supplement to Field Sales," *Industrial Marketing Management*, Vol. 14, No. 3 (August 1985), pp. 213–216.

[27]Kevin T. Higging, "Rep's Fears of Telemarketing Present Management Hurdle," *Marketing News*, Vol. 20, No. 9 (April 25, 1986), p. 8.

while they are traveling. Chapter 16 will cover the important uses of the telephone in selling.

People-Oriented Training

Today's sales training teaches salespeople to be sensitive to the needs of others, to be knowledgeable about products, and to be more of an advisor–consultant or counselor than a pusher of products and the quick sell. Increasingly, companies are training salespeople to put themselves in the client's shoes, ask questions, probe, listen, and determine the customers' needs. These people-oriented skills are used to build long-term relationships.[28]

Many of these people-oriented skills are covered in Chapter 6, Understanding the Buyer as an Individual; Chapter 7, Different Approaches to Selling; and Chapter 11, Securing Feedback.

Stress on Relationships

In their efforts to build long-term relationships with their key customers, companies must provide them with incentives to remain customers.[29] Firms try to create the customer satisfaction that will foster long-term relationships. To do this, they must become very customer-oriented and concentrate on really satisfying customer needs.[30]

AMERICAN HOSPITAL SUPPLY LETS HOSPITAL PURCHASERS HAVE PRODUCT ASAP

American Hospital Supply has established a network of computer terminals with key hospitals, which enables the hospitals to order supplies directly from American's distribution centers. The system, called ASAP (analytical systems automated purchasing) eliminates hours of paper shuffling and rubber stamping in ordering the thousands of items a hospital needs. For American Hospital Supply, ASAP means orders, for it is easier and faster for hospitals to place orders with American than with anyone else.

SOURCE: Anne B. Pillsbury, "The Hard-Selling Supplier to the Sick," *Fortune,* Vol. 106, No. 2 (July 26, 1982), pp. 56–61. Reprinted with permission of *Fortune.* Copyright © 1982, by Time, Inc. All rights reserved.

---

[28]Jeremy Main, "How to Sell by Listening," *Fortune,* Vol. 111, No. 3 (February 4, 1985), pp. 52–54.

[29]See, for example, Leonard L. Berry, "Relationship Marketing," in *Emerging Perspectives on Services Marketing,* Leonard L. Berry, G. Lynn Shostack, and Gregory D. Upah, eds. (Chicago: American Marketing Association, 1983), pp. 25–28.

[30]See Barbara Bund Jackson, "Build Customer Relationships That Last," *Harvard Business Review,* Vol. 63, No. 6 (November–December 1985), p. 126.

TABLE 1.4
ACTIONS THAT AFFECT RELATIONSHIPS

POSITIVE ACTIONS	NEGATIVE ACTIONS
■ Initiate positive phone calls.	■ Make only call backs.
■ Make recommendations.	■ Make justifications.
■ Use candid language.	■ Use accommodative language.
■ Use phone.	■ Use correspondence.
■ Show appreciation.	■ Wait for misunderstandings.
■ Make service suggestions.	■ Wait for service requests.
■ Use "we" problem-solving language.	■ Use "owe us" legal language.
■ Get to problems.	■ Respond only to problems.
■ Use jargon or shorthand.	■ Use long-winded communications.
■ Air personality problems.	■ Hide personality problems.
■ Talk of "our future together."	■ Talk about making good on the past.
■ Routinize responses.	■ Fire drill/emergency responsiveness.
■ Accept responsibility.	■ Shift blame.
■ Plan the future.	■ Rehash the past.

SOURCE: Theodore Levitt, "After the Sales Is Over," *Harvard Business Review*, Vol. 61, No. 5 (September–October 1983), p. 91.

HOW SALESPEOPLE ESTABLISH TRUST

- ■ Establish expectations and demonstrate dependability.
- ■ Offer sources of proof to back up statements.
- ■ Be honest and candid.
- ■ Be businesslike and professional.
- ■ Give pros and cons of product.
- ■ Create a perception of quality.
- ■ Be honest.
- ■ Use technical knowledge.
- ■ Demonstrate competence.
- ■ Emphasize availability and ability to get the job done.
- ■ Stress benefits.
- ■ Stress meeting unique customer needs.
- ■ Be friendly.
- ■ Establish common ground.
- ■ Be polite.

SOURCE: John E. Swan, I. Frederick Trawick, and David W. Silva, "How Industrial Salespeople Gain Customer Trust," *Industrial Marketing Management*, Vol. 14, No. 1 (April 1985), pp. 203–211. Copyright © 1985, by Elsevier Science Publishing Co., Inc. Reprinted by permission of the publisher.

There are a number of things you can do as a salesperson to affect relationships. Some of the positive and negative actions are outlined in Table 1.4

Another factor that affects relationships is trust. If trust is established between buyer and seller, it is much easier to communicate and buyers are much more likely to let you help them. Trust, however, can only be built up over time, and it must be earned.

National Accounts

Another trend that some companies have followed is to establish a separate sales force for their national or major accounts. Companies such as IBM, AT&T, Union Oil, and Xerox have salespeople who specialize in handling their key customers and large national accounts.[31] National accounts sales forces try to meet the special needs of these key customers by becoming specialists in the customers' business. It is hoped that specializing in this way will improve communications with customers, will enable the company to give better service, and will thus improve relations between buyers and sellers.

SUMMARY

Personal selling skills are important for you whether or not you choose selling as a career. If you do not choose selling as a career, these skills will help you to sell your ideas and to be a good people-oriented communicator. If you do choose selling as a career, there are many opportunities open to you to use these skills. Several positive aspects of selling as a career are the social contributions to be made, the opportunity for continuing growth, the financial rewards, the freedom from direct supervision, and an opportunity for advancement.

The job of the modern salesperson has changed since earlier times. Modern selling tends to be more customer-oriented; the sales person discovers needs through discussions with customers and tries to build long-term relationships with customers by adjusting to their needs.

As a modern salesperson you will assume a number of roles, including educator, change agent, problem solver, innovator, manager, communicator, researcher, informant, forecaster, modifier, and psychologist.

A number of the many different types of sales positions were described, including route selling, retail selling, inside order taking, trade selling, missionary selling, technical selling, selling of tangibles, and selling of intangibles. Additional factors that differentiate various sales jobs were also highlighted. These include types of accounts, types of customers within accounts, types of products, size of orders taken, the degree of problem solving involved, the geographical extent of a territory, and the amount of nonselling

[31]John Barrett, "Why Major Account Selling Works," *Industrial Marketing Management*, Vol. 15, No. 1 (February 1986), pp. 63–73.

duties. In reality there is no single occupation of selling; rather, there is a
wide spectrum of work opportunities that require vastly different skills for
success.

Next, some qualities of successful salespeople were examined. It is important to point out that there are no universally accepted qualities that relate to all selling jobs. Instead, essential qualities depend on what you are selling and to whom you are selling it. However, a number of desirable qualities were examined, including intelligence, knowledge, verbal skills, information-gathering skills, and planning skills. Personality characteristics of good salespeople were also examined, including social sensitivity, flexibility, durability in relationships, empathy, drive, enthusiasm, and motivation.

Finally, a number of trends in selling were reviewed: greater numbers of women in selling, increased use of personal computers, greater use of the telephone, people-oriented training, a stress on building relationships, and a reliance on national accounts sales forces.

PROBLEMS

1. Are any of the characteristics of the traditional salesperson evident in certain types of sales positions today? What types of salespeople are liable to possess the characteristics of the modern salesperson?
2. In your own words, describe how salespeople could assume each of the roles of the modern salesperson?
3. Describe how important you consider empathy to be to a career in selling. Would empathy be more or less important to a salesperson than to an accountant or an engineer?
4. How do you think you would do as a salesperson? What are some potential negative aspects of a selling career?
5. Drive and motivation would seem to be interrelated. Do you think that both are equally important to a sales person's chances of success? Do all sales representatives need the same amount of these two characteristics to be successful?

EXERCISE 1

Objectives: To increase your understanding of the personal selling function and the great variety of selling jobs.

To gain insight regarding the vocational opportunities in personal selling.

PART A Interview with Salesperson

Choose a salesperson to interview. Your instructor may wish to designate a particular interviewee; otherwise, select a salesperson that you know and ask him or her the following questions.

1. How would you describe your principal duties?
2. How would you describe your customers and prospects?

3. What do you sell?
4. Who is your greatest competition?
5. What do you like most about your job? Least?
6. What qualifications are needed for your job?

After the interview, prepare a summary description of the salesperson's job.

PART B **Self-analysis**
From your reading of Chapter 1 and the interview with a salesperson, ask yourself the following questions.

1. What kinds of selling jobs are you most suited for?
2. What personal qualities do you have that relate to successful sales performance?

Case 1-1 Jason's Dilemma

Jason Smith is about to graduate from a midwestern college with a degree in marketing. His father owns a large used-car dealership outside of Detroit and has asked Jason to become part of the business. He is trying to decide whether to go to work for a large pharmaceutical firm as a detail salesperson or to work for his father in the car lot as a salesperson, with the possibility of taking over the business some day. His father has been relatively successful and considers that, with Jason's education, the business could be really successful. When discussing his options with several of his friends, Jason hears the following comments: "Used-car salesmen are nothing but high-pressure con artists" and "How would you ever be able to force people to buy cars they didn't need?" This disturbs Jason, and he is trying to decide whether he could apply to used cars the more modern approach to selling that he learned in school.

1. Would the more modern approach to selling work for a used-car salesperson?
2. How would Jason apply the modern selling concept to selling used cars?

Case 1-2 Meadow Brook National Bank

Meadow Brook is a white-collar bedroom community near New York City. The National Bank enjoys the largest share of business, although there are two other prosperous banks in the community.

Jack Diamond is the founder and head of National and, to many, *he is the bank*. He is a member of virtually every voluntary group and avidly supports local high school athletics. He makes good press, having become famous for his quotable quotes. Here are some examples.

"National is a high-class, well-managed hock shop."

"We buy and sell money. Bring yours to us or buy some from us."

"Everyone in National sells; if they don't, we don't want them around."

"Customers are the most important people in the world."

"Full service at one stop."

National has flourished under his leadership although some of the more conservative citizens are of the opinion that Jack runs a circus rather than a bank. National is always promoting something—new accounts, vacation club membership, certificates of deposit.

Jack insists that all members of the management team devote at least one day a week to making calls on customers and prospects among local businesses. Each person is also required to play an active role in at least one community organization.

1. What do you think about National's policies? What are the hazards?
2. Would you like to work there?

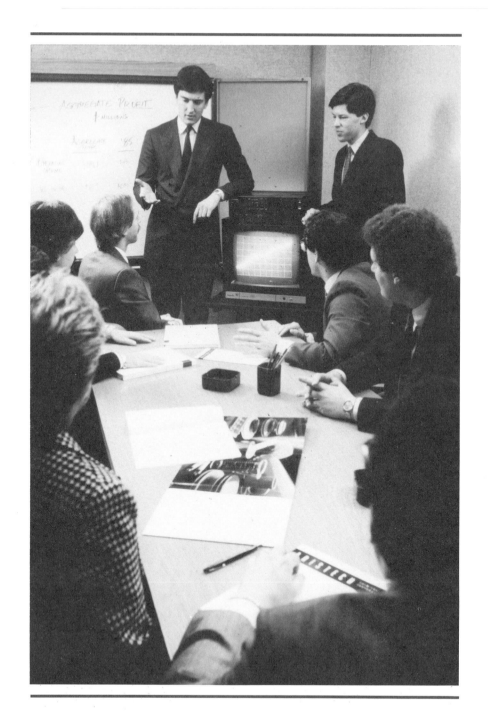

Selling and the Marketing Effort

After studying this chapter, you should be able to

1. Define the marketing concept.
2. Understand the key principles of the marketing concept.
3. Recognize the importance of uncontrollable factors to a firm's marketing efforts.
4. Specify the elements of a firm's marketing mix: product, price, promotion, and distribution.
5. Understand the roles of the sales manager.

As a salesperson you are an integral part of your firm's marketing program, and thus you must coordinate efforts with the rest of your firm's marketing activities.[1] In this chapter the importance of marketing and the marketing concept will be examined. It is critically important to have a clear understanding of the marketing concept, because the entire firm's sales and marketing efforts are usually based upon it. Factors beyond the control of the marketing manager that may vitally affect the success of the sales program will also be examined. In addition, the interaction between the tools the marketing manager uses to compete effectively in the marketplace and the firm's personal selling effort will be analyzed. Finally, the functions and responsibilities of sales managment will be reviewed.

Before the development of the marketing concept, most firms were oriented toward production or sales. That is, they were more interested in producing their products and selling them to customers than they were in actually satisfying the customer. The marketing concept, on the other hand, takes a different perspective.

THE MARKETING CONCEPT

The marketing concept, as a management philosophy, states that the integrated efforts of the firm should be directed toward satisfying customers as a means of generating profits. As such, the marketing concept has several key principles: (1) consumer orientation, (2) integrated effort, (3) belief that change is inevitable, (4) broad definition of mission, and (5) profit orientation. If a firm is to be truly marketing-oriented, it must adopt each of these principles.

Consumer Orientation

The idea that the entire firm focuses on the satisfaction of customer needs does not imply just taking a customer out for a fancy dinner in the industrial selling world, or smiling and being pleasant in retail sales situations. Rather, it means that through various types of marketing research, including feedback from salespeople, the firm will attempt to determine what it can offer its customers that will meet their needs as closely as possible. However, some products that would satisfy a few customers' needs completely the firm would not want to supply because they lack the required profit potential.

No one company can satisfy all potential customers and markets at once. Therefore, at any one point in time, the firm must strive to serve specific markets and specific customer needs. Examples of firms that try to meet limited markets at particular points in time are Southwest Airlines, which flies a commuter service between San Antonio, Dallas, and Houston; Fiat, which primarily produces economy-oriented automobiles; and McDonald's, which primarily sells fast-service meals. Adopting a customer orientation usually means spending money to determine what the market really wants. Often this means surveying final users to find out what they want and their attitudes toward different messages.

---

[1] For an interesting discussion of the relationship of sales and marketing, see "When Sales Meets Marketing," *Sales and Marketing Management*, Vol. 134, No. 7 (May 13, 1985), pp. 59–65.

Provide information on need In order to be a customer-oriented salesperson you must provide your firm with information about customers' needs and try to satisfy these needs. Compared with the survey researcher, you have several substantial advantages in obtaining data about future projects, customers, and competition. First, the additional cost incurred to collect information is relatively low, because you are meeting with customers anyway. Second, you can transmit the information you obtain on your regular calls back to your firm with little extra effort. Third, you normally have a well-established relationship with your customers and are therefore aware of their needs and wants. Finally, as a salesperson for a respected company you are usually perceived by customers as a potential supplier of problem-solving products and services. Prospective customers are therefore normally willing to provide you with information that they might not give to a survey researcher.[2]

Satisfy real needs Another responsibility of the marketing-oriented salesperson is to provide customers with products that satisfy their real needs. Because you pay attention to these needs, it will often take you longer to sell products than it takes product-oriented salespeople. Sometimes it takes months to determine the precise needs of the customer, but the payoff comes

---

WHO ARE YOUR CUSTOMERS?

CUSTOMERS ARE
- The most important people to your company.
- Not dependent on you; you are dependent on them.
- Not an interruption of your work; they are the purpose for it.
- Not outsiders to your business; they are part of it.
- Doing you a favor by doing business with you; you are not doing them a favor by serving them.
- Not cold statistics, names on filing cards or ledger sheets; they are flesh-and-bone human beings, with biases, prejudices, feelings, and emotions like your own.
- Not someone to argue with; no one ever won an argument with a customer.

CUSTOMERS ARE
People who bring you their wants. It is your job to fill these wants.

SOURCE: Unknown.

---

[2]See Kenneth R. Evans and John L. Schlacter, "The Role of Sales Managers and Sales People in a Marketing Information System," *Journal of Personal Selling and Sales Management,* Vol. 5, No. 2 (November 1985), pp. 49–58.

in having really satisfied customers. In industrial selling, this process may require that the seller provide enginering assistance to build new products or modify existing ones to fit the needs of the customer.

As a marketing-oriented salesperson, you should also realize that you will not make every sale, for there will be situations in which your company does not provide a product that would solve the customer's problems. When this happens, you should point this out rather than have the customer buy a product and then become dissatisfied with it.

If you take the time required to determine the customer's actual needs and then recommend your products only if they are capable of meeting such needs, you will find that you are welcomed and trusted by the prospect when you call. Your recommendations will carry significantly more weight in the purchase decision process than those of the salesperson who tries to push merchandise regardless of its ability to satisfy the customer's needs.

Integrated Effort

In an integrated effort all departments within the firm work in a coordinated fashion to satisfy customers and at the same time generate profits. If a firm produces the best products in its industry but delivers them late or delivers them in damaged condition, customers will not be satisfied. Similarly, if all the marketing activities of the firm are performed well but customers are not satisfied with their treatment by credit personnel, effectiveness will suffer. Thus, implementation of the marketing concept requires coordination between departments and a solid commitment to satisfying customer needs. It also requires you to integrate activities before and after the sale.

Before the sale As a salesperson, you are one of the most important individuals involved in integrating the entire firm's efforts to solve a customer's problem. At times you will have to put together a team of production, research, service, and even accounting or finance people from your company to assist a customer. Assume, for example, that you are working for a firm that is bidding on a large industrial contract. You may have to ask the research department to design new plans to fit the exact specifications of the customer. You would then present the plans to the customer for approval. Frequently you would be accompanied by a representative of the research department during this crucial stage of the sales process.

Additionally, a customer who has a problem financing a project may need the assistance of your financial people, who may be able to show the customer how a project can be financed. In some circumstances your firm may provide the capital for the project. Thus, you make certain that the efforts of your entire firm are directed toward satisfying your customers.

After the sale Once the sale has been made and the equipment installed, you will probably become concerned with its long-term service requirements. If a problem develops, the customer's first reaction may be to call you. Although it may not be your formal responsibility, long-term relationships with your accounts are important and you should become personally involved in major service problems.

Belief That Change Is Inevitable

The firm adopting the marketing concept understands that even its most successful product will some day be obsolete. Unfortunately, many firms with products generating substantial profits year after year are lulled into the belief that their products will never become obsolete. These firms will eventually face a rude awakening when their products are displaced from the market.

Products such as slide rules and adding machines quickly became obsolete with the advent of the calculator. The firm with a marketing orientation anticipates this problem and constantly monitors changing consumer needs so that it, not one of its competitors, will be the firm to develop the new product that makes the old product obsolete. In this way, the firm will be able to generate profits in the future.

Broad Definition of Mission

Realization that competitive substitutes exist causes the marketing-oriented firm to take on a broad definition of its mission. Such a broad definition encourages the firm to monitor its methods continually in order to adjust to the current market environment and to take advantage of new opportunities. Several examples of narrow versus broad definitions of missions are given in Table 2.1 An industry that suffered from not taking a broad look at its mission was the railroads, which considered themselves to be in the railroad business rather than the transportation business. Yet their major competition came not from other railroads but from other forms of transportation such as trucking and air. The transportation market has continued to expand, but the railroads have faltered.[3]

On the other hand, some of the petroleum companies exemplify firms that are taking on a much broader definition of mission now than they did in the past. Most of the forward-thinking companies in this industry now perceive themselves to be in the energy business rather than in the oil business. They have diversified in areas such as coal, nuclear power, and solar energy research. This change in emphasis will put them in a much better position to adjust to the world's future energy needs.

TABLE 2.1
NARROW VERSUS BROAD MISSIONS OF THE FIRM

NARROW DEFINITION OF MISSION	BROAD DEFINITION OF MISSION
Oil	Energy
Telephones	Communications
Computers	Problem solving
Airlines	Transportation
Dairy	Nutrition

SOURCE: Adapted from William H. Cunningham and Isabella C. M. Cunningham, *Marketing: A Managerial Approach* (Cincinnati: Southwestern, 1981), p. 18.

[3]For a good discussion of this, see Theodore Levitt, "Marketing Myopia," *Harvard Business Review*, Vol. 38, No. 4 (July–August 1960), pp. 45–56.

Profit Orientation

If a firm cannot make a profit, the question of whether it is satisfying a customer need is irrelevant because the firm will not be in business for long. In this sense, profit is not so much an objective as it is a constraint; in short the firm must first survive. In the evaluation of a business, it is not how many sales a product generates but how much profit it contributes. There are many examples of products that sell well but are unprofitable.[4] The marketing-oriented firm seeks only profitable growth. As a result, the firm may be forced to abandon a product that generates sales but not profit. However, sometimes it is necessary to continue selling a marginal product to accommodate the rest of the line or to satisfy customers.

Your responsibility as a marketing-oriented salesperson is directed more to profit than to sales volume. Your company should encourage you to sell products that are profitable, rather than just those that might be easy to sell, and to call on customers who would seem to have the greatest long-run profit potential for the firm. As a marketing-oriented salesperson, you should realize that there will be accounts without enough potential business to warrant your efforts. Your firm's compensation plan may reflect these objectives, with management offering higher commissions based on the relative profitability of particular products and particular types of accounts. Marketing and selling are also appropriate for nonprofit organizations. The objective of these organizations would not be profit but would center around some other factor. For instance, a hospital might try to raise money to build a new wing. The hospital administrator's objective in selling would then be to raise funds, perhaps by naming the new wing after the donor.

UNCONTROLLABLE ENVIRONMENTAL FACTORS

Each firm, regardless of products, markets, or management philosophy, faces a number of largely uncontrollable environmental factors such as culture, technology, legal constraints, competition, economic forces, and limited resources. These are uncontrollable in the sense that your firm has little power over them, and yet they may affect the very survival of your firm. Thus, a firm must monitor these factors closely so it can adjust its operations as quickly as possible to fit the changing environment.

Figure 2.1 illustrates the interaction that takes place among the largely uncontrollable factors and marketing management. As can be seen, these environmental changes affect each firm's market. Thus firms must constantly monitor their markets and the environmental factors that influence their markets. Finally, actions the firm takes may influence the environment. For example, as a result of a recent economic recession (economic environment), the federal government passed laws (legal factors) that were designed to stimulate the construction of new plants and equipment (technology) and consumer spending (culture). Consequently, companies' top management ad-

---

[4]"Owens-Illinois: Giving Market Share to Improve Profits," *Business Week*, No. 2687 (May 11, 1981), pp. 81–82.

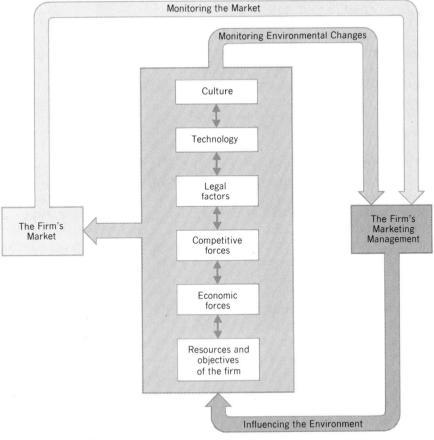

FIGURE 2.1 Uncontrollable environmental factors.

justed their plans for the succeeding year (objectives of the firm). Not only did most marketing executives monitor the developments in each of these areas, but they also tried to influence their top management in terms of what plans they felt the firm should adopt (objectives of the firm). In addition, many of these marketing executives also lobbied in Washington either through their corporate offices or through trade associations to try to get laws passed (legal factors) that would be beneficial to their organizations. Each of the uncontrollable variables will be examined briefly from the perspective of the marketing department and the salesperson.

Culture

Culture consists of the values, ideas, attitudes, and other symbols that are created by people to regulate their behavior, and that are passed from one generation to the next.[5] As an example, in Latin America being thirty minutes

[5]James F. Engel and Roger D. Blackwell, *Consumer Behavior,* fourth edition (New York: Holt, Rinehart and Winston, 1982), p. 72.

late for a sales call is not considered to be in bad taste, whereas being more than five or ten minutes late to a similar meeting in New York would be. In a somewhat different example, certain products are consumed by one segment of society and not by others: in many southern states, grits and hush puppies are very popular; in the Southwest, Mexican food is eaten regularly. In major cities, some newspapers are published in other languages to appeal directly to certain subcultures among cities' residents. As a salesperson, you must adjust your behavior to fit the particular cultural situation in which you find yourself.

Technology

New technology is responsible for many of the inventions and innovations that are developed by industry. Manufacturers have learned that products are frequently the most profitable in their early stages of production, before a great deal of competition exists. Therefore, it is important that a firm continue to develop new products that will satisfy consumer needs. Such products as nylon, television, and the computer have dramatically changed our life-styles while producing substantial profits for business. Two of your prime functions as a salesperson are to provide the necessary information to the technical staff to help them understand what the market is likely to need and to keep management informed of technological breakthroughs of competitors.

Technology also affects you in your role as a salesperson. New technological developments such as personal computers, pagers, cellular telephones, and answering machines all make your selling job more efficient.

Legal Factors

Many laws regulating the practice of business have been passed by local, state, and national governments. On the federal level, for example, the Sherman Antitrust Act (1890), the Clayton Act (1914), and the Federal Trade Commission Act (1914) make it illegal for two or more firms engaged in interstate commerce to conspire to fix the prices of a product. Several years ago General Electric, Westinghouse, and 29 other corporations were convicted of fixing the prices of electrical generating equipment.[6] These companies paid millions of dollars in fines for their involvement in the conspiracy and paid out much larger sums in damages to the utilities that purchased merchandise at inflated prices. Salespeople from each of these firms were intimately involved in establishing the price-fixing arrangements.

The Robinson–Patman Act makes it illegal for the firm or its representatives to provide price discounts or other concessions to one retailer that it does not provide to another retailer. Most states have now adopted the Uniform Commercial Code, which regulates trade practices with individual states. These state laws directly affect your day-to-day activities as a salesperson. Finally, local, municipal, and county governments have passed laws dealing with all aspects of selling ranging from the days when certain prod-

---

[6]Richard A. Smith, "The Incredible Electrical Conspiracy," *Fortune*, Vol. 63, No. 4 (April 1961), p. 132.

ucts can be sold (so-called blue laws) to how and where products can be displayed. (Chapter 17 covers in greater detail the pieces of federal legislation and sections of the Uniform Commercial Code that directly affect selling activities.) As a salesperson, you must be aware of the law and how it affects selling your products. In one firm all salespeople go through a study course developed by their legal department, so that they by their actions will not get themselves or their company into trouble.[7]

Competitive Forces

A firm's offerings will always be compared to competitors, and those competitive activities will influence how a firm is perceived in the marketplace.[8] Therefore, one key element in the marketing strategy of your firm will be information about your firm's competition. Global competition and deregulation mean that competition is becoming increasingly important in many industries, and firms need to monitor competitive activities and choose markets where they can compete.[9]

Your management will want to know such factors as geographical coverage of each competitor, products sold most effectively by competitors, industries in which competitors are active, after-sale service capabilities of competitors, major strengths and weaknesses of competitors, and the image of competitors in the marketplace.[10]

Economic Forces

When the economic environment fluctuates, major changes take place in the level of profitability of various sectors of the economy. For example, when the United States experienced a high level of inflation during a period of economic recession, the situation hurt the home-building and automobile industries. Apparently, during periods of economic uncertainty most Americans do not spend money on purchases that can be postponed. Although most products sell better during periods of economic prosperity, if you wish to make the best of a bad situation, during periods of recession, you should try to sell products of your firm that are more basic in design and less costly. Then, as the economy turns upward, you can begin to emphasize the more sophisticated and expensive items. Another example of economic forces affecting selling is that in times of rising interest rates many firms find capital hard to come by and may tend to lease equipment rather than to purchase it. A knowledgeable salesperson can often ensure that the deal goes through by describing the leasing option.

---

[7]Terry Parker, "At Signode, Field Salespeople Play a Key Role in Tracking Competitors," *Sales and Marketing Management,* Vol. 126, No. 4 (March 16, 1981), p. 91.

[8]For an extensive list of questions you can ask about competition, see Ted Pollock, "How Well Do You Know the Competition," *The American Salesman,* Vol. 29, No. 12 (December 1984), pp. 26 – 30, 42.

[9]See, for example, Philip Kotler and Ravi Singh, "Marketing Warfare in the 1980's," *Journal of Business Strategy,* Vol. 1, No. 3 (Winter 1984), pp. 30 – 41.

[10]Terry Barker, "At Signode, Field Salespeople Play a Key Role in Tracking Competitors," *Sales and Marketing Management,* Vol. 126, No. 4 (March 16, 1981), p. 94.

Resources and Objectives of the Firm

Even though the resources and objectives of a firm are somewhat controllable by the firm's top management, they are not within the control of marketing management. The resources needed to succeed in the marketplace—such as financial strength, physical plant, raw materials, personnel, patents, and the goodwill of the public—are critical to a firm's success. For instance, if a business does not have the required line of credit to borrow enough money at a competitive interest rate, it may not be able to survive. In the same way, if it does not have innovative research and development along with adequate production facilities, it may not be able to succeed. Finally, if a firm has developed a reputation for producing poor-quality products, it will have great difficulty in successfully introducing a new product, even if it is of high quality and represents a genuinely good buy.

The objectives determined by the firm's top management will also affect the marketing department. For instance, several years ago General Electric decided to get out of the computer business. Similarly, Motorola decided to stop producing television sets. These top-management decisions affected the marketing efforts at these companies by changing directions and by creating resources that could be used in other segments of the firms' businesses.

THE MARKETING MIX

Although marketing management does face a series of uncontrollable variables, it also has a set of marketing tools that it can use to compete effectively in the marketplace. These tools represent factors that the marketer can control; they are called the marketing mix.

Elements of the Marketing Mix

Marketing mix decisions revolve around four basic questions[11]: What constitutes the product? How much will it be sold for? How will it be distributed? How will it be promoted to customers? Although the questions seem simple enough, the answers may be difficult and complex.

Product Although it might seem self-evident that the product or service is the physical object being sold, in reality it is much more than that. Specifically, a product consists of all the factors that the customer considers when making a purchase.[12] How is the item serviced? Does it have a warranty? What is its reputation? The answers to these questions also constitute the product. In marketing, the term product may also be used to describe a service such as insurance or banking.

---

[11]Adapted from William H. Cunningham and Isabella C. M. Cunningham, *Marketing: A Managerial Approach* (Cincinnati: Southwestern, 1981), p. 35.

[12]For an extensive list of questions you should be able to answer about your product, see Ted Pollock, "How Well Do You Know Your Product," *The American Salesman*, Vol. 30, No. 3 (March 1985), pp. 24–27.

Price The pricing decision is rather straightforward if the product in question is very much like others currently on the market. In this situation, the firm sets the selling price roughly equal to the market price of competitive products. However, if the product has features that differentiate it from similar products, or if it is a new product, a firm must make a series of pricing decisions. Should the item be priced to generate immediate or long-term profits? Should demand or cost factors be used in setting price? Most prices consist of a base amount plus the cost of the things like accessories and delivery. Often prices are adjusted to give discounts for paying early or for volume purchases, and to give allowances for promotion. Thus, pricing is often complex. Frequently, the firm will try to use marketing tools other than price to attract its customers, because a reduction in price is easily matched by competition.

SELLING: THE HEART OF MARKETING

According to Arch McGill, formerly of IBM, Marketing is an art, the art of selling the benefits of your product and, by contrast, making it clear that your benefits are more relevant than the competitor's. The heart of marketing is not computer-based segmentation. As we seem to have ignored in the last twenty-five years, the heart of marketing is selling. Selling is a fine thing! We love salespersons! We continue to believe that a good candidate for the single most significant strength of the all-powerful IBM company is the fact that it has always been run by former salesmen.

SOURCE: Tom Peters and Nancy Austin, *A Passion for Excellence* (New York: Random House, 1985), pp. 91–92. Copyright © 1985, by Thomas J. Peters and Nancy K. Austin. Reprinted by permission of Random House, Inc.

Distribution Distribution refers to the members of the distribution channel who sell the product. These members might be wholesalers, distributors, or retailers. They are involved in moving the product from the manufacturer to the customer. Many times, the most important factor in determining the success of a product is not the product itself, but rather where and how it is sold. Firms such as Gillette, Procter & Gamble, and General Foods are much more likely to introduce new products successfully than are small local companies, simply because of their large, already established national retail networks. Some of the more important decisions affecting distribution are determined by the following questions. Who should distribute the product? Should the distribution structure be owned by the manufacturer, or should independent intermediaries be utilized? What amounts of inventories should be maintained at each level in the distribution organization? At what locations should a firm sell its products?

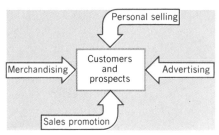

FIGURE 2.2 Various forms of promotion.

Often as a salesperson you will have to work directly with other members of the channel. For instance, a salesperson working for a manufacturer might participate in the training of distributor salespeople and in trying to motivate them. You might also make sales calls with them and act as a source of technical support.[13]

Promotion It is somewhat naive to think that a good product *always* finds a market. Buyers must be made aware of the product before they can purchase it. As can be seen from Figure 2.2, there are a number of different forms of promotion and they should all be aimed at customers or prospects. Usually, personal selling and mass media advertising campaigns must be employed to acquaint potential buyers with the product and to convince them of its merits. For example, when a firm uses radio, television, magazines, newspapers, or billboards to announce a new product or a price reduction, it is using advertising. Sales promotions are activities other than advertising or selling that stimulate consumer purchasing and dealer effectiveness. Trade shows, exhibits, coupons, special sales or deals, and demonstrations are all forms of sales promotion. Another form of promotion is called merchandising. Merchandising includes anything done to enhance the attractiveness of the product and would include such things as packaging, displays, the way the products are shelved, and store windows.

The Marketing Mix and the Customer
Figure 2.3 illustrates the relationship between the various marketing-mix elements. The middle of the figure represents the overall needs and wants of a firm's present and potential customers. Notice that the customer portion is located in the middle to emphasize that the company cannot afford to forget its present customers in its efforts to attract new ones. All too often, a firm begins to take its established accounts for granted and then finds itself in substantial difficulty as these accounts are wooed away by competitors.

Needed marketing information is provided by marketing research and marketing intelligence. The top part of Figure 2.3, shows the efforts of the marketing research staff, and the bottom portion represents the additional ef-

[13]For a good discussion of these interfaces, see Bert Rosenbloom and Rolph Anderson, "Channel Management and Sales Management: Some Key Interfaces," *Journal of the Academy of Marketing Sciences*, Vol. 13, No. 3 (Summer 1985), pp. 97–106.

Marketing executives discussing the marketing mix.

forts of the sales force and others in collecting useful information. The information flow is continuous and includes data about what types of products the market wants, what changes should take place in the firm's product offering, the levels of competitive activity that exist for the firm's various products, and what changes should take place in distribution and pricing.

The outer portion of the figure represents a firm's marketing effort. Notice that it includes the four elements of the marketing mix: product, price, promotion, and distribution. With the information provided by marketing research and the sales staff, a firm should be in a position to design and then market a product successfully. Product management consists of first designing

FIGURE 2.3 The marketing system.

the proper product for the market and then positioning it to meet the needs of specific market segments. Virginia Slims, for example, was positioned in the market to try to attract female smokers. Pricing represents a powerful marketing tool, and every firm needs to establish a policy for product pricing. A combination of personal selling, advertising, sales promotion, and merchandising may also be used to communicate with the market.

Finally, the firm must decide how its products are to be distributed. It must determine the channels of distribution that the firm will use to move its merchandise from the plant to the consumer or the locations the firm will choose should it decide to market directly to its customers.

Interaction among Selling and Other Marketing Tools

If firms are to market effectively, they must recognize that each one of their marketing tools interacts with the others. For example, in an effort to develop a successful promotional program, the wise marketing manager will consider the relative emphasis to place on selling, advertising, sales promotion, and merchandising in each of the firm's markets. The manager will also take into account specific plans, decisions, and actions when chosing media, merchandising aids, and kinds of sales promotional activity. Similarly, when defining the distribution structure, firms must consider the strength of their own sales force and how well recognized their products are. The manner in which various marketing tools interact with selling activities is explored next.

Marketing research There are two primary ways that your selling activities and the marketing research functions interact. First, you provide a portion of the input that the marketing research department needs in order to prepare its reports. At times, the marketing research department may ask you to report on customers' answers to specific questions. In addition, the marketing research department will analyze the regular data that you send back to the firm, such as sales reports, new sources of competition, and sales orders, to determine whether any patterns have developed that may necessitate changes in the company's marketing strategy.

The second means of interaction is your use of the reports developed by the marketing research staff in your selling activities. As an example, if you are a salesperson for an electronics firm, responsible for selling electrical switching gear, you will want to have information on new competitors, types of competitive changes in pricing and service policies, and new uses for the switching gear, in order to design the most effective sales approach. Moreover, if you know that a specific firm is your major competitor for a specific contract and that this competition offers primarily low-cost items, you may want to stress that quality, reliability, and service are critical in the long run for a firm that is considering new electrical switching gear.

Channels of distribution The salesperson has a great deal to do with the firm's channels of distribution for a product. If you work for a firm such as Motorola that sells its merchandise through distributors, you are the link between these distributors and your firm. It is your responsibility to supply the distributor with the right quantity and types of products for the market. In addition, you would frequently work with the distributor's promotion and sales staff, providing display materials and conducting sales clinics. These tools increase the salespeople's knowledge of the product, thus making them more effective. Finally, you would make sales calls with the distributor's staff. The objective of such sales calls is to contact the distributor's customers and to try to get them to place an order for your firm's product through the distributor. This maneuver is not an effort on the part of your firm to steal customers from the distributor; rather, it is the recognition on the part of your firm that a sale is really not made until the distributor's accounts have purchased the product.

Sales promotion As a salesperson, you are frequently responsible for the implementation of your firm's sales promotion campaign. If a firm that sells packaged foods to grocery stores wants to run a special on cake mixes, it might try to get each local supermarket to provide room for a special display rack to promote the product. If you work for such a firm and call on supermarkets, you will frequently be asked to "sell" the idea to the supermarket. In this same manner, you can determine whether point-of-purchase displays sent to a market by your firm are actually set up, the dealers' reactions to them, and how long the displays are used. If the materials were not well received by dealers, you can find out why and pass the information back to your management. Other sales promotion activities that you as a salesperson might engage in are organizing display windows for retailers and providing information and literature at exhibits and tradeshows.[14]

Advertising In contrast to selling, the main effort of advertising must be exerted before an actual sale. That is, advertising is used to convince the potential customer to consider the purchase of a product. As Figure 2-4 shows, advertisements may make your job as a salesperson easier by providing the prospect with information prior to your call. The McGraw-Hill advertisement shows a prospect who needed information before the salesperson arrived in his office.

Only in rare instances, however, does advertising bring about a purchase without being accompanied by personal selling. Even at the retail level, many advertising campaigns are designed not to sell one particular product but to attract consumers to the store where a salesperson can assist them in making a purchase. Advertising does, however, have secondary, after-sale function in helping customers rationalize their purchases. For instance, many readers of advertisements are recent purchasers of what is being advertised.

It is clear that advertising and selling are interdependent and complementary.[15] References to your firm's advertising and actual samples of ads are

---

[14]For information on selling at trade shows, see Nancy Day, "Ten Ways to Stop Customers at Your Booth," *Marketing Times,* Vol. 29, No. 5 (October 1982), p. 26; or Allen Konopacki, "The Different Sell at Trade Shows," *Industrial Marketing,* Vol. 69, No. 7 (July 1984), pp. 71–74; or Archie Jordan, "Trade Shows as a Powerful Sales Tool," *The American Salesman,* Vol. 28, No. 7 (July 1983), pp. 14–18.

[15]For an interesting discussion of the sales–advertising interface and how firms actually interrelate them, see Alan J. Dubinski, Thomas A. Barry, and Roger A. Kerin, "The Sales–Advertising Interface in Promotion Planning," *Journal of Advertising,* Vol. 10, No. 3 (1981), pp. 35–41.

"*I don't know who you are.*

I don't know your company.

I don't know your company's product.

I don't know what your company stands for.

I don't know your company's customers.

I don't know your company's record.

I don't know your company's reputation.

Now–what was it you wanted to sell me?'

MORAL: Sales start **before** your salesman calls–with business publication advertising.

McGRAW-HILL MAGAZINES
BUSINESS • PROFESSIONAL • TECHNICAL

FIGURE 2.4 Advertisement helps the salesperson.

important selling aids in many situations, particularly when your firm uses intermediaries. Armed with the advertising plans of your company and samples of that advertising, you can show how much impact your firm is going to exert on the ultimate users who are the customers of the retailer. For instance, you might show a retailer an advertisement that will run in *Newsweek* and *Time* magazines in order to influence the retailer to stock your product.

It is relatively common in industrial firms to use advertising to generate leads, which are followed up by salespeople. This is accomplished by means of coupon returns and, in the case of some industrial trade media, by reader service cards—often referred to as "bingo" cards.

Just as advertising helps you, so can you help your firm in appraising the impact of its advertising. You can determine how many of your customers and prospects have actually seen or heard an ad. By questioning them carefully, you can also learn their reactions to the advertisements. This information, along with your comments pertaining to the ads, will provide valuable feedback for your firm's marketing management.

Pricing Generally, you would have relatively little input into the final pricing decisions for a product. One study found, for example, that firms giving salespeople the highest degree of pricing authority generated the lowest sales and profit performance.[16] This does not mean that you might not be asked how a product should be priced; you might even be given some price flexibility when negotiating with your customers. However, the pricing decisions normally are made by executives within the marketing organization. You may have some direct interaction with the pricing decisions if you find that your merchandise is continually overpriced compared with the competition. This situation might imply that you are trying to sell your customers a better-grade product than they feel they need, or that the product is simply overpriced.

Product management As with the pricing function, you are not usually involved with the decision to introduce a new product in the market, relative to your firm's other products and the competition's products. However, you interact regularly with the product because you are responsible for selling it. Thus, you may be a key to determining how successful the new product is. If there is unexpected market resistence to a product, you are the first to learn of it, and you should try to determine what the problem is and communicate it back to management. You also have a responsibility for identifying customers' needs that your firm can profitably serve or for suggesting modifications in existing products that would serve your customers better.

SALES MANAGEMENT'S FUNCTIONS AND RESPONSIBILITIES

As a salesperson you interact regularly with your immediate superior—the field sales manager.[17] Futhermore, many salespeople aspire to management positions. For these reasons the job of sales manager is reviewed. Five of the most important functions of the sales manager are discussed along with how

[16]P. Ronald Stephenson, William L. Cron, and Gary L. Frazier, "Delegating Pricing Authority to the Sales Force: The Effects on Sales and Profit Performance," *Journal of Marketing*, Vol. 43, No. 2 (Spring 1979), pp. 21–28.

[17]For an interesting discussion of the sales manager, see Bert Rosenbloom and Rolph E. Anderson, "The Sales Manager: Tomorrow's Super Marketers," *Business Horizons*, Vol. 27, No. 2 (March–April 1984), pp. 50–56.

they relate to you as a salesperson. These five functions are planning, people management, communications, selling, and leadership.

Planning

Sales managers frequently participate in the development of the firm's marketing strategy, and very few people have as good a perspective of market conditions as they do. As a result, they will counsel the firm's marketing and top management concerning new-product development, price changes on existing products, delivery and production schedules, and advertising activities. In addition, sales managers are responsible for designing territories for their own sales force in a way that will generate profitable sales for the firm. This planning function requires that sales managers perform sales forecasts on a district-by-district basis to determine how often each account should be called on, to ascertain how much time should be spent on each call, and to calculate the travel time from one sales call to another.

People Management

In their role of managing people, sales managers are responsible for hiring, training, and promoting salespeople.

Hiring Frequently, members of the personnel staff will do the initial screening of applicants. However, after this screening, applicants are normally interviewed by a sales manager, who often makes the final decision of hiring. This is important, because experienced sales managers are in a good position to judge your chances of success in selling and in getting along with the firm's customers.

Training Sales managers train employees in several ways. If you have not sold before, you frequently begin your career with the firm by spending several weeks in the district sales office. At this time sales managers and staff provide you with the product knowledge and with an understanding of the firm's basic approach to selling. After this introductory period you are frequently assigned to work with an experienced salesperson for several weeks. Then you are assigned a territory. Normally, the sales manager or training officer will then spend several weeks making joint calls with you to introduce you to clients and to help you improve your sales tactics.

Sales managers also perform training services for experienced sales representatives by holding regular sales meetings in which members of the sales staff discuss mutual sales problems. At this time sales managers also explain new products and any marketing programs the firm is introducing. In addition, most sales managers try to spend several days each month making calls with their salespeople. This puts sales managers in the best possible position to advise the individual salesperson on how to improve selling. After having observed several calls, the sales manager will often have a "curbstone conference" with the salesperson to suggest strengths and weaknesses in the presentation. Giving such advice is sometimes called coaching.

Evaluations Sales managers are also responsible for evaluating salespeople. In this capacity they counsel with each salesperson, encourage improvements in weak performers, terminate unqualified people, and promote qualified salespeople. Evaluation is made more difficult by the fact that each salesperson faces a different territory. They have different customers, face different individuals, and often encounter different competitors. Consider, for example, two salespeople for a copier firm, one of whom has a territory in North Dakota and another who has a two-block area in New York City. Since the two territories would differ so much in size and potential, evaluating these people on a similar basis would be impossible. Table 2.2 includes some measures sales managers use to evaluate salespeople.

Communications

Field sales managers are the personal link between salespeople and headquarters, ensuring that information flows in both directions. Sales personnel are a vital source of information to top management. Because they spend a great percentage of their working day meeting with customers, trying to determine what problems the customer has and how their firm can best go about solving these problems, the sales personnel are in an excellent position to provide management with input for sales forecasts, ideas for new products, customer-identified problems of existing products, and reports of competitive activity. Such information is of critical importance to the development of the firm's overall marketing strategy. Sales managers must also communicate top management's policies, objectives, and strategies to the field sales force.

Selling

One survey indicated that sales managers spend approximately one-third of their time on selling activities.[18] Some sales managers have several house accounts of their own for two reasons. First, the firm may feel that a particular account is so important that it deserves the best sales representation. If the most qualified individual is the sales manager, then responsibility for selling to this account will be given to the manager. Second, in that most managers were salespeople before they were promoted to their current positions, they understand the importance of keeping in close contact with the marketplace. If sales managers lose touch with customers' problems and the activities of the competitors, they will be ineffective as counselors to management and to their sales team. Other selling activities in which sales managers participate include handling problem accounts, expediting customer orders and deciding on customer requests for special sales terms.[19]

There are, however, a number of companies that specifically exclude actual selling from a sales manager's responsibilities. These companies argue that this eliminates conflict for the sales mangers and ensures that they will do what they are paid to do—manage salespeople.

Leadership

It is critically important for the firm that sales managers be leaders. The morale of the sales representatives frequently depends on how effectively sales

[18]Rodney Evans and William J. E. Crissy, "The Field Sales Manger. Part 1," *Sales Management,* Vol. 103, No. 9 (October 15, 1969), pp. 51–54.

[19]Ibid.

TABLE 2.2

MEASURES USED TO EVALUATE SALESPEOPLE

PERFORMANCE MEASURE	PERCENTAGE OF SALES MANAGERS USING	PERFORMANCE MEASURE	PERCENTAGE OF SALES MANAGERS USING
Sales		Calls	
Sales volume in dollars	81	Calls per period	57
Sales volume to previous year's sales	78	Number of calls per number of customers (by product class)	17
Sales volume by product or product line	69	Selling expense	
Amount of new account sales	58	Selling expense to sales	41
Sales volume in units	54	Selling expense to quota	22
Sales volume to dollar quota	54	Average cost per call	13
Sales volume by customer	49	Ancillary activities	
Sales volume to market potential	34	Number of required reports turned in	44
Sales volume to physical unit quota	24	Number of customer complaints	31
Sales volume per order	15	Training meetings conducted	28
Sales volume by outlet type	11	Number of letters and phone calls to prospects	25
Sales volume per call	10	Number of demonstrations conducted	25
Percentage of sales made by telephone or mail	8	Number of service calls made	24
Market share		Number of dealer meetings held	15
Market share per quota	18	Advertising displays set up	12
Accounts		Attitude	90
Number of new accounts	71	Product knowledge	89
Number of accounts lost	43	Selling skills	85
Number of accounts on which payment is overdue	22	Appearance and manner	82
Number of accounts buying the full line	16	Communication skills	81
Profit		Initiative and aggressiveness	80
Net profit dollars	26	Planning ability	78
Return on investment	16	Time management	73
Net profit contribution	14	Knowledge of competition	72
Gross margin	14	Judgment	69
Gross margin per sales	14	Creativity	61
New profit as a percentage of sales	13	Knowledge of company policies	59
Orders		Report preparation and submission	59
Order–call ratio	26	Customer goodwill generated	50
Net orders per repeat order	17	Degree of respect from trade and competition	34
Number of canceled orders per orders booked	14	Good citizenship	23

SOURCE: Donald W. Jackson, Jr., Janet E. Keith, and John L. Schlacter, "Evaluation of Selling Performance: A Study of Current Practices," *Journal of Personal Selling and Sales Management*, Vol. 3, No. 2 (November 1983), pp. 42–51. Reprinted by permission from *Journal of Personal Selling and Sales Management*.

managers perform this function. Sales personnel may not see their managers for several days or weeks, so it is not the presence of an authority figure that keeps them working up to standards; rather, it is their own professionalism, combined with inspiration from an effective leader to do the job successfully. Thus, the sales manager is often called on to provide long-distance motivation and direction, encouraging salespeople to perform well without day-to-day supervision. The sales manager must also see to it that each salesperson has a clear picture of the company's broader marketing objectives in order to pursue those goals in the field.[20]

SUMMARY

The objective in this chapter has been to provide an overview of the relationship between selling and marketing. The marketing concept was explored as a way of life for the firm. It was pointed out that the most significant difference between the old production orientation and the new marketing orientation is the firm's realization that it must focus its efforts on the needs of the consumer rather than on its own products. It is your responsiblity to determine the needs of your prospective customers and then sell them a product or service only if it truly meets their needs. Although this process may be time-consuming, it generates substantially more long-term business than a strategy that is based on "hard-sell" tactics.

A challenge to marketers is that they must accomplish their task despite environmental factors over which they have little or no control. Among these factors are the culture of the society, the laws that govern business activities, competitive forces, company resources and objectives, and the changing economic environment. In contrast to the uncontrollable factors, the marketing mix contains tools that the marketing manager can use to compete effectively in the marketplace. Relationships between the firm's salespeople and marketing research, product, pricing, promotion, and distribution were illustrated. In addition, the relationship between selling and the uncontrollable variables *and* selling and the other marketing tools was discussed.

The basic sales management functions—of planning, people management, communication, selling, and leadership—were reviewed. Each specific managerial function was discussed to elucidate the relation between salespeople and their immediate superior, the sales manager.

PROBLEMS

1. Has the American automobile industry historically been marketing-oriented? Explain.
2. Describe the different functions salespeople have if they sell for a marketing-oriented firm rather than a firm that is not marketing-oriented.

---

[20]Donald W. Jackson, Jr., and Ramon J. Aldag, "Managing the Sales Force by Objectives," *MSU Business Topics,* Vol. 22, No. 2 (Spring 1974), p. 53.

3. What kinds of marketing information might be better obtained through marketing research? Through the field sales force?
4. If you are operating a small real estate agency, which of the uncontrollable factors discussed will have the greatest impact on your sales force?
5. Describe in your own words the interaction that salespeople have with the rest of the elements in the marketing mix.
6. If you are a sales manager, which of the functions that you perform do you feel would be the most important to the prosperity of the firm? How do these functions affect your sales representatives?

EXERCISE 2

Objective: To apply marketing concepts to one national advertiser.

Choose a firm that engages in heavy national advertising. Analyze a sample of its ads on radio, television, newspapers, and magazines, and then answer the following questions.

1. What are the principal appeals used in the ads?
2. Who are the key targets of the ads?
3. What mention is made, if any, of competitiors and competitive products?
4. How attention-compelling are the ads?
5. What are your personal reactions to them?

Case 2–1 Beech Aircraft

Joel Snyder sells for the Beech Aircraft dealership in Las Vegas. After graduating from the Air Force Academy, he spent the next six years flying jet attack aircraft for the Air Force. When his tour was up, Joel returned to Las Vegas and began working for a local bank. After three years as an investment officer, he quit the bank and went to work for the local Beech dealer. He stated, "I found banking just too confining. I enjoy meeting people and flying, and now I am doing just what I want to do—what comes naturally to me. In addition, I get to work closely with the most advanced general aviation company in the world—Beech Aircraft." Joel is earning good money, consisting of base salary plus commission. His commissions last year made up 50 percent of his income.

Three companies account for over 75 percent of all the general aviation aircraft units sold in the United States. They are Beech, Cessna, and Piper. The general aviation market is segmented: business, commercial, personal, and instructional. The business market consists of aircrafts used by firms to transport their executives, the commercial market primarily of air taxis. Aircraft owned for personal use constitute the personal market; units used to teach people to fly are the instructional market.

More than 80 percent of the planes Beech sells are used for business purposes. It is also known that less than 15 percent of their twin-engine planes are purchased by "Forbes TOP 125 Industrialists," less than 28 percent of them are sold in cities of population greater than 500,000, and more than 63 percent of the twin-engine planes are sold in cities with a population of less than 250,000.

Traditionally Beech had concentrated its efforts on the high-performance single-engine and twin-engine aircraft. This left Piper and Cessna virtually alone to compete for the lower-priced aircraft market. However, at about this time Piper and Cessna both began to upgrade the quality of some of their models to compete with the Beech twin. Beech brought out a trainer called the Musketeer, which was later renamed the Sport-Trainer, to compete with the low-priced Cessnas and Pipers.

Part of Beech's rationale for introducing the Musketeer was that research had shown that there was a high degree of brand loyalty among pilots. As a result, it was felt that an individual was more likely to purchase a plane manufactured by the company that made the plane in which he or she had learned to fly. The Musketeer was initially priced almost $5000 higher than its competition. A Beech executive explained the price differential by stating that all their planes are produced in the "quality Beech tradition." The plane is first manufactured and then a price is set that reflects the true cost of the airplane. Several Beech executives felt that this approach might not be applicable for the low-priced market.

Beech sells its nonjet aircraft through approximately 150 dealers, but Cessna and Piper each have more than 500 dealers. Beech dealers are primarily interested in selling new planes, whereas Cessna and Piper dealers are more oriented toward aircraft maintenance and flying instruction. Most of the Cessna and Piper dealers operate flying schools as a part of their dealer operation.

Joel has been asked by his boss to push the Musketeer; however, Joel feels that this will be difficult, because the plane is too expensive and because the local Piper dealer has traditionally gotten most of the "trainer market." Joel told his boss, "Listen Fred, my contacts are in the business community. I know what their needs are and I continually work on them to upgrade their aircraft. I have a great following in Nevada that provides me with lots of leads to other businessmen. I just do not feel it makes any sense for us to fool around with this inexpensive airplane." His boss countered by stating, "Joel, I understand your point of view. However, I am getting pressure from Beech to help make the Musketeer sell, and I may want to open a training school of my own."

1. Was Beech Aircraft marketing-oriented when they introduced the Musketeer?
2. How should Joel handle his boss's request?[21]

---

[21]Taken in part from Stephen A. Greyser, *Cases in Marketing Management* (Englewood Cliffs, N.J.: Prentice-Hall, 1972), pp. 39–72.

Case 2–2 Quality Craftsmen of North Carolina

Florence Escott has been selling furniture for Quality Craftsmen of North Carolina for 11 years. She calls on accounts in Washington, Oregon, and northern California, and is considered an above-average salesperson by her superiors. She is at present preparing to make a call on Kaplan's furniture store in Portland.

Quality Craftsmen is an old furniture company with a complete line of solid-wood furniture. Most of the units are relatively expensive and compete directly with high-quality nationally advertised brands such as Henredon and Heritage.

In the furniture industry most of the buying is done at "market." The various furniture companies display their merchandise in four or five central cities across the United States. Some of the "markets" are permanently set up, but others are in operation only during the buying season. As a result, salespeoples' roles in this industry are unique. It is their responsibility to visit the company's customers to try to keep in touch with what is happening in their territories and to help solve any problems their customers may have with the company. Although salespeople will try to get the retailer to buy more of their mechandise between trips to the market, this sales function is often of secondary importance to the other activities.

Kaplan's furniture store is owned by William J. Kaplan, who has been moderately successful over the years. He describes his customers as those in the "value market." Actually, they are mainly lower-middle-income to middle-income families who buy on credit and extended terms. In addition, his customers are younger than average. One of Kaplan's main appeals has always been that it discounts its products 20 percent off list price. In addition, his salesclerks provide interior decoration suggestions to their customers.

Florence has two objectives to meet on her present swing through the territory. First, she has been asked by Quality's market research department to obtain information concerning what the firm's present competition is at the retail level, and what the dealers estimate future sales will be. This unfortunately will not be easy to obtain from Mr. Kaplan, a very guarded person who feels he is competing as much with his suppliers as he is with other furniture stores. In the past he has not generally been willing to talk about his present sales patterns or what sales growth he projects for the future.

Florence's second objective is to generate participation in a spring sales promotion campaign for Quality's outdoor furniture. Quality is planning to run a series of advertisements on network television and in national magazines to promote its outdoor furniture line. In addition, Quality will provide ad mats to local dealers and will pay half of the cost of local advertising. In turn, Quality is asking each of its dealers to provide space for a floor display and carry a warehouse inventory worth at least $25,000.

On hearing Florence's explanation of the program, Mr. Kaplan's reaction was, "Are you kidding? I only stock $60,000 worth of outdoor furniture in the first place, and you want me to tie half of it up in Quality's line. As far as I am concerned, you people still want too much money for your product.

And, frankly, you are the only furniture company that refuses to give me a price break if I order in volume from you."

1. Have Florence Escott and Quality Craftsmen been marketing-oriented?
2. How should Florence respond to Mr. Kaplan's last statement?
3. What sources, other than Mr. Kaplan, can Florence tap to secure the information her marketing research department has requested?

Setting Objectives: The First Step in Self-management

After studying this chapter, you should be able to

1. Understand the process of self-management.
2. Differentiate between the four levels of self-management.
3. Recognize the advantages of self-management.
4. Identify the criteria of objectives.
5. Determine the information needed to set objectives.
6. Formulate territory objectives, account objectives, call objectives, and personal development objectives.
7. Differentiate between overall strategies, account strategies, call strategies, and personal development strategies.
8. Understand the process for evaluating your results.

The modern salesperson must be an effective manager to survive and prosper in today's marketplace.[1] Increased competition, spiraling costs and increasingly sophisticated buyers demand a new breed of salesperson who must manage in much the same way as other executives.[2] As a salesperson, you are responsible for the business in your territory, and you often operate without day-to-day supervision. Therefore, to ensure your success you should manage yourself, your time, your territory, and your customer relationships. To do this you have to organize your activities, develop plans of action, and monitor your results; these are management tasks.[3]

Regardless of how closely a salesperson is supervised, selling tasks must still be planned and controlled. This chapter presents a framework you can use to manage your efforts and focuses on a key ingredient of that framework—setting objectives.

THE SALESPERSON'S SELF-MANAGEMENT

Effective self-management requires setting objectives, developing strategies to reach those objectives, and evaluating results. The steps provide a systematic framework for improving your performance. The process is shown in Figure 3.1. This chapter discusses all three components.

Setting Objectives

The first step in effective self-management is to set objectives. An objective is a statement of a desired accomplishment; it represents something for you to shoot for and gives you a sense of direction and purpose. Trying to sell without clearly defined objectives results in a lack of direction. An old axiom says, "If you don't know where you are going, any road will get you there."

You should set objectives for each of the key tasks contributing to your success.[4] These objectives might concern the number of calls you wish to make, the number of new accounts you wish to close, the products you wish to sell, and the results you wish to achieve on a particular sales call. It is important that objectives be specific and be set for each of your many responsibilities. Several examples of objectives for a salesperson of an industrial lubricant firm might include:

Increase the average number of calls per day to five for the next quarter.

Generate four new accounts this month.

---

[1]Parts of this chapter are adapted from Donald W. Jackson, Jr., "Managing the Sales Territory," Annual Educator's Conference, Pi Sigma Epsilon (Chicago, 1977), pp. 1–8.

[2]For an interesting discussion of the salesperson's role as a manager, see "The Salesman as Marketer," *Industrial Distribution,* Vol. 74, No. 2 (February 1984), pp. 39–43.

[3]Thomas R. Wotruba, "The Changing Character of Industrial Selling," *European Journal of Marketing,* Vol. 14, No. 5/6 (1980), p. 298.

[4]See, for example, W. H. Weiss, "Planning and Setting Goals for Yourself," *The American Salesman,* Vol. 29, No. 2 (February 1984), pp. 36–39.

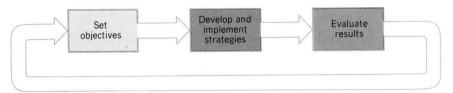

FIGURE 3.1 The process of self-management.

Increase sales volume by 10 percent this year.

Increase commissions to $40,000 this year.

Get General Electric management to put us on their bid list by the end of the next quarter.

Developing Strategies To Reach Objectives

The second component of your management system is to plan strategies to reach your objectives. This planning requires a change in perspective from determining where you are going (your objectives) to focusing on how you will get there (your strategies). After you have set good measurable objectives, you need to identify the steps necessary to attain those objectives. Strategies do not develop themselves; they must be carefully formulated.[5] They are a series of statements of what you plan to do, how you plan to do it, and also of what you want to avoid doing.

For example, on a particular account you might determine that it is necessary to make a formal presentation to the decision makers, develop a formal proposal for the presentation, and cover several points. At the same time you would want to have a very tight agenda and avoid any small talk. This would be your strategy for dealing with this account.

Planning and adjusting strategies are critical in selling. A truly effective salesperson is usually a planner, a person who thinks ahead. Because selling requires flexibility, you must also have contingency plans to use if your initial strategy fails. Contingency plans are one aspect of tactics—the shifts in strategy you must make in the field if you are to succeed. Contingency plans are possible shifts that you may anticipate making because something may happen before the call. For instance, you may plan to close a sale on a particular call but anticipate that your prospect may be distracted by a particular problem. A tactical adjustment would now be necessary. You may choose to schedule a later call or shift your focus during this call to another product that may solve the prospect's problems. The other aspect of tactics concerns the shifts you must make in the field in response to unforeseen events. Despite the possiblity that adjustment will be necessary, it is still important to have a plan of action before you go into the field. One author states, "plan-

---

[5]Marge Figel, "Using a Game Plan to Become a Self Starter," *The American Salesman*, Vol. 28, No. 4 (April 1983), pp. 36 – 42.

ning is necessary, but flexibility is essential. . . . Plan for everything that might happen but don't expect everything you anticipated to happen."[6]

Once your strategy has been developed, it must then be implemented or carried out. This is an important step, because even the best strategy will not be successful if it is not carried out correctly.

Evaluating Performance

In evaluating performance, the final component of your management system, you compare actual results with each objective to determine *where* you need improvement and *why* you did or did not reach your overall objective. Failure to reach a single overall objective, such as a sales quota, does not tell you what you must do to improve your performance. However, by evaluating your results in several areas of activity, you will see *where* you need improvement and *why* you missed your overall objective. You should be constantly looking for situations where your actual results do not coincide with what you wanted to accomplish. The discrepancies will give you direction for self-improvement. For example, if your objective is to make two more calls per week, and it is frequently not met, perhaps your scheduling or routing strategies should be reexamined. You might find that using the telephone more often would enable you to reach this objective.

Failure to reach an objective may be caused by several factors. First, the objective may have been set too high, in which case you would have to set a new objective. Second, your objective may have been set appropriately, but your strategy may have been faulty. Often, this can be determined by comparing your results with those of other salespeople in your company. Third, you may not have implemented your strategy correctly, in which case you would need to do a better job of carrying out your strategy. Finally, environmental factors, such as a poor economy, may have kept you from realizing your objective. In this case, you may have to change either your strategy or your objective.

Evaluation is an ongoing process, for you should be constantly monitoring progress toward your objectives and noting deviations from expected results. Self-evaluation is also the first step in developing your new plan. It gives you information about the success or failure of previous strategies and provides a starting point for new objectives.

FOUR DIFFERENT LEVELS OF SELF-MANAGEMENT

Setting objectives, developing strategies, and evaluating results must be done on four distinct but interacting levels. As a salesperson you must manage (1) your overall territory, (2) each account in your territory, (3) each sales call, and (4) your personal development. Thus the steps just described must be expanded as shown in Figure 3.2. The results at each level are determined by how well you have managed the underlying levels. At the territory level you manage the activities carried out for all customers and prospects. Overall

---

[6]William S. Howell, *The Empathic Communicator* (Belmont, Calif.: Wadsworth, 1982), p. 5.

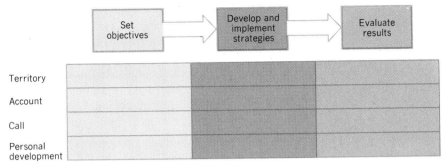

FIGURE 3.2 An expanded view of the salesperson's self-management.

territorial results are determined by the results you achieve with each account in the territory. Therefore, the account level consists of managing each customer or prospect account. Furthermore it may take several sales calls to close each sale with an account, and you may make several sales over a year. Thus, each sales call must also be managed. Similarly, in order to improve your performance on sales calls, you must continue to develop as a person. How these various levels of self-management relate to one another is shown in Figure 3.3

Enhanced personal development leads to more effective sales calls, which in turn improve your results with your accounts. Finally, the accumulated success with accounts brings overall territory success. Thus, what you accomplish on each level builds a foundation for the work you are to do on the next level. Each of these levels will now be described.

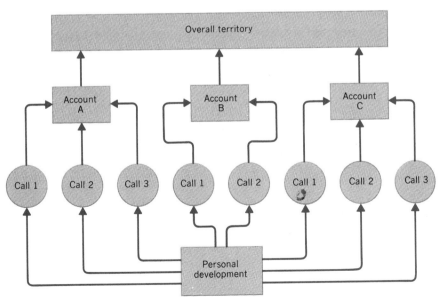

FIGURE 3.3 Relationships between the different levels of self-management.

Overall Territory Management

At the overall territory level, objectives should be set for measures such as total sales, number of sales calls per day, the mix of customer versus prospect sales, and other factors that cut across the entire territory. Strategies to reach these objectives—including time management strategies, routing strategies, prospecting strategies, and others designed to improve overall performance—should also be developed. These strategies are discussed in Chapter 4. Finally, overall performance should be monitored to determine how you are progressing.

Account Management

Objectives should also be set for each account or group of accounts in your territory. For instance a machine tools salesperson might want to specify objectives for major accounts such as Chrysler, General Motors, and Ford. Similarly, strategies should be developed for each account (account strategies are discussed in Chapter 5). Account performance should also be monitored in order to give you insight on your progress with each account.

Sales Call Management

In order to improve your performance, you must also manage each sales call. Again, this consists of setting objectives for each call you make, and then developing a call strategy that specifies what you will say and do on a particular call and what you will avoid saying and doing. Finally, you must critically evaluate your results on each call in order to develop your selling skills and continue to improve.

Personal Development Management

To manage your personal development you must set objectives for improving particular skills and gaining knowledge. You might wish to improve interpersonal skills, develop more management potential, or improve your technical background. Strategies for acquiring skills and gaining knowledge might include attending seminars, reading books, or listening to career-oriented tapes. Finally, you must periodically evaluate your personal development to ensure that you continue to improve.

ADVANTAGES OF SELF-MANAGEMENT

Self-management has several advantages. First, it forces you to focus on the results you expect to achieve. You must state your objectives explicitly and develop strategies designed to reach them. These steps are important because they force you to think about where you are going and how you will get there. The significance of this emphasis on results is made very evident by the high cost of sales calls. For instance, the average cost of an industrial sales call as estimated by McGraw-Hill Research has risen to $205; therefore, every sales call has to count.[7]

[7]Jeremy Main, "How To Sell by Listening," *Fortune*, Vol. 111, No. 3 (February 4, 1985), p. 52.

The second benefit of this multilevel self-management system is in forcing you to set objectives for your activities at these several levels. Thus after evaluating performance, you can pinpoint where you are not reaching your objectives and need improvement. Similarly, the continuous monitoring of results may also serve to motivate you, since achieving specific results provides encouraging feedback.

Finally, self-management may also enable you to fulfill your career goals more effectively. If you decide to go into sales management, these skills will be invaluable. If, on the other hand, you decide to seek out a career as a salesperson, these self-management skills will help keep you more productive.

In summary, a self-management system of setting goals, planning strategies, and evaluating achievements should improve your efficiency. You should become better able to set priorities and to organize your time more effectively. The remainder of this chapter explores objective setting in greater depth.

GUIDELINES FOR SETTING OBJECTIVES

Setting objectives is an important component of your self-management, because objectives give you direction. Without clearly defined objectives, you may waste time on unimportant activities, and setting priorities becomes difficult. In order to set useful objectives you must carefully consider the criteria for objectives as well as the information that will be needed.

Criteria for Objectives

Several factors should be considered when setting objectives. You should make sure that the objectives are congruent, compatible, specific, measurable, set for a time frame, realistic, and written.

Congruent Objectives must fit together and not conflict with one another. An obvious example of incongruent goals would be to wish to cut travel expenses while desiring to spend more time in the field. Attaining both of these objectives simultaneously would be very difficult. Thus, you must step back and examine how your objectives fit together rather than setting them independent of each other.

Compatible Your objectives must also be compatible with the broader corporate and marketing objectives of your firm.[8] Salespeople do not function in isolation. To be most effective, you must act in conjunction with your firm's broader efforts. Your firm's marketing objectives, for instance, may specify which products and customers are to be stressed. If you are trying to sell products that are not promoted or produced in sufficient quantity, or if you call on accounts that cannot be reached economically with the firm's planned

---

[8]Bruce D. Buskirk, "Make Sure Sales Force Tactics, Firm's Goals Don't Conflict," *Marketing News*, Vol. 16, Section 1 (March 18, 1983), p. 20.

distribution or promotion, your efficiency will decline regardless of how hard you try to improve your sales presentation.

Specific Broadly stated goals such as "to increase sales" are so vague that they are difficult to evaluate. For instance, would a 1 percent increase in sales meet this objective? Or should a 10 percent increase be sought? It is important that objectives specify the exact amount of sales increase you wish to achieve or the precise number of new accounts you wish to open. Without the guidance of specific objectives, it is difficult to determine whether you have accomplished what you set out to do.

Measurable Goals such as to "sell better" offer no means of measuring whether the objective has been achieved. Instead you must establish a method of measuring your success or failure before you go out into the field. For instance, if an objective is to average five sales calls per day over the next month, you must keep a record of the exact number of calls you make each day. Failure to record the calls will make it impossible to track your accomplishments.

Specific time period Even specific and measurable goals such as increasing sales by 10 percent must be expressed for a definite time period, such as during the next quarter or month, if they are to provide direction. If a time frame is not set, you may be tempted to postpone action. Thus, the time frame gives you an indication of when you should evaluate your results and provides an appropriate sense of urgency for attaining your objective.

Realistic Keep your objectives realistic as well as ambitious. For instance, it would be unrealistic for a salesperson selling word-processing equipment and making her first call on a prospect to set as her objective to sell a system. But the first call can have a specific, attainable objective such as to get permission to do a survey of the prospect's word-processing requirements or to arrange for the prospect to visit a current user of her system.

Written Finally, your objectives should be written down so that you have no trouble remembering them. Writing the objectives also tends to make you feel more committed to them. Having your objectives in writing keeps them in perspective and also allows you to review them easily.

Information Needed

Several key pieces of information may be utilized when developing objectives. These include past trends, market conditions, economic conditions, and competition.

Past trends Previous performance in a territory gives an indication of the size and direction of the results you might expect in a territory. Although it is important not to be restricted by past trends, they do serve as a starting point. For example, if last year's sales in a territory were one million dollars an objective of five million dollars for this year might be unreasonable unless there were some special circumstances.

Market conditions Another factor is market conditions. You should carefully examine your market to determine trends and factors that might expand or inhibit demand. Factors such as unemployment, labor strikes, unavailability of raw materials, or social trends might all affect demand for a particular product. In addition, various locations within the country will have unique conditions. For example, the demand for many products in Detroit is influenced by the automble industry; similarly, the Pacific Northwest market is affected by the lumber business.

Economic conditions The economy will often influence results in your territory. Some products will be adversely affected by a poor economy, whereas other products actually do better in a poor economy because they represent cost savings or substitutions for more expensive products. Economic factors such as inflation, interest rates, and construction activity should be considered when establishing objectives.

Competition Finally, you must examine competition prior to setting objectives. This will enable you to capitalize on your own advantages and counter your competitors' strengths. Factors such as new entrants into the market, new models, or a competitor's promotional campaign should all be considered.[9]

KINDS OF OBJECTIVES

Remember, objectives should be set for the entire territory, for each account or class of accounts, for each sales call, and for your personal development. Determining which objectives are appropriate for a particular territory will depend on the unique characteristics of the territory and on past performance in the territory. Sometimes your manager or other salespeople in your company can suggest areas in which to set objectives. Each of these objectives should be put in writing before you go into the field.

Territory Objectives
Territory objectives are overall objectives and might include such things as which products to stress, which customers to pay particular attention to, the desired number of accounts, and others. Several examples of territory objectives are given in Table 3.1.

These overall objectives, whether developed by management or by you, provide you with broad direction. They indicate the overall achievement lev-

---

[9]For more insight on how to get information on competition, see William A. Clark, "Where to Get Information from Your Competitor," *Marketing Times,* Vol. 30, No. 2 (March–April 1983), pp. 19–22.

TABLE 3.1

EXAMPLES OF POSSIBLE TERRITORY OBJECTIVES[a]

Increase sales volume by 10 percent.

Keep average gross margin on goods sold at 20 percent.

Increase the number of calls per day to six.

Increase order–call ratio to 50 percent.

Increase average size of order to $5000.

Reduce the ratio of selling expense to net sales to 2 percent.

Generate 20 new accounts.

Keep the number of lost accounts below 10 percent.

Earn at least $40,000 in commissions over the next year.

[a]Unless otherwise noted, each of the objectives in the table would
be for a certain planning period, which might be a quarter of a year.

els desired for the territory. After territory objectives have been set, the next
step is to establish objectives for each account or classification of accounts.

Account Objectives

Account objectives should be similar to the territory objectives and may concern products, volume, or profitablitity. They should be set for each customer
and prospect in your territory. Examples of objectives for a specific account
are given in Table 3.2.

Although these objectives are only examples of the many that might be
used for a specific account, they do point out the varied efforts you must
make in order to get the job done. Again, they serve as a source of direction
to you when planning your time and efforts.

Achieving account objectives is critical to achieving the territory objectives outlined earlier. If territory objectives and account objectives are not
harmonious, you must look for ways to reconcile the differences. For in-

TABLE 3.2

EXAMPLE OF OBJECTIVES FOR WORD
PROCESSING, INC. ACCOUNT[a]

Achieve $50,000 sales per year.

Get them to buy at least 50 percent of our total line.

Increase average order size to $5000.

Become sole supplier for a particular product.

Increase gross margin to 21 percent.

Get them to consolidate orders to 10 per year.

Get collection time down to 30 days.

Reduce expenses to 1 percent of sales.

[a]Unless otherwise noted, each of the objectives in the table
would be for one planning period, whether it might be one
quarter or a year.

stance, if the sum of all the account sales turns out to be less than the total territory sales, you should explore such avenues as finding new prospects or expanding sales to existing customers. If goals are still not in line, territory objectives may have to be revised.

In addition to the many factors noted earlier, another useful piece of information when setting account objectives is an analysis of past sales. These allow you to project what you might achieve if you continued to sell in the same manner as in the past. A prerequisite to this kind of analysis, however, is information on who is buying what. Many companies have computerized sales analysis systems that provide salespeople with this information.[10] However, when this is not available, you may also develop your own filing system for classifying sales by product, customer, or both.

In some sales jobs, because of the sheer number of customers, it is impossible to set account objectives for each customer in a territory. In these situations customer groups or key customers may be used instead.[11] These groupings may be based on type of business, geography, use of the product, or size of orders. An example of this type of account objective would be "increase sales to hardware stores by 10 percent over the next year."

Sales Call Objectives

Objectives must also be set for each call and should come naturally from account objectives, so that each call contributes to the final account objectives. Although you may set overall and even account objectives with your sales manager, you are usually responsible for setting call objectives. These objectives should be specific and should be stated in writing before the call. According to David Stumm, "One of the biggest negative factors in selling is in the failure of the salesperson to have a specific objective for every single call."[12] It is too easy to rationalize the results achieved as being those expected if goals are not clearly set beforehand. Call objectives could range from closing a sale to informing a recent buyer of the use and maintenance of a product. What is important is that before you walk through your customer's door, you are aware of what you hope to accomplish. Table 3.3 illustrates some specific call objectives that might be used. It is important to note that the call objectives need not always be to close the sale.

In many situations purchase, as such, is not the call objective. In such situations, reaching objectives is more complex and the salesperson has less conclusive evidence of having achieved objectives. The two principal situations in which purchase is not the objective are (1) when more than one call will be required to complete the sale, and (2) when the salesperson is not dealing with the ultimate user.

The first situation, knowing in advance that several calls will be needed before a purchasing decision can be expected, is more common than the

---

[10]See, for example, Peter Finch, "How Computers Are Reshaping the Sales Process," *Business Marketing,* Vol. 70, No. 6 (June 1985), pp. 108–118.

[11]Donald W. Jackson, Jr., and Lonnie L. Ostrom, "Grouping Segments for Profitability Analysis," *MSU Business Topics,* Vol. 28, No. 2 (Spring 1980), pp. 38–44.

[12]David A. Stumm, *Advanced Industrial Selling* (New York: Amacom, 1981), p. 30.

TABLE 3.3

EXAMPLES OF POSSIBLE SALES CALL OBJECTIVES

Close the sale for at least 500 units.

Demonstrate a product.

Present technical information and leave a sample.

Check to see whether an order has been received and installed.

Convince a prospect to put you on the bid list.

Show the buyer a new product.

Obtain a trial order of at least 100 units.

Determine who the decision makers are within an account.

Qualify a prospect.

second. Under these circumstances you must have specific objectives to achieve on each individual call. The objective for each consists of obtaining agreement up to a particular point. Between calls, however, you can expect changes in the situation: decision makers may forget; competitors may shift their efforts; new personnel may need to be influenced. Therefore, on each succeeding call you must determine the extent to which agreement still does exist; and where it does not, you must rebuild the relationship.

The second situation not expected to conclude with a sale is a call to a person who does not actually make the purchase but only prescribes the product or recommends the purchase to others. An example of this situation is the pharmaceutical salesperson who calls on a physician. The main call objective is to convince the doctor to prescribe the firm's products for patients. Similarly, the textbook salesperson hopes to convince instructors to use the firm's textbooks in their courses. In industrial selling, where there are often two or more decision makers in a given account, it is common for one

Pharmaceutical salesperson calling on a physician.

of them to be designated as the person who finally places the order. Thus, the industrial salesperson cannot expect purchase from each person seen. For example, it would be rare for the director of research to place an order. The objective of meeting with such people is to convince them they should recommend the products for use by the firm.

It is the nature of the selling job that you should not expect to reach your objectives on every call. You are dealing with people, and unexpected circumstances may come up that force you to alter your behavior and revise your objectives. However, it is important for you to start each call with a clear idea of what you want to accomplish.

Personal Development Objectives

You should also set objectives for your personal development. Although achievement of these objectives is more difficult to measure than achievement of territory, account, and call objectives, they are important none-the-less. Only through continual improvement will you grow. Furthermore, because the marketplace is constantly changing, it is important that you continually develop with it and remain knowledgeable.

Objectives can be set for the development of four kinds of skills: interpersonal skills, technical skills, selling skills, and skills that will prepare you for advancement.

Interpersonal skills The interpersonal skills to be improved might be your listening skills, your speaking ability, and your ability to read nonverbal clues, as well as overcoming personality deficiencies or learning to evaluate prospects more effectively.

Technical skills You may wish to improve your technical skills. You may, for example, lack the ability to write effective reports, be deficient in your knowledge of the product, or be slow in writing your orders. You can set specific objectives for improving these skills and your knowledge of the product.

Selling skills Particular selling skills you might wish to improve are overcoming objections, closing, and prospecting.

Preparation for advancement You may also wish to prepare yourself for advancement—perhaps into a higher-level sales job or into management. Objectives of this sort might include acquisiton of supervisory skills, attending management seminars, or acquiring greater breadth of knowledge concerning your firm's markets.

DEVELOPING STRATEGIES

Strategies are the steps necessary to reach your objectives and are an important component of your self-management system. They have two important aspects. First, you must distinguish and understand the various kinds of strategies—overall strategies, account strategies, sales call strategies, and personal development strategies. Second, you must view planning and developing these strategies from a cost–benefit standpoint and justify these activities as investments.

Kinds of Strategies

Territory management strategies Strategies that must be developed for managing your overall territory include your account analysis, your prospecting strategy to develop new accounts, your routing strategy to schedule movements in your territory, and your time management strategy. These aspects of your territory management strategy are covered in Chapter 4.

Account strategies You should set out specific steps for working with each customer and prospect in your territory.[13] With established customer accounts you are already getting business from the account; thus, your major strategic goals are to protect your position from competitors and to get a larger share of the customer's business. On the other hand, with prospect accounts, you are trying to persuade the prospect to adopt your product or service.

Sales call strategies On each call you need to decide what you will say and do and what you will avoid saying and doing. These decisions make up a blueprint or rough script for how you think you will handle the call. But, of course, you must also be prepared to adjust your approach to meet the customer's needs. Guidelines for developing account and call strategies are covered in Chapter 5.

Personal development strategies The final kind of strategy consists of the actions you take to develop yourself as a professional salesperson. Specific steps to ensure your development might be continuing your education, reading, taking training programs, and becoming active in the community. Various steps you might take to develop yourself are covered in Chapter 18.

The Cost–Benefit Trade-off in Planning

Developing strategies is a very complex process that requires a substantial amount of time, but the time must be considered as an investment. You should recognize that planning enables you to change course faster and to react more correctly than if you merely tried to react to every event in the field. Planning is most justified and most critical when it will have the largest payback in improved results.

Because a salesperson is under time pressure, the total amount of planning you will do for one situation will be a function of how much potential business you feel the prospect has to offer. As an example, an individual who sells paper and office supplies will spend more time planning a call to a large department store than one to a small neighborhood store.

---

[13]See, for example, Daniel Caust, "A Plan for Every Customer," *Sales and Marketing Management,* Vol. 125, No. 1 (July 7, 1980), pp. 36–37.

Evaluating your results allows you to determine which objectives you have reached, where you failed, and where you excelled. In this stage you compare your actual results to your objectives, which serve as a measuring stick. Evalution allows you to identify your strong and weak points, highlights the areas needing improvement, and reveals strengths that should be capitalized on. Evaluation should be made of your entire territory, of each account, of each sales call, and of your personal development.

Territorial Evaluations

Territorial evaluations compare your overall results to your overall objectives. In order to evaluate your performance, you must plan in advance to collect information on your actual performance. Some firms have sophisticated computer systems to help their sales forces evaluate their performance.[14] When a computer is not available, you must collect your own information on sales by product, customer, geographical area, and other important aspects. Often, a simple analysis of your orders will enable you to derive much of this information.

An example of a simple form that may be used to evaluate your overall results, along with several sample entries, is given in Figure 3.4. Territorial objectives should be listed at the beginning of the time period and actual results inserted at the end of the period. Further analysis will enable you to determine the reasons for your successes or failures. Analysis of territorial performance reveals your strong and weak points and gives you a summary form to use for your future planning.

Evaluation of Overall Performance

FOR TIME PERIOD FROM ___1/1___ TO ___12/31___

FOR SALESPERSON ___Mary Smith___

TERRITORIAL OBJECTIVES	ACTUAL RESULTS	REASONS FOR DIFFERENCES
Increase sales by 10 percent over the next year	Sales increased by 12 percent	Closed two large new prospects
Average 6 calls per day over the next year	Averaged 5 calls per day	Need to make more early morning calls
Get 50 percent of customer base to try the new X-72	Half tried it	Mission accomplished: Now start working on the other half.

FIGURE 3.4 Form for evaluation of overall performance.

[14]See, for example, Peter R. Finch, "How Computers Are Reshaping the Sales Process," *Business Marketing,* Vol. 70, No. 6 (June 1985), pp. 108–118.

Account Evaluations

Actual results from each account should also be compared to your account objectives. Evaluating account performance enables you to determine your most successful accounts. You may then ask yourself *why* they are more productive. If the account was simply a better prospect, you should change your prospecting habits to concentrate on the more productive type of account. On the other hand, if your *strategy* for dealing with the more productive type of account was superior, you should incorporate that strategy into dealing with your other accounts. Basically, this sort of analysis enables you to determine which accounts were the most productive and enables you to direct your activities toward productive accounts or accounts with the most potential.

Call Evaluation

You should also evaluate the results of each sales call. Evaluating each call allows you to determine what you have learned and what you can use in the future with the same account or with others. Without evaluating calls and incorporating what you have learned into future calls, you will not improve or use new found knowledge to your advantage. The procedure is to compare your call objectives with your actual performance. One method of doing this is to use a call report, which is your record (for yourself, management, or both) of your actual achievements in your calls: when you made them, whom you called on, and what you achieved.[15] An example of a call report with a sample entry is given in Figure 3.5. An abbreviated summary may accompany the call report to highlight your weekly progress, as depicted in the lower part of Figure 3.5. Some fims such as PPG have actually computerized their call reports so that the sales person can virtually eliminate paperwork, allowing more time for selling.[16]

When evaluating your call report, you should compare your objectives and your actual accomplishments even if you are not required to do so, in order to determine areas of deficiency. For instance, do you constantly fail to get appointments to demonstrate your product, to secure call-backs, to close? Each of these failures would point out an area for improvement. For instance, the following information may be available from your call report.

Prospect's name and title The name and title of your prospect are important because they tell you whether you are actually talking to the person you had planned to call on.

Number and type of call By looking at the number of calls and whether the calls are on customers or prospects, you can see whether you are being active enough to reach your objectives and whether you are making a sufficient number of new calls.

---

[15]For an interesting discussion of call reports, see Hal Fahner, "Call Reports That Tell It All," *Sales and Marketing Management*, Vol. 133, No. 6 (November 12, 1984), pp. 50–52.

[16]Thayer C. Taylor, "Paperless Call Reports Bring PPG More Data," *Sales and Marketing Management*, Vol. 131, No. 8 (December 5, 1983), pp. 52–56.

Call Report for Salesperson _____ *Mary Smith* _____

For the Week of _____ *7/7* _____

Date	Time From	To	Account	Prospect Talked To	Results	To Do Next
7/7	8:00	9:00	ABC Distributor	Don Jordon	Received order for $10,000	Follow up by 7/14

Weekly Summary

Calls Actual _____ versus Calls Planned _____

Results Actual _____ versus Results Planned _____

Calls to Next Week's Itinerary _____

FIGURE 3.5 Example of a call report.

Continued failure to meet a specified objective Failure to meet a specified type of call objective, such as closing, being allowed to make a demonstration, or getting on a bid list, may signal that you function poorly in particular activities; you may need help from your manager or the counsel of other more experienced salespeople. Of course, you will never reach your call objective on every call, but continued problems can be a signal for you to seek help.

Another useful approach is self-analysis. After every call you should analyze what was said and done; decide what you could have done better what strategies were successful enough to be used again later. In analyzing your sales call performance, you may need to ask questions similar to the ones in Table 3.4.

TABLE 3.4
QUESTIONS FOR EVALUATING THE CALL
_____

Was the call objective realistic?
Did I call on the right person?
Did I prepare sufficiently?
What additional preparation would have improved the sales call?
What should I have done differently?
What did I do well that I should try again?
What was accomplished on this call?
Were visual aids used? If so, were they used properly?
Was the prospect allowed to express his or her views openly?
Did I ask for the order or for other appropriate commitments?

Several benefits accrue to you from such a system. First, you have a clear picture of your performance on a call-by-call basis. Second, you have a clear statement of what you will do next, which makes your next call more productive. Finally, you have a periodic review of your achievements.

Evaluating Personal Development

The final step is to evaluate your personal development. The procedure is the same as in other evaluations: you compare your personal development objectives to your results. Nevertheless, this analysis is perhaps the most difficult to do. Most salespeople find that it is difficult to be objective in evaluating their personal development. Often, day-to-day pressures force you to put off attending to personal development in favor of more pressing operating efforts.

There are several steps you may take to solve these problems. First, you can obtain a more objective appraisal of your personal development by asking an outsider to assist you. Sales managers, friends, associates, or other salespeople are often willing to help. Second, you should set aside some specific time during the year, presumably not prime selling time, to be spent in evaluating your personal development. An objective, conscientious, periodic look at your personal development may pay off handsomely in the long run by forcing you to plan and evaluate your development.

Evaluation allows critical analysis of your strategies and their implementation. When evaluating your performance, note the strategies that were successful and continue them; discontinue unsuccessful strategies. This conscious attempt to evaluate the soundness of your strategies should help you to be more efficient. Evaluation is also the first step in setting new objectives, as you answer questions like these: Were my old objectives realistic? Given last year's results, what can I expect next year?

Thus, you have come full circle. You set objectives, developed strategies for reaching these objectives, and evaluated your results. You are right back to setting objectives. Such a procedure is the basis for an effective self-management program. Consciously followed, it will improve your results, give you direction, and enable you to succeed.

SUMMARY

In this chapter a three-pronged framework for managing the sales territory was examined: setting objectives, developing strategies to reach these objectives, and evaluating results. Each of these steps is carried out on four different levels: for the territory as a whole, for each account or group of accounts, for each sales call, and for your personal development. Each level builds upon the others. Personal development leads to better sales calls, which lead to improved account activity, which ultimately means better territory performance.

Objectives should be congruent, compatible, specific, measurable, realistic, written, and set for a specific time period. Several bits of key information—such as past trends, market conditions, economic conditions, and competiton—should be examined when setting objectives.

Guidelines and examples were presented for territorial objectives, account objectives, sales call objectives, and personal development objectives. A clear delineation of objectives will help you in planning and organizing your time and efforts. You will know where you are going and will have a yardstick for measuring your results.

After goals have been set for your overall performance in your territory, for the customers and prospects in the territory, for each call, and for your personal development, you are ready to plan strategies for reaching these goals. Planning needs to be viewed as an investment. You must seek to maximize the return on the time you invest in planning.

The final step in your self-management program is to evaluate your results. This step helps you to build upon your strengths and correct your weaknesses.

PROBLEMS

1. What are the roles of top management, marketing management, sales management, and the salesperson in setting objectives?
2. Explain in your own words the key elements in the salesperson's self-management. In what ways do the elements interact?
3. Differentiate between the concepts of strategy and tactics.
4. What are the differences in setting objectives and developing strategies for serving current customers in contrast to prospective customers?
5. Explain, in your own words, differences between territorial objectives, account objectives, call objectives, and personal development objectives. Give an example of each.

EXERCISE 3

Objectives: To increase understanding of the self-management process.

To apply knowledge of self-management to the sales call.

PART A Personal Application
What is the most important thing you hope to achieve tomorrow? Outline your plan, noting

1. Your objective.
2. Your strategy.
3. Your results.

Note: You will have to wait until tomorrow night to specify your results.

PART B Call Objectives
The following are statements of possible call objectives. Select the one you think best meets the critera discussed in the text. How would you adapt the others to make them meet the criteria?

1. To obtain more business.
2. To introduce one or more products.

3. To seek information about the account.
4. To convince the purchasing agent to test a sample of our product X by next Thursday.
5. To sell at least a trial order of our product Y.

Case 3–1 Satellite Stereo, Incorporated

Tom Swift represents RTA, a multinational manufacturer and marketer of electronic devices and components. Other divisions of his firm produce and sell end-products for use in navigation or control systems in plants.

Tom is reviewing his accounts and making plans for the upcoming quarter. Of his key prospects, he decides that Satellite Stereo will be his prime target. He faces a difficult problem: RTA was once a major supplier of Satellite, before he was assigned the territory. However, Satellite dropped RTA and vowed never to do business with the firm again.

RTA's version of what happened is as follows: Satellite was developing a miniaturized inexpensive tape recorder. It was to be supplied to a national discount chain and marketed under the chain's label. This represented a radical departure for Satellite. At that time they were producing only high-quality, costly products under their own label. RTA manufactured devices for the new product to Satellite's specifications. At the time they alerted Satellite to the hazards of printed circuits and inexpensive power units. The upshot was that many of the units were returned to the chain and caused considerable trouble and loss of goodwill.

Satellite's version of what happened is that RTA, in a bid to be price-competitive, cut corners in production and failed to maintain quality control. Furthermore, Satellite accused RTA of shipping devices without final inspection.

Tom has called on Satellite monthly for the eighteen months he has been in the territory. Bill Lynch, number two in purchasing at Satellite, has been willing to see Tom but has told him, "My hands are tied. Our production manager, George Young, can't bear to hear the name RTA." Tom pointed out to Bill that RTA furnished items to Satellite for use in other products and as far as can be determined only good results were obtained. Bill has indicated that Dick Zimmerman, Satellite's vice-president of marketing, is also anti-RTA.

RTA's engineering department, at Bill's request, thoroughly analyzed specimens of Satellite's leading products and gave him a rundown on which RTA products might be used in various parts of the line. Wherever possible, they have also told Tom whose competitive products are now being used.

Tom recently learned that Satellite is phasing out of the private-label recorder–player business. Thus, the disagreement that lost the account has little or no significance today.

Tom jots down the best description he can make of Bill Lynch, the purchasing manager.

Background: Engineering graduate; went to work at Satellite right out of college; married; about 35 years old; active in the local chapter of purchasing agents.

Personality: Mild, cheerful, conventional, serious, practical, dependent, courteous.

Motivation: Seeks status with own management and peers in purchasing. Aspires to be number one. (His boss, Mr. Baker, is 55.) Great personal integrity which influences how he does business.

As Tom sees it, unless he can find some way to reach and influence George Young and Dick Zimmerman, he cannot crack the account.

Outline an objective and strategy for Tom's next call.

Case 3–2 Ross Brothers Sporting Goods

Mary Smith just went to work for Ross Brothers, a wholesaler serving a three-state area. The firm carries a full line of athletic and outdoor recreational equipment. Most of its customers are retail stores, but it does sell goods to the athletic departments of high schools and colleges. Mary has been hired to replace Tom Evans, who was released because he did not seem to be doing a good job. Jim Ross, the sales manager, has given Mary a folder containing information about her territory and some records Tom had left. In the folder she finds a list of Tom's territorial objectives for the last year. The list is as follows.

1. Sell more baseball equipment.
2. Show each of our accounts the new running outfits.
3. Try to make more calls.
4. Concentrate on the large accounts in the territory.

What should be Mary's reaction to the objectives?

Territory Management Strategies

After studying this chapter, you should be able to

1. Understand how to analyze the accounts in your territory.
2. Identify strategies for handling unprofitable accounts.
3. Describe various forms for generating leads.
4. Know how to qualify leads.
5. Recognize various routing methods.
6. Understand key concepts for managing time.
7. Appreciate specific strategies for managing selling time.

A salesperson must follow several broad territory management strategies in order to reach overall objectives. These include account analysis, prospecting, routing, and time management strategies.[1] Each of these is explored in this chapter.

ACCOUNT ANALYSIS STRATEGIES

In order to be effective and efficient in your territory, you must allocate your time to accounts with the most potential. To single out these accounts, you need to have a thorough understanding of all present accounts.[2] Without this understanding, it is impossible to plan future efforts effectively. The questions set forth in Table 4.1 provide a quick test to use in assessing your current business. If you are unable to answer these questions, you are probably taking your established accounts for granted. Yet they represent the foundation for the present and future business of your firm.

ABC Analysis

In order to allocate your time and to spot trends in your territory, it is important to conduct account analysis, which means classifying present accounts on the basis of their volume and potential. One way of assessing accounts is ABC analysis.[3] Accounts are first classified on the basis of their present volume. Thus, accounts generating sales over $100,000 for one salesperson might be A accounts; accounts falling between $50,000 and $100,000 might be B accounts; and those under $50,000 might be C accounts. It is important to recognize that these cutoff points depend on the specific territory. For a salesperson in another business the cutoff point for A accounts might be over $1 million in sales. After accounts have been classified by volume, the next step is to adjust the classifications on the basis of account potential. Thus, a C account with very high potential might be reclassified as an A account, or a B account that is about to file for bankruptcy might be reclassified as a C account. The net result is that A accounts have a high volume of sales or high potential, B accounts have a medium volume of sales or medium potential, and C accounts have a low volume of sales or low potential. When most salespeople perform ABC analysis on their territories, they find they are spending a disproportionate amount of time with C accounts and not nearly enough of their time with A accounts.[4]

---

[1]For a good overview of territory management strategies, see Ron Kolgraf, "Strategies of Territory Management," *Industrial Distribution,* Vol. 67, No. 5 (November 1978), pp. 35–40.

[2]See, for example, Thomas A. Whitty, "Focusing the Sales Effort," *Sales and Marketing Management,* Vol. 123, No. 4 (September 17, 1979), pp. 57–60.

[3]For an alternative way of analyzing customers, see Gordon Canning, Jr., "Do a Value Analysis of Your Customer Base," *Industrial Marketing Management,* Vol. 11, No. 5 (April 1982), pp. 89–93; or Raymond W. LaForge and Clifford E. Young, "A Portfolio Model to Improve Sales Call Coverage, *Business,* Vol. 35 (April–June 1985), pp. 10–16.

[4]For more information on ABC analysis, see Porter Henry's "The Important Few—The Unimportant Many," 1980 Portfolio of Sales and Marketing Plans (New York: Sales and Marketing Management 1980), pp. 42–45.

TABLE 4.1
A SALESPERSON'S TEST FOR ASSESSING
CURRENT CUSTOMERS

How many customers do you have?

Which are your key accounts?

Which are unprofitable for you?

How often do each of your major types of customers need to be called on?

How many hours does each type of customer require?

How many selling hours are needed to service your present business without wasting precious time in overlong calls?

SOURCE: Adapted from *Sales Management: The Marketing Magazine,* Vol. 106, No. 7 (April 1, 1971), p. 17.

The typical salesperson has a large number of accounts; yet only a very small percentage of these usually represent a large proportion of sales and profits. For example, a cosmetics salesperson who has 150 accounts might find that the accounts are distributed as shown in Table 4.2. This particular salesperson has 15 A accounts, which make up 50 percent of volume, and 69 C accounts, which make up 10 percent of volume.

You must spend proportionately more time on accounts that represent a large portion of your business. You should not spend time trying to get a small, low-potential account to buy more merchandise if it means neglecting one of your larger accounts. Many sales representatives base their planned call frequencies on the amount of business the customer does with them. Table 4.3 continues the example of the cosmetics salesperson. This salesper-

TABLE 4.2
COSMETICS SALESPERSON'S CATEGORIZATION OF CUSTOMERS

ACCOUNT CLASSIFICIATION	NUMBER OF CUSTOMERS RANKED BY VOLUME (OR PROFIT)	VOLUME (OR PROFIT) FOR TOTAL TERRITORY, PERCENT
A	15	50
B	66	40
C	69	10

TABLE 4.3
COSMETICS SALESPERSON'S COMMUNICATION WITH ACCOUNTS

ACCOUNT CLASSIFICATION	PERSONAL VISITS	TELEPHONE CALLS
A	Three per month	Three per month, or as often as necessary
B	One per month	Three per month
C	Four per year	One per month

son visits A accounts on average three times per month and telephones them three times per month or as often as necessary. At the other extreme, the C accounts are visited only four times each year and telephoned only once a month. Of course, if a C customer telephoned, you would return the call or possibly even visit with the customer. You have a limited amount of time, and you must try to spend a proportionately large amount of it with key accounts.

Handling Unprofitable Accounts

Unprofitable accounts are accounts for which the investment of your time does not justify the return.[5] Thus, even a large account may be unprofitable for you if it takes a disproportionate amount of time, and a small account may be profitable if it does not take much time. Because you have only a limited amount of time, your objective should be to maximize the return on the time you invest in selling. It is important to note three things about classifying unprofitable accounts. First, it may be appropriate to continue serving an unprofitable account if it has enough potential. Second, in order to drop an unprofitable account, a more profitable account must be available that will enable you to sell more in less time. Third, some of the strategies used to handle unprofitable accounts may result in your losing them. This is inevitable and is acceptable as long as it is done professionally and with the knowledge of the consequences. With this in mind, several strategies are available for handling unprofitable accounts.

Call on them less frequently Unprofitable accounts may become more profitable in terms of an investment of your time if you can call on them less frequently. If you can get the same amount of business from the account with fewer calls, the account will be more profitable to you. Encouraging the account to consolidate orders may make the account more profitable for you. Thus, instead of calling on a small account once a week, calling on them once a month may be more appropriate.

Use the telephone Often unprofitable accounts, especially small remote ones, may be profitably served by telephone. Replacing in-person calls with telephone calls is certain to cut costs and may make the account profitable if this procedure is acceptable to the account.

Sell at trade shows Some unprofitable accounts may be handled at trade shows, where the customer comes to you rather than you visiting the customer. This dramatically reduces the time invested and may increase the attractiveness of the account. It may be possible to encourage these accounts to use this procedure by personally inviting them to your booth and giving them careful personal attention when they are at your display.

---

[5]For more discussions on the return on time invested in a customer, see Robert F. Vizza, "ROTI: Profitable Selling's New Math," *Sales and Marketing Management—Special Report: Time and Territory Management*, Vol. 116, No. 8 (May 24, 1976), pp. 17–22.

Mail-in order It may be possible to have some accounts, mail in routine orders rather than your having to call on them to take these orders. This may be a way to save valuable time.

Drop them Some accounts are simply unprofitable. If you have tried all the preceding strategies, it may be appropriate to turn them over to distributors or wholesalers or stop selling the account, providing there are more profitable uses of your time. You should be careful not to cause any bad feelings that may be conveyed to other customers.

PROSPECTING STRATEGIES

Many times it is important to look for new business. For example, no matter how well you monitor existing accounts, you will occasionally lose some of them to competition. Futhermore, some of your accounts may go out of business or relocate to another area. In addition, your firm may ask you to attract new business as plant capacity increases or as new opportunities become available. In some markets, such as residential real estate, there is very little repeat business, and salespeople are always looking for new accounts. Several definitions are appropriate when examining sources of new business.

A *prospect* is a person or institution with a need for your product or service, the authority to buy, and the ability to pay for the product or service. A *lead,* on the other hand, is a person or institution that might be a potential prospect. Thus, in order to turn a lead into a prospect, the lead has to be *qualified.* This is the act of determining whether a lead has a need for your offering, the authority to buy, and the financial resources to be able to pay for it. Until leads are qualified they are suspects, not prospects.

Generating Leads
Several avenues are available to you in generating leads. You should examine each carefully and then select the method or source or combination of methods and sources that best fits your needs. The nine basic ways to generate leads are listed in Table 4.4.[6]

Endless chain When you use the endless chain, each prospect is asked to provide you with three or four names of individuals who might be interested in purchasing your product or service. A professional salesperson makes the prospect feel the visit was worthwhile even if no purchase is made. Thus, you can ask for leads even if you did not successfully complete the sale. A good example of this approach is a local lawn service that asks each of its customers for the names of their immediate neighbors. The lawn service then mails each a notice about the service and offers a free estimate.

[6]There are also other sources for generating leads. See, for example, "Sales Leads: They're Everywhere," *Industrial Distribution,* Vol. 76, No.2 (February 1983), pp. 35–39.; "21 Sales Door Openers," *Industrial Distribution,* Vol. 76, No. 5 (May 1983), pp. 88–90.

TABLE 4.4
METHODS OF GENERATING LEADS

Endless chain
Referrals
Important people
Noncompeting sales representatives
Junior sales representatives
Acquaintances and friends
Telephone and mail
Directories
Cold canvasing

Referrals Referrals involve asking the customer to go one step further than with the endless chain. That is, you ask the customer not only to provide names of individuals who might be interested in your product, but also to contact these individuals for you.[7] Often the customer can say things about experience with you and with your products and services that would not be believable if they came directly from you. Obviously, this approach works only if you and the customer have a positive, long-standing relationship.

When business is referred to you by a customer, you should be sure to thank the referrer.[8] A telephone call, small business gift, or a short note may be appropriate, but you do want to thank them for the business.

Important people Most sales territories have individuals or firms whose buying behavior directly influences others. If you are to maximize your success within your territory, you will want to identify and cultivate such influential accounts, even if it means spending more money and time on them then they justify on their own merits. Several years ago, for example, investigators observed that air conditioners occurred in clusters rather than being randomly distributed throughout the market. The research found that in each instance one individual began the buying process in each cluster. Once this key person had purchased an air conditioner, neighbors, who viewed this person as a trend setter, purchased theirs. Research in the medical field supports these findings. Certain physicians tend to be viewed by their colleagues as leaders in the use of new, successful medical practices.[9] As a result, their behavior

---

[7]For background and exploration of why buyers will give referrals, see John R. Stuteville, "The Buyer as a Salesman," *Journal of Marketing*, Vol. 32, No. 3 (July 1968), pp. 14–16.

[8]Hank Tresler, "Selling Referrals: Where the Rubber Meets the Road!," *Insurance Sales*, Vol. 126, No. 9 (September 1983), p. 26.

[9]Raymond A. Bauer and Lawrence H. Wortzel, "Doctor's Choice: The Physician and His Source of Information about Drugs," *Journal of Marketing Research*, Vol. 3, No. 1 (February 1966), pp. 40–48.

is often followed. In the industrial marketplace, small firms frequently look to the large ones to determine what to buy and whom to buy it from.

Noncompeting sales representatives Noncompeting sales representatives are particularly useful if you both provide leads for each other and thus both feel a need to continue the relationship. However, this source may not provide enough information for you to classify the leads as likely prospects, and you may need to tap additional sources of information. One company, Great Lakes Supply Company, encourages its salespeople to develop close relationships with manufacturers' representatives so that they can get leads.[10]

Occasionally, the noncompeting salesperson may be able to furnish a direct entree, either through a joint call or through permission to be a reference. Before this entree is used, however, you should make sure that your colleague has a favorable relationship with this account. If this is not the case, the reference may have a very negative effect. Usually leads from noncompeting sales representatives are suspect and should be examined very closely to determine how much potential business is available and how the account should be approached.

Some salespeople have formed networking associations where they meet to exchange leads and to socialize. These networking associations are a good way to gather information about potential prospects, perhaps over a breakfast meeting. Salespeople or business owners can get together, describe their business, and get sales leads from other members of the network. The national organization, National Business Executives, was formed exclusively for networking.[11]

Junior sales representatives Inexperienced sales representatives are frequently used as "bird dogs" to determine how much business might be available from a number of accounts. This activity gives the newer sales person good experience in the field and avoids wasting the experienced salesperson's time on unproductive leads. Normally, when this procedure is followed, the junior salesperson turns any good leads over to an experienced salesperson, who then attempts to make a sale.

Acquaintances and friends Bankers and other people in the financial community are extremely valuable to the salesperson whose products represent substantial capital outlays. Executives of trade associations, industrial groups, and chambers of commerce can also be useful in providing information concerning new businesses and shifts in the objectives of existing firms. Frequently, these people do not want to be cited as having furnished informa-

[10]"Sales Leads: They're Everywhere," *Industrial Distribution,* Vol. 76, No. 2 (February 1983), p. 36.

[11]"Networking: The Essential Arm of Marketing," *Marketing Times,* Vol. 30, No. 6 (November–December 1983), p. 5.

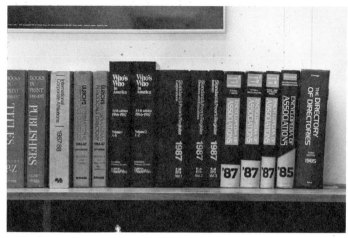

Directories are a good source of leads.

tion, since they work with many businesses; you must respect this confidence if you want to maintain this source of information.

Telephone and mail Telephone and mail inquiries and responses to advertising constitute another important source of leads.[12] When following them up, you must carefully screen good leads from those that have little potential, and you must do so with a minimum investment of your time and effort. It may be useful to phone or write such prospects before making personal calls. In one case a sales manager gave an electronics equipment salesperson an advertisment coupon that an individual had mailed in. The salesperson drove more than 30 miles only to find that the coupon had been sent by a high school student writing a science paper.

Directories In some areas of selling, special directories, reports, and open-to-bid announcements constitute an important source of leads.[13] The categories vary greatly from industry to industry. You should acquaint yourself with such resources if they exist in your field, and through your own experience and the experience of your fellow sales representatives, you should determine whether or not they are valuable sources of leads.

Directories such as *Dunn and Bradstreet's Million Dollar Directory* and *Dunn and Bradstreet's Middle Market Directory* classify firms by the type of product they sell, give company sales figures, and provide other important information. Another valuable prospecting tool used by many salespeople is the white and yellow pages of the telephone directory. Other information on

---

[12]Jack Pitchon, "How to Use Telemarketing for Inquiry Handling and Lead Fulfillment," *Telemarketing*, Vol. 1, No. 3 (November–December 1982), pp. 9–11, 33; see also Alfred P. Thode, "Get Ready, Get Set, Deal," *Real Estate Today*, Vol. 15, No. 8 (October 1982), pp. 55–57.

[13]Leonard E. Malherbe, "Prospecting in Your City Library," *The American Salesman*, Vol. 21, No. 1 (January 1976), pp. 38–41.

specific industries may be obtained from directories provided by trade associations. Specific trade associations may be found in the *Encyclopedia of Associations* distributed by Gale Research Company, Detroit, Michigan. Information on key individuals in business and industry, education, and science, may be found in directories such as *Who's Who*. Finally, certain types of salespeople find membership rosters of clubs or organizations useful. For instance, a hotel salesperson might find the membership roster of Sales and Marketing Executives clubs a good source, since sales managers often hold meetings in hotels.

Although the number of directories available is very extensive, one useful summary of various directories is the *Directory of Directories,* Distributed by Gale Research Comapny, Detroit, Michigan. This directory provides information on general business directories on the local, state, national, and international levels categorized by region. Addresses, telephone numbers, coverage, and other information is provided.

Cold canvasing Cold canvasing consists of calling on people who may or may not be potential users of your product or service without having qualified them first. The term "cold call" refers to a call made to a person with whom you have had no earlier contact and for whom you have no background information. If this method is to be used effectively, you should have at least some criteria to apply before investing your time in an actual interview. Before making the call, you should observe the size of the establishment, the traffic flow there, the amount and type of inventory in sight, and the general appearance and upkeep of the premises. In effect, you are segmenting the market by trying to identify groups of prospects that will have the most potential for your offering. Then, if you feel that an account is worth calling on, you must have a quick method of determining whether it has any real potential for profitable sales. A good way to do this is to develop a series of questions to ask that will identify how much potential business the account has, who its present supplier is, and how happy the prospect is with the present supplier.

Qualifying Leads

Once you have generated some leads, you need to collect information on each one. This information will permit you to qualify the lead, to determine its real needs, and to decide the best way to approach the account. You should try to gather as much of this information as possible before you make the actual call.[14] Sometimes, during cold canvasing or when using the telephone, you call on someone and qualify them on the same call. Doing an effective job of researching the prospect and qualifying has two major benefits. It allows you to determine the prospect's needs better, and it helps you to improve your sales effectiveness by concentrating on factors that are important to the prospect.

[14]See, for example, Ted Pollack, "How to 'Case' a Prospect," *The American Salesman*, Vol. 28, No. 1 (January 1983), pp. 27–31.

Evaluating or qualifying leads is one of the most important aspects of a salesperson's job. At this stage, you are trying to learn which leads are really worth pursuing. If this is done well, you will neither waste time working on leads that do not have the potential to be profitable, nor overlook leads that might become profitable accounts. Factors you will want to evaluate include financial ability, potential business, special requirements sought by the prospect, the likelihood of a long-term relationship, and the prospect's location.

Financial ability Information on the financial ability of the lead can be obtained through observation, questioning, references, and credit-reporting agencies. Whichever sources of information you use, you must learn to rely on sound business judgment. Many salespeople have a natural tendency to discount or override adverse credit information; they may do so because they feel that they are in the business of selling, not financing. Such an attitude is reinforced by the fact that they are paid a commission based on sales. How-

OTHER INFORMATION USEFUL FOR QUALIFYING A LEAD

Name
Age
Education
Possessions: gives you an indication of their preferences.
Purchasing power: do they have the authority to buy?
Family data
Routine: when is the best time to call on them?
Memberships and affiliations
Interests
Aspirations: personal ambitions
Self-image: what is their image of themselves?
Quality of mind: how intelligent are they?
Type of business involved
Size of business
Location of office
Type of management of the company
Names of key people in the company
Company's previous experience with yours
Terminology of the company
Problems the company is facing
Company's credit rating
Future prospects of the company
Pattern of buying

SOURCE: Ted Pollack, "How to 'Case' a Prospect," *The American Salesman*, Vol. 28, No. 1 (January 1983), pp. 27–31.

ever, professional salespeople are aware that, in the long run, they will run
into problems if they make too many sales that cause collection problems.
Thus, you must make sure that your leads have the ability to pay for your
product.

Volume of business When you evaluate business available, it is important to
keep in mind your company's best interest. Every account incurs fixed costs,
such as billing expenses: these exist regardless of volume. Some accounts are
so small, however, that their business would not cover these fixed costs'
therefore, they do not warrant your attention. You may, however, see future
potential in some small accounts, even though their present volume is small.
Account potential may be determined by observing such things as the quality
of management, the state of the industry, and the strength of product lines.
Insights gained by such observations often allow you to acquire an important
account that your competitors have overlooked. You should carefully weigh
each prospect's current potential against fixed costs for your company, but
you should also keep in mind the prospect's future potential when you make
the decision whether to pursue a small account.

Special requirements Some accounts require unique service such as special
deliveries or modified products. It is important to remember that product
modification may cause substantial production costs for your company. In the
final analysis, you must weigh the costs of special services or production
modifications against the benefits that your firm will obtain in the long run,
and then decide whether the account is worth pursuing.

Continuity For many firms, maintenance of long-term business with customers is a vital consideration. There may be little chance to make a profit on an
account until several orders have been written. One specialty chemical company, for example, estimates that it must receive three orders before a profit
is generated. Thus, it is up to you to estimate whether the new account has
a substantial chance of becoming a long-term customer. If it does, you will
be willing to spend more time and effort working with the prospect.

Location A new customer may buy in one office but have shipments made
to its other sites. If a large amount of follow-up service and contact is required, you will want to balance the extra cost of traveling to a customer
against the expected profit that should develop from your efforts. For example, if two leads have the same potential and one is located far away from
your office and away from other prospects and accounts, this lead would be
less desirable than one close to your office or near a large existing customer.

ROUTING STRATEGIES

Routing is the formal procedure used to determine which customers and prospects the salesperson should call on during a particular time period. A salesperson's route may be established for as short a period as an afternoon or for

as long a time as several weeks. Responsibility for the salesperson's routing is examined first; then six specific routing techniques are discussed.

Responsibility for Routing

There are at least two perspectives on who is responsible for routing the salesperson. Some think it is strictly management's responsibility; others feel the salesperson should play the major role in determining routes. Each of these perspectives is examined along with some special circumstances that may influence routing policy.

Management responsibility Those who believe it is management's responsibility to handle routing feel that salespeople, left on their own, will not make a full, systematic coverage of the territory. They also contend that a proper mix of customer and prospect calls will not be maintained, assuming that most sales representatives prefer to call where they are already established and that personal convenience will influence the salesperson's decisions. For example, advocates of this perspective suspect that salespeople who are left to handle their own routing will backtrack and move back and forth across their territory in an attempt to be home every night. Some companies have pointed out this problem by analyzing the percentage of potential business realized from each account. They find that a circle can be drawn around the salesperson's home that represents the maximum distance the salesperson can travel and still be home at night. Accounts within the circle yield a disproportionate amount of business compared with those outside the circle.

Salesperson's responsibility A case can also be made for salespeople determining their own routes; they are, after all, the territory manager. One way to handle this problem is to have salespeople plan their routes subject to approval by management. Not only does this system give salespeople a great deal of responsibility in planning activities in their territory, but it also helps management know where sales representatives are in case they need to be contacted.

Those who recommend giving salespeople the routing responsibility argue that they are professionals who know their territories better than any management personnel possibly could. The salesperson knows how much time should be devoted to each account, the optimum times to call, which accounts expect entertainment, and what the current sales potential of each account is. As an account becomes more active, the salesperson who monitors the market closely will be in the best position to adjust call patterns to this new development.

Other special considerations There is no one best answer for determining who should do the routing. The overriding factor may be how good a sales force the firm has and what its members want to do. A truly topflight sales organization that wants to do its own routing should be given a chance to do so. There are, however, two other factors to be considered—the nature of the product and the extent of market development.

When the product is a frequently purchased one, such as foods, drugs, tobacco, fuel, and hardware, it is best to have a detailed routing plan worked out by management. If the salesperson misses a call with these types of products, a competing salesperson is likely to take over the account very quickly. One of the most important benefits a firm can offer is the regularity of its visits. Management cannot afford any mistakes in this area. In contrast, if a firm sells products that are not purchased regularly, a good salesperson does much better by relying on experience and judgement rather than on some predetermined route set up by management.

Similarly, the extent of market development and the identification of potential buyers are related factors that influence who is responsible for the routing. In the early stages of developing a market, when efforts are directed toward locating new customers, the salesperson must be prepared to spend as much time with each account as the situation requires. This type of selling does not permit extremely close supervision by management. The salesperson will have to make scheduling changes as new circumstances develop. In contrast, if the market is highly developed and prospects and customers have already been identified, it may be possible for management to determine who the salesperson should call on and at what time intervals.

Special Routing Techniques

Virtually any systematic routing plan is superior to a haphazard coverage of the territory. The size of the territory, concentration of business, number of accounts, call frequency, expected length of each call, and mode of transportation are factors that must be considered in deciding on the best method to use. When deciding on your routing strategy, you should also remember your account analysis discussed earlier, in order to ensure that adequate time is spent with accounts having high potential and that a disproportionate amount of time is not spent with low-volume accounts with low potential. Six routing plans are examined: circular, cloverleaf, leapfrog, straight line, skip-stop, and computerized models.

Circular The circular approach to routing is appropriate when your accounts are distributed uniformly, when there are few limitations on their accessibility, and when the frequency of calls is about the same for each account. With this approach, you draw concentric circles, or a spiral, around your accounts. You then begin calling on the accounts closest to your office and work out around the circle until you have called on each account. Or you could begin at the edge of the outer circle and spiral you way back to your office. Figure 4.1 illustrates the circular approach.

Cloverleaf The cloverleaf approach is useful when there are concentrations of accounts in specific parts of the territory. A hub point is chosen in each area and calls are made in loops. Alternate sales calls and those made less frequently can be placed on the schedule for each loop. This technique is illustrated in Figure 4.2.

Leapfrog When it is important that you maintain a frequent call pattern on each account, leapfrog routing is feasible. With this approach, you drive to a distant point in your territory and work back to your office, making sales calls as you go. It would appear that you are jumping to each account in a random

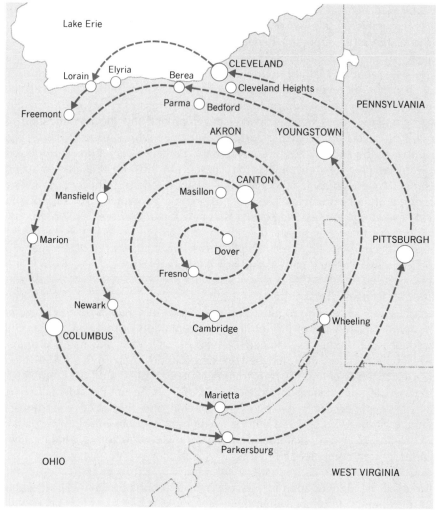

FIGURE 4.1 Circular approach to routing.

manner; yet this is not the case. Rather, you have figured out the best route to return home that will at the same time take you through each of your accounts. The key point about the leapfrog approach is that because you start at a distant point, should you fail to have time to call on any accounts before you have to return home, they are near your home base and thus are easy and inexpensive to call on. Figure 4.3 demonstrates leapfrog routing.

Straight line The straight-line approach works best when business is concentrated in several clusters that are scattered from one another. You travel in a straight line to the first cluster; you call on each account within that cluster and then travel in a straight line to the next cluster. The principle here is that by traveling in a straight line you minimize the distances traveled in your territory. This approach is illustrated in Figure 4.4.

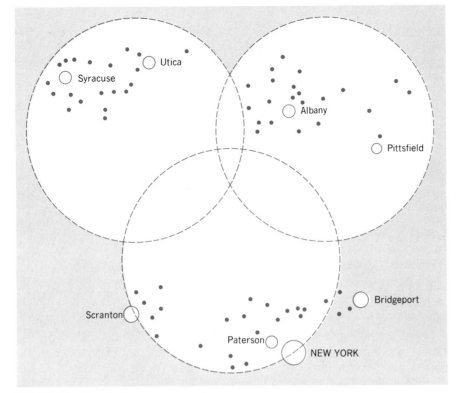

FIGURE 4.2 Cloverleaf approach to routing.

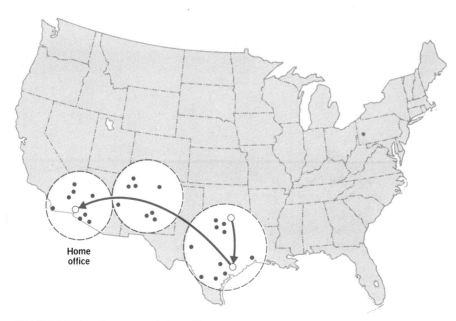

FIGURE 4.3 Leapfrog approach to routing.

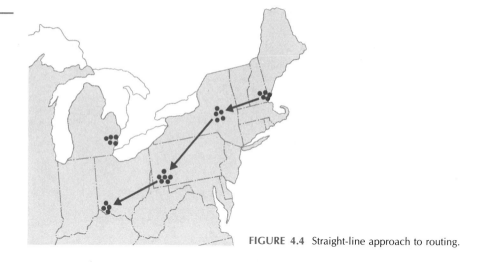

FIGURE 4.4 Straight-line approach to routing.

Skip stop With the skip-stop approach, you route yourself through all your accounts during one sales trip. However, the next time through the territory you will skip the accounts that are not among your most profitable or that do not have the potential to become more profitable. During this follow-up trip through the territory, you may visit only 10 to 20 percent of your accounts. For instance, you might only call on the A accounts in your ABC analysis. Figure 4.5 illustrates this skip-stop approach.

FIGURE 4.5 Skip-stop approach to routing.

Computerized models Mathematical models, such as linear programming, also help the salesperson or management develop a routing plan. Normally, these models are programmed for use on a computer because they require a great number of calculations. The inputs to such a model would include length of call, number of accounts, location of accounts, and when specific accounts wish to be visited. A number of models have been developed that will help minimize total travel time or cost.[15]

TIME MANAGEMENT STRATEGIES

Time management is a critical aspect of a salesperson's self-management; the old axiom, "Time is money," is especially true for salespeople. Time management is explored from two perspectives. First, some overall time management concepts are reviewed; then some specific concepts for managing selling time are explored.

TOP TEN TIME WASTERS RANKED BY SALES REPRESENTATIVES

1. Telephone interruptions.
2. Drop-in visitors.
3. Lack of self-discipline.
4. Crises.
5. Meetings.
6. Lack of objectives, priorities, and deadlines.
7. Indecision and procrastination.
8. Attempting too much at once.
9. Leaving tasks unfinished.
10. Unclear communication.

SOURCE: Michael LeBoeuf, "Managing Your Time Managing Yourself," *Business Horizons,* Vol. 23, No. 1 (February 1980), p. 42. Copyright © 1980, by the Foundation for the School of Business at Indiana University. Reprinted by permission.

Key Concepts for Managing Time

Several key concepts are common to most time management programs: time analysis, consolidation, the quiet hour, the daily reminder, a to-do list, the 80/20 principle, value of time, and planning. Each of these concepts will be explored.

---

[15]For discussion of the role of the computer in routing planning and sales analysis, see James Comer, "The Computer, Personal Selling and Sales Management," *Journal of Marketing,* Vol. 39, No. 3 (July 1975), pp. 27–33.

Time analysis The first step in managing your time effectively is to analyze how you are currently spending your time. This involves keeping some type of daily log of your activities. There are two basic rules for time analysis: (1) your activities have to be written down, and (2) they have to be recorded as you are working rather than from memory.[16] You might, for instance, break the day into fifteen-minute segments and record on a calendar how you actually spend your time. Most salespeople who perform such an analysis are surprised by how little time they spend in actual selling. This analysis also allows you to identify time wasted.

One hypothetical salesman, Walt Joyce, broke his daily activities down into the categories of travel, waiting, contact, service, and administration. He found that on one day he spent his time as shown in Figure 4.6. Mr. Joyce also sampled his work over a 10-day period and found that he spent his time as follows.

Average calls per day	six
Average travel time	160 minutes (31%)
Average waiting time	65 minutes (13%)
Average contact time	145 minutes (28%)
Average service time	100 minutes (19%)
Average administration time	45 minutes (9%)
Total	515 minutes (100%)

Walt is now in a position to evaluate his time and figure out how to use it better.[17]

Consolidation You can consolidate your work by grouping similar tasks and handling all tasks of one type during a single period of time. For instance, you might group telephone calls and handle them at one sitting, or you might do all your paperwork at one sitting. Grouping of similar tasks lets you concentrate on one activity, and you benefit by being more efficient.

Quiet hour Another useful concept in time management is the quiet hour.[18] This is a time you should set aside for yourself when you will not be interrupted, and you should spend it where you can concentrate. It is important that the quiet hour not be selling time, but it is amazing how productive you can be when you can concentrate on your work without interruptions. Tracy Adams, a successful copy machine salesperson, comes into the office early

[16]George H. Labovitz and Lloyd Baird, "Managing Time: Positive Clock-Watching," *SAM Advanced Management Journal,* Vol. 46, No. 3 Summer (1981), pp. 4–8.

[17]From Jack Schiff and Michael Schiff, "A Stitch in Time Saves Sales, Too," *Sales and Marketing Management—Special Report: Time and Territory Management,* Vol. 116, No. 8 (May 24, 1967), p. 59.

[18]For more information on the quiet hour, see Merrill E. Douglas and Donna N. Douglas, "It's About Time Quiet Time Increases Productivity," *Personnel Administrator,* Vol. 25, No. 3 (March 1980), p. 22.

Time	Activity					Remarks
	Travel	Wait	Contact	Service	Administration	
8:30–9:15	■					Customer W
9:15–9:30		■				To resell
9:30–9:50			■			Product A
9:50–10:00	■					
10:00–10:05		■				Prospect T
10:05–10:50			■			Group presentation
10:50–11:30	■					
11:30–11:40		■				Customer Z
11:40–12:55			■			Lunch with P.A.
12:55–1:40				■		Technical service
1:40–2:05	■					Monthly order
2:15–2:30		■				Customer R
2:30–3:30			■			Plant Supervisor re
2:05–2:15				■		Product B
3:30–4:05	■					
4:05–4:15		■				Customer P
4:15–4:45			■			Trial order·
4:45–5:05	■					Product B
5:05–5:35					■	
Date: November 12 Day: Wednesday Calls: five						Summary: Travel: 175 minutes Wait: 50 minutes Contact: 185 minutes Service: 105 minutes Administration: 30 minutes

FIGURE 4.6 Activity analysis. SOURCE: Jack Schiff and Michael Schiff, "A Stitch in Time Saves Sales, Too," *Sales and Marketing Management—Special Report: Time and Territory Management* (May 24, 1976), p. 59.

each morning and utilizes this time before anyone else arrives to plan, do her paperwork, and prepare. By the time her customers come into their offices, she is ready to start selling; she is prepared and has done her homework.

Bill Kule, another successful salesperson, does all his paperwork at home at night after dinner. Each night, for his quiet hour, he goes to his study, writes his orders, and does his paperwork.

Daily reminder Effective salespeople generally utilize a daily reminder on which they write down appointments and schedule meetings. They always have these calendars with them, so they know in advance what their day looks like and can schedule appointments. The reminder also gives you an opportunity to follow up. If a prospect says, for instance, "I don't need anything, but I may be in the market after the first of the year," you should enter in your daily reminder to call the prospect early in the year to see whether the firm has a need. It would be very difficult to remember such facts, but when committed to writing, you have a good source of follow-up.

THINGS TO DO TODAY

Date _____   **Completed**

1 _____ ☐
2 _____ ☐
3 _____ ☐
4 _____ ☐
5 _____ ☐
6 _____ ☐
7 _____ ☐
8 _____ ☐
9 _____ ☐
10 _____ ☐
11 _____ ☐
12 _____ ☐

Notes

To-do lists and daily reminders can help you to organize your time.

To-do list Making lists of important things you need to do is another motivator. As you accomplish each task, you can cross it off your list; this is a form of positive reinforcement. The busier you are, the more important it is that you write down your "to do's." You should never trust your memory to remember these details. As one successful salesperson was overheard saying, "If you are not busy enough to write it down, you probably are not busy enough." It is also important, however, that you rank the items on your list by priority, or you will cross off many activities but may neglect the really important tasks. Management experts have suggested three categories of items. "Must do" items are critical and must be done today, "should do" items should receive priority but could be put off a day, and "could do" items have to be done but can be put off with no negative consequences.

80/20 principle The 80/20 principle states that a small proportion of your actions, 20 percent, account for a large proportion of your results, 80 percent.[19] Applied to selling, this might mean that 20 percent of your customers might account for 80 percent of your sales, or 20 percent of your product line accounts for 80 percent of your sales. It is important that you concentrate your efforts on these critical few customers and products and not neglect

[19]For a discussion of the 80/20 principle, see Alan J. Dubinsky and Richard W. Hansen, "Improving Marketing Productivity: The 80/20 Principle Revisited," *California Management Review,* Vol. 25, No. 1 (Fall 1982), pp. 96 –105.

Reprinted with permission, Universal Press Syndicate.

them. This is not to say that the other products and customers should be ignored, but they should not receive a disproportionate amount of your time.

Value of time Putting a value on your time tends to make you very conscious of time.[20] As you can see from Table 4.5, if you earn $20,000 per year, your time is worth $10 per hour. When you earn $50,000 per year, your time is worth $25 per hour. The $20,000-a-year sales trainee who spends an hour on a coffee break has just spent $10.50 on coffee, which is rather expensive. As another example of expensive activity, a life insurance salesperson earning over $50,000 a year on straight commission took a two-week vacation to paint his house. He was very proud that he had saved several hundred dollars by painting the house himself. In effect, he was giving up more than $25 an hour to save approximately $10 an hour for a housepainter—and doing something that he did not even enjoy. Putting a value on your time allows you to see the earnings you forgo when you spend time doing nonproductive things.

Planning A critical concept in time management is the importance of planning. It must be looked at as an investment of your time. As in an investment of your money, every hour you spend in planning should return to you saved time in execution. You will be able to react faster, with better responses and more accuracy, if you plan. For instance, if you carefully route yourself through your territory and try to minimize traffic congestion and excess travel,

[20]William J. Tobin, "Make Sure Sales Time Equals Sales Revenue," *Telephony*, Vol. 201, No. 12 (September 14, 1981), pp. 140–142.

TABLE 4.5

VALUE OF TIME[a]

ANNUAL EARNINGS	VALUE OF ONE HOUR'S TIME
$ 20,000	$10
$ 30,000	$15
$ 40,000	$20
$ 50,000	$25
$ 60,000	$30
$ 80,000	$40
$100,000	$50

[a]Based on 40 hours per week, 50 weeks per year.

the planning will take time, but you can expect to save many more hours of travel time as a result of this planning.

Managing Selling Time

In addition to these general concepts of time management, some specific guidelines are also useful for managing selling time. These include extending call time, planning your itinerary, determining call frequency, scheduling your calls, having alternative calls, organizing selling aids, utilizing waiting time, utilizing travel time, and using the telephone. These are explored next.

Extend call time Often it is possible to extend your day by having early-morning meetings with clients, breakfast meetings, luncheon meetings, dinner meetings, or evening meetings.[21] Of course, customers and prospects will differ in how receptive they are to meetings at various times of the day, but these special meetings may often be valuable ways to extend your day. Sometimes calling at these unconventional times is a way to increase your productivity and see the customers when they are receptive and not likely to be interrupted. One potential problem with meetings over meals is that business matters may not be covered. There is sometimes a need for a social business luncheon, but this may not substitute for a sales call. One suggestion is to cover the business part of the call first and then eat the meal. This ensures that you reach your call objective.

Plan sales itinerary. One activity that consumes considerable time for many salespeople is travel. It is a necessity in most sales jobs, but travel time can be time wasted. You should plan your itinerary so that you have no back-tracking, and so that your calls fall as close to a straight line as possible. Another suggestion from leapfrog routing, is to drive out to the farthest call in

[21]See, for example, Archie Jordan, "How to Get More Actual Selling Time from Each Day," *The American Salesman*, Vol. 27, No. 5 (May 1982), pp. 17–19.

Sales Itinerary for Salesperson _____ John Doe _____

For the Week of _____ 7/25 _____

Date	Time From To	Account	Location	Prospect's Name	Call Objective
7/25	8:00 9:00	Safeway	First and Mill	Bill George	Get permission to reset dairy case
7/25	9:00 10:00	Bayless	Second and Broadway	Sam Jones	Try to receive an order for 10 cases of cheese

FIGURE 4.7 Example of a sales itinerary.

your territory and work back towards your office so that any calls you do not make are near your office and can be easily reached without a great deal of travel.

One useful device to help you plan your schedule through your territory is the sales itinerary.[22] Even if not required by their firms, many salespeople have found it useful to develop a written _sales itinerary_ highlighting _whom_ they will call on, _where_ they will be, _when_ they will call, and _what_ the objective of each call is. An example of a sales itinerary is given in Figure 4.7. Because it deals with the ordering of your calls, the sales itinerary is closely related to your routing strategy discussed earlier but it also includes the time spent in the call, the location, the prospect's name, and the call objective. Many salespeople find that the sales itinerary gives them direction and something to strive for. In addition to promoting examination of individual call objectives, several territorial objectives, such as number of calls and type of accounts called on, are summarized on this form.

Determine call frequency A technique that saves a great deal of time is determining how frequently customers should be called on. One method for doing this is ABC analysis referred to earlier. Calling on customers too frequently can be just as counterproductive as calling on them too infrequently.

Schedule calls It is often useful to schedule calls and make appointments rather than just dropping in on customers. Even if you routinely call on customers at a regular time, reconfirmation can be useful and can save a great deal of unproductive travel time and waiting time.

Have alternative calls Regardless of how well you plan your calls, set appointments, and reconfirm, there will be times when you are unable to see the prospect you wanted to see and occasions when the appointment takes

[22]See, for example, Mike Shatzkin, "Planning a Sales Itinerary: A How-To Guide for Today's Conditions," _Publishers Weekly_, Vol. 216, No. 5 (July 30, 1979), pp. 44 – 47.

less time than you had expected. For these occasions it is important that you have some alternative calls.[23] These may take several forms: you might call on someone else within the account; you might make a goodwill call; or you might make another call in the vicinity. The important point is that you can use this unplanned break productively if you have a contingency plan.

Organize your selling aids Not having your selling aids in good order, your charts, brochures, samples, and models, will cause you to fumble around and waste time—both yours and your customer's. In addition, you may lose credibility in the customer's eyes and even overlook a key sales point. Therefore, you want to be sure to organize your selling aids.

Utilize waiting time Every salesperson spends time waiting to see prospects, even if appointments have been scheduled. This waiting time can easily be wasted or it can be spent productively, studying the next account, studying materials, reading company literature, getting background information on the account from the receptionist, doing your expense account, or doing other paperwork. One good suggestion is always have some small projects to do. Keep these projects readily accessible in your briefcase so that when you have waiting time, you can spend it productively. You will also release other time for important activites.

Utilize travel time Many salespeople do a great deal of their traveling either by car or by airplane.[24] Several productive activities that can be done during travel time are critiquing your last call, thinking through the next call, dictating correspondence, or listening to career-oriented tapes. Cellular telephones also enable you to make telephone calls while you are in your car. Thus much business can be conducted during travel time.

Use the telephone The telephone may often be used as a substitute for traveling, thus saving time. Telephone calls can be used for prospecting, to identify decision makers before making an initial call, to replace routine calls, to handle small or outlying accounts, to make appointments, to reconfirm appointments, and to follow up on orders. Although telephone selling is covered in Chapter 16, several time-saving suggestions include planning to make a number of calls at one sitting and having telephone numbers readily available, thus saving time.

SUMMARY

In this chapter territory management strategies—such as account analysis, prospecting, routing, and time management—were examined. Reviewing

[23]See, for example, Gerson Goodman, "Filling Holes with Cold Calls," *Sales and Marketing Management,* Vol. 122, No. 3 (February 5, 1979), pp. 46 – 47.
[24]See for example, Merrill Douglass and Donna Douglas, "How to Make Travel Time More Productive," *Marketing Times,* Vol. 30, No. 1 (January 1983), pp. 17–18.

present accounts by ABC analysis of current volume and potential is one strategy for managing the territory. In addition, various strategies were given

present accounts by ABC analysis of current volume and potential is one strategy for managing the territory. In addition, various strategies were given for handling unprofitable accounts: calling on them less frequently, using the telephone, selling at trade shows, having them mail in orders, and dropping them.

Nine methods and sources for generating leads were examined: the endless chain, referrals, important people, noncompeting salespersons, junior salespersons, acquaintances and friends, telephone and mail, directories, and cold canvasing. You must evaluate these ways to generate leads and determine which combination will work best for you.

The types of information you must collect on each lead were also discussed. Before you qualify the lead as a potential customer, you must investigate the lead's financial ability, the current and potential volume of business, any special requirements the account may demand, chances for a long-term relationship, and whether the firm's location will cause problems.

Routing was also discussed. A good case can be made for either management or salespeople having primary responsibility for routing. Several special considerations that would influence this decision were examined. Six techniques for routing were outlined: circular, cloverleaf, leapfrog, straight-line, skip stop, and computerized models.

Finally, time management strategies were explored. Overall strategies for managing time are: time analysis, consolidation, the quiet hour, the daily reminder, a to-do list, the 80/20 principle, putting a value on time, and planning. In addition, suggestions were also made for managing selling time: extending call time, planning the sales itinerary, determining call frequency, scheduling calls, having alternative calls, organizing selling aids, utilizing waiting time, utilizing travel time, and using the telephone.

PROBLEMS

1. Why is it so important that many salespeople spend a large proportion of their time on a few "key accounts"? Under what circumstances would salespeople have few if any key accounts?
2. Compare and contrast the endless-chain method to the referral method for generating new leads.
3. Under what type of selling situations is cold canvasing the normal method for generating new leads?
4. What are the most important factors in qualifying a prospect? Is determining who the key decision makers are in the prospect's firm a part of the process? Explain.
5. Explain the advantages and disadvantages of having salespeople do their own routing. Under what conditions should management perform this function?
6. Which of the key concepts for time mangement do you feel would be most useful to you in managing your time?

EXERCISE 4

Objective: To appreciate the importance of routing as a means of covering existing accounts and prospective accounts.

Assume that you are a salesperson and that the accompanying map is your territory. Key customers are depicted by ●; other customers, ○; key prospects, □; other prospects, ■. You see key customers and prospects at least twice a month. You call on other customers and prospects at least monthly. Your home is your office and is in suburban Detroit.

1. What method or methods of routing would you use?
2. Would you use the same route each time? If not, why not?
3. Plot your progress through the territory, bearing in mind prescribed call frequency.

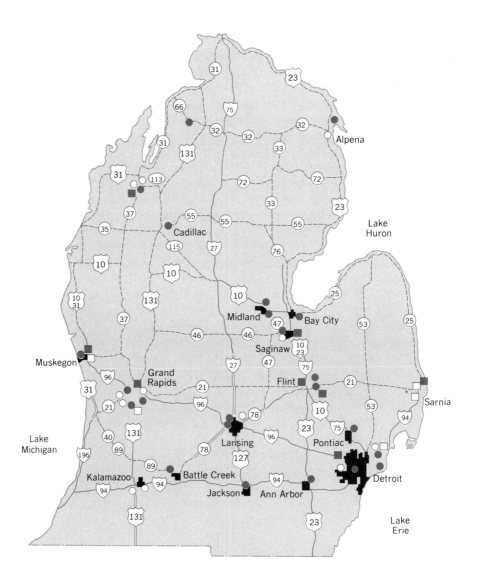

Case 4–1 Beatty Chevrolet

David Johnson is in charge of the new-car fleet-leasing program for George Beatty Chevorlet of Houston. At one point in time, Beatty Chevrolet did a substantial business in fleet leasing. About two years ago, the firm had thirty-two customers who leased an average of 23.5 vehicles for one year or longer.

However, their fleet-leasing manager recently retired and business slipped substantially. Beatty felt that he would try to cut costs and take over the leasing business himself. Unfortunately, he did not have the time or the flair for running this side of his dealership, and as a result the fleet-leasing business fell off substantially. In the six months before hiring David Johnson, Beatty Chevrolet received only one contract for fleet vehicles. This order was for twenty Caprices, which were leased to a cousin of George Beatty.

David has been with Beatty for two months. In this time he has established a fleet-leasing service program and has received two contracts for a total of fifty units. The fleet-leasing service program consists of little more than a half-time service representative who deals with all the service problems of the fleet customers. David believes the reason Beatty lost so many contracts so fast was that there was no one person in service who worked solely on fleet leasers' problems.

The two new contracts that David landed are Dix's Delivery Service for thirty delivery vans and Houston Oaks Bank for ten Caprices. David became aware of the Dix's contract through a public announcement that they would be accepting bids on the vans. David knew Dix's reputation for leasing strictly on price; and because he needed to land a good contract to build momentum in the leasing program and to show Mr. Beatty he was making progress, he bid very low on the contract and was the winner.

David became aware of the Houston Oaks Bank's need for ten vehicles from Mr. Beatty, who is a friend of the bank's senior vice-president. Only one other firm bid on the vehicles, and Beatty Chevrolet received the order. David's bid was not quite so low as it had been for the Dix contract, and as a result the firm made a good profit.

Mr. Beatty thinks David is doing a good job with the leasing business. However, he feels that David's performance must continue to improve if Beatty is to stay in the new-car and truck fleet-leasing business. Beatty feels that the firm's break-even point for this segment of the business is approximately 400 new vehicles leased each year for a period of one year. Beatty told David that he will have at least one year to build up to this point, but at the end of this period, he will have to review the fleet-leasing business to determine whether it can be profitable again.

1. What can David do to attract new customers?
2. Is there any possibility that some of Beatty's old customers can be lured back to the firm?
3. What techniques would be useful for David in generating new leads for Beatty Chevrolet?

Case 4–2 The Magic Screen Corporation

Magic Screen Corporation is a small consulting firm located in Austin, Texas. It was founded several years ago by two professors of the University of Texas,

Dr. William Witt and Dr. Edward Alpert. Both men had been researching and developing teaching systems that would be effective for large classes (from 200 to 1000 students).

Witt and Alpert have written several articles on the subject and investigated proven teaching methods for large classes.

The present policy of state and other public universities forces colleges to increase class sizes in order to serve an ever-larger number of students with limited budgets. However, very few teaching innovations have been introduced, and the professors lecture to 400 or 500 students with very poor results. Witt and Alpert experimented with several types of audiovisual aids, such as overhead transparencies, slides, television cassettes, and movies. After a full year of research, they developed a package that combined all these techniques in what they thought was an optimum and most effective manner.

As professors of marketing at the University of Texas, they saw the opportunity for developing their idea into a small consulting business. This is how Magic Screen Corporation originated. After one year the firm was ready to proceed and market its services, which were divided into four different package offerings.

The major problem facing Magic Screen Corporation is to identify and contact their prospective customers. The academic community is close-knit and not very sensitive to commercial appeals. The two professors are convinced that personal calls are the best way to get the job done.

1. What should Witt and Alpert do in order to contact the major public universities, which appear to be their target market?
2. Whom should they contact within those universities?
3. Design a presentation for the Magic Screen Corporation services.

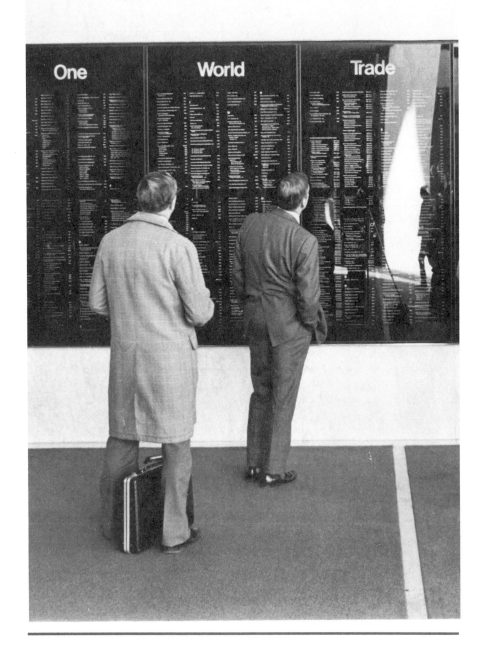

Developing Account and Call Strategies

After studying this chapter, you should be able to

1. Identify important information necessary to develop strategies.
2. Develop strategies in customer accounts.
3. Formulate strategies in prospect accounts.
4. Describe outside influences on strategies.
5. Recognize account strategies involving several decision makers.
6. Create a call strategy.
7. Understand the importance of planning in team and group selling.

Not only are strategies necessary for managing the territory, but they are also critical in developing each account and planning each sales call. Well-developed strategies enable you to focus your activities on the specific steps necessary to reach your objectives. Without them, your activities may lack direction and purpose.

Most field salespeople have businesses and organizations rather than individuals as customers and prospects. These organizations are of course made up of individuals, but there are usually several individuals who are responsible for the firm's purchasing. Even the salesperson calling in the home should view the family as a buying unit or "account." For instance, a life insurance salesperson calling on a young couple in their home should have a strategy for this call and a strategy for dealing with this account.

Your strategic objective is to recognize the unique characteristics of each account. This means that you must be aware of each decision maker's role in the buying unit and become familiar not only with their personal needs but also with what they feel are the needs of the organization. In order to do this, you must have information.

INFORMATION THE SALESPERSON MUST KNOW

In order to identify the uniqueness of each account, the salesperson needs a system for gathering information about each customer and prospect. Table 5.1 provides some data that might be useful in developing an account strat-

TABLE 5.1
SELECTIVE INFORMATION ABOUT A CUSTOMER OR PROSPECT'S BUSINESS

- *Organizational considerations* reveal how the account's business is organized. Factors such as whether buying is centralized or decentralized and the reporting procedures within the organization are useful in determining whom to call on.

- *Financial facts* about the account's business are useful in qualifying the account and in determining account potential. The financial statements of public companies are available through annual reports. Other sources include Dun and Bradstreet reports or articles in trade journals.

- *Marketing approaches* utilized by the firm to market its products are also useful to know. Knowledge of the account's target markets and which product the firm is stressing will give insight into where a product or service fits into the account's business. It is especially important to know what items become part of firm's final product—what raw materials, component parts, or other materials the firm is buying.

- *Company policies* reveal the way the account does business. Knowledge of these policies are helpful to the salesperson in figuring out how to meet the firm's needs. Often these policies will be in written form for vendors and will specify such things as when to call and conditions and timing of plant visits.

- *Technological data* about an account's manufacturing operations would include changes in production machinery, changes in their product line, and whatever new production processes or components the account might use in producing their products. These data are useful because technological changes of one kind will often mean that other components will have to be changed to keep them compatible.

egy. The exact information needed will vary, but the account's organizational considerations, financial facts about the business, its marketing approaches, company policies, and technological data about the firm's manufacturing operations are all useful to understanding the account and seeing where your offering fits in. For example, a firm selling life insurance to businesses would want to know the number of employees, their ages, the type of work they do, the other fringe benefits the employees receive, and the financial health of the company, before proposing an insurance package as a fringe benefit. You should expend every effort to learn about three additional aspects of a business: the account's buying patterns, its procurement policies, and the level of competition in the account.

Account Buying Pattern

An important step in customer account planning is to determine your share of the customer's business. This is done by first learning how much total business has existed, not only for you but for your competitors. You can ascertain the total business of a firm by asking questions, observing, researching sales and other information given in the customer's annual report, and by talking to knowledgeable people. You then determine how much business your firm has with the account. The ratio of these two items is your current share of the customer's business.

Next, you must project the future for this account. You make a forecast of the total business available in the time period for which you are now planning and you predict what your sales will be to the account. The ratio of these two figures is your projected share of the accounts' future business.

Finally, you must try to determine trends. For example, you must determine whether the total business available is increasing, declining, or holding steady. If the data suggest a sharp increase in business, you may have to allocate proportionately more effort to the account. In contrast, if the account's business appears to be decreasing, you may lessen your efforts. In the extreme case, after your sales manager has agreed, you may drop the account altogether. You should also evaluate your own firm's current business relative to your potential sales and potential business with the particular account. If your projected share of the business in that account is greater than your current share, it means that you hope for additional penetration within the account. If your projected share is less than your current share of the account, it means that you are gradually being displaced by competitors. Figure 5.1 is a matrix illustrating the information required for individual account planning.

This analysis must also be applied to prospective accounts, although you will have fewer details on these businesses. You can, however, make an educated guess of how much business currently exists in a given prospective account, what the future holds, and what the trends are. Knowing which competitors are currently getting the firm's business can help you to forecast the amount of business you hope to cultivate during the period ahead.

In addition, you can make reasonably accurate estimates of the quantities of a product required by calculating the quantity of goods manufactured or sold by the customer or prospect. Some firms will permit a tour of their premises, giving you an opportunity to observe what goods are in inventory,

	PAST	FUTURE	TREND
Industry sales to the account	Total sales by all suppliers ($)	Future total sales ($)	Increase, decrease, no change
Our company sales to the account	Our sales ($)	Future sales for our company ($)	Increase, decrease, no change
Our company share of the account's business	Share of account (%)	Future account share (%)	Increase, decrease, no change

FIGURE   Account buying patterns.

what production lines are running, and the volume of outgoing orders. Of course, you may not get all this information in one tour. You may also engage in casual conversation with plant supervisory employees, a source of information not otherwise available. Even though such personnel do not contribute directly to purchasing decisions, their unfavorable comments can block purchases.

Procurement Policies

It is also necessary to learn as much as possible about the operation of the account. You need in-depth knowledge of the procurement policies and procedures of the account and of the departments that are likely to use your product. You have to see how your offering fits with the buying firm's business. If the prospective account is a manufacturer, you must discover how your products and services fit in as ingredients or components of the company's products and services. You may be able to demonstrate that the products you offer can give the firm a competitive advantage in its own markets. If the company is a reseller, you may show how your offering enhances or rounds out the product–service mix of the reseller. Often the service offered the reseller is assistance in the promotion of the line to ultimate purchasers. Cosmetics sales representatives, for example, can make slight product mix changes so that their line can fit into parts of a store other than the cosmetics department, such as departments selling sports equipment, sportswear, and high school and college fashions.

Level of Competition

You must also learn who your direct and indirect competitors are. You must find answers to such questions as these: How much business of the kind you are seeking does each competitor enjoy? How long has each competitor been doing business with the account? What is each competitor doing to develop and sustain their place in the account? Then, you must make a detailed study of each competitor to determine strategic areas in which you can achieve the greatest advantage. This information may be obtained by asking questions, listening, observing, and talking to other competing salespeople. You can use it to answer questions and objections raised by the customer concerning experiences with competing products and services.

Most of this information about accounts and competitors must be generated through your own observation and inquiry, although your firm may acquire some knowledge through executive-level contacts, marketing research, and trade and industry sources. You may also gain information by talking to noncompeting sales representatives and by reading trade publications.

STRATEGY IN CUSTOMER ACCOUNTS

It is important not to neglect your existing customers. Your objective is to render these accounts as invulnerable as possible to competitors. The stance is protective. This does not mean that you may not seek to cultivate and increase the amount of business, but your prime concern is to prevent any loss of business.

What you should strive for with your customers is to develop a relationship. In order to do this, you need to provide service, be dependable, keep the customer informed, and help build the customer's business. A good relationship will be an added incentive for customers to continue to do business with you and to increase their dependence on you.[1]

Sometimes, salespeople feel there is more potential for new business in competitors' accounts than in their own, and they work at opening up new accounts. Unfortunately, this is sometimes done at the expense of the salesperson's existing accounts. Thus, while you are out generating new business, one of your competitors may be lining up one of your present accounts.

You must take two inputs into consideration when developing your strategy for customer accounts: (1) the interaction among key decision makers and (2) the movement of your product or service within the customer's business. Because you have been doing business with the account, you will have access to information and will have contacts in the account that will provide you with information.

Interaction among Key Decision Makers

Generally speaking, in most accounts purchasing decisions are made by a group of people rather than by an individual. This group is called the buying center.[2] The more you know about the relationships between the various participants who influence the purchase, the better you will be able to solve their problems, meet their individual needs, and tailor your presentation to include the information they want.

[1]See, for example, Leonard L. Berry, "Relationship Marketing," in *Emerging Perspective on Services Marketing*, Leonard L. Berry, G. Lynn Shostack, Gregory D. Upah, eds. (Chicago: American Marketing Association 1983), 25–28.

[2]Yoram Wind, "The Boundaries of Buying Decision Centers," *Journal of Purchasing and Materials Management*, Vol. 14 (Summer 1978), pp. 23–29.

The interaction of decision makers in one account is illustrated in Figure 5.2. Assume that you are a salesperson for a large semiconductor manufacturer and have determined that the key decision makers for these products are the purchasing executive, head engineer, plant manager, and director of research. In this particular account one member of this decision-making group, the director of research, is a key entry point. Since additional orders for your semiconductors depend on influencing the director of research, you normally begin your round of calls with this person. In addition to being a key decision maker, the director of research may also act as a gatekeeper by controlling the information that is given to other executives. Thus, you must also make an effort on each visit to see the other key decision makers, the plant manager, purchasing executive, and head engineer. Monitoring changes in the composition of the group are critical steps in effective account management.

DIFFERENT ROLES WITHIN THE BUYING CENTER

ROLE	DESCRIPTION
Users	Will be using the product in question.
Gatekeepers	Control information to be received by other members of the buying center.
Influencers	Affect the purchasing decision by supplying information for evaluating alternatives or by setting buying specifications; typically technical people.
Deciders	Actually make the buying decision, whether or not they have the formal authority. Purchasing agents may have formal authority to buy, but the president of the firm may actually make the decision.
Buyers	Often a purchasing agent; has formal authority for selecting a supplier and implementing all procedures connected with securing the product.

SOURCE: Adapted from Frederick E. Webster, Jr., and Yoram Wind, *Organizational Buying Behavior* (Englewood Cliffs, N.J.: Prentice-Hall, 1972), pp. 77–80. Adapted by permission of Prentice-Hall, Inc., Englewood Cliffs, N.J.

Movement of the Product or Service

You must be aware of the cycle of events that your products and services move through in each organization you sell to. These events are illustrated in Figure 5.3, using the semiconductors as an example.

You have determined that the purchased semiconductors arrive by common carrier on the receiving dock of the company and are then moved to

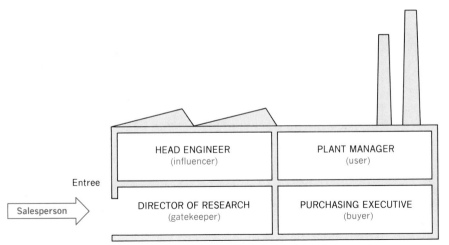

FIGURE 5.2 Interrelation of key decision makers in the buying center.

inventory. As the mechandise is needed, it is moved to ready-use inventory on the production line. These goods then become a component in the account's products. You must ensure that no troubles or difficulties come up as your goods pass through these steps. Whatever the situation may be, you know that each competing salesperson is seeking weak spots in the physical flow cycle of events. For example, suppose your firm has trouble with deliveries, your products are difficult to unload, or your packages are difficult to store; competitors may try to make inroads into the account by using this information to strengthen the case for their products. With customer accounts, then, the objective is to prevent trouble. This means that you must thoroughly follow through on all transactions.

Specific Strategies

Several specific strategies may be used with customer accounts in order to increase your share of the customer's business and to discourage competitors. These strategies include stressing customer service and follow-up, cultivating the entire buying team, and looking for additional competitive advantages.

Stress customer service and follow-up Satisfied customers tend to be loyal to you and to your company. Thus, you must make every effort to provide your customers with better service then they can get from your competition.

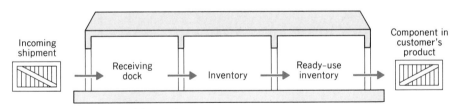

FIGURE 5.3 Movement of the product.

You must get orders in on time, make sure they are accurate, keep customers informed about the status of their orders, help customers with installation of the product, ensure that service people follow up with the customers, and check to make certain they are satisfied. Many of these ideas are expanded in Chapter 14. The important point is that your customers know you care about their business and that you will do everything you can to keep them satisfied.

Cultivate the entire buying team All things being equal, each competing salesperson is seeking to identify the person who is least pleased with things as they are. This is the person most vulnerable to the competitor. Accordingly, you should make every effort to leave no weak link in this people cycle. You should also be on the lookout for "comers" in the organization, individuals who will be part of the decision-making group in the future. If you can cultivate these subordinates now, you will have an advantage when they move up and can contribute to the buying decisions. You should also be alert to any impending shifts or changes in the organization that may influence the composition of the decision-making groups.

Look for additional advantages As your products or services pass into a customer's business, you have an opportunity to view them in actual use. Thus, you may be able to show that your products, in contrast to those of your competitors, are easier to unload and require less handling in getting them into inventory. You may be able to demonstrate that they are easier to stack. You may also have learned that on the production line your firm's goods have greater uniformity of quality from batch to batch and as a result there are fewer production stoppages. If you are selling services, you may be able to show that your services are faster, more accurate, or more complete than your competitors.

Two important points should be made here. First, the burden of proving these advantages lies with you; that is, you may have to take the initiative in showing your offering's superiority. Second, it is important that you make sure that these advantages are communicated to the key decision makers, who are often not the actual users of the products or services.

STRATEGY IN PROSPECT ACCOUNTS

Even though maintaining present customers is critically important to you, often it is important to prospect for new accounts. Prospecting is important because you might lose an account to a competitor; or, after examining your total situation, you may feel you can open new accounts while keeping your present customers satisfied. With prospect accounts, you are the outsider trying to get in. Your objective is to find some way to change the present situation.

Your first task is to identify the decision makers.[3] As you call on decision makers, you seek ways and means of showing them that they are not as

---

[3]Marvin Berkowitz, "New Product Adoption by the Buying Organization: Who are the Real Influencers," *Industrial Marketing Management,* Vol. 15, No. 1 (February 1986), pp. 33–43.

well off by purchasing from your competition as they believe they are. In prospect accounts, orders have not been placed. Thus you should be looking for a key entry point into the decision-making team. If you are unable to locate such a person, you may have to take a longer-term view and give your attention to the up-and-coming managers in the account. However, if you are successful in locating one or more persons in the current decision-making team who are favorable to what you are offering, you then attempt to make each of these persons an internal salesperson. You hope that they can influence the other decision makers who are satisfied with their present suppliers.

You must also concern yourself with how the product might be used. Your objective is to find difficulty or trouble in the present situation. For example, you may gain entry by suggesting an improved work method on the production line, even though you have been unable to demonstrate that your product alone is superior.

PATIENCE MAKES THIS PROSPECT A CUSTOMER

J. Michael Curto, then a group vice-president of U.S. Steel, related how keeping in contact with a prospect got him an order.

Several years ago, when I was a sales vice-president in the East, I used to call on a major steel buyer who was giving all of their business to another steel company. They were very loyal to our competitor because, when their own company was just beginning, it received financial help from them. I continually called on this company, but I could sense that the owner's loyalty to our competitor was so strong that I would have overstepped my bounds had I tried to aggressively pull him away from them. I could also sense that if I stayed in there, I would eventually get some business.

I continued to call on him, and we become personal friends, but still I wasn't getting any business. In a low-key manner, I would subtly sell him on U.S. Steel. Now what did happen was the competing steel company was taken over by a conglomerate, and the new management fired all the customer's old friends. When that happened, he no longer felt any obligations to that company. Well, there I was . . . just sitting there in the wings, very eager to do business with him. And, sure enough, he swung all of the business over to us. I want to point out that all of this took place over a period of two years, and knowing that any kind of selling pressure on my end would have ruined the relationship I was building, well, I played it very low key. I just waited, and when he finally did call to give us the business, we became his major supplier.

SOURCE: Robert L. Shook, *Ten Greatest Salespersons: What They Say about Selling* (New York: Harper and Row, 1978), pp. 155–164. Copyright © 1978, by Robert L. Shook and Roberta W. Shook, Trustees. Reprinted by permission of Harper and Row Publishers, Inc.

Identifying the Key Decision Makers

A critical element in all prospect accounts is identifying the key decision makers. Most purchasing decisions are typically made or influenced by several participants. While your first contact may be with the purchasing agent, it is unusual for the purchasing agent to be the only influence in the purchasing process. In the purchase of heavy machinery, for example, production people, engineers, financial people, and maybe even top management will get involved with the purchase in varying degrees.

As indicated earlier, the key decision makers in the account are generally referred to as the buying center. The salesperson must determine who constitutes the buying center for a particular product, and the amount and type of influence possessed by each of the individuals. It is naive to assume that each decision maker has equal influence on what is purchased.[4] It is equally naive to assume that the influence of each decision maker remains constant over time. For example, if an account is experiencing difficulty in meeting production schedules, it is likely that the plant manager will have a major voice in purchasing, and the vendor who offers time saving and labor-saving ideas is likely to be strongly considered. Similarly, if a company is finding it increasingly difficult to obtain the necessary skilled labor for its operation, the human resources director may have a strong voice in purchases. Here, the vendor firm that offers products and services that save on labor and are easy to use may have the competitive advantage.

You are thus forced to maintain a current picture of conditions in each account and to formulate a strategy based on them. Strategies for identifying the key decision makers include asking questions, calling a meeting, entering at the top, and sending literature.

Ask questions One question that is useful in determining the key decision maker is, "Who, besides yourself, must approve this type of purchase?" Notice that the question is not aimed directly at the purchase under discussion. In this way, the salesperson will not seem pushy, and yet will learn a great deal about who, under what conditions has the authority to make the purchase decision.

Call a meeting A second strategy is to call a meeting and ask, "Who else should be invited to the meeting about this product?" or "Are there other people in your organization who would need to know about this?" This leaves the door open for you to ask what their interest or responsibility with regard to your product would be.

Enter at the top A third strategy is to enter the prospect organization by contacting the highest-level person you can get access to. This strategy has two advantages. First, if you are referred to someone in the organization by a member of top management, you will usually gain credibility and the atten-

---

[4]Donald W. Jackson, Jr., Janet E. Keith, and Richard Burdick, "Purchasing Agents' Perceptions of Industrial Buying Center Influence: A Situational Approach," *Journal of Marketing*, Vol. 48, No. 4 (Fall 1984), pp. 75–83.

tion of lower management. Moreover, top management can specify several people who should be contacted, whereas lower-level management might lose face by having to admit that they could not actually make the decision. There are two possible negative outcomes to this strategy. Lower-level management may resent your not going through channels, and you may be unable to gain access to top management.

SIX CLUES FOR IDENTIFYING KEY DECISION MAKERS

1. Although power and formal authority often are related, they are not the same. Thus, you must determine where the true decision making lies.
2. One way to identify decision makers in the buying company is to monitor communications.
3. Decision makers may be disliked by those with less power. Thus, when other people express concern over one member's opinions, you may have a strong indication of who is powerful.
4. High-powered decision makers tend to get information from others. The executive who doesn't come to meetings but who receives copies of all correspondence about a purchase may be a key figure.
5. Often decision makers with a great deal of power are not the most easily identified or the most talkative. Sometimes powerful decision makers send others to critical meetings, knowing that little will happen without their presence.
6. There is little relationship between the managers' functional areas and their power.

SOURCE: Adapted from Thomas V. Bonoma, "Major Sales: Who Really Does the Buying?" *Harvard Business Review,* Vol. 60, No. 3 (May–June, 1982) p. 116.

Send literature The final strategy is to ask the prospect, "Are there other people in your organization who should receive this literature on our product?" Again this is nonthreatening and leaves the door open to probe about the nature of their interest in your product. Even if you do not succeed in getting an order, your literature is in the hands of other key decision makers.

Specific Strategies in Prospect Accounts
After you have identified the key decision makers, several specific strategies are open to you in your efforts to convert the prospect into a customer. These include stressing competitive advantage, accepting trial orders, giving free samples, inviting prospects to your plant, offering technical assistance, and furnishing testimonials.[5]

[5]Some of these same strategies might be used in customer accounts when trying to introduce a new product.

Competitive advantage In your initial efforts, you may stress an item in your product line that has the greatest competitive advantage compared to the goods now being purchased. It may not be the product with the greatest volume or profit potential, but it may be the product most amenable to a dramatic presentation. Once the prospective customer sees the advantage of the first product, there may be a tendency to buy the rest of your product line. The important point is that you use the product that looks best compared to competition to sell the rest of the product line.

CINCINNATI MILACRON SALESPEOPLE GET CLOSE TO THE BUYING CENTER

Cincinnati Milacron salespeople sell robots—a very competitive business. In order to do this well, they need to work closely with various departments with different needs and perspectives. They must work with top management, engineering, production managers, purchasing, machine operators, and shop foremen. All these people may be involved in the decision to purchase a robot. The salespeople even work with employees on the shop floor. As one Milacron executive noted, "We know the guys who wear the bowling shirts and the baseball caps."

SOURCES: Paul Ingrassi and Darmon Darlin, "Cincinnati Milacron, Mainly a Metal-Bender, Now Is a Robot Maker," *Wall Street Journal* (April 7, 1983), p. 110. Copyright © 1982, by Cincinnati Milacron Marketing Company. Reprinted by permission of the *Wall Street Journal*. Also *Robots: A Managers Guide*. Copyright © 1983, by Dow Jones and Company, Inc. All rights reserved.

Trial orders Under certain circumstances, you may settle for a trial order. This means that the customer is willing to purchase enough of the product to test it under actual conditions but is not ready to purchase large quantities. If this procedure is followed, you must make sure your goods are given a through objective test on a comparative basis with the products now in use. Ideally, you should be on hand for such testing, not only to observe and inquire about procedures in the prospect account, but also to establish face-to-face contact and interchange ideas with people in the firm other than your entry person.

Free samples Another possibility, one not quite as desirable as the trial order, is to furnish the prospect with a sample for testing purposes. Although you are not really selling the product, you may favorably affect the buyers' attitude by getting them to try the product. It is possible that products obtained at no cost may be seen as having less value than those paid for. Thus, if samples are furnished, it is even more imperative that they are tested and that you are furnished with the results. You must also be wary that you do not supply free goods beyond those needed for trial and evaluation.

Plant visit In some situations it is sound strategy to invite one or more decision makers to visit your plant or home office. You can give them the VIP treatment and show off the many people and physical resources backing you up in the field. Guests on such occasions are likely to feel an obligation to give a fair trial to your company's products. Technical personnel from the prospective account can meet and exchange ideas with the specialists in your firm. Ball Corporation salespeople, for instance, explain their entire product line and then invite potential customers to headquarters for plant tours. They feel this builds customer confidence in the selling organization.[6]

Technical assistance If the potential in the prospective account warrants it, you may, on a speculative basis, commit technical assistance on problems that are of concern to the prospect. You must plan the arrangement with care, however, and inform your technical personnel about the people in the account as well as the background of the account. The technical people need to realize that their knowledge and efforts are being committed with the hope of generating a lasting relationship. It is important that they build favorable personal relationships with their counterparts in the account.

Testimonials Recognizing the impact of testimonials from satisfied users, you may arrange for a prospect to visit a customer's installation. This has the advantage of letting the prospective customer see the product under "real-world" conditions. The prospect will have a chance to talk not only with plant executives, but with the people who are responsible for the day-to-day handling of the product. Such a visit obviously requires advance clearance and careful planning with the customer. You must also make sure that the customer you choose will have prestige in the eyes of the prospect and that the visit will not prove disruptive to the customer's business.

Other forms of testimonials are also useful. For example, you might ask a satisfied customer to write a letter of introduction or recommendation for you to a prospective customer. Or you might ask the satisfied customer whether prospective customers could telephone for a recommendation.

You must, of course, use good commercial judgment in the efforts you expend to open a new account. The important thing to remember is that you will not always be successful. Therefore, you must know when to quit as well as when to persist. Sometimes a salesperson becomes so ego-involved in the challenge provided by a prospect that undue effort is devoted to attempt to gain an order. Careful examination of the situation many well reveal that the same energies expended in other directions might provide far more business than could possibly be achieved in that single account.

[6]Clifton J. Reichard, "Industrial Selling: Beyond Price and Persistence," *Harvard Business Review*, Vol. 63, No. 2 (March–April 1985), pp. 127–133.

OTHER INFLUENCES ON STRATEGY

If this discussion of account strategy ended at this point, it would be oversimplifying the selling–buying relationship. Regardless of what is being considered for purchase, it is unlikely that final buying decisions are independent of other influences. External factors such as the degree and types of competition, engaging in reciprocity, the desire of an account to have multiple sourcing, the influence of important companies and individuals, and publicity all play important roles in the purchasing decision process.

Competition

The ingredients in each competitor's promotional mix—personal selling, advertising, sales promotion, and merchandising—exert varying degrees of influence on each member of the decision-making group. This means that you must be alert not only to your own firm's promotional forces but also to those being used by each of your competitors. You should continually look for the advantages you have over each competing salesperson and the advantages your firm has over its competitors. You will learn what you should stress in your presentations, and you will become keenly aware of the specific points your different competitors are likely to use to sell their products.

If company A's advantage is its delivery time, for example, company B's salesperson will not want to talk about delivery; rather, company B's person will want to stress other important areas, such as service. However, if company B's salesperson were competing with company D, whose delivery was extremely slow, it might be wise to stress company B's three-week delivery schedule.

Reciprocity

Many industrial sales are set in motion by reciprocity. A company may buy from a given supplier because the supplier is also a customer for the company's goods and services. Sales made on the basis of reciprocity confront you with one of two strategic situations. In the first situation your company buys from the customer or prospect. You now have another source of information about the company you are calling on—namely, your own purchasing department and others who have become involved with procurement. You can also find out what volume of business the account enjoys with your firm. You are then in a position to use this information as reinforcement for a customer account or as a basis for entry for a prospect account.

In the second situation the prospective account is buying from one or more of your competitors owing to reciprocity. Your strategy then is to convince the customer that they may not be buying the best products for their firm and to imply that captive purchasing may not be profitable purchasing. You may encourage the purchasing department to compare your products carefully to the competition's products. (This procedure, called value analysis, is discussed in detail in Chapter 15.)

Multiple Buying Sources

Many purchasers desire multiple buying sources and divide their business between a number of vendors. Generally speaking, this purchasing policy is justified; a firm may not wish to become too dependent on any one of its suppliers. A natural catastrophe, such as flood or fire, or a strike might curtail or even eliminate supplies from a sole source. It is also argued that when a firm has several suppliers, they will compete to provide maximum value.[7]

A firm that buys from multiple sources poses two distinct sales situations: (1) you now have an assigned share of its total business, and (2) you are the outsider trying to get in. In the first instance, your likely objective is to increase your share of the total business. To accomplish this you must show that buying a fixed share from you has limited benefit for the account. To acquire a larger share of the business, you may build your strategy around the economic stability and favorable labor conditions of your firm as well as the savings available when large orders are placed with your firm.

When you are trying to get a share of the business, you will want to know on what basis the allocations have been made. Your strategy may be to change the prospect's assumption that it is now doing business with the best combination of sources. In this instance, you may seek a trial order or even ask that a free sample be evaluated in comparison with the products now in use. For instance, Jenny Smith, a sales representative for an office supply firm, was trying to get her paper products line into the approved list at a particular university. After considerable work, she finally convinced purchasing that it made sense to have her product lines included in case the existing source had delivery problems.

Important Companies and Individuals

Every market is likely to have influential people and organizations that set purchasing patterns. These persons and accounts warrant an effort to cultivate them that is beyond their direct payoff. If you can establish a selling–buying relationship with several of these in each part of your territory, you have a real promotional asset. A sales manager once referred to these prestige accounts quite appropriately as an "unpaid sales force." A textbook sales representative may find that a text adoption by a prestigious institution, such as Harvard Business School, may help adoptions at other universities.

Publicity

An important outside influence is the unsolicited favorable publicity that may occasionally come from the media. You must be alert to this publicity when it occurs, so that you can exploit it with both customers and prospects. For example, a major oil company received widespread national publicity for its "drive safely" campaign. In one state the governor declared a day in honor of the firm, and there was an immediate boost in the firm's market share. Salespeople need to be aware when their firm receives public praise so that they can share it with their customers.

It is also important for you to be able to handle unfavorable—and at times unfair—criticisms of your firm. In the event the unfavorable publicity is true, you should admit that, like most human beings, people in your com-

[7]For an interesting discussion of multiple sourcing, see Oliver W. Wight, "Multiple Vendors—A Sacred Cow?" *Purchasing*, Vol. 95, No. 1 (July 14, 1983), p. 31.

pany make some mistakes. Hopefully, you will be in a position to assure the customer that your firm is doing all it can to correct past problems and to ensure that they do not occur again. But if the criticisms are truly unfair and unfounded, you should respond to questions about your firm's problems by stating clearly and unemotionally, within the bounds of good taste, why the publicity is in error. When handling publicity, you should consult with your firm and ask for advice.

ACCOUNT STRATEGIES INVOLVING SEVERAL DECISION MAKERS

Account strategy gets even more complex when the nature of the marketplace is such that two or more independent individuals or firms become directly or indirectly responsible for purchasing decisions. The following examples illustrate some of the complexities that exist in selling consumer and industrial goods to more than one decision maker.

HOW TO SELL THE BUYER TO SELL THE BUYING COMMITTEE

Sometimes you must not only convince the buyer, but also help the buyer convince the buying committee. Here are some tips.

1. Provide the buyer with all the facts summarized.
2. Be enthusiastic—it's contagious.
3. Get the buyer's commitment.
4. Supply the buyer with the same selling tools you used.
5. Provide the buyer with a one-page summary of the facts with enough copies for each member of the committee.
6. Give the buyer enough copies to cover the entire committee.
7. Get to know all members of the committee. Sell as many as you can individually.
8. Offer to make the committee presentation yourself.
9. Follow up with the buyer to determine the outcome of the committee meeting.
10. Follow up after the sale.

SOURCE: Reprinted with permission of The Dial Corporation

Consumer Goods Example

Jane Evans, a pharmaceutical salesperson, seeks to influence each of three physicians who practice noncompetitive medical specialties and who share a common suite in the Medical Arts Building. She has several products that fit the practices of each of these doctors, as well as some general-purpose pharmaceuticals that each of them might have occasion to prescribe. In formulating her strategy, Jane assumes that these three physicians discuss common professional problems and that each one influences to some degree the prescribing habits of the other two. But there are other aspects to the situation facing her. These physicians are affiliated with two local hospitals.

Jane has the task of influencing each of these institutions to place her products on the approved list of the hospital pharmacy. In each institution she has a decision-making group to influence. This may include, among others, the hospital administrator, the chief pharmacist, and the purchasing agent. Assuming she is successful in each hospital, Jane still has not concluded her task with these physicians.

She must also make sure that the local retail drugstores patronized by the physicians' patients stock her products. If a physician prescribes one of her products and it is not in stock, the pharmacist may call the physician for permission to substitute a competitive drug. Thus, Jane must influence the decision-making group in each retail drugstore so that her products are in inventory. If Jane allows a weak spot to develop in this complex system, she can be reasonably sure that a competitor will discover and exploit it.

Industrial Goods Example

The same kinds of complications caused by independent individuals or accounts interacting in consumer goods buying decisions also occur in the industrial sector of the economy. For instance, Jim Washington, a salesperson representing an air-conditioning equipment manufacturer, seeks to have his equipment purchased for a new office building. Jim learns about the impending construction from a newspaper article describing the land purchase and notes the names of several realty developers and an insurance company which are jointly engaged in the undertaking. His task is to identify and penetrate the decision-making group in each of these participating firms, and to show each of them the benefit of designating his firm as the preferred supplier. It is likely, however, that the persons called on will indicate that they are going to be guided by the recommendations of their architects when the firm is appointed. He then has to learn which firm it will be, hopefully before his competitors do.

Jim's next step is to meet with the firm's architects. Obviously, the needs and wants of the architecture firm are quite different from those of the promoters. It may be that Jim will seek to give technical assistance to the architecture firm in designing the air-conditioning system of the projected building. Certainly, Jim will want the resulting design to incorporate his own firm's products. At a minimum, Jim would hope that the design will enable his products and services to have a competitive advantage.

The next step is to learn which contractors are likely to get the contract for the building. Several will probably put in bids. At this stage, Jim has the task of cultivating each of these general contracting firms. Again, he is likely to encounter a unique pattern of needs, different from those of the architectural and financial interests. Each general contracting firm may then have its own view about the subcontractors it wants to work with.

When the bid is finally let, Jim must call on each firm involved to ensure, if he can, that he gets the business. Notice in this example that it is not enough for Jim to achieve favorable results internally in each of these varied firms; he must see each of them as part of an interlocking, decision-making whole. It would not be unusual for the sales effort in a project like this to extend over a period of one or two years. In addition, thousands of dollars worth of technical assistance could be committed on a speculative basis. The decision-making group for a project such as this one could undergo many changes from the time Jim made his first call on the financial interests to the day when an offer was finally obtained.

DEVELOPING A CALL STRATEGY

The sales call is the keystone of effective selling. Each call represents a step in a larger plan for the particular customer or prospective account. In order to reach your account objective, you have to go through a series of calls that might include personal calls, telephone calls, and mail. Thus it is important that calls be planned so that they contribute to the overall effort with the account. The sales call consists of three phases: (1) the "before" stage, when you develop an objective and strategy; (2) the "during" stage, when you engage in face-to-face tactics; and (3) the "after" stage, when you evaluate or follow up. Obviously, a key consideration for the "before" phase of developing a strategy for a call to an individual is the "after" phase of the last call to the individual. This information and experience enables you to make your next visit more effective. In the "during" phase, you replan and adjust to the unforeseen and unanticipated. In the "after" phase, you determine the lessons learned and, in reality, begin planning your next call on the account even though it may be weeks or months away. When you are developing a call strategy, there are two types of situations to consider—calls to customers and calls to prospects.

Call Strategy for Current Customers

In planning calls to current customers, you have many things in your favor. The most important is that you know the customer's problems and how your products can be used to help solve them. You also know who your major competitors are and how much of the customer's business you are getting compared to the competition. The only way to improve your position is to sell a larger quantity of what you are currently selling or to sell additional items in the line that the customer is not presently purchasing.

Before making the actual sales call, you should check your last call report to determine whether there were any unanswered questions, commitments, or unfinished items that should be part of the present visit. In addition, you should review what you know about each individual with whom you will be talking—the individual's motivational patterns, outstanding characteristics, idiosyncrasies, position in the firm, and likely influence on purchasing decisions. Realize that every person wants to be treated as a unique individual and that nothing is likely to turn the person off faster than a lack of per-

sonal interest and attention. Good record keeping enables you to be aware
of the unique characteristics of each of your customers.

Your call strategy outlines what you plan to say or do on a particular
sales call and what you plan to avoid saying and doing on a particular call.
The purpose of your strategy is to achieve your call objective. A call strategy
for an existing account might consist of checking on the shipment that was
delivered last week, showing them a new product, giving them literature on
a new product, and not talking down to them.

Call Strategy for Prospective Customers

When you call on a prospective account, your problem is incomplete information. You may not even know whom to see. Often your only insights are
derived from secondary sources. You may not know what role the various
members of management play in purchasing decisions, whom the company
is currently doing business with, what the firm likes about its current suppliers, or what problems the prospective customer has that you might be able
to solve.

Several sources of information are available to you before you call on a
prospective account. Such services as Moody's, Standard and Poor, and Dun
and Bradstreet provide analyses on most U.S. firms. Industry directories supply similar information for particular industries throughout the country, usually including the firm's financial status, its primary operating location, its
major product line, and the name of the chief executive officer. If your firm
does not have this reference material, it is available in most public libraries.
In addition, you may know sales representatives of noncompeting companies
who call on the prospective account. It is quite ethical to exchange ideas
about a firm, including information about current problems and key developments.

The important point is that on an initial visit to a prospective account,
you may accomplish nothing more than obtaining information about the firm.
Nevertheless, it is still important to plan your call carefully so that you will
ask the right questions, obtain pertinent information, and appear knowledgeable and interested in helping the prospective customer. One firm that sells
copiers uses the form in Figure 5.4 to collect information on prospective customers.

TEAM AND GROUP SELLING

Strategy development and planning are particularly important in two types of
sales calls involving several people. These two types are *team selling,* in
which persons from your firm accompany you on your call; and *group selling,* in which you make a presentation to a group of buyers.

Team Selling

Although you plan and conduct most sales on your own, occasionally you
must plan for a joint call. Your supervisor may schedule a "work with" period
in your territory, or it may be appropriate for you to bring additional person-

Date of contact_____

In person _____
By phone _____

Company_____

Address_____

City _____ Zip code_____

Telephone_____

Contact_____ Title _____

Decision maker _____ Title _____

Existing equipment, type and make _____

Approximate age_____

Monthly volume _____

Average number of copies per original _____

Own_____ Rent_____ Lease_____ Expiration date_____

Use of outside printer or quick copy shop:

A great deal _____ Some_____ Rarely_____

Type of printing done outside:

Direct mail _____ Flyers_____ Internal forms_____ Form letters _____

Instruction sheets or books _____ Surveys _____ Inventory sheets _____

Remarks_____

_____

_____

Date of follow-up _____

Results _____

Reprinted with permission of Gestetner Corporation, Yonkers, New York.

FIGURE 5.4 Sample form used for gaining information on prospective copier customers.
SOURCE: Reproduced with permission of Gestetner Corporation, Yonkers, New York.

nel from your firm. These additional people might be experts from within
your company or support people whom you want to assist you.

When more than one person goes on a call, a strategy must be developed and communicated to the other individual so that the call will be coordinated. First, you need to determine in advance what role each person
will play. Who will be in control? Who will answer what questions? It is
useful to have either you or your manager act as a quarterback, to be in

Salespeople making a joint call on prospects.

control and act as a focal point for questions. Second, the other person should be thoroughly briefed on the background of the account, including prior calls, background of key people, previous discussions, and any unique circumstances of the account. This briefing will ensure that the other person is informed and will minimize the possibility of conflicting stories. Third, it is especially important to have a call objective and to have mutual understanding of this objective. Fourth, you should anticipate objections and determine who will handle them and how. For instance, you might agree that if a question comes up about price, you will handle it and state an agreed-upon amount. Finally, if the call is important enough, you may wish to do a dry run of the call, that is, role-play it. Even less important calls, however, should be coordinated, with all people participating in the call being informed. If you are really behind in your planning, you can do the coordinating in the car while driving to the account.

Supervisor-initiated joint calls When your boss accompanies you on a call to a customer, you are sometimes confronted with the difficult problem of preventing your boss from taking over the face-to-face meeting. If you handle the call effectively on your own, the supervisor is likely to be impressed both by your knowledge of the account and by the care with which you plan your calls. It is your responsibility to brief your supervisor so that the "during" phase of each joint call goes smoothly. You may have more tolerance for joint calls if you recognize that your boss has a responsibility to observe your work, to evaluate it, and to assist you in being even more effective.

Salesperson-initiated joint calls Sometimes joint calls are initiated by you, usually to achieve some combination of the following objectives: (1) to reinforce your own personal selling effort, (2) to provide the account with technical information beyond the scope of your own knowledge, (3) to have someone in your own firm gain information on how the customer has applied the company's product line, and (4) to help in the training of other sales representatives. In each instance, it is important for you to keep in mind that you are the account manager and that it is your responsibility to plan such calls. You must brief the other person sufficiently so that together you can obtain the impact desired.

If the call objective is to *reinforce your own selling effort,* you will likely bring in a member of your firm's management. To get maximum benefit from this reinforcement, you should arrange specific appointments with key decision makers within the account. Then, as part of the "before" phase, you can brief your associate on each person to be seen and what you hope to accomplish with them.

If the objective of the joint call is to *provide technical information,* it is critically important in the planning stage to brief the technician from your firm on the people you will meet as well as the technical side of the account. It is particularly important for your technical helper to know the level of sophistication of each person to be contacted. Otherwise, the technician may talk over the heads of the decision makers.

If the objective of the joint call is to help someone within your own firm *obtain information,* you should be careful which accounts you call on, for the customer is providing a favor. You certainly do not want to upset a favorable relationship with such a call. In addition, you must be sure to brief your colleague about the customer, the buying history of the account, and the specific applications the account is making of the company's product line. It may also be pertinent to inform your colleagues about any directly competing products being used by the account. Tactful questions regarding these products can then be raised, and comparative evaluations can be developed from the customer's point of view.

If *training* is the objective of the joint call, it should never be attempted at the expense of a favorable account relationship. You should brief the sales trainee fully before the face-to-face meeting. If the trainee is sufficiently advanced in knowledge and skill to make presentations, these may be arranged for selected accounts in advance. Alternatively, training calls may be made on prospective accounts of low potential.

Selling to a Group

Another situation for which it is especially necessary to have a clearly defined call strategy is convincing a group to make a purchase.[8] Group selling occurs in industrial selling when you make a presentation to a buying committee or the board of directors, in consumer selling you make a presentation to a family. Another form of presentation consists of seminars prepared for groups of prospects. This is called seminar selling and is covered in Chapter 7. Several suggestions for group selling follow.

[8]For an interesting discussion on making presentations, see Peter Rogen, "How to Design and Deliver a Convincing Presentation," *Business Marketing,* Vol. 65, No. 7 (July 7, 1980), pp. 36 – 37.

Salesperson selling to a group.

Use visual aids One important aspect of your call strategy when selling to a group is the use of visual aids. The larger the group, the more effective and necessary are such aids as charts, posters, flip charts, slides, overhead transparencies, filmstrips, and movies. Specifics of using these and other visuals are covered in Chapter 10.

Get involvement Another important aspect of group selling is getting the involvement of the entire group and not letting anyone feel ignored. Answering all group questions and asking questions of various individuals are strategies for involving participants.

Note nonverbal responses Groups are typically made up of members with different backgrounds, personalities, and motivations; therefore, it is also important to note nonverbal responses of group members in order to spot potential objections, or to note communication difficulties or misunderstandings and thus get a sense of how to proceed.[9] The larger the group, the more difficult it is to read all nonverbal responses and avoid misunderstanding.

Limit topics Because of the potential for miscommunication and the differing backgrounds and interests of group members, one sound strategy is to keep the number of topics to a minimum. You should also draw the conclusions for the group rather than relying on them to do so. Given their potentially

[9]See for example, John Franco, "Making Effective Presentations: Learning to Recognize and Address Audience Needs," *The American Salesman,* Vol. 29, No. 12 (December 1984), pp. 22–25.

different perspectives, they may come to different conclusions unless you summarize and specifically state your conclusions.

Rehearse When making group presentations, you should be thoroughly rehearsed for the presentation and should know the information well enough to be able to field questions. This preparation will make your presentation smooth and professional.

Note power structure When planning your strategy, you should also take into account the power structure and roles of the various group members. In group selling to a customer account, these would generally be known beforehand. When dealing with a prospect group, some of these things will have to be determined by analyzing nonverbal reactions of the group. Even in prospect group selling, however, the more information you have on various group members' backgrounds, personalities, motivations, and their status and role within the group, the better off you will be. You can acquire some of this information by visiting the individuals in the group separately before the

If the Key Decision Makers Are	Your Presentation Should Be
Analytical	Highly logical
Orderly and precise	Neatly structured
Conceptual; prefer the "big picture"	Built around a framework
Long-range-oriented	Amplified by trends, projections, and predictions
Short-term-oriented	Related to impact, bottom line
Highly social, warm, and affiliative	Laced with anecdotes, acknowledgments, and accolades
Intellectual, abstract, and intuitive	Broad-brushed with references to its being on the cutting edge, in the vanguard, and so on
Uncomfortable with yes–no decisions	Concluded with many options
Uncomfortable with options	Concluded with request for a yes–no decision
Perfectionist	Neat and accurate, but containing small flaws
Skeptical and suspicious	Supported by irrefutable proof, high-quality references
Controlling and power-oriented	Interactive and concluded with recommendations

FIGURE 5.5 Analyzing key decision makers for group presentations. SOURCE: Chip R. Bell, "Let Your Presentation Dazzle Top Management," *Personnel Journal*, Vol 63. (February 1984), pp. 26–30. Adapted with permission of *Personnel Journal*, Costa Mesa, Calif. All rights reserved.

group presentation or by persuading your initial contact person in the prospect's organization to describe the group members and their interests to you. Using this knowledge, you can then adapt your presentation to fit the needs of key decision makers. As can be seen from Figure 5.5, your presentation should be tailored to the nature of the key decision makers.

SUMMARY

Your objective with accounts is to recognize uniqueness. To accomplish this, you must identify the decision-making groups. You must also know the steps your products (and those of competitors) go through following purchase. Finally, you need to find out as much as possible about direct and indirect competition in each account.

The strategy for customer accounts is to make the account impenetrable by competitors. You should emphasize the personal follow-up designed to maximize satisfaction. Several strategies can be used to keep customers happy: stressing customer service and follow-up, cultivating the entire buying team, and looking for additional advantages of your product or services. In contrast, for prospects sales strategy is aimed at disturbing the status quo and thus gaining entree. The six specific methods for winning new accounts are stressing competitive advantage; accepting trial orders, giving free samples, inviting prospects to visit your plant, offering technical assistance, and furnishing testimonials.

Circumstances and priorities within each account change with time, and strategy must be modified accordingly. In addition to internal influences, several external factors affect strategy: a competitor's promotional efforts, engaging in reciprocity, a desire for multiple buying sources, the influence of important companies and individuals, and publicity.

In addition to developing a strategy for each account, you also need to have a strategy for each sales call, a plan of what you will or will not say and do in order to reach your call objective. Call strategies are much easier to develop for current customers than for prospects, since you have much more information and experience with current customers.

Two kinds of calls that require special preparation are team selling and sales to a group. In team selling, it is important to define each person's role, brief the other person, have a call objective, anticipate questions, and go over the call carefully. This should be done whether the joint call was initiated by management or by you. When you sell to a group, visuals will be useful, and group members should be involved; you should limit the number of topics, take the power structure of the group into account, and rehearse your presentation.

PROBLEMS

1. Why is it important for salespeople to know their market share for each of their accounts?

2. Differentiate between the strategy used in customer accounts and that used in prospect accounts.

3. What are the most important differences, from salespeople's perspective, between a trial order and a free sample?

4. How important are the external influences on account strategy? List the most important external influences for a particular account.

5. Which external influence on strategy would be most difficult to counteract? Why?

6. Referring to the industrial goods example in the text, what are some of the changes that might occur during the time the salesperson is engaged in the project?

7. Why might salespeople initiate a joint call? What steps should they take before the joint call?

8. How would you feel about having your sales manager travel with you as part of your regular evaluation? Do you feel the sales manager has anything personal to gain from such visits?

EXERCISE 5

Objectives: To obtain a salesperson's views about account strategy.

To compare this with what was learned from the text.

You are to interview a salesperson (may be arranged in class) and learn how he or she penetrates each account in sufficient depth to achieve effectiveness. Cover all questions set forth in the following, supplementing each where necessary to obtain full response.

Name of salesperson _____

Company _____

Product line _____

1. Who are your key customers and prospects?
2. In the largest accounts, how many people must be seen?
   What positions do they hold?
   a.
   b.
   c.
   d.
3. In a new account, how do you determine which persons to see?
4. What kinds of things do you try to find out about each person?
5. How do you learn about the competition in these accounts?
6. What steps do products such as yours pass through once they are purchased?
7. What kinds of problems or difficulties might occur at each step?
8. How many calls are usually required before you obtain the first order?
9. Please describe the sales strategies you used to obtain a specific new major account.

Elite is a highly regarded wholesaler that provides a full line of printed and engraved products, ranging from business cards to wedding invitations. Elite has two broad categories of accounts: business and professional organizations, which are sold direct; and gift and stationery shops and stationery departments in large stores. This second category accounts for about 75 percent of total sales. Ina Kahn has a territory in which most of the potential is accounted for by retailers.

One of Ina's prospects is the Atkin Card and Gift Shop. At present Atkin does not offer such personalized items, and Ms. Elizabeth Atkin has been reluctant to carry such a line.

On earlier calls Ms. Atkin told Ina that she has all she can handle now. She operates the store herself except at peak hours and in the holiday seasons, when she uses part-time help.

Ina feels the Elite line would do well with Atkin's. The store is in a shopping mall that serves a fairly affluent surrounding area. True, it is small and space is at a premium. However, the Elite catalog and sample books could be stored out of the way when not in use. Besides, Ina is sure that the limited variety of gift items does not add too much to profit. On her calls to Atkin's she noticed that most of the traffic is focused on cards. Atkin's carries the best label in the industry. Two barriers face Ina: (1) the store as it is now run provides Ms. Atkin an adequate livelihood, and (2) Ms. Atkin is change-resistant. But Ina has observed Ms. Atkin closely and overheard conversations between Ms. Atkin and her customers. Many patrons compliment Ms. Atkin on her excellent taste in the cards she stocks as well as in the other items in the store. Ina has noticed how Ms. Atkin beams when complimented or when asked for advice. Ms. Atkin seems to be ideal for her job; she really loves people and has a wonderful way with them.

What type of strategy should Ina use in making her next call on Atkin's?

Case 5–2 Joseph Shanks of Austin

Mr. John Murphy, a sales representative for Joseph Shanks of Austin, is preparing for a very important sales call on Lake Travis West—a resort community located in the Texas hill country. Mr. Murphy has worked for Shanks for five years, and his familiarity with the Austin area has helped him become one of the store's more successful salespeople.

Joseph Shanks is a large furniture store that sells middle- to upper-quality furniture. Most of its business is with private individuals who purchase furniture for their homes. However, Shanks always bids on institutional orders such as furniture for banks, state office buildings, and large apartment complexes if the management feels they "have a reasonable chance of winning a profitable bid."

Lake Travis West is a resort complex being built on Lake Travis. When the first section is completed, there will be eighty apartment units for rent. The developer plans eventually to develop two additional areas on Lake Travis West; these will have seventy-five apartment units each. When the resort complex is finished, it will have a full array of water sports facilities along with tennis, golf (an eighteen-hole course is currently under construction), and horseback riding. The complex is designed to cater primarily to wealthy families in Houston and Dallas.

Murphy had never made an institutional bid for Shanks before. He became involved in Lake Travis West because a fraternity brother of his, Jerry Jones, is handling the decoration and furniture selection for the complex. When Murphy told his boss, William Sinclair, that he had been invited to submit a bid for the furnishings of the apartments, Sinclair instructed him to go ahead and offered to help him with negotiations if necessary. Sinclair would have to approve the final bid before Murphy could submit it to Lake Travis West.

Murphy provided a great deal of technical assistance to his friend Jones. He spent countless hours working on room designs and furniture layouts. In addition, he investigated practically all the nation's major furniture manufacturers so that he would be able to get Lake Travis West the most furniture for its money. He presented four room "concepts," which included all the furniture, draperies, carpeting, and wall decorations. In order to give the complex some variety, he suggested they adopt all four concepts, rather than just one room design for each of the apartments.

Murphy thought everything was going well until he got a call from Jones. He explained that he had presented the four concepts and the total price to his boss, Mr. Caskey, whose initial reactions were "The price is too high" and "I just do not like the concepts Shanks has come up with."

Jones thought that it would be desirable to have a joint meeting between Mr. Caskey, Murphy, and himself. After Murphy related these developments to his boss, Sinclair suggested that it would be best for Shanks to be represented by Murphy, himself, and Bob Taylor, Shanks's number one designer. (Taylor had worked on the concepts behind the scenes with Murphy, so he was aware of them.)

Murphy was a little nervous about Sinclair's going with him. He felt that Sinclair did not trust him with such a big order and this would give Sinclair a chance to observe him in action.

1. What role should each of the people from Shanks play?
2. Should Murphy alert Jones of his fear of Sinclair?
3. What types of planning should go into this call on the part of Shanks employees?

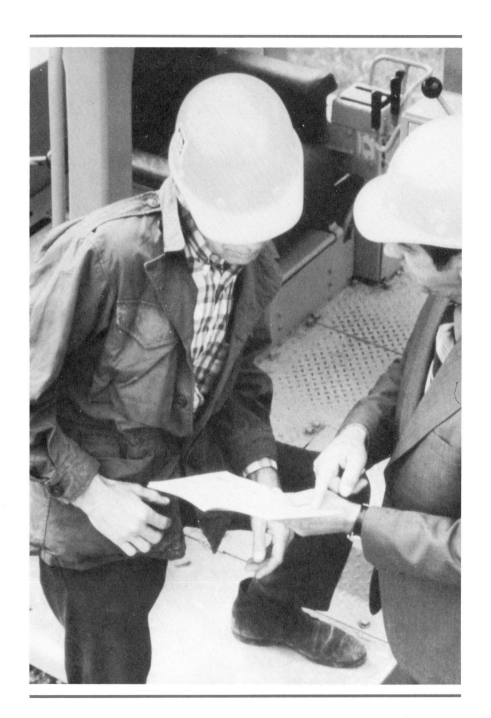

Understanding the Buyer as an Individual

6

After studying this chapter, you should be able to

1. Understand the importance of treating the prospect as a unique individual.
2. Recognize key elements that determine a person's background.
3. Differentiate between typecasting and the trait approach for understanding the prospect's personality.
4. Develop a strategy for handling an individual based upon personality traits.
5. Identify various motives for purchasing your product or service.

In order to make an effective sales call, it is important to understand the buyer as an individual. You must understand buyers as individuals if you are to adapt to their style and needs. In the selling situation you must be flexible and adapt; the buyer does not have to change.

An important characteristic of human nature is the desire for individuality. Because of this desire, the universal objective in all interpersonal relations is to treat the other person as a unique individual; salespeople who are able to treat people on an individual basis are likely to be successful.

ON THE IMPORTANCE OF UNDERSTANDING THE BUYER

According to Joe M. Gandolfo, one of the world's top salespeople of life insurance, Selling is 98 percent understanding human beings and 2 percent product knowledge. You'll never really understand people unless you go out and meet them. Asking a lot of questions and doing a lot of listening, well, that's the best way to understand people. Because if you do all the talking, how can you understand 'em? You'd never get to know anyone if you did all the talking. And another thing: I'm genuinely interested in this guy. I really want to know how he got into business, and I want to know all about his philosophies. I want to find out everything I can about him, because I think he's an interesting person. And, I'll tell you something else, I come away a better person because I learned a lot from this man.

SOURCE: Robert Shook, *Ten Greatest Salespersons: What They Say about Selling* (New York: Harper and Row, 1978), pp. 34–35. Copyright © 1978, by Robert L. Shook and Roberta W. Shook, Trustees. Reprinted with permission by Harper and Row Publishers, Inc.

To respond to this desire for uniqueness, you should maintain a file on each individual you visit. Figure 6.1 gives an example of a customer file. A customer file usually includes such information as age, position, hobbies, buying habits, education, and unusual or particularly strong personality traits. It might also include dominant motives of purchase. You should refine and amend this information as you gain new insights into the individual. If other people in your company contact this person, their observations can also be added. Given the large number of people you will meet and the diverse characteristics of each person, it is wise to write down the information rather than trying to remember such details. Therefore, before each visit you should review the customer's file, and after the call you should add any new information you might have learned.

1. Name: *Mary Worthington*

2. Address: *875 Montgomery St., San Jose, Calif.*

3. Position: *Production Manager, Moss Publishing, Inc.*

4. Background information: *From small town in midwest—lived on farm,*
   conservative

5. Personality traits: *Outgoing, charming, but hard to know.*

6. Motives: *Quality, appreciates technical knowledge.*

7. Hobbies: *Loves animals, tennis, interested in stock market.*

8. Buying habits: *Very shrewd and budget-oriented.*

9. Family: *Not married, boyfriend is Gene Daily (Journalist).*

10. Religion: *Doesn't seem to be affiliated.*

11. Needs and problems: *Needs quick turnaround time.*

12. Usual objections: *Defensive.*

FIGURE 6.1 Example of a customer file.

There are even microcomputer systems available that keep basic information on prospects. One software program, for example, The Dow Jones Prospect Organizer, enables the user to track prospects from initial inquiry to the time they became a customer. This program also allows salespeople to generate corresponding form letters and scripts for telemarketing.[1]

In order to treat the customer or prospect as a unique individual, you must understand the person's background, personality, and motivation. These are factors that tend to differentiate people and are keys for developing a strategy for handling the person as an individual.

BACKGROUND

The prospect's interests, vocabulary, and knowledge will depend to a considerable extent on his or her background. You may determine a person's background by asking questions and listening, for people generally like to talk about themselves. Sometimes this information is gathered during a business lunch or through business entertaining, when you can learn key aspects of the customer's or prospect's background that you might never have noticed in the office. Another way of discovering aspects of background is to observe a person's office or home. Diplomas, certificates, reading materials, plaques, trophies, pictures, and furnishings all give important clues to a person's back-

[1]Robert H. Collins, "Microcomputer Systems to Handle Sales Leads: A Key to Increased Salesforce Productivity," *Journal of Personal Selling and Sales Management,* Vol. 5, No. 1 (May 1985), pp. 77–83.

What can you tell about the person from this office?

ground or interests. Often these clues can be used as icebreakers to build rapport with the prospect. For instance, if you noticed a golf trophy on a prospect's desk and you have some knowledge or interest in golf, you might ask about her golf game or where she plays. Sometimes, however, these clues can be misleading; a prospect may put books on her desk to impress visitors rather than because of her own interest. Nevertheless, several factors are normally good clues to people's backgrounds. These factors include their formal education, work experience, cultural background, and activities.

Formal Education
The kind and extent of formal education customers or prospects have may be some clue to their intelligence and may dictate the vocabulary and level of your presentation. Several cautions are in order, however. First, many people without formal education are very intelligent, very successful, and possess a great deal of practical knowledge. Second, formal education should be viewed in relation to the products or services being offered. An insurance salesperson would have to treat a doctorate holder in English very differently from a doctorate holder in finance, even though they have the same amount of formal education.

Work Experience
Work experience can often be an important determinant of the strategy to use with a person. People, especially successful people, often like to talk about their business experience. Often a simple question such as, "How did you first get started in this business?" is all that is necessary to get a person talking. It is also important to find out that one key contact had work experience in marketing whereas another had experience in engineering. These experiences will reveal the aspects of your product in which they will be interested and also how you approach them.

Cultural Background
Cultural background consists of such things as race, religion, and the region of the country in which the person lives. Cultural background will often influ-

ence how people conduct business and how you deal with them. Observation of two salespeople from the same firm who have territories in New York City and New Orleans revealed very different approaches to selling, primarily because of the differences in the regional cultures of these two areas. The New Yorker's approach was very fast-paced, formal, and businesslike. On the other hand, the sales representative from New Orleans spent much more time with small talk and personal business, and was much more casual and relaxed before getting down to business. Although these stereotypes do not always hold true, they often do. The business customs in various parts of the country and in foreign countries should be taken into account.[2]

Activities

Cultural, recreational, and social activities are the final aspects of background. Knowledge of these activities is usually used to establish mutual interests and rapport, or as icebreakers to start off a call. To the extent that you share mutual interests with a prospect, it will be easier for you to communicate with that person. That is why having a broad background is important or desirable. You will find that the more interests you share with prospects, the easier it will be to establish rapport with them.

PERSONALITY

Personality is the "how" of behavior. It tells you how a person interacts with his or her environment, and it reflects distinguishing qualities—the qualities that make a person different from other people. Two buyers with different personalities would have to be handled quite differently. For instance, a prospect who is forceful must be handled quite differently from a prospect who is timid. The forceful prospect might be given information and asked to make a decision, whereas the timid prospect might have to be given reassurance, told about other successful purchasers, and provided with testimonials. The key point is that your strategy with an individual will be influenced by the person's personality. Analyzing a buyer's personality tells you how to sell the prospect and tells you what approach to take in dealing with the buyer as an individual.

There are two methods of identifying a customer or prospect's personality, typecasting and trait analysis.

Typecasting

When asked to describe someone, you might respond by saying "She is an extrovert," or "She is shy." This is typecasting the person. Although this approach is of some use in comparing one individual with another, it is less helpful in planning a strategy to influence a particular person. The task is to learn what makes a person different, not what the person has in common with other people.

---

[2]For an interesting discussion of cultural aspects of international business, see Edward Hall, *Beyond Culture* (Garden City, N. Y.: Anchor, 1977).

Typecasting has several potential limitations. First, it tends to hide rather than highlight the variety of characteristics of an individual. When an individual is classified as an extrovert, attention tends to focus on this characteristic rather than on the many other facets of the individual's personality. In addition, there are vast differences in the amount of a characteristic a person possesses. Few people are truly either extrovert or introvert; most people fall somewhere in between.

Despite these potential disadvantages, the approach has been widely used, and there are a number of different typologies for classifying personalities.[3] One of these typologies classifies prospects' personalities according to their assertiveness and emotional responsiveness.[4] As shown in Figure 6.2, this approach depicts behavior as ranging from high assertiveness to low assertiveness, and from highly controlled to emote. A highly assertive person is competitive, fast-acting, directive, and takes risks—a real take-charge person. On the other end of this continuum is the unassertive person who is cooperative, slower-acting, and nondirective, avoids risk, and is a follower. A highly

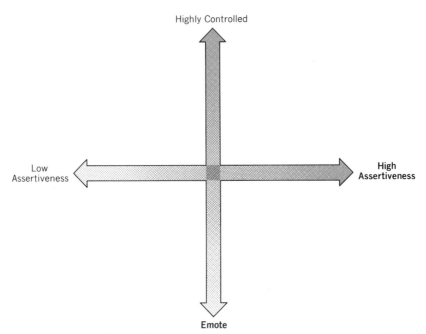

FIGURE 6.2 Personality classification according to degree of assertiveness and emotional reponsiveness.

[3]Hugh J. Ingrasci, "How to Reach Buyers in Their Psychological 'Comfort Zones,'" *Industrial Marketing,* Vol. 66, No. 7 (July 1981), pp. 60–64; Dudley Lynch, "Getting 'In Sync' With the Customer," *Management* (May 19, 1980), pp. 42–46; Sally Scanlon, "Every Salesperson a Psychologist," *Sales and Marketing Management,* Vol. 120, No. 2 (February 6, 1978), pp. 34–36; Anthony J. Alessandra and Phillip S. Wexler, *Non-Manipulative Selling* (San Diego, Calif.: Courseware, 1979), pp. 13–41.

[4]This discussion generally follows Hugh J. Ingrasci, "How To Reach Buyers in Their Psychological 'Comfort Zones,'" *Industrial Marketing,* Vol. 66, No.7 (July 1981), pp. 60–64.

controlled person is rational, disciplined, task-oriented, formal, independent, and businesslike. The opposite, an emote person, is very friendly, informal, open, emotional, undisciplined, and relationship-oriented. Crossing these two characteristics gives four personality types: analyticals, drivers, expressives, and amiables (see Figure 6.3).

Analyticals Analytical people are not very assertive and are very controlled in their behavior. They are often financially or technically oriented. These buyers are very logical and like appeals that acknowledge their technical expertise and stick to the facts. Warranties, independent tests, and testimonials may be good strategies for working with analytical people.

Drivers Drivers are also very controlled, but they are highly assertive. They are the hard-chargers, the achievement-oriented buyers. They are very hard workers and are very highly motivated. Drivers need to be shown the payoff. They will want quick answers to their questions and quick follow-up on their orders. They also like you to be businesslike, provide them with facts, and be organized.

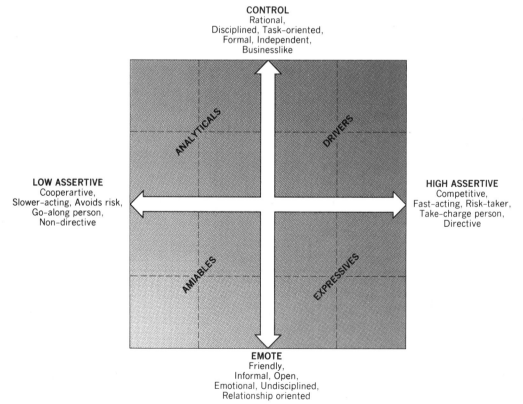

FIGURE 6.3 Social style matrix. SOURCE: Hugh J. Ingrasci, "How To Reach Buyers in Their Psychological 'Comfort Zones,' " *Industrial Marketing*, Vol. 66, No. 7 (July 1981), p. 61. Copyright © 1981, by Crain Communications, Inc. Adapted with permission of *Business Marketing*.

Expressives Expressives are very open in their behavior but also very assertive. They are people-oriented as opposed to technically oriented. They are idea people who like to work with others. They should not be given very technical information or other demanding, detailed data, for they will tend to ignore this information. Instead, very personalized, people-oriented presentations should be made. Testimonials may work well with expressives; however, they like to be innovators and seek approval from others for their purchases.

Amiables Amiable people are very open but not very assertive. They are loyal, dependable team workers. They need personal attention, and your appeals should stress human considerations. You would need to show them the effect that your product would have on their personnel. Because amiables are not assertive, they may find decision making difficult and risky. You need to stress dependability and your firm's reputation. Amiables may also like guarantees and warranties.

The strategies for dealing with the four types of personalities are summarized in Figure 6.4.

Trait Analysis

Trait analysis is an alternative to typecasting. This approach recognizes that people have multifaceted personalities. Although all human beings have personality and behavioral traits in common, no two people are alike, for they possess different amounts of these traits. Traits are enduring or persistent characteristics of a person. For instance, you might describe a person as aggressive, sarcastic, shrewd, and formal. In using trait analysis, you identify traits that the person possesses to a great extent, compared to people in general.

ANALYTICALS	DRIVERS
• Stick to facts. • Use warranties. • Provide independent tests. • Use testimonials.	• Show them bottom line. • Answer questions. • Follow up their orders. • Be businesslike. • Be organized.
AMIABLES	EXPRESSIVES
• Give personal attention. • Stress human consideration. • Stress your firm's dependability and reputation. • Use guarantees and warranties.	• Avoid technical information. • Avoid detail. • Personalize presentation. • Use testimonials.

FIGURE 6.4 Strategies for dealing with various customer personality types.

These are the traits that set this person apart as a unique individual. To the degree that these traits can be identified in the customer, you have a basis for your strategy for dealing with the person. From another standpoint, it would be impossible for you to treat a prospect as a unique individual if you did not know what characteristics made the individual different. You use a number of factors to help you identify the traits of a customer or prospect.

Factors Influencing Trait Analysis

Many factors—your experience, your attentiveness, and the inputs of third parties—affect the accuracy with which traits are identified.

Experience The most important factor is the sheer amount of evidence on which the analysis is based. Every time you call on a person, you increase your knowledge of that person. In fact, as you complete a call you should ask yourself, "What have I learned about this person that I didn't know before?" Some traits become evident almost immediately, others not until much later. Seeing a person under a variety of circumstances may bring out traits that otherwise would not be seen. For example, light talk over lunch may reveal interests that would never come to the surface in a more formal atmosphere. A prospect may behave far differently at an industry meeting than she does behind her own desk. Thus, it is important to observe a person under varying conditions to get as full a trait picture as possible.

Your attentiveness Another factor that is bound to influence the accuracy of identifying traits is the degree of your attentiveness toward the other person. You are likely to arrive at a more accurate assessment of the customer if you go into the call well prepared and with a conscious objective of learning all you can. If you have to direct too much of your attention inwardly to think about what to say or do next, you cannot give full attention to the other person; hence, you miss cues concerning the person's behavior.

Third-party inputs You may learn some things about the customer by questioning other people who have had contact with the person. Of course, caution must be exercised in using this source of information, for a third party's opinion may bias your own judgment favorably or unfavorably and lessen the likelihood that you can approach the customer with an open mind. More often than not, however, another person's point of view is useful. A third party might observe some aspects of the customer's behavior that you miss. Therefore, it is probably sound practice for you to check with other people who have had contact with the person you are seeking to influence.

Steps in Trait Analyses

With these factors in mind, there are five steps in handling a person on the basis of their personality traits: (1) identify outstanding traits, (2) note evidence for those traits, (3) develop a strategy for each trait, (4) group traits into patterns of behavior, and (5) develop an overall strategy on the basis of behavior patterns.

TABLE 6.1

COMMON PAIRS OF TRAIT TERMS TO HELP SIZE UP PEOPLE

1. Adaptable / Inflexible	33. Fatalistic / Self-controlling	65. Open-minded / Opinionated	81. Self-pitying / Spartan
2. Affected / Natural	34. Feminine / Masculine	66. Opportunistic / Nonexploiting	82. Self-respecting / Shameless
3. Alert / Sluggish	35. Fluent / Inarticulate	67. Optimistic / Pessimistic	83. Self-sufficient / Dependent
4. Apathetic / Enthusiastic	36. Forbearing / Complaining	68. Persuasive / Yes-man	84. Sensitive / Callous
5. Argumentative / Agreeable	37. Foresighted / Hindsighted	69. Pliant / Stubborn	85. Sincere / Hypocritical
6. Ascetic / Sensuous	38. Formal / Informal	70. Practical / Theoretical	86. Strong-willed / Suggestible
7. Autocratic / Democratic	39. Forgetful / Retentive	71. Practical joker / Considerate	87. Talkative / Close-mouthed
8. Benevolent / Malevolent	40. Frigid / Amorous	72. Price-minded / Quality-minded	88. Teetotaler / Alcoholic
9. Blundering / Tactful	41. Gay / Serious	73. Progressive / Reactionary	89. Treacherous / Trustworthy
10. Boastful / Self-effacing	42. Generous / Stingy	74. Rash / Cautious	90. Trusting / Suspicious
11. Bold / Retiring	43. Grateful / Ungrateful	75. Realistic / Self-deceiving	91. Unconcerned / Curious
12. Bungling / Clever	44. Habit-bound / Venturesome	76. Reliable / Undependable	92. Unrestrained / Inhibited
13. Charming / Repugnant	45. Harsh / Mild	77. Remorseful / Conscienceless	93. Unsure / Self-confident
14. Cheerful / Gloomy	46. Honest / Deceitful	78. Rude / Courteous	94. Vacillating / Decisive
15. Complacent / Ambitious	47. Humble / Overbearing	79. Sarcastic / Gentle	95. Vindictive / Forgiving
16. Confused / Clear-thinking	48. Humorous / Somber	80. Satisfied / Displeased	96. Worrying / Indifferent
17. Considerate / Selfish	49. Imaginative / Plodding		
18. Conventional / Nonconforming	50. Imitative / Original		
19. Cooperative / Obstructive	51. Inexperienced / Sophisticated		
20. Courageous / Cowardly	52. Industrious / Indolent		
21. Crude / Polished	53. Interests-wide / Interests-narrow		
22. Cruel / Affectionate	54. Intuitive / Logical		
23. Defiant / Obedient	55. Irreverent / Pious		
24. Deliberate / Impulsive	56. Jealous / Well-wishing		
25. Depressing / Stimulating	57. Leisurely / Hurried		
26. Derogatory / Complimentary	58. Light eater / Gluttonous		
27. Distant / Friendly	59. Loyal / Unfaithful		
28. Estranged / Sociable	60. Mature / Childish		
29. Evasive / Frank	61. Modest / Conceited		
30. Excitable / Calm	62. Moody / Stable		
31. Extravagant / Thrifty	63. Naive / Shrewd		
32. Extreme / Temperate	64. Negativistic / Agreeable		

SOURCE: Harold C. Cash and William J. E. Crissy, *The Psychology of Selling Series*, Vol. 4, "Personality and Sales Strategy" (Flushing, N.Y.: Personnel Development Associates, 1965), pp. 56–58.

Identify outstanding traits The first step in your analysis of the prospect's personality is to identify the several traits that make the prospect unique. Table 6.1 presents 96 pairs of traits that help to evaluate an individual.

Suppose a large number of people are examined with respect to one trait, their intelligence. You would find the intelligence trait distributed along a normal distribution as in Figure 6.5. Some people would have very high intelligence and some very low; however, most people would have average intelligence. When examining a prospect with respect to intelligence, if the person has average intelligence, you would not have to consider this trait when developing a strategy for this prospect; you would treat their intelligence the same as you would that of most other people. If, on the other hand, this person possesses a great deal of intelligence or very little, they would have to be treated differently. This would be an outstanding trait—a trait that a person possesses to such a degree that the trait makes the person different. When examining a prospect, you should seek to find the six to ten traits that serve to make the prospect a unique individual.

Note evidence It is important when making a trait analysis of a person to ask the question, "What evidence do I have for each of the traits I have identified?" The evidence for each trait is likely to be a combination of the prospect's nonverbal behavior obtained by observation as well as verbal statements generated by asking questions. Generally speaking, nonverbal cues are much more important than verbal cues in arriving at an accurate assessment of the other person's personality. People are generally less aware of their nonverbal messages and are not as capable of guarding them as their verbal messages. Evidence is important because it lessens the tendency to "type" the other person. Moreover, as evidence accumulates, refinements and changes can be made in assessing traits.

Develop a strategy for each trait Your next task is to consider each prominent trait you have identified and then ask yourself, "Knowing this, what should I do or avoid doing?" It is important to remember that you will have examined a large set of traits, but you are only interested in those that help identify the particular individual as a unique person.

Figure 6.6 lists the dominant traits of a customer, Mr. Quickslip. How would you deal with him? Write down how you would react to each of his traits, and then compare your responses with those given in the following list.

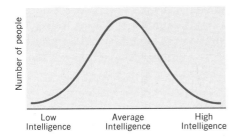

FIGURE 6.5 Distribution of intelligence trait.

1. Intelligent	4. Dominant
2. Technically competent	5. Bold
3. Interested in technical aspects of your product	6. Impulsive

FIGURE 6.6 Characteristics of Mr. Quickslip.

DEALING WITH MR. QUICKSLIP

- **Intelligent.** If the customer possesses a superior amount of intelligence, you may reason on the basis of this trait that you do not need to go into great detail in making your presentation. If you hit the highlights, Mr. Quickslip, being very intelligent, will fill in the specifics. You may also reason that you had better be prepared for difficult questions. In fact, part of your preparation for the call may very well include trying to anticipate difficult questions that are likely to be asked so that you can have answers ready.

- **Technically competent.** If Mr. Quickslip is also very knowledgeable concerning the technical aspects of your product, you may use technical jargon peculiar to the products and services. You are also forewarned that you had better be extremely well prepared on the technical aspects of the presentation. You certainly should not attempt to give answers that are not well thought out.

- **Interested in technical aspects of the product.** In addition, if Mr. Quickslip is extremely interested in the technical aspects of the product, you can explore them in depth without losing his attention. Knowing his great interest and superior knowledge and experience, you may question Mr. Quickslip on his views about the technical side of the product and related services rather than attempt to give him information with which he is probably already familiar.

- **Dominant.** If Mr. Quickslip has an outstanding amount of dominance in his personality, he might react adversely if you cite favorable experiences that other customers have had with the product. Instead, you might capitalize on this trait by seeking his opinion about the product and by encouraging him to be the first to use it. This strategy would certainly be sound if you sense that Mr. Quickslip is striving for status in his industry and prides himself on scoring firsts.

- **Bold.** If Mr. Quickslip is a bold individual, there is every reason to believe that he is not only confident in his actions but also willing to try new things that many prospective customers would consider too risky. As a result, when you have a truly new product with substantial promise, Mr. Quickslip will be a good prospect for it.

- **Impulsive.** Finally, if Mr. Quickslip can be described as impulsive, you should be able to close the sale more quickly than you might with a more deliberative customer. This does not mean that you should push

Mr. Quickslip too fast. When it becomes apparent that he has thought over the proposition and is favorably disposed to it, however, you should try to complete the sale.

Therefore, you have the task of thinking through your best course of action to appeal to each distinguishing characteristic that you have identified in the customer. But you must also recognize that this is an analytical procedure and that you are dealing with a whole person—not with a combination of separate traits.

Group traits into patterns of behavior You must now go back to the dominant traits that make up the prospect's uniqueness and ask yourself, "Which of these traits interact with one another?" "Which ones suggest a common strategy?" Looking at Mr. Quickslip again, you find that superior intelligence plus in-depth knowledge of the technical aspects of the product and an interest in such matters constitute an interactive pattern of traits. In addition, the traits of dominance, boldness, and impulsiveness constitute a second interactive pattern. Once these patterns are identified, you are ready for the next step; mapping your strategy.

Develop an overall strategy on the basis of behavior patterns You should plan your strategy on the basis of *patterns* of behavior. By reviewing each *individual trait*, you know what to do and what to avoid doing. Referring again to Mr. Quickslip, the combination of superior intelligence, an unusual amount of technical expertise, and an interest in the technical aspects of the product might call for a high-level, carefully conceived, technical presentation. If you do more listening than talking, Mr. Quickslip may easily sell himself the product. Finally, his combination of dominance, boldness, and impulsiveness suggest that Mr. Quickslip might be interested in purchasing products that provide new ways of solving old problems. He probably has confidence in his own decision-making ability, and may be willing to purchase the product without a great deal of fanfare on your part.

Difficulties in Understanding Personalities
The method just suggested for mapping strategy and influencing the prospect or customer may seem thorough and straightforward, but in actual practice these principles are sometimes difficult to apply. There are several reasons for this: lack of psychological maturity on the part of the customer, the customer's reluctance to participate actively, and your own projection, type thinking, and tendency to rely on first impressions.

Psychological immaturity If customers lack psychological maturity, behavior may be inconsistent and their reactions highly unpredictable. It may be difficult to determine customers' positions because their thought processes are not orderly and jump from idea to idea. Propects might lose their temper, or become very depressed or withdrawn. Psychologically immature people frequently lack emotional control; hence, their behavior is impulsive and based on the feelings of the moment.

Lack of active participation Another factor that influences the effectiveness with which strategy can be formulated is the extent to which the customer participates. It is difficult to plan strategy for dealing with someone who fails to react at all. As you enter the selling situation, you cannot really tell how you are progressing in your relationship with the unresponsive individual, so it is important to ask, "Why is this person unreactive?" A cosmetics salesperson cites this example. When the cosmetics buyer failed to react, the salesperson asked, "What have I done to cause you to dislike talking to me?" The other person pointed out that the salesperson parked his car directly in front of the store on each visit. The buyer had mentally reserved the spot for customers.

Projection Projection is the tendency to see your own traits—especially those considered desirable—in each person with whom you interact, whether the traits are there or not. Furthermore, when such traits are actually present, they may bias your judgment about other characteristics of the individual. For this reason it is important to have adequate evidence for trait analysis and to remain objective and open-minded about the person being analyzed.

Type thinking There is a natural tendency for you to engage in *type* thinking rather than *trait* thinking when analyzing the customer. We all tend to group specific information into a generalized concept or into a type of individual. For instance, it is more difficult to remember that a customer has four specific traits, such as being clever, stingy, formal, and alert, than simply to recall that the customer is economy-minded. Each of us wants a definitive, simple answer with regard to human behavior—including our own. Conscious effort is required to remain open-minded about each person to be influenced.

Tendency to use first impressions Another difficulty is that you may rely on first impressions, reliance on them has several potential problems. First, prospects may not show their entire self on your first meeting. Second, they may be nervous and act differently than they will when they get to know you. Third, they may hide their real feelings from you as a relative stranger. Fourth, their immediate past behavior may influence their present behavior. For instance, if they are in a bad mood, it may color their behavior. All these factors mean that you have to be careful not to let first impressions of prospects cause you to size up their personalities incorrectly.

Additional Help

There are software programs available to help you size up the prospect's personality. A example, Sales Edge matches the psychological traits of the buyer and seller. With the aid of this software and a personal computer, you answer a number of multiple-choice and agree-or-disagree questions about the customer. These are then compared with information you have already entered about yourself. The computer then prints out a detailed sales strategy from opening to close.[5] The strategy includes what to expect from the customer;

---

[5]Peter Finch, "Software That Probes the Psychology of a Deal," *Business Marketing*, Vol. 70, No. 6 (June, 1985), p. 111.

how to succeed with the customer; and a customer-specific preparation strategy, opening strategy, presentation strategy, and closing strategy.[6] _____153

MOTIVATION

MOTIVATION

Motivation is the "why" of behavior. Human motives sometimes stem from physiological needs and sometimes from psychological or social needs. When the physical or emotional state of balance is disturbed, you feel a need of some kind. The awareness of such a need is also called a "want." When people attempt to satisfy a want, they experience motivation. Figure 6.7 illustrates this concept. In this example, when the individual feels hunger, the physical balance is disturbed, causing a feeling of uneasiness and a desire for food. The individual will then selectively respond to agreeable cues—for example, a hamburger stand. This is a simple example of physiological need—want satisfaction.

Other needs of people, however, are many and far more complex than those of a physiological nature. A number of questions could be asked concerning motivation, such as why do people drink alcoholic beverages? They certainly do not do so to satisfy the physiological need of thirst. Nor do women who wear dresses appear to do so mainly to protect themselves from the cold. The same could be said of those who wear platform shoes; they do not appear to wear these shoes to protect their feet! Other variables are therefore also responsible for motivating people to buy specific products. Many aspects of motivation will be examined as they affect buyer behavior, including learned drives, different types of motives, and different types of needs.

Learned Drives

The psychological and social needs of people are related to their environments. The cultural background, education, family life, and personality of

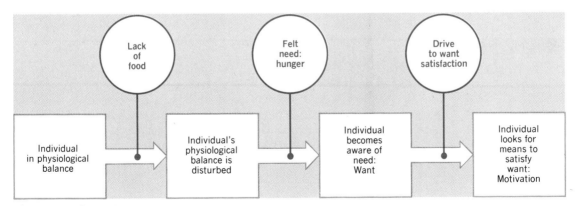

FIGURE 6.7 The motivation process.

[6]Robert H. Collins, "Artificial Intelligence in Personal Selling," *Journal of Personal Selling and Sales Management*, Vol. 4, No. 1 (May 1984), pp. 58–66.

individuals determine the types and intensity of their psychological and social needs. These needs then motivate the individuals to move toward achieving goals that are acceptable in their environment. They are called learned drives.

The concept of learned drives explains many things, for example, why people in different countries consume different products to satisfy their hunger. Although the physiological need is the same in any country, the people have different learned drives. Therefore, an Italian will probably feel a desire for pasta, a Chinese person to eat rice. Learned drives are very difficult to alter because they are an integral part of a culture, and as such they resist change. You should be aware of the nature of these drives in order to give them major consideration when approaching customers.

Different Types of Buying Motives

Buying motives may be classified into two groups; operational motives and sociopsychological motives. This classification is based on the idea that some products are purchased because of their intrinsic qualities, others in response to social or psychological needs.

Operational motives Motives that are directly related to the anticipated performance of the product are called operational motives. For example, a consumer who wants to put a nail into a wall to hang a picture may need a hammer. The motive to purchase the hammer would be based on the expectation that it will be an instrument capable of driving the nail into the wall. Most purchases of industrial goods can be classified as responses to this category of motives. As a result, when you feel that an operational motive is stimulating the buyer to act, you will want to stress the practical and functional aspects of the product.

Sociopsychological motives A consumer may buy a product because of the social and psychological significance associated with its purchase or owner-

---

MOTIVES FOR BUYING CORPORATE JETS

When a firm buys a $3 million business jet, a salesperson who relies solely on depreciation schedules and minimum runway statistics will almost certainly not sell an airplane. The salesperson must not overlook the psychological and emotional motives in the buying decision. For the chief executive, you need the facts for support, but if you cannot excite the CEO about the sheer beauty and prestige of the airplane, you will never sell the equipment. If you appeal to psychological motives, you sell the jet.

SOURCE: Adapted from Thomas V. Bonoma, "Major Sales: Who Really Does the Buying?" *Harvard Business Review*, Vol. 60, No. 3 (May–June 1982), p. 112.

ship. The operational performance of the product is only an indirect factor in the purchase. Buyers may be consciously or unconsciously aware of the social and psychological motives that have influenced a particular purchase. For example, a woman who purchases a mink coat may do so because she feels that the garment will convey an image of elegance, distinctiveness, and social prestige, even though she may use the coat only when the weather is cold. The function of protecting her from the bad weather is related only indirectly to the purchase. A salesperson selling this coat would want to stress its "rich and distinctive appearance" rather than its ability to keep the individual warm.

In reality, products are usually purchased to satisfy both operational and sociopsychological motives. For example, a coat is generally purchased for use as protection against cold weather, but the choice of color, length, style, and material will often be made on the basis of a person's likes and dislikes, notion of style, and the like.

Different Types of Needs

A number of different types of needs can be identified. Hanna, for example, identified seven different types of consumer needs: physical safety, material security, material comfort, acceptance by others, recognition from others, influence over others, and personal growth.[7] These needs are described in Table 6.2.

TABLE 6.2
A TYPOLOGY OF CONSUMER NEEDS

TYPE OF NEED	DESCRIPTION
Physical safety	The need to consume products in order to avoid harm or danger and to preserve clean air and water in the environment.
Material security	The need to consume an adequate supply of material possessions.
Material comfort	The need to consume a large or luxurious supply of material possessions.
Acceptance by others	The need to consume products in order to be associated with a significant other or a special reference group.
Recognition from others	The need to consume products in order to be acknowledged by others as having gained a high status in one's community.
Influence over others	The need to feel one's impact on others' consumption decisions.
Personal growth	The need to consume products to be or become one's own unique self.

SOURCE: Janice G. Hanna, "A Typology of Consumer Needs," in J. N. Sheth, ed., *Research in Marketing* (Greenwich, Conn.: JAI Press, 1979).

[7]Janice G. Hanna, "A Typology of Consumer Needs," in J. N. Sheth, ed., *Research in Marketing* (Greenwich, Conn.: JAI Press, 1979).

Although this classification was developed for consumer buying, it has also been extended to industrial purchasing.[8] In addition to individual needs, an industrial buyer is also influenced by the needs of the organization, the needs of the job function, and personal needs. Each of these is discussed in the following paragraphs.

Organization needs Every company has specific needs that must be satisfied. These needs may change over time or they may be stable. Organization needs may vary from company to company. For instance, one company may base buying decisions on the need for economy, whereas another company's major need may be quality or dependability.

Job-related needs A buyer has needs with respect to the job of purchasing, and they are not necessarily different from organization needs. Job-related needs include such things as the need for recognition from others, the need to keep his or her present job, and the need to get promoted. If you suspect that these needs are present, you may want to relate your offering to show how it will help fulfill the person's job needs. You may also build up the buyer in front of his or her supervisor or boss. These strategies may help to satisfy job-related needs.

Personal needs The buyer's personal needs must also be examined. Thus, two individuals within the same organization with the same job title may buy for very different reasons. One may have a need for expressing creativity in purchasing products and another may be very risk-averse in purchasing.

All three of these types of needs—organization needs, job-related needs, and personal needs—interact with one another. In most situations, all three exist and you must consider them.

Importance of Various Types of Needs
In order to build interest for your product when making a sales presentation to a customer or prospect, you may want to use some of the insights provided by the examination of needs. It is usually easier to justify basic needs, such as physical safety, than the more complex higher needs, such as personal growth. A rationalization of the reasons for the purchase of a product may therefore bring quicker and more favorable results.

Difficulties in Discovering Motives
It is critical for you to identify a buyer's motives, for they tell you what to sell and what aspects of your firm's offering you should stress to satisfy needs and gain attention. However, there are several difficulties in identifying motives.

Lack of awareness Prospects may not be aware of their motives. That is, they may not be consciously aware of why they are buying. This is especially likely when buying simple products or when buying products that are bought routinely.

---

[8]See, for example, Michael A. Belch and Robert W. Haas, "Using the Buyer's Needs to Improve Industrial Sales," *Business,* Vol. 29, No. 5 (September–October 1979), pp. 8–14.

Noncommunicativeness Prospects may be aware of their motives but may be unwilling to tell you why they are buying. The person who is buying a new automobile to impress others is not likely to offer this as a reason for purchasing a car.

EXAMINING VARIOUS NEEDS FOR A COAT

Jeff Schroeder enters a clothing store to purchase a fall coat. The salesperson shows him four different lightweight tweed coats, reasonably priced and very traditional. Jeff examines them. The coats are the type of product he needs— not too expensive, long-lasting, practical, and with a nonpretentious look.

The salesperson then takes from a rack a luxurious dark-brown pigskin coat and shows it to Jeff, saying, "This is one of our newest models, very stylish and beautifully tailored." After trying it on, Jeff decides that the coat is attractive. Of course, it costs about four times as much as the tweed coats. The decision is very difficult. The salesperson, noticing Jeff's preference, stresses the elegance, the durability, and the general appearance of the coat. She adds that, although the coat is considerably more expensive than other models, it is a more fashionable item, and it would also be appropriate for more formal occasions. Jeff buys the coat.

In this example, the salesperson has shown sensitivity to the customer's felt needs. Although some of the determining factors of the purchase were operational in nature, Jeff also felt some sociopsychological desires. The salesperson was able to point out clearly how the product might satisfy Jeff's operational and sociopsychological motives, therefore supplying him with a suitable solution for his problem—the purchase of the coat. Had the salesperson stressed the coat's capability of fulfilling status needs only, the sale might have been lost. Although Jeff felt the desire for social status, other more basic needs had to be satisfied first, such as durability and versatility.

Complexity Motives are also very complex; thus it may be difficult to identify all the reasons why a person buys. Two prospects can have very different motives for buying. For instance, one prospective buyer for a Cadillac may be attracted to the car's luxury, and another may be interested in the car's roominess. A prospect's motives may also vary over time. At one point in time a person may buy a car primarily for economy reasons, later for the image the car conveys. Given the multiple motives for buying products and the interactive nature of these motives, buyers seldom buy for any single reason. Rather, their motives tend to be complex, and several are likely to be operative in any one purchase. For instance, the primary motive in shopping for a stereo may be the quality of the sound, but the buyer may also be interested in the size of the speakers or the look of the components.

Another contributory factor in the complexity of motives is that purchases are often made by groups of people rather than individuals. Families must be influenced to buy consumer goods, and the buying-center participants must be influenced to buy industrial goods. The problem is that the motives of each of the participants may be different. In the purchase of a home, for instance, the wife may be interested in the kitchen and laundry room and how the home entertains, whereas the husband is interested in the landscaping, workshop, and family room. As a real estate salesperson, you must identify and satisfy these various needs if you are going to sell this family a house.

The most important points for you to remember are that the prospect will generally not purchase because of one motive alone, but some motives will be more important than others.

How To Discover Buyers' Motives

There are three methods you can use to obtain a good understanding of what motivates a particular individual: use feedback, utilize past experience, and use published materials.

Use feedback Probably the most useful way to discover motives is to listen and watch prospects, analyze the questions they ask, and ask questions yourself. This feedback is invaluable in determining what prospects are looking for. It is very important to hear what prospects are saying. The ability to do this may be critical to your success. If you listen, most prospects will tell you what they want in a product or what motivates them.

As an example, a prospect might ask such questions as "What mileage does this car get on the highway and in town? How often does the car need service? Is the car designed to permit the amateur mechanic to repair it?" You will logically conclude that this individual is interested in an economical automobile. In the same manner, a purchasing agent might ask "How long is the service policy on the equipment? Can the service policy be extended by a fee? How long does it take to get parts? Where is the service center located?" You can reasonably conclude that the purchasing agent is concerned about service. In order to get feedback you must learn to ask questions that will unveil individuals' motives, then listen and observe their nonverbal reactions.

Utilize past experience You should make full use of your past experience. After dealing with a customer for a period of time, you learn the customer's behavior patterns.

As an example, an industrial salesperson may be selling identical products to three different accounts. One account may be interested in service, another in delivery speed, and the third in price. Although the product is the same, the salesperson will want to stress different aspects of the product and features of the company when calling on each of the three accounts.

Most organizations operate in a very dynamic world; you must therefore be aware of shifting motives on the part of the buyer. Nevertheless, your past experience will give you some very good clues about how an account should be approached.

_____**159**

SUMMARY

Use published materials Finally, you should continually monitor trade magazines and other applied journals to keep up with the latest theories about individual behavior. Through proper use of published studies, you can improve your selling techniques and obtain a significant advantage over your competitors. Advertisements also sometimes give you insight into buyers' motives. Looking at the major themes of your firm and of competitors' advertisements may help you to understand motives for buying your product type.

SUMMARY

The universal objective in dealing with people is to recognize their uniqueness. People all need to feel that they are unique individuals. To the extent that you can make each of your customers feel this way, you will find it much easier to accomplish your sales objectives.

Treating prospects as unique individuals requires that you take into account their background, personality, and motivation. A person's background consists of his or her formal education, work experiences, cultural background, and cultural, recreational, and social activities.

There are two methods for analyzing a person's personality; a typecasting classifies individuals into certain types, and trait analysis identifies the many facets of personality. When you apply the trait approach, there are five steps for handling each potential customer: (1) identify outstanding traits, (2) document each with evidence, (3) develop a strategy for handling each trait, (4) group traits into patterns, and (5) develop an overall strategy on the basis of these patterns.

Certain characteristics that make some individuals difficult to understand or influence were discussed. The psychological immaturity and unresponsiveness of customers will make it almost impossible for you to develop a strategy to influence them effectively. Your own projection, type thinking, and tendency to rely on first impressions may keep you from defining a customer's personality.

Motivation explains "why" a prospect buys. Motives may be physiological, psychological, or social. Many motives have learned aspects, which explains why two individuals satisfy the same need differently. Two different types of buying motives prevail, operational motives, which are directly related to the performance of the product, and sociopsychological motives, which relate to the customer's social and psychological expectations of the product. Furthermore, there are a number of different types of needs: physical safety, material security, material comfort, acceptance by others, recognition from others, influence over others, and personal growth. Both consumer and industrial buyers have these needs. Industrial buyers also have organizational needs, job-related needs, and personal needs.

Several difficulties in discovering buyers' motives were pointed out, including the buyer's lack of awareness of needs, the buyer's unwillingness to

communicate, and the complexity of needs. In order to uncover needs, you should make use of feedback, past experience, and published materials.

PROBLEMS

1. How do typecasting and trait analysis differ?
2. Assume that you are a life insurance salesperson and that you are planning a strategy to influence a friend of yours to buy insurance. Do a complete trait analysis of this person. How do the results of this analysis vary from how you might have typecast the person?
3. Referring to your answer to problem 2, was the person you selected difficult to understand for any of the five reasons stated in the text? If so, how did you overcome the problem?
4. You are selling life insurance to a man with a wife and three little children. What motives and needs might you appeal to?

EXERCISE 6

Objective: To illustrate trait analysis and sales strategy.

A salesperson notes that a key decision maker in an account possesses each of the traits in column 1, in extreme amount. In column 2 indicate for each listed trait the evidence that might underlie it. In column 3 indicate for each listed trait what the salesperson ought to do or avoid doing.

TRAIT	EVIDENCE	WHAT TO DO OR NOT TO DO
Intelligent		
Quantitative thinker		
Widely read		
Able conversationalist		
Honest		
Religious		
Charitable		
Mature		
Self-possessed		
Sincere		
Sociable		
Friendly		
Sensitive		
Emphatic		
Industrious		
Open-minded		

Now indicate the traits that form *patterns* of behavior and what the salesperson's strategy ought to be.

PATTERNS	STRATEGY

Case 6-1 The Madison Glove Company (A)

The Madison Glove Company manufactures high-quality industrial gloves. Its products are used by many firms to protect their employees' hands from harsh objects and high temperatures. In addition to its standard line of gloves, the company regularly designs special-order gloves to fit a customer's unique problem. The firm's gloves range in price from $1.50 per pair for its regular workgloves to $65.00 per pair for its thermal-insulated gloves. The company always felt that it should have a complete line of products, but that it had the most to offer over competition in the high-price, high-quality lines.

Joseph Baker has worked for Madison Glove as a salesperson for twenty-one years. He calls on a number of accounts, including Claymore Steel, Inc., which is a steel service center located in Houston. Steel service centers handle about 20 percent of the nation's total mill output. They, in turn, sell to firms that require smaller quantities than can be furnished directly by the manufacturer.

Mr. Baker has done business with Claymore for five years, yet he has never had more than 25 percent of their glove business. The purchasing agent, Mr. Waxley, has resisted Mr. Baker's efforts to obtain a larger proportion of their business.

Mr. Baker decided that he must obtain more business soon from Claymore or he will have to discontinue selling to the firm. His cost of calling on Claymore is too high to continue his present sales efforts. Baker has done a trait analysis on Mr. Waxley and feels that Waxley's outstanding traits are the following: distant, impulsive, agreeable, alcoholic, frigid, narrow interests, special interest in family, serious, evasive, self-sufficient, unconcerned, and little mechanical ability.

1. How do you suggest that Mr. Baker deal with each of these traits?
2. Develop a strategy for dealing with Mr. Waxley.

Case 6-2 The Brown–Talleyrand Encyclopedia

The Woods are a young couple living in the suburbs of Phoenix, Arizona. They are both highly educated. Jim Wood has a doctorate and teaches at the local university. Liz, his wife, has a master's degree and works as a consultant for a local firm. They have two children, Peter and Gregory, ages nine and seven, respectively. The Woods are very concerned about their children's education and make sure the best schools and programs in the city are available to them.

In October, Liz decided that the children were old enough to make use of encyclopedias. While reading a magazine, Liz noticed an advertisement for encyclopedias and called the local representative for an appointment.

Two weeks later Mr. Rudolf Schick, the encyclopedia salesman, called on her. Liz explained that she wanted him to show her all the advantages of owning such a collection. The resulting dialogue went as follows.

MR. SCHICK: Very well, first of all let me show you one of our sample volumes. As you can see, the binding is all in genuine leather with gold-leaf engraving. All fifty volumes are bound in this same way, and they look marvelous in the showcase.

LIZ: I see. Can you tell me something about the books?

MR. SCHICK: Certainly. The books are organized in alphabetical order, so that it becomes easy to find information on a specific item. The pictures and illustrations are all in beautiful color. As you can see, this is the picture of all the flags of South America; look at the sharp colors!

LIZ: I can see that, but I am more interested . . .

MR. SCHICK: I know what you mean! The books are concerned with many different aspects of knowledge. For instance, you have here a beautiful atlas, with detailed geographical charts. It is really a very useful source of knowledge for adults.

LIZ: I am really concerned about my children!

MR. SCHICK: Sure! I can understand that! Bless their hearts, if they decide to play with the books and scratch them with crayons or paste peanut butter all over them! This is why our company makes this special bookcase with glass doors and key lock, so that the little angels will not ruin your marvelous investment.

You know, of course, this is a very valuable investment. This collection has a high resale value. It becomes more valuable as time goes by. It is also a beautiful decoration piece. We hardly get back the money we spent in having the cabinet made. May I write up your order?

LIZ: Well, Mr. Schick, I really would like to think it over. Maybe you could leave me some literature about the collection, so that I could learn more about it.

MR. SCHICK: I really do not have any supplementary literature with me. Also, I would like to mention that we are offering a special easy-payment plan this week only, and I would suggest that you take advantage of it.

LIZ: I am afraid that I am not really ready to purchase the product now. I should think about it a little further . . .

MR. SCHICK: Shall I call you tomorrow? It would be a very nice gift to your husband . . .

LIZ: Well, no, not really. I don't think we are interested right now. Thank you so much.

MR. SCHICK: Thank you and good-bye. Please give me a call if you change your mind.

LIZ: Good-bye.

1. What did Mr. Schick do wrong?
2. What would have been a motive for Liz to buy the encyclopedia?
3. What would you have done if you had made this sales call?

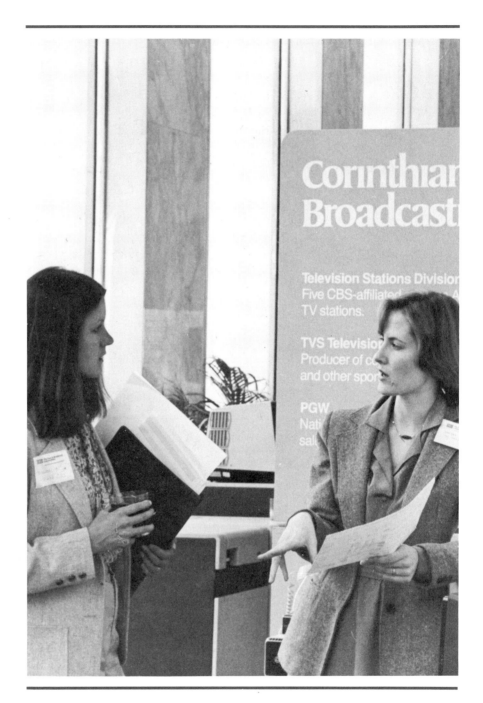

Different Approaches to Selling

After studying this chapter, you should be able to

1. Recognize situations where stimulus–response selling is applicable.
2. Understand formula selling.
3. Specify the components of need satisfaction selling.
4. Determine situations when need satisfaction selling is appropriate.
5. Identify the various styles of selling.

Sales calls can be categorized into three fundamental approaches: stimulus–response, formula, and need satisfaction. A number of styles are also available to use in structuring the sales call, including consultative selling, systems selling, negotiation selling, non-manipulative selling, seminar selling, and team selling. Each of these is reviewed in this chapter.

THE STIMULUS-RESPONSE APPROACH

The stimulus–response approach, the simplest of the three approaches, has its psychological origin in Pavlov's experiments with animals. Pavlov found that a given stimulus, food, would cause a given response, salivation, in his subject, a dog. If the food was offered at the same time that a bell rang, the dog could be conditioned to respond to the substitute stimulus. When the bell rang, the dog would salivate. Figure 7.1 shows the stimulus–response approach. The sales application of this theory is that if you say and do the right things, that is, provide the appropriate stimuli, the prospect or customer will buy, that is, respond to the stimuli.

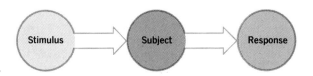

FIGURE 7.1 Stimulus–response approach.

In stimulus–response selling memorized "canned presentations" designed to include the major sales points (stimuli) are used to get the prospect to buy (response). Here is a brief, simplified example of a canned stimulus–response presentation.

SALESPERSON'S STIMULUS: You would want your family taken care of in case you were injured, wouldn't you?

PROSPECT'S RESPONSE: Yes.

SALESPERSON'S STIMULUS: And you want your children to be able to go to college, don't you?

PROSPECT'S RESPONSE: Yes.

SALESPERSON'S STIMULUS: Then don't you think you'd better have life insurance?

PROSPECT'S RESPONSE: Well, yes.

The process is shown in Figure 7.2; as you can see, most of the participation is done by the salesperson. The advantages, disadvantages, and uses of the stimulus–response approach will be discussed. It is best used for selling low-priced products, when time is critical and when prospects' motivations are relatively simple. This stimulus-response method is effective for door-to-door selling of products such as magazine subscriptions, books, cookies, candy, or other relatively simple consumer household products. Another application of stimulus–response selling is telephone selling, for which a script may be used.

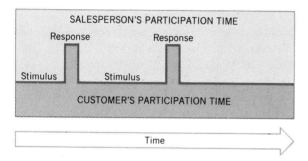

FIGURE 7.2 A stimulus–response approach as applied to a sales presentation. SOURCE: Adapted from G. M. Grikscheit, H. C. Cash, and W. J. E. Crissy, *Handbook of Selling: Psychological, Managerial, and Marketing Bases* (New York: Wiley, 1981), p. 24. Copyright © 1981, by John Wiley & Sons, Inc. Used with permission.

Advantages of the Stimulus–Response Approach

For the stimulus–response approach the salesperson memorizes a canned sales presentation.[1] This ensures a relatively complete presentation covering most, if not all, of the key points. Training is easy, for salespeople simply memorize a script. Because this approach utilizes mainly one-way communication—sending stimuli with only minimal responses (see Figure 7.2)—it also saves time for both the salesperson and the prospect. Developing a presentation customized to the needs of the customer would be much more time-consuming. After considerable practice, the canned presentation may become quite smooth; and having a clear knowledge of what to say boosts the salesperson's self-confidence. In addition, companies can hire people with fewer specific skills; because they need only memorize, salespeople need less creativity and fewer people skills.

"I've heard of canned sales presentations, but this is ridiculous."

[1]For a discussion of the canned presentation, see Marvin A. Jolson, "Should the Sales Presentation Be 'Fresh' or 'Canned.'" *Business Horizons*, Vol. 16, No. 5 (October 1973), pp. 81–88.

Limitations of the Stimulus–Response Approach

The stimulus-response approach to selling is useful in situations in which the unit sale is low and the time devoted to the sales effort is very brief. This selling–buying process has six primary limitations, however. First, the stimulus–response approach is controlled by the salesperson and is not very customer-oriented. It does not concentrate on the unique needs of the customer. Notice that many of the advantages accrue to the salesperson or the salesperson's firm, not to the customer or prospect. Second, the stimulus–response approach runs counter to what is known about individual differences in people. According to the stimulus–response approach, a given word, phrase, or action should cause the same response from a prospect, regardless of who the respondent is; yet it is known that prospects may react very differently. The third shortcoming, which is closely related to the second, implies that a given stimulus will yield the desired response with the same person in varying circumstances. Yet every salesperson knows that prospects may behave quite differently at lunch than at their desk, or when colleagues are present in a conference room. A fourth limitation is that this approach does not take into account what is going on inside the prospect's mind; it merely deals with outward behavior, ignoring motivational factors and eliminating choice as a consideration. The fifth limitation is that salespeople who rely on this approach do not improve their performance on the basis of experience. Instead, with different types of customers or situations, they continue hoping that the magic words or phrases will guarantee success. Finally, because it uses a canned presentation, the method is not very flexible. The presentation does not handle interruptions, unexpected replies, or different situations very well.

THE FORMULA APPROACH

The formula approach assumes that to make a sale, you must take the customer through a series of steps that are the same for all customers and for all selling–buying situations. The *formula* most frequently cited is AIDA, which stands for *attention, interest, desire,* and *action.* Advocates of this approach claim that the customer or prospect must be taken through a series of stages— namely, paying attention to the product or service, becoming interested in it, desiring what is being presented, and acting by purchasing what you are promoting (see Figure 7.3). Sometimes the additional steps of satisfaction and conviction are included.

If you are using the formula approach, in each sales presentation you will make statements designed to attract attention, arouse interest, create desire, and obtain action. The formula approach is shown in Figure 7.4. Like

FIGURE 7.3 The AIDA steps.

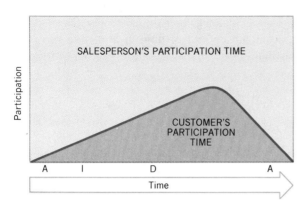

FIGURE 7.4 Formula selling as applied to sales presentation. SOURCE: Adapted from G. M. Grikscheit, H. C. Cash, and W. J. E. Crissy, *Handbook of Selling: Psychological, Managerial, and Marketing Bases* (New York: Wiley, 1981), p. 24. Copyright © 1981, by John Wiley & Sons, Inc. Used with permission.

the stimulus–response approach, it is obviously very dependent on the participation of the salesperson. It is suitable for more complicated products and is often used in industrial sales or for selling consumer durables such as cars, appliances, and furniture.

Advantages of the Formula Approach

The formula approach has several advantages. First, it is simple to remember. Second, it encourages preparation on the part of salespeople, because it forces them to think about strategies to gain attention, interest, desire, and action. Third, it encourages salespeople to observe the prospect to determine which of the four stages the prospect is in. Finally, it is more flexible than the stimulus–response approach because it allows salespeople to use different strategies for reaching different stages in the process, depending on the prospect or situation.

Limitations of the Formula Approach

The chief weakness of the formula approach is that a particular customer is not likely to move smoothly from step to step, despite the best efforts of the salesperson. Moreover, because it lists four specific steps, salespeople may tend to become overanxious to move from step to step and thus not really meet the customer's needs. This approach, like the stimulus–response approach, assumes a similarity of reaction by prospects that does not exist. Salespeople could therefore begin to believe that by following a standard procedure, they can induce the customer to make a purchase. As Figure 7.4 clearly shows, this approach is dominated by the salesperson's participation and is thus controlled by the salesperson rather than the customer.

Another limitation is that, although salespeople question, listen, and observe, it may be difficult to tell when prospects move from stage to stage: from attention to interest, or from interest to desire. In some situations the steps do not come in order. Some knowledgeable customers will approach the salesperson ready for action. By trying to gain this prospect's attention and interest, the salesperson may talk the prospect out of a sale. A final disadvantage is that the steps may not all be of equal importance. For instance one company that sells industrial chemicals to maintenance people considers the most important aspect of making a sale to be gaining the prospect's attention. They devote a disproportionate amount of time to attracting prospect attention, on the assumption that, once this is accomplished, the products practically sell themselves.

THE NEED SATISFACTION APPROACH

Philosophically, need satisfaction selling is more customer-oriented than the two approaches just outlined. As shown in Figure 7.5, this approach requires much more customer involvement, especially in the initial stages. Need satisfaction selling is made up of three steps: need development, need awareness, and need fulfillment.[2] These are discussed in the following paragraphs.

The Three Steps of Need Satisfaction

Need development The first step in need satisfaction is to identify the customer's needs. You can do this in three ways: (1) ask questions; (2) observe the customer's present situation, as you might do if you were selling clothing; or (3) conduct a survey of needs, as you would do if you were selling copiers, accounting equipment, or computers. The most frequent approach is to ask questions. Table 7.1 lists questions used by Sylvania salespeople to stimulate their thinking about customers' needs. You as a salesperson may find these questions useful to ask to help determine the real needs of individual customers. (Chapter 11 also discusses questioning techniques in some depth.) The goal is to stimulate prospects to talk about their needs. Once you understand these needs, you can base your presentation on how your product meets them.

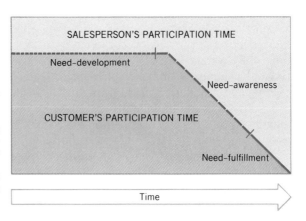

FIGURE 7.5 Need satisfaction theory as applied to sales presentation. SOURCE: Adapted from G. M. Grikscheit, H. C. Cash, and W. J. E. Crissy, *Handbook of Selling: Psychological, Managerial, and Marketing Bases* (New York: Wiley, 1981), p. 23. Copyright © 1981, by John Wiley & Sons, Inc. Used with permission.

[2]See, for example, G. M. Grikscheit, H. C. Cash, and W. J. E. Crissy, *Handbook of Selling: Psychological, Managerial, and Marketing Bases* (New York: Wiley, 1981), pp. 23–26.

TABLE 7.1

_____171

SYLVANIA ELECTRIC PRODUCTS QUESTIONS USED TO
DETERMINE A CUSTOMER'S NEEDS

1. What is the account's total annual production?
2. What percentage of total production was made with our competitor's machines? With ours?
3. What acceptance does the customer's product line have in the market?
4. What equipment does the customer use—both Sylvania and competition? The *why* of each?
5. Is production off in any of the product lines? Why?
6. Is the customer ahead of or behind last year's production? Why?
7. Are standard manufacturing costs in line?
8. Are there any control figures on downtime, reject rates, maintenance cost?
9. Is the company strong on new-product innovation?
10. Is the company entering new markets?
11. Does the firm have adequate and competent production personnel?
12. Is the firm losing customers? Why?
13. Do employees have a positive attitude toward the employer's business and Sylvania?
14. Are they adequately informed and trained to use our equipment?
15. What is their credit or financial condition? If in a tight position, is the customer reluctant to mention it? How can we help without causing embarrassment?
16. Is the person you deal with progressive?
17. What is the position of the company's marketing department on packaging?
18. What is the customer's attitude toward Sylvania's competition. Why?
19. Who is the competition—what are their strengths and weaknesses?
20. What is the customer's attitude toward their *own* competition?
21. What are the relationships between members of your competitors' organizations and your customer or your customer's people?
22. What poor experiences has your customer had with competitors' equipment or services? How about yours? How does the customer feel now?
23. What is the customer's rate of growth? Prospects for future growth? Market potential? How can we help the customer to grow?
24. Has the customer budgeted for new-equipment purchases?
25. Specifically, who makes the buying decisions in the customer's firm (R&D, plant manager, product design, general manager, P.A., etc.)? What are their basic motives in making a buying decision?
26. Are expense requisitions required? Who must approve?
27. Who are the key influencers on the decision maker? What needs do they have as individuals for recognition, credit, or other psychic (status) satisfactions? How can you supply them?
28. What is the customer's relationship with our headquarters personnel? Can they help you?
29. Does the customer have a habit of spreading purchases among manufacturers? If so, what is the customer's real reason for doing so?
30. If the customer is manufacturing private-label products, what is the reaction of customers toward current packaging?
31. What special projects are anticipated or in progress?
32. What business losses has the customer suffered? How recently? How have these affected the customer's philosophy of operation or relationship with us—or with the competition?
33. If the individual with whom you must do business must in turn sell others in the organization, what information, help, or support is required from you?
34. Does the customer have any problems in the following areas that you (with or without help from others in the company) can help solve: Space facilities? Packaging materials? Packaging design? Location? Production methods or costs? Finan-

cial inexperience? Disposing of used equipment? Can you (or the company) help in these areas?

35. Will the customer welcome help in any of these areas or will it cause antagonism or embarrassment if offered?

36. Does the customer's long-range buying potential justify the time it will require to get the answers, or does it justify any compromise you are expected to make in your work schedule?

37. Have you lost any previous orders? Why? . . . be honest now!

38. When the customer asks for a quote, is it to do business or just for ballpark figures?

39. Have you recorded key information in your customer file for future reference in your sales planning?

In a larger context, this step can be thought of as your marketing research function. For example, if you are a salesperson calling on a food store, you might inspect the frozen-food stock on display before interviewing the prospect. Much of what you learn may be useful to your company, in addition to providing you with a basis for a personalized presentation.

Deciding which questions to use will depend on the particular situation you face. Several guidelines for asking questions are given in Chapter 11. However, if you were selling copiers, you might use questions such as the following to determine needs.

"What types of documents do you copy?"

"What quality of copies do you need?"

"How quickly do you need the copies?"

"What type of equipment do you have at present?"

"What do you look for in a copier?"

These questions and similar questions can go a long way toward giving you insights into which copier to suggest to the prospect and which benefits to stress.

Need awareness Even though you understand customers' needs, it does not necessarily mean that customers actually realize that they have these needs. Customers may not recognize their real needs for three reasons. First, they may not have fully examined their situation. Second, they may not be aware that there are products or services available that could solve their problems. Third, they may have identified other needs and may require redirection. The best way to promote customers' awareness of needs is to ask questions designed to get customers to specify their own needs. At this point both you and the customers are aware of these needs. This joint awareness tends to build rapport, and customers feel that you are taking a genuine interest in them.

You may also have to point out that there are products available to solve customers' needs. For example, you might say, "Would you be interested in a desktop copier that would give you letter-quality output?" This might make customers aware that something is available to meet their need, even though they were unaware of it.

Need fulfillment The final step in need satisfaction selling is need fulfillment. In this step you show customers how your product or service can satisfy their needs as they perceive those needs. As a salesperson, you might have twenty benefits to using your product; however, if a customer is interested in only a few aspects of your offering, you should confine your presentation to these. You are thus customizing your presentation to the unique needs of the prospect. Using what you learned in need awareness, you present your offering in a way designed to meet the wants of customers or prospects *differently* from and *better* than what they are currently using or competitors are offering. Thus, you must make customers or prospects feel that your products and services are superior to alternative offerings. Unless you accomplish this, you will not make a sale. It is important for you to single out a relatively small but important number of benefits that make your products better than alternative offerings. An acid test is to pick aspects about which the prospect is most concerned, and the benefits that will have the greatest impact on the prospect.

To illustrate need fulfillment, let us continue with our copier example. If you find that the person has a need for a small, compact desktop copier that will make letter-quality copies without too much need for speed, you will present this model, stressing the benefits in which the prospect had earlier indicated an interest. In this case, perhaps the *small size* means that the copier will fit into the prospect's limited space, and the *letter quality* means that important documents can be copied for customers.

Advantages of the Need Satisfaction Approach

Because this approach to selling is more comprehensive than the other two, it has unique advantages. First, it is customer-oriented; it emphasizes the point of view of customers or prospects by accounting for their needs, perceptions, thoughts, and feelings. Thus, it is more compatible with the marketing concept than the other appeals. Second, because both parties are active participants, you must be an attentive observer and an astute questioner, which makes the sales presentation more of a sales interview. Third, this approach accounts for individual differences and recognizes the need to personalize the presentation. The key to personalization is using what has been learned about the other person's needs and wants. Need satisfaction is therefore flexible and is likely to build rapport between the salesperson and the prospect. Fourth, it provides a basis for determining what the salesperson should say and do and how to say and do it. Fifth, the approach is more likely to be perceived as low pressure and thus is more likely to build long-lasting relationships. In general, need satisfaction should be used for selling when transactions are relatively large and a lasting relationship is desired. Examples of products and services might be computers, real estate, heavy equipment, office equipment, and financial services.

Limitations of the Need Satisfaction Approach

The need satisfaction approach does have limitations. Inasmuch as it places far more responsibility and freedom of action in the hands of the salesperson than do other selling approaches, sales personnel must be relatively sophisticated. It also implies that the stake in the potential transaction is high enough for both buyer and seller to invest significant time and effort in the sale. Since it involves questioning, participation, and two-way communication, the need-satisfaction approach is likely to take more time than other approaches, and thus is more costly.

Need satisfaction selling is very effective because it is flexible and customer-oriented, it stresses factors that customers feel are important, and it is low pressure. This selling does get the job done; it results in sales. However, it may not be the most efficient approach when sales are small, because it may be too time-consuming and costly. Therefore, when order sizes are small or needs are simple, need-satisfaction selling would not be appropriate, and the stimulus–response or formula approach would be preferred. On the other hand, need satisfaction is the most appropriate approach when (1) there are marked individual differences in customers and prospects; (2) there is great diversity of needs to be met; (3) the products and services are complex and technical; (4) the level of knowledge and skill of sales personnel is high; (5) the unit transaction is large enough to cover the cost; (6) an entire product line is being sold so that various needs, once uncovered, can be met; and (7) the likelihood of a continuing selling–buying relationship warrants the effort.

STYLES OF SELLING

Several styles of selling have evolved that build upon a need satisfaction type of base. All are low pressure and highly professional; all stress working with the customer in jointly solving the customer's problems and improving the customer's business. These styles are consultative selling, systems selling, negotiation selling, non-manipulative selling, seminar selling, and team selling. Often they are combined or used interchangeably; however, for ease of presentation each is explained separately.

Consultative Selling

In the consultative style of selling, a salesperson acts as a consultant to the potential buyer who becomes a client; thus you focus on solving your client's problems. Instead of recommending single products in isolation to accomplish this, you recommend various combinations of products and services. As a consultant, you will have to possess many skills in addition to selling. You must work with nearly all facets of a prospect's business that bear on the product that you are selling—ranging from equipment depreciation and inventory control to distribution.[3] In your consulting capacity, you might also call on other specialists in your firm to provide help with technical aspects if the customer has engineering or financial problems.

[3] See "The New Supersalesman: Wired for Success," *Business Week* (January 6, 1973), pp. 44 – 49.

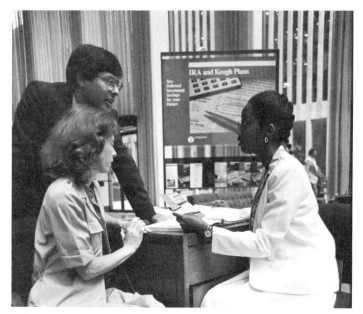

Salesperson consults with her client.

Consultative selling is buyer-oriented. After asking questions to determine your prospects' needs, you listen. Only after having discovered all of their needs would you present a solution.[4]

In order to succeed as a consultative salesperson, you must become an expert in your client's business operations, so that your consulting advice is more valuable than that of your competition. Some of the things that clients expect from a consultative salesperson are explained in Table 7.2.

Consultative selling has been criticized as being too sophisticated, too difficult to manage, and too dependent on technical specialists for results.[5] Nevertheless, it is one style of selling that may be adopted by sophisticated, complex, multiline companies.

Systems Selling

A systems salesperson, instead of merely selling a product, sells an interrelated group of products to perform a complete function or service for the customer.[6] Such a salesperson for an office products firm would not sell a customer just a desk. Rather, he or she would sell a system of office furniture designed to make a total work environment for the customer. In order to be effective in systems selling, your firm needs to develop or acquire lines of

[4]Jack R. Snader, "Consultative Selling for Real Estate," *Real Estate Today* (February 1982), p. 6.

[5]See Dan T. Dunn, Claud A. Thomas, and James L. Lubawaki, "The Pitfalls of Consultative Selling," *Business Horizons*, Vol. 24, No. 5 (September/October 1981), pp. 59–65.

[6]For a good discussion of conditions in which systems selling is appropriate, see Dan T. Dunn, Jr. and Claud A. Thomas, "Strategy for Systems Sellers: A Grid Approach," *Journal of Personal Selling and Sales Management*, Vol. 6, No. 2 (August 1986), pp. 1–10.

TABLE 7.2

FIFTEEN THINGS THAT CLIENTS EXPECT OF CONSULTATIVE SALESPEOPLE

1. "Cure Me"
Get things done—respond to my needs.
Produce results fast because I have more needs.

2. "Talk My Language"
Speak to me in profit–improvement language.
Show me you identify with me and that you know my business.

3. "Don't Surprise Me"
Install a control system so I can be comfortable.
Let me share in evaluating our work together.

4. "Level with Me"
Tell it like it is.
Criticize constructively. Tell me what's wrong, but let me know what's right, too.

5. "Get into My Business"
Become a part of my team.
Be around—ask questions. Don't be disruptive.

6. "Be Reasonable"
Give a superior value in relation to your superior price—superior service makes a high price reasonable.

7. "Be Competent"
Give me the best you have.
Be a real professional.

8. "Teach Me"
While you sell or perform, teach me how.
Share some of your experience and expertise with me.

9. "Take Leadership"
Get out in front of my problems.
Roll up your sleeves and get your hands dirty in my operations.

10. "Worry for Me"
Think hard about my problems.
Let me know what you think even without my asking.
Give me immediate access to you when I am worried—be available.
Put my needs first—never mind anyone else.

11. "Innovate"
Give me something that's better than you give anyone else.
Make me proud—make me stand out.
Apply yourself in a way that transcends normal boundaries.
Offer me options.

12. "Be Faithful"
Keep our business confidential.
Make your relationship with me personal and continuous—don't pass me along to others.

13. "Be Motivated"
Show a strong desire to achieve our objectives.
Be really interested in my problems.
Don't leave a single stone unturned in looking for solutions.

14. "Be Flexible"
Compromise with me once in a while but don't give in on what you know is vital.

15. "Treat Me Like a Person, Not Just a Client"
Treat me like an equal—deal with me one-to-one.
Don't talk down to me.
Throw in a few "little extras" every now and then.
Advise me on closely related matters, even if you're not being paid for them.

SOURCE: Mack Hanan, James Cribbin, and Jack Donis, *Systems Selling Strategies* (New York: by AMACOM, 1978), pp. 30–32. Copyright © 1978, by AMACOM, a division of American Management Association, New York. All rights reserved. Excerpted by permission of the publisher.

products that are interchangeable with one another and that can be tailored to meet customers' needs and marketed as one package—that is, a system. An IBM sales representative says, 'I get inside the business of my key accounts. I uncover their key problems. I prescribe solutions for them, using my company's systems and even, at times, components from other suppliers.

I prove beforehand that my system will save money or make money for my accounts. Then I work with the account to install the system and make it prove out."[7]

When properly done, selling systems of products to solve customer problems is profitable for both the buyer and the seller. From the seller's perspective, premium prices can be charged because systems are unique and distinctive from the competition, whereas individual products may be subject to more price competition. From the buyer's perspective, a system that is designed to solve problems and is oriented toward improving the bottom line is a profitable purchase.

Consultative selling and systems selling are closely related. As a consultant, you will normally recommend systems of products to your clients; and in order to sell your customers a system, you will have to be viewed as knowledgeable enough and trustworthy enough to be a consultant.

Systems selling is well known in data-processing and aerospace industries which routinely buy groups of products as systems. Industrial supplies are also being sold as systems by industrial distributors. When this is done, inventories are retained by distributors. Inventories are often ordered automatically, and one-day deliveries are not uncommon.[8] Thus, a salesperson for a distributor of this type sells not only operating supplies or maintenance supplies, but also a system designed to make the customer's paperwork easier and reduce storage needs.

Negotiation Selling

Negotiation selling is a selling style designed to produce a "win–win" outcome for you and the customer, you both benefit from the sale. According to one authority, "Negotiation is the art of making mutually profitable sales agreements"[9] Thus, the objective of negotiation selling is to make the customer and salesperson into partners. The three characteristics of the partnership are being equals, winning together, and setting up a counseling relationship that is devoted to problem solving.[10]

Negotiation is important when the terms of sale are important, as when prices, delivery dates, or financing arrangements must be jointly determined. Negotiation is also important (1) when complaints occur; (2) when customers request special treatment or consideration in product specifications, credit, and other services; or (3) when your company introduces an innovation and you must negotiate with the customer to get the product adopted.[11] A prospect who says something like "I might be interested in purchasing that if you would lower your price by 5 percent," is leaving the way open for negotia-

---

[7]See Mark Hanan, "Join the Systems Sell and You Can't Be Beat," *Sales and Marketing Management,* Vol. 109, No. 3 (August 21, 1972), p. 44.

[8]See William J. Hannaford, "Systems Selling: Problems and Benefits for Buyers and Sellers," *Industrial Marketing Management,* Vol. 5, No. 1 (1976), p. 139.

[9]See Mack Hanan, James Cribbin, and Howard Berrian, *Sales Negotiation Strategies* (New York: AMACOM, 1977), p. viii.

[10]Ibid., p. ix.

[11]Ibid., pp. 8–9.

tion. Here the salesperson would have to strike a deal that was acceptable to the prospect and to his or her own firm. A reply such as "We can't lower our price by 5 percent, but if you order a carload we can reduce the price by 3 percent" might be a possible alternative.

In the situation just described, your skill as a negotiator will directly affect your firm's profitability; therefore, it is important for you to negotiate a profitable arrangement. But it is also important to have a satisfied customer who is likely to be a candidate for repeat purchases. For this reason the win–win perspective is taken rather than hard negotiations, which might tend to damage the relationship you have with the customer.

Negotiations often have a negative connotation because negotiators are seen as either hard or soft.[12] The hard negotiator uses high pressure and views the negotiation as a contest of wills. The soft negotiator wants to avoid personal conflict and thus gives in readily in order to reach agreement. Clearly, neither of these approaches will lead to profitable, long-term relationships in selling. Another approach, developed by the Harvard Negotiation Project, is called principled negotiation and tries to decide issues on their merit rather than haggling; it suggests you look for mutual gains whenever possible and stresses looking for fair, independent standards when your interests conflict with the customer's. It is very open and uses no tricks. As can be seen from Table 7.3, principled bargaining is very different from hard or soft negotiation.

Principled negotiation is based upon four major premises. You should strive to have a situation in which you and the prospect are working side by side, attacking the customer's problem and not each other. The method tries to be hard on solving the problem but soft on the people. Thus, the first premise is to separate the people from the problem. Second, you should try to negotiate with the aim of improving the customer's and your interests rather than taking positions. Once someone has taken a position, it becomes difficult to compromise. Rather than being tied to a position, it is better to try to work out agreements that serve the interests of both sides. Therefore, the second premise is to focus on interests, not positions.

You should also think up as many alternative solutions as possible. This ensures that you have a better chance of effective problem solving and may enable you to consider better alternatives than your competition. When developing alternative solutions, you should try to invent options that focus on mutual gains. Thus, the third premise is to generate a variety of possibilities before deciding what to do. Finally, rather than insisting on getting your own way or conceding to the customer's will, it is often better to develop objective criteria. By discussing such criteria rather than what you and the customer are willing or unwilling to do, neither you or the customer need to give in; both of you can look for a fair solution. You might say, for example, "Look, you want a low price and I want a higher price. Let's figure out what a fair price would be. Would it be fair if we earned 10 percent over our cost?" Thus, the final guideline is to use objective criteria.

---

[12]This section is based on Roger Fisher and William Ury, *Getting to Yes* (New York: Penguin, 1981).

TABLE 7.3
DIFFERENT TYPES OF NEGOTIATIONS

PROBLEM Positional bargaining: Which game should you play?		SOLUTION Change the game— negotiate on the merits.
SOFT	HARD	PRINCIPLED
Participants are friends.	Participants are adversaries.	Participants are problem solvers.
The goal is agreement.	The goal is victory.	The goal is a wise outcome, reached efficiently and amicably.
Make concessions to cultivate the relationship.	Demand concessions as a condition of the relationship.	Separate the people from the problem.
Be soft on the people and the problem.	Be hard on the problem and the people.	Be soft on the people, hard on the problem.
Trust others.	Distrust others.	Proceed independently of trust.
Change your position easily.	Dig into your position.	Focus on interests, not positions.
Make offers.	Make threats.	Explore interests.
Disclose your bottom line.	Mislead as to your bottom line.	Avoid having a bottom line.
Accept one-sided losses to reach agreement.	Demand one-sided gains as the price of agreement.	Invent options for mutual gain.
Search for the single answer—the one *they* will accept.	Search for the single answer—the one *you* will accept.	Develop multiple options to choose from; decide later.
Insist on agreement.	Insist on your position.	Insist on using objective criteria.
Try to avoid a contest of will.	Try to win a contest of will.	Try to reach a result based on standards independent of will.
Yield to pressure.	Apply pressure.	Reason and be open to reason; yield to principle, not pressure.

SOURCE: Roger Fisher and William Ury, *Getting to Yes* (New York: Penguin, 1981), p. 13.

There is a great deal of literature on negotiation that you can use to improve your negotiation skills.[13] Generally speaking, these skills are all learned traits that you can practice. The literature suggests several traits you should possess to negotiate effectively. The most important are preparation and planning skill, knowledge of the subject matter being negotiated, the

[13]See, for example, Herb Cohen, *You Can Negotiate Anything* (Secaucus, N.J.: Lyle Stuart Inc., 1980); and Ross R. Reck and Brian G. Long, *The Win–Win Negotiator* (Escondido, Calif.: Blanchard Training and Development, Inc., 1985).

ability to think clearly and rapidly under pressure and uncertainty, being able to express your thoughts verbally, listening skill, judgment and general intelligence, integrity, the ability to persuade others, and patience.[14]

Non-Manipulative Selling

In non-manipulative selling you build trust between you and your prospect while avoiding high-pressure tactics that create tension in the buying–selling situation.[15] Using non-manipulative selling, you would spend time understanding and solving prospects' business-related problems. "In non-manipulative selling, more time is spent defining needs than on any other stage in the sales process. . . . this allows a sales presentation which is 'custom tailored' to the client and participants."[16]

The non-manipulative selling process is shown in Table 7.4. As can be seen, non-manipulative selling stresses problem solving, follow-up, and building trust. Notice how building trust is a key element in each stage of the process.

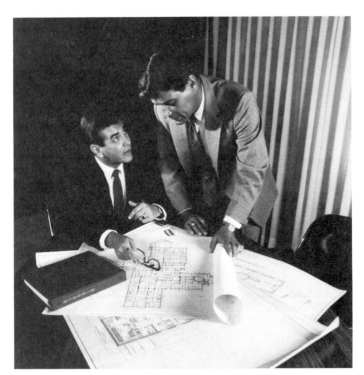

Non-manipulative style encourages trust.

[14]See Chester Karrass, *The Negotiating Game* (Cleveland: World, 1970), pp. 242–244.

[15]See Anthony J. Alessandra and Phillip S. Wexler, *Non-Manipulative Selling* (San Diego, Calif.: Courseware Publishers, 1979).

[16]See Anthony J. Alessandra, "Non-Manipulative Selling," *The Insurance Journal* (January 26, 1981), p. 22.

TABLE 7.4

_____**181**

STYLES OF SELLING

THE NON-MANIPULATIVE SELLING PROCESS[a]

1. Define the need(s) and problem(s).
  a. Establish the trust bond.
  b. Determine the current situation.
  c. Determine client goals and objectives.
  d. Identify client needs and problems.
  e Agree on the needs and problems to be worked on.

2. Find a solution.
  a. Check the trust bond.
  b. Determine decision-making criteria.
  c. Solicit potential solutions.
  d. Suggest potential solutions.
  e. Agree on the best solution(s).

3. Implement the solution.
  a. Check the trust bond.
  b. Outline each other's tasks and responsibilities.
  c. Work out an implementation schedule.

4. Track the results.
  a. Check the trust bond.
  b. Identify criteria for successful results.
  c. Determine how and when to measure results.
  d. Monitor the results.

[a]All steps are to be done mutually with the client.

SOURCE: Anthony J. Alessandra and Phillip S. Wexler, _Non-Manipulative Selling_ (New York, NY: Prentice-Hall Press, 1975), p. 9

Non-manipulative selling stresses being very client-oriented and involving the customer in the problem-solving process by probing, asking questions, and noting nonverbal cues in order to get feedback. This feedback from the client allows you to modify your behavior so that it fits in with the behavioral style of the client. This is called behavioral flexibility and is a very important concept in non-manipulative selling.

Seminar Selling

Seminar selling brings together prospects for your firm's products to attend a seminar presenting up-to-date information about your product and related topics. "Properly planned, developed and executed, a seminar can shorten decision-making time, reduce the number of sales calls required for major purchasing decisions and improve your image in the marketplace for technical and product leadership."[17] Two additional benefits are speaking to a targeted audience and being able to deliver a common message to several clients at once.[18]

[17]See G. A. Marken, "The Sales Seminar," _Industrial Marketing,_ Vol. 66, No. 6 (June 1981), p. 46.

[18]See Kevin Higgins, "Selling by Seminar' Lets Customers Learn in Nonthreatening Environment," _Marketing News,_ Vol. 14 (March 6, 1981), p. 16.

Salesperson conducting a sales seminar.

The seminar establishes you and your company as experts on the topic. For instance, a company marketing a software system to protect computer information in case of fires or floods conducted a seminar in disaster preparation for potential clients. They mentioned their software and its advantages but also had experts talk about insulation, fireproofing, backup systems, and planning.

When planning such a seminar, be sure to get the decision makers to attend; if they are absent, you will waste time and money.[19] Those invited to the seminar generally pay their own travel; this assures that only those who are really interested attend. Your firm will pick up the costs of the meetings and perhaps lunches. To add credibility to such seminars, bring in outside experts or users. You should give the participants significant information, so their attendance is worthwhile; you can also give them handouts to take home. It is critical that you be thoroughly prepared and that you put on the most professional presentation possible. Your presentation should not come across as a sales pitch and should be as informative as possible. Finally, it is necessary to follow up after the seminar to ensure that your prospects are contacted. The sooner you follow up, the better.

Team Selling

Given the technical complexity of many products and their sophisticated applications, it is often necessary for a wide variety of personnel from your firm

---

[19]For a good overview on selling by seminar, see John Farac, "Business Seminars: An Exciting Marketing Approach," *Real Estate Today* (February 1980), pp. 45–49.

to become involved in the sale. The sales team might include technical specialists, financial people, top management, and others. In many of these complex situations it would be impossible for you to be an expert in all these areas. Given that industrial purchases are typically made by individuals from various departments such as purchasing, engineering, and production, it is important to have highly trained specialists who can communicate with these individuals. Although joint calls are common in many sales situations, team selling is a more formalized approach making routine use of several specialists.

GUIDE TO THE SALES SEMINAR

The seminar should do all the following things.

- It should break down barriers. No one expects to be sold that night.
- It should present an atmosphere in which to meet a new prospect that is much less threatening than the normal first interview.
- It should entice people to come who would not agree to a sales interview.
- It should motivate the prospect to see you privately.
- And not least of all, the seminar should entertain the prospect. Everyone should have a good time.

SOURCE: "Seminars Lauded as Superb Prospecting Tool," *National Underwriter* (July 5, 1982), pp. 52–53.

One company, Allied Chemical Corporation, has developed sales teams to sell to power plants and smelters their service to abate sulfur dioxide pollution. Each team consists of a financial specialist, a technical specialist, a specialist in sulfur dioxide reduction, an operations specialist, and three engineers. The teams are orchestrated by an experienced salesperson. A team can provide detailed studies and other assistance to potential customers.[20]

In other situations teams are even larger and more complex. Boeing, for example, uses team selling when calling on airlines. These teams might consist of twenty to thirty specialists in financial analyses, engineering, aircraft maintenance, scheduling, forecasting, and marketing. The specialists work with their functional counterparts in the airlines.

SUMMARY

Several approaches to examining the selling–buying process were explored. The stimulus–response approach is based on the theory that if the salesperson

---

[20]See Benson P. Shapiro, *Sales Program Management: Formulation and Implementation* (New York: McGraw-Hill, 1977), p. 77.

says and does the right things, the prospect will purchase the product. The chief weakness of this "canned" approach is that it does not recognize individual differences. Its major use is for simple products that do not generate complex buying motives, such as door-to-door sales of household products.

The formula approach is based on the assumption that to complete a sale a salesperson must take the customer through a series of steps that are the same for all individuals: attention, interest, desire, and action. The weakness of this approach is that an individual customer may not move smoothly from step to step.

The need satisfaction approach is the most comprehensive of all approaches. Although it incorporates both selling and buying ingredients, it approaches the process from the prospect's or customer's point of view. The process has three steps: need development, need awareness, and need fulfillment. This approach is very professional and very effective for larger sales and when long-term relationships are desired. Limitations are that it is time-consuming and expensive; thus it should be reserved for larger purchases.

Several selling styles are often utilized within a need satisfaction framework. These styles are consultative selling, systems selling, negotiation selling, non-manipulative selling, seminar selling, and team selling.

PROBLEMS

1. What are the major advantages and disadvantages of using the stimulus–response model in the selling–buying process? When would the model be used?
2. You are a salesperson for a manufacturer of home care products selling to hardware stores. You want to develop a sales presentation applying the formula approach to the selling–buying process. Describe your plan and illustrate what tactics you will use to gain your customer's attention, interest, desire, and finally action.
3. Define in your own words the need satisfaction model.
4. Your firm has just developed a new energy-generating instrument that uses solar energy to supply single housing units with the electricity necessary for normal living conditions. Explain how the need satisfaction approach could be used to sell such a product to individual home-owners.
5. Apply the same principles used in question 4, but this time tailor your sales appeal to housing construction firms.
6. How do consultative selling and systems selling fit together?

EXERCISE 7

Objective: To understand the selling–buying process along with the advantages and disadvantages of the stimulus–response model, the formula approach, and the need satisfaction model.

Here is a segment of a sales interview. Indicate for each statement by the salesperson what theory of selling is illustrated and, where possible, what phase.

(1) SALESPERSON: Good morning, Mr. Black, I represent Cresco and I want to tell you how we can make money for you.

BLACK: Well, I'm never too busy to hear how to make money. What's your proposition?

(2) SALESPERSON: I'm sure you have a lot of "do-it-yourselfers" coming in to buy tools. We sell our tools singly and in various kit combinations.

BLACK: Hold on. I wish we did have a big demand like you describe. I think most of our tool sales are for fixing things around the house.

(3) SALESPERSON: Well, Cresco tools are great for that, too. However, I think our window display material and cooperative advertising will flush out more "do-it-yourselfers" than you think are around. Besides, wives will buy tool kits as gifts for their husbands.

BLACK: I don't know how I'd squeeze another thing in our windows. I've noticed, too, that both the local discount houses carry your line. How can I compete with them if I do stock Cresco?

(4) SALESPERSON: Don't you carry other items that are available in the discount stores? How do they sell?

BLACK: Well, some move pretty well; some don't.

(5) SALESPERSON: What advantages do you offer a customer who shops with you rather than a discounter?

BLACK: The big edge we have is that we give our customer personal treatment.

(6) SALESPERSON: That's great. We have a retailer's guide from which you can get a lot of ideas for helping people use tools.

1. Indicate what you might have said had you been the salesperson.
2. Do you think Mr. Black will buy? Defend your answer.

Case 7-1 Fleur De Lis Jewelry

Fleur de Lis Jewelry manufactures and markets a fine line of costume and semiprecious jewelry and sells it direct to consumers. It advertises heavily in women's magazines, and the brand name is well known and highly regarded. It has a large nationwide sales force of part-time and full-time representatives who work on a straight commission basis. Incomes range from $6000 to $60,000 a year.

Actual sales are made at "parties" hosted by former purchasers of the jewelry, who are also induced to stimulate future "parties." Thus the sales representative has two kinds of selling to accomplish: first, to sell as much jewelry as possible at each party; and second, to line up future hostesses at each "party." Each hostess receives "free goods" as an incentive, the amount depending on how many sales are made.

The market consists of two segments: young married housewives with children who find the morning coffee or the afternoon tea fun, and young working women—single and married—who enjoy a social evening. The firm's prime source of salespeople are former hostesses who find the selling job a pleasant way to earn either a primary or a supplemental income.

1. Which theory of selling would seem to be most applicable in selling jewelry at a party and convincing a party guest to be a hostess at a future party?
2. What should Fleur de Lis look for in selecting hostesses?
3. What should Fleur de Lis look for in recruiting salespeople?

Case 7-2 Institutional Foods, Inc.

Manufacturers of kitchen equipment for large commercial operations, such as restaurants, hotels, and cafeterias, or for institutions, such as hospitals and schools, produce all types of machinery and accessories. Although there is little differentiation with respect to the types of products offered, the quality of service performed by such equipment and its durability and reliability are very important considerations for the purchase.

There are several manufacturers of kitchen equipment for commercial or institutional organizations, and the prices of their products are very comparable. Two of them, however, The Kitchen Company and Institutional Foods, Inc., price their equipment at about 10 percent above the other competitors in the market. The two organizations rationalize the price difference by stating that their products are more durable and more reliable than those of competitors.

The management of Institutional Foods, Inc., is aware that institutional buyers are very cost-oriented when purchasing equipment for their operation. They also know that the durability and reliability of the equipment are advantages difficult to prove because the average life span of such goods is eight to ten years.

It was clear that to achieve a competitive advantage, an additional effort had to be made by Institutional Foods, Inc. They decided to train their sales representatives so that they could quickly diagnose each customer's equipment needs on the basis of the accounts' estimated production needs and time constraints. For three months, each salesperson attended a highly specialized course in food management at the University of Houston Hotel and Restaurant Management School.

Last May, the sales manager of Institutional Foods, Inc., received a memo from the president indicating that once the specialized training of salespeople has been completed, management expects representatives to concentrate all their efforts into using such knowledge. This means that the sales representatives are expected to use their skills and sell equipment to potential customers by acting almost as consultants to them.

The sales manager likes the idea of using the problem-solving approach to sales in order to build a unique image for her firm in the market. She is faced, however, with the task of developing a semistructured sales presentation in order to make the best use of the rep's skills; planning forms, information leaflets, and slide presentations have all been prepared to aid in the sales task. It is a matter now of putting it all together in the best possible form.

1. Assume that you are the sales manager. How will you proceed?
2. How can commercial kitchen equipment be differentiated? Explain.
3. If you were the president of Institutional Foods, Inc., would you have taken another approach to differentiate your products?

The Contact

After studying this chapter, you should be able to

1. Understand various direct methods of making contact and their advantages and disadvantages.

2. Recognize the advantages and disadvantages of indirect methods of making contact.

3. Remember things to do just before the interview.

4. Identify the elements of a contact, including preliminary conversation.

5. Describe various approaches to the selling portion of the contact.

Before each call, all the factors that need to be considered in calling on a particular customer or prospect are planned. Once the call plan is determined, you must consider your *approach*—the strategy and tactics you will use to gain entry and establish rapport. No matter how carefully you have planned your call, you may have to make adjustments once you are face to face with the prospect. As the call progresses, you must continue to adjust tactically to the other person's reactions. This chapter will discuss situations the salesperson encounters when calling on accounts, the direct and indirect methods the salesperson may use to gain entry, and the beginning of the face-to-face interview.

ESTABLISHED VERSUS PROSPECTIVE CUSTOMERS

With established customers, a salesperson usually has no difficulty in arranging a call. Your main concern is what to say in order to give the interview a favorable start. There will usually be one or more matters to discuss from the previous call; perhaps you need to provide some technical information requested by the customer, or if you left technical information on the last call, you might begin by asking, "Did you get a chance to examine the literature I left last time?" Delivery of an order may also provide a topic for opening the conversation. You could ask about delivery or how the customer is enjoying the product. These "bridges" or "links" that join calls are invaluable in making the ongoing relationship smooth and continuous.

If you have done business with the other person for a period of time, you have accumulated reliable, comprehensive information on which to base your strategy and can size up the situation very quickly. At the other extreme, your first call on a prospect is mostly a reactive situation. You are likely to have, at best, only limited information about the person and the firm to use for openers, assuming you are granted the interview. The most difficult approach situation is when the call represents the first face-to-face contact and there has been no prior communication by telephone or correspondence. This is referred to as the "cold call."

DIRECT METHODS FOR MAKING CONTACT

In trying to gain access to a new prospect, you must first decide whether to attempt to make contact directly through your own efforts or indirectly through the efforts of others. Although the indirect method has several advantages, more often than not you must make contact on your own. There are three direct methods available to you: a telephone call, a letter, or a personal visit. Each has unique advantages and disadvantages.

Generally speaking, two and sometimes all three of these methods are used in conjunction with one another. That is, you would probably use a telephone call or a letter to set up an appointment for a personal visit.

The Telephone Call

A common direct method of making contact is to phone in advance for an appointment. The advantage of this method is a greater likelihood that you will be able to see the prospect than if you walk in off the street to seek an interview. Furthermore, if the prospect adheres to an appointment calendar, this method will result in far less waiting time; thus, you may be able to schedule more calls closer together than you would otherwise be able to do. In addition, there is some evidence that out-of-town calls requesting appointments are honored more frequently than local calls. (Chapter 16 deals in depth with effective use of the telephone in selling.)

Other advantages to calling ahead Another advantage to calling ahead is that you can usually get through to the person you want to talk to, rather than having to depend on the receptionist to get you in. Should you be unable to talk to the decision maker directly, you can usually speak with that person's private secretary and arrange for the visit. Still another advantage is that at the time of the actual interview, both parties are aware of the purpose of the visit. This allows you to get down to business more quickly than you would otherwise be able to do.

ATTENTION TO DETAIL HELPS MAKE HIS CONTACTS

Martin D. Shafiroff, a top securities salesperson for Lehman Brothers Kuhn Loeb, is very conscious of how he makes contacts. When Martin is on the telephone, everything he does has a definite purpose. For instance, he jots down the name of his client's secretary. He always calls her by name.

I treat every person as an individual. Besides, there's many little helpful things his secretary can do for you, and she'll more than likely have an influence on her boss. So you want her on your side. After all, it certainly can't hurt, can it?

Another thing about the secretary, I always state my name and company when I start talking with her, and I do it nicely, so she'll announce me in a favorable way. Sometimes, just her enthusiasm in telling the executive that I am on the wire can make a difference. For example, if she didn't like the person calling, she might say, "Oh, that Mr. Jones is on the phone, should I tell him you're busy?" But if she's in the caller's corner, she can say it in an approving fashion, such as "I'm sorry to interrupt, sir, but Mr. Shafiroff is on the telephone, and it sounds important. He would like to speak with you."

SOURCE: Robert L. Shook, *Ten Greatest Salespersons: What They Say about Selling* (New York: Harper and Row, 1978), pp. 135–146. Copyright © 1978, by Robert L. Shook and Roberta W. Shook, Trustees. Reprinted by permission of Harper and Row Publishers, Inc.

Disadvantages to telephone calls There are, however, some problems in using the telephone call method. For example, you may not know in advance who would be the most appropriate person to see. A personal visit will often permit you to obtain this information from the receptionist. Although this problem can sometimes be solved by seeking information over the phone from the switchboard operator or receptionist, there is always a danger that your call will be directed to the wrong person. Another problem is that the prospect may not be available to receive telephone calls when you phone.

In addition, you may ask for more information over the phone than is necessary. It is usually sound strategy not to give out or ask for too much information in a telephone call; you can talk your way out of an appointment.

If you are calling a business, you almost always talk first to a subordinate, usually a receptionist or secretary. You must persuade that person to arrange the actual interview. Your objective with such persons is to convince them that they are fulfilling their responsibility by *getting you in* rather than *by keeping you out*. Even though receptionists may not participate in the actual buying decisions of their firm, they are important to you. The way in which the receptionist or secretary indicates your presence, the impression the receptionist conveys of you to a buyer, may determine whether you get the interview or not and how you will be received.

In general, it is not a good practice to deceive the receptionist. If the receptionist asks directly, "Are you a salesperson?" you should indicate that you are. You might want to add that you are trying to help the company make a profitable purchase. Your behavior in this situation may have greater impact than what you actually say. If you can generate confidence, sincerity, and

HOW TO SELL THE APPOINTMENT

A critical aspect in many types of sales is getting the prospect to see you and to want to listen to you. Here are several ways to sell the appointment.

- Ask questions to arouse interest and curiosity.
- Get something of interest into the prospect's hands—even if you must mail it.
- Send an advance letter.
- Use the "Your time is important" method. State the high value of the prospect's time and request a future appointment when neither of you will be rushed.
- Supply testimonials to show the prospect how others are using the product or service.
- Ask for five minutes, and spend that time listing reasons why an appointment would make sense.

SOURCE: L. Perry Wilbur, "Sell the Appointment First," *The American Salesman*, Vol. 29, No. 1 (January 1984), pp. 40 – 42. Reprinted with permission of *The American Salesman*, by The National Research Bureau, Inc., 424 North Third Street, Burlington, Iowa 52601.

conviction, you are more likely to see the decision maker. It may be a good tactic, before asking for the actual interview, to get information about the company from the receptionist. For instance, you might say: "Who in your firm is responsible for handling semiconductors?" A question such as this opens the way for you to inquire about other aspects of the firm's business.

Often it is necessary for you to sell the appointment. You will need to provide the prospect with sufficient information to generate interest but not so much that he or she feels no need to see you. In addition to having to sell the appointment to the person you want to see, you often have to sell the appointment to a secretary or a receptionist. Again, stressing the benefits of the appointment and not providing too much information are solid advice.

Personal Letter

If you are covering a large territory, you will often find it effective to write to prospects well in advance of your planned calls.[1] This is a particularly appropriate method if products and services offered are technical in nature and represent large dollar outlays. You may enclose appropriate company literature with your letter requesting the interview (see Figure 8.1). A personal letter may also be used in combination with the long-distance telephone request as a confirmation and reinforcement of arrangements. This method can save time, and the likelihood of gaining entry is even greater with arrangements made by mail than with those made by telephone.

SEVEN WAYS TO IMPROVE YOUR WRITING SKILLS

1. Jot down notes of what you want to cover in your communication.
2. Put the most important point first.
3. Express your thoughts clearly and concisely.
4. Use concrete words that involve seeing, tasting, touching, smelling, and hearing.
5. When writing to individuals in another field, keep their vocabulary in mind.
6. Use live verbs that convey action.
7. Place the person doing the action (the doer) before the verb. For example, "We invite you to visit our booth at the trade show" is stronger than "Our booth is easily located; you're invited to visit it."

SOURCE: Bruce B. MacMillan, "Seven Ways to Improve Your Writing Skills," *Sales and Marketing Management*, Vol. 134, No. 4 (March 11, 1985), pp. 75–76.

---

[1]For advice on how to write sales letters, see Timothy J. Conner, "Writing Sales Letters and Proposals," *The American Salesman*, Vol. 29, No. 3 (March 1984), pp. 10–15; Ted Pollock, "Thirty-One Tips on Writing Sales Letters That Sell," *The American Salesman*, Vol. 26, No. 2 (February 1981), pp. 28–32.

MULTIMOWER CORPORATION
1711 E. Apache Blvd.
Tempe, Arizona 85282
(602) 838-1516

Dear Mr. Hutchins:

When you show a customer a Multimower—a lawnmower completely new in design and principle, which cuts, trims, and "rakes" a lawn in one operation, you have a quick sale, a satisfied customer, and a $46.65 profit.

Your customers will like the Multimower because it gives them more time to spend in enjoyable summer recreation. It cuts right up to walls, fences, trees, and flowerbeds and thus eliminates the need for hand trimming in spots not reached by ordinary mowers. Its easily adjustable cutting-height regulator and self-sharpening cutters that slice down the toughest kinds of grass, dandelions, and weeds will assure them of having a trim, neat lawn in half the time they've formerly spent.

Both men and women like the Multimower because its light weight—only 58 pounds—means easy handling. The quiet operation of the interlocking cutters has won approval of 8000 Multimower users. They like it, too, because it is permanently lubricated and self-sharpening. With a minimum of care it's always ready for use. So normally you just put in the gas and it's ready to go.

No doubt many of your customers have been reading about the Multimower in the full-page, four-color monthly ads that started running in *Homeowners* and *Vacation* magazines in March and will continue through July. A reprint, along with testimonials and conditions of our guarantee, appears on the next page. Note the favorable guarantee and servicing arrangements.

In these days of high prices, the $139.95 retail cost of the Multimower will be popular with your customers. Our price to you is only $93.30.

Early next week I will be in contact with you to set up an appointment to talk to you about Multimowers so that you can have a supply of Multimowers on hand when your customers begin asking for them.

Cordially,

Sally De Michael

Sally De Michael
Sales Representative
Multimowers Corporation

FIGURE 8.1 An example of a business letter asking for an appointment. Adapted from C. W. Wilkinson, Peter B. Clarke, and Dorothy C. Wilkinson, *Communicating Through Letters and Reports*, eighth edition (Homewood, Ill.: Richard D. Irwin, 1983), p. 262.

It is imperative that you construct the letter with considerable care. It is wise for you to have one or more persons in your firm read the letter and make suggestions before it is sent. The letter, like the telephone request, should not go beyond determining how the prospect's needs are being satisfied. It should be designed to accomplish the following objectives.

- Let recipients know that you are aware of their needs.
- Raise doubts and questions in their minds about how best to fulfill their needs and wants.
- Request the interview.

ERRORS TO AVOID IN WRITTEN COMMUNICATION

Some common errors to avoid in written communication are

- Using industry slang.
- Choosing words that can have double meanings.
- Expressing yourself in negative words.
- Resorting to highly technical jargon.
- Choosing words that force people to think, as opposed to feel.
- Using geographical colloquialisms.
- Constructing long sentences and paragraphs.
- Extensive use of first-person pronouns (I, me, my, mine).

SOURCE: Timothy J. Conner, "Writing Sales Letters and Proposals," *The American Salesman,* Vol. 29, No. 3 (March 1984), pp. 10–15.

In connection with the third objective, it is a good practice for you to offer two alternative dates. You are more likely to get the interview with this approach than if you ask, "When can I see you?" A second approach is to indicate that you will be telephoning to set up an appointment. When you plan the interview, it is unwise to assume that the person will have read all the material you furnished. Your plan should include a tactful review of the basic points in your literature.

One disadvantage of a letter is that many executives' secretaries or assistants screen their mail and may keep such a letter from reaching the executive. Personalizing the letter as much as possible and stressing benefits will help it reach its intended destination.

Personal Visit

Some salespeople make personal visits without setting up appointments. These calls are being discouraged by many companies because of the high cost of selling and because in many industries professional buyers expect salespeople to make appointments. In these instances, unannounced calls may be taken as rude and unprofessional.

Company policies differ on whether to see salespeople who have not made appointments.[2] If you fail to make appointments you may get any of the following responses.

"I'm sorry but Miss Rick is tied up in a meeting all day; you can't possibly see her."

"Miss Rick is out of town today and won't be back until tomorrow."

"Miss Rick is busy right now. Would you like to wait?"

If you do get in to see the prospect for a personal visit, you have several advantages. First, it is harder for them to say no when you are face to face. Second, you have an opportunity to see the physical facilities of the prospective account.

If you do visit personally, be careful not to waste time. Occupy your waiting time productively by reviewing printed information on the prospective account, tactfully questioning the receptionist, talking with noncompetitive sales representatives, making sure that you are well organized, or doing something else associated with work. In some fields of selling, the actual "wait time" exceeds the total amount of time you spend in face-to-face interviews. This large portion of your working time must be *invested* rather than *spent*.

You should also plan alternate calls with nearby prospects in order to gain a payoff from the travel time in case the first interview does not occur. You must recognize that even though a prospect wishes to see you, it often happens that the prospect cannot arrange this on the spur of the moment.

INDIRECT METHODS OF MAKING CONTACT

In the indirect method of making contact, a third person makes a referral and paves the way for an appointment. This may be done by face-to-face contact, by correspondence, by a phone call, or simply by the intermediary giving you permission to use his or her name in making the request.

You should weigh two considerations before deciding to take an indirect course of action: (1) the impact on your relationship with the referrer if you ask for such a favor, and (2) the effectiveness of the other person in dealing with the prospect versus the results you might obtain on your own. The first of these two considerations is, of course, not appropriate if the referrer is the one who has taken the initiative and has suggested the particular prospect. The second consideration, the referrer's entrée to the prospect, is greatly affected by the reputation of the referrer.

---

[2]"New Suppliers Visiting Less: Prefer to Phone," *Purchasing*, Vol. 95, No. 3 (September 29, 1983), pp. 23–24.

Referrals from Customers

The indirect method can have a decided advantage over the direct method because it has all the impact of a testimonial. For this reason, the best possible person to refer you is a satisfied customer who is willing to share with the prospect the benefits derived from the selling–buying relationship. An additional advantage of having the customer pave the way is that the customer is equipped to handle technical questions with confidence and can do this from the buyer's standpoint.

Referrals from Other Persons

Having a mutual friend or a key person in the community refer you represents a different referral situation. If you ask such persons to help, you should make sure that they are given sufficient briefing so that they do not misinform the prospect or make commitments that you are unable to fulfill. Your banker, lawyer, or CPA, for example, may be able to introduce you to a prospect.

Other Important Considerations

If a person agrees to write to a prospect, you should request a copy of the letter to make sure you personally follow up. Routing a copy of the letter to you lets the prospect know that you are aware of the request that has been made on your behalf. If the referring person handles the matter by telephone or personal contact, be sure that you have some way of knowing when the contact is made, so that you may follow up at an appropriate time.

Sometimes a person is unwilling to become directly involved in setting up the appointment but may give you a business card with a personally written note to the contact in the prospective account. This card then becomes a means of entry that you can use directly. Or you may receive permission to use the intermediary's name and the name of the company as a means of getting the appointment.

In some sales situations there is another indirect method open to you: you may have an appropriate executive of your company's management write a letter of introduction for you or make a telephone call to the executive in the prospective account. The advantages here are the impact of the executive and the opportunity afforded your management to elevate you in the eyes of the prospect.

PRIOR TO THE FACE-TO-FACE INTERVIEW

Before you begin the interview, you should remind yourself of several critical factors, such as the basic assumptions underlying each sales call, the importance of first impressions, the possibility that perceived similarity may breed success, and the call objectives.

Basic Assumptions

There are five basic assumptions to remember before the interview starts: (1) you are interrupting the prospect, (2) you must invest your time and the prospect's time, (3) the prospect is gathering information, (4) the prospect is at present satisfied, and (5) the prospect wants to buy profitably.

Interruption Generally, when you call on an account, you will be interrupting some activity of the other individual, even when you have an appointment. Therefore, you have an immediate objective of tactfully redirecting the person's attention to the matters you wish to discuss. Given that you have a valuable product or service to offer the prospect, you have a strong reason to be there, but you must gain the prospect's attention. Another thing you can do to get people's attention is to remain silent until they recognize you.

Investment of time You need to remind yourself that the person you call on is as busy as you are. You have an obligation to invest the face-to-face time, not spend or waste it. Thus, you have an objective of making every minute count, both for the prospect and for yourself. This places a premium on being carefully prepared and well organized.

Interest in information The third assumption you must keep in mind is that the individual being called on is a key avenue of information about products or services. Thus, prospects are the "eyes and ears" for their company as you are for your firm. Accordingly, one basis prospects will have for deciding on the worth of your visit is the *amount, relevance,* and *value* of the information gained from it. Your knowledge and expertise may differentiate you from competition.

Present satisfaction You also must assume that prospects are satisfied with things as they are. Of course, sometimes you will obtain a lead because a prospect is dissatisfied. Very often, however, your prime prospects are satisfied customers of your competitors. Thus, your immediate tactical objective is to disturb prospects' needs and gain their attention as quickly as possible. Questions are a key method of doing this. If you are selling a self-correcting typewriter, for instance, you might ask, "How much time does your staff spend in making corrections?" or "How would you like to have all your correspondence done without having to use liquid correction fluid?"

Buy profitably Finally, prospects are as desirous of buying profitably as you are of selling profitably. If the call is to be effective, it must be mutually beneficial. For this reason it is often said that the effective salesperson is a good buyer for the prospect.

First Impression
As a salesperson, you should view first impressions in two lights: (1) you must try to have the best possible impact on the other person, and (2) you must guard against jumping to conclusions concerning the prospect.[3]

---

[3]For an interesting discussion of first impressions, see Ron Kolgraf, "Three Minutes to Sell: Why First Impressions Count," *Industrial Distribution,* Vol. 70, No. 1 (January 1980), pp. 79–80.

Personal appearance is superficial, but it has considerable initial influence. Your grooming and attire should be consistent with the expectations of your clientele. One successful construction equipment salesperson called not only on the heads of road-building firms and members of city, county, and state road commissions, but also on job bosses on construction sites. He carried a hard hat, overalls, and work shoes in his car, and changed whenever he made field calls.

SOME THINGS YOU CAN DO TO CREATE A GOOD FIRST IMPRESSION

- Keep up on current events, especially sports, national news, and news that could affect your field.
- Be curious and unafraid to ask questions.
- Let the prospect know you are genuinely interested in hobbies, community activities, travel, and family.
- Remember that what you do and how you do it must be tailored to the individual you are meeting.

SOURCE: Matthew J. Culligan, "What It Takes to Succeed in Sales," *Nation's Business*, Vol. 70 (April 1982), pp. 44–45.

Your behavior should be responsive to the other person. For example, you should wait for your prospect to ask you to be seated. In addition, throughout more and more offices smoking is taboo. Therefore, you should not smoke unless the host takes the initiative and invites you to smoke. Good manners add to your favorable impact.

On the other hand, as was stressed in Chapter 6, it is critically important that you do not jump to initial conclusions when dealing with the customer. If you do, all too often you will later make errors based on an initially incorrect perception of the customer.

Similarity May Breed Success

Although evidence is not completely conclusive, a number of studies have indicated that the more similar the salesperson and the customer are, the more likely it is that a sale will result from the meeting.[4] For instance, early research showed that prospects who purchased life insurance were more similar to their salespeople than prospects who did not purchase with respect to age, height, education, income, religion, political affiliation, and even smok-

---

[4]For a review of this literature, see Robert J. Zimmer and James W. Taylor, "Matching Profiles for Your Industrial Sales Force," *Business*, Vol. 31, No. 2 (March–April 1981), pp. 2–13.

ing habits.[5] It is important to note that the *perceived* similarities in religion and politics were much higher and of seemingly more importance to the sale than was *actual* similarity. Thus, you should try to appear to be as similar as possible to your prospects.

These findings on similarity, of course, do not mean to imply that you should call only on prospects who are similar to you. However, you should attempt to minimize the perceived differences between yourself and the customers in ways that you have some control over. As an example, if you are a smoker and a customer is not, you should not smoke while calling on the customer. In addition, if your political views differ from those of the customer, you should keep them to yourself.

Thus, when first meeting a prospect, you should look for similarities of background and interest. There are almost always some areas, such as hobbies or sports, in which you both have enough in common that you can emphasize your similarities rather than your differences. These areas may be found through conversations or from noticing pictures or other cues in the prospect's office or home. For instance, if you play golf and notice a golf trophy in the prospect's office, you might bring up the subject of golf. This mutually shared interest gives you something to talk about and tends to build rapport.

You should also be careful not to wear any item that identifies a personal association or belief, unless you are absolutely sure that the prospect shares these beliefs. Remember, it is perceived association that is important, not actual association. Therefore, you should avoid religious or political topics unless you are sure your prospect shares the same belief.

Review Call Objectives

Just before you make the contact, it is important to review your call objectives and call strategy so you will have a clear impression of what you want to accomplish, what you want to say and do, and what you want to avoid saying and doing. For instance, your call objective may be to ''demonstrate the new software package to the prospect and get them to commit to a trial of the package.'' This gives you an idea of what you must accomplish on the call. All of the earlier planning and organization will not help if you do not have a fresh picture of what you want to do in the actual call. This review will also help you to be more confident and to conserve both your own time and the customer's time.

THE CRITICAL BEGINNING OF THE INTERVIEW

It is obvious that you have many things to accomplish in the first few seconds of the interview. You must gauge the mood of the prospect. Is the emotional climate favorable for a presentation? You must also gain the prospect's atten-

---

[5]Franklin Evans, ''Selling as a Dyadic Relationship: A New Approach,'' *American Behavioral Scientist*, Vol. 6 (May 1963), pp. 76–79.

tion. Finally, you must determine the prospect's level of satisfaction with present suppliers. How can you best open the interview? A number of elements should be a part of each contact, including preliminary conversation and a number of methods are available to begin selling.

ATTENTION GETTERS

Here are some suggestions for getting a customer's attention.

- Many customers like yourself find themselves in the position . . .
- I suspect that you've encountered the problem of . . .
- What most people want in a . . .
- The inconvenience and lost time many people experience . . .
- I've found that many customers are looking for . . .
- One of the biggest problems with . . .

SOURCE: Reprinted with permission of Formica Corporation.

Elements of the Contact

Although there are no hard and fast rules about what should be said during a contact with a prospect, there are a number of elements that probably should be included especially with prospect accounts or with accounts that are called on infrequently (see Figure 8.2). With customer accounts called on frequently, you may not need to include each of the elements.

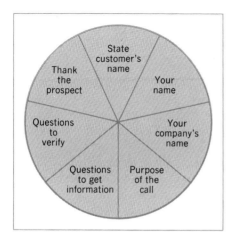

FIGURE 8.2 Elements of contact with a prospect.

TABLE 8.1

TRICKS TO HELP YOU REMEMBER NAMES

Respecting, acknowledging, and treating the prospect as a unique individual are basic to effective selling. Remembering names is a tangible indication of this respect. Here are six tips to help you remember names.

- Make yourself interested in the person.
- If this is a new prospect, get a business card and take a long hard look at the name right away.
- Listen carefully to the name—especially if the pronunciation is difficult.
- Repeat the name. Repetition reinforces the idea in your mind. Try to use the name once or twice in the conversation, especially as you part company.
- Without sounding too contrived, try to make a comment about the name. Ask how it is spelled or about its family origin.
- Try acronyms. If your new contact's name, for instance, is Brian Evans, see a buzzing bee when you think of him—based on the B and E of his initials.

SOURCE: Adapted from "Six Tricks Help You Remember Names, Facts," *Successful Meetings* (May 1982), p. 66.

Customer's name An important element of any contact is to state the customer's name. This serves three very important functions: it helps you to remember the prospect's name, it adds a personal touch, and it is also polite. People like to have you remember their name and personalize your contact with them. Many people have trouble remembering names; Table 8.1 gives some suggestions for helping you remember them.

Your own name You should also introduce yourself to the prospect, even if this is not the first call. Do not expect the prospect to remember your name or put them in the embarrassing position of having to ask your name. Providing the prospect with your business card is also a useful way to ensure they remember you.

Your company's name Be sure to mention your company's name early in the interview. Prospects, especially professional purchasing agents, see many people. Thus, you must remind them whom you represent.

Purpose of the call You should state the purpose of your call so that the prospect has an idea of what to expect. You probably will not want to reveal your call objectives, but you may wish to give the prospect a general idea of what you hope to accomplish. If you represent a copier firm, you might say for example, "I would like to explore with you your copying needs and see whether we can be of service to you."

Questions to get information You may wish to develop several questions to get information from the prospect in order to know which products and which benefits of these products to stress. Questioning techniques are reviewed in depth in Chapter 10, but here are several questions you may wish to ask.

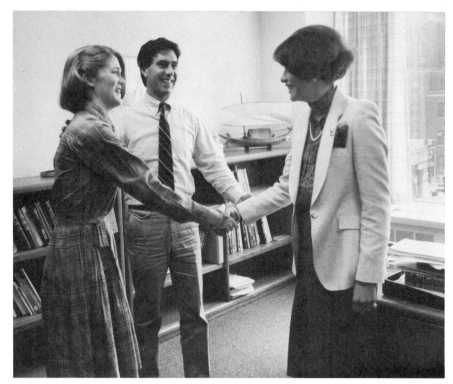

Greeting the client.

- How would you describe your current system?
- What problems are you currently having?
- What are you looking for in a new system?
- What is your time frame for making a decision?

If prospects have little or no information about the products now in use or the competing companies serving their firm, the questions asked must be broad and general. On a cold call, you must guard against asking questions that might seem to the other person presumptuous on short acquaintance. In the early stages of the call, the questions should be ones the prospect can answer without difficulty or hesitation. They should deal with matters of fact rather than opinion.

Questions to verify precall information You should also have developed questions to verify precall information. These questions serve a dual purpose. They make sure that your information is correct so that you do not make false assumptions, and they demonstrate that you have done your homework. Examples of verifying questions are

"I read in the newspaper that your company is planning a major new expansion. Is that correct?"

"Our records show that you bought our line until several years ago. Is that correct?"

Thank the prospect You should be sure to thank prospects for the interview, preferably at the beginning of the call. You might begin by saying, "Mr. Jones, I am Sally Smith of Computech Corporation and I'd like to thank you for your willingness to see me. I will do my best to make this visit profitable for you and your company." At the end of your interview you will probably want to thank prospects again for their time. For example, you might end a call by saying, "I really enjoyed finding out about your needs, Mr. Jones. Thank you so much for your time. I will send you a catalogue and will have a proposal for you before our next meeting."

SOME GREETINGS THAT SHOULD NEVER BE USED

"Working hard?" (Considered a worn-out phrase by 1920.)

"Well, if it isn't old blankety-blank." (Nickname givers are unloved.)

"Do you really WORK here?" (A real heartwarmer, especially if said within earshot of the person's superior.)

"You look like death warmed over." (Be prepared to duck.)

"What's new?" (If he answers, "New Guinea," that's where you both should be.)

"Thought you'd been fired by now." (Be prepared to lose the big order.)

"Looks like you lived it up last night." (What business is it of yours? He could be dying of cancer.)

SOURCE: Paul Ferris, "The Greeting," *The American Salesman,* Vol. 27, No. 2 (February 1982), p. 19. Reprinted by permission of *The American Salesman,* by the National Research Bureau, Inc., 424 North Third Street, Burlington, Iowa 52601.

Preliminary Conversation

Since the selling–buying process consists of social interaction, the question of preliminary conversation or light talk is a pertinent issue. From a practical standpoint, you are safer to be guided in conversation by the prospect. Obviously, if the prospect takes the initiative, you should join in. If you take the initiative, you should be alert to the other person's reaction to the topic. In addition, it is good practice to avoid topics that are controversial. Topics such as sex, religion, and politics can only cause difficulty. Finally, just as you view the occasion as a business appointment, it is reasonable to assume that the prospect has the same perspective. If too much time is devoted to light talk, the prospect may resent it later, even though it was accepted at the time.

Furthermore, if you carry light talk to an extreme, you may find yourself investing more time on a call than the potential sale warrants.

To be a good conversationalist, you must be *receiver-oriented*. This implies, first, that you will treat the other person as a unique individual and talk about topics of interest to that person. Second, you must have something to say. This puts a premium on being as broadly based as possible in your knowledge about contemporary happenings and business news. Third, it is up to you to avoid argument. If controversy develops, you should be mature enough to shift to another topic, which requires a fourth condition: you must be tolerant of the other person's point of view.

There is one other aspect of light talk that deserves special consideration. If you have paid attention and remember what the other person likes to talk about, you have a basis for accomplishing a smooth transition from one visit to the next. For example, if a prospect has discussed a favorite sport, you may pave your way on the next visit by mentioning recent news item relating to this sport.

You should have ways and means on tap to turn light talk to the business at hand. Any conversational topic you initiate ought to have some direct or indirect relation to your call agenda. In our business culture, light talk is so likely to occur that it underscores the need for you to be a good conversationalist.

Approaches To Begin Selling

Several approaches are available to you in beginning the actual selling aspect of the contact, and none is universally right or wrong. The right approach depends on what you feel comfortable with, what will make the customer feel comfortable, what you are selling, and the situation. Your objective is to gain the prospect's attention and interest, and there are six ways to do this: the question approach, the benefit approach, the new products or news approach, the picture or sample approach, the compliment approach, and the success story approach. Of course, these approaches are generally utilized only after you have introduced yourself and after any light talk.

These are by no means the only ways to begin—nor should they be used by everyone in sales. The need to develop personal "door openers" is very important for two reasons. First, your own personality and other characteristics may make it difficult to adopt the methods of other people. And second, because of the individual differences that are sure to exist among prospects, you must have different approaches for different persons. What might be appropriate for one person may be very inappropriate for others.

Question approach The question approach begins the selling part of the interview by asking prospects a question. This has the benefit of involving prospects and getting the information you need to customize the interview to their unique needs. It is important that the questions be broad enough to have application to prospects' situations and not be too prying. You might ask, for instance, "What type of product are you presently using?" Or, if you know that a prospect is in the market for a new word processsor, you might ask, "What will you be using the word processor for?" These broad questions allow you to find out prospects' needs and gets them involved.

Benefit approach A second approach is to bringing a key benefit of your offering to the attention of prospects, with the aim of gaining their interest. If you are offering a tax shelter to a wealthy investor, you might begin by saying, "How would you like to save up to $15,000 in income taxes next year?" Although the benefit approach has the advantage of trying to appeal to the customer's needs, it does have two disadvantages with prospect accounts. First, given the many buying motives for purchasing a product or service, you do not know at the beginning of a call which benefit to stress. Second, even if you happen to stress a benefit that is important to a prospect, you may not choose the wording that will have the greatest impact until you have gotten to know the prospect. Therefore, the benefit approach should be used cautiously with prospects you do not know. On the other hand, when you do have some idea about your customer's motives, this approach may be useful.

New products or news approach Sharing new products or news is a very good approach for salespeople who call on the same customers over long periods of time. Although long-term calling on customers has the benefit of your getting to know them well and building long-term relationships, you may tend to get into a rut. Thus, you might begin by saying "John, I'm really excited about this new semiconductor our company has developed. I think you will find it useful in your product line . . ." Or, "Our company has just instituted a new advertising campaign and we want you to be the first to hear about it . . ." The important thing is to share something new with the prospect and thus have an opportunity to build enthusiasm. Of course, you must be selective in the products or information you share, depending on the prospects' needs and interests. Simply showing prospects a new product that you know they will not be interested in is a waste of time.

Picture or sample You may open with a display or sample designed to attract the attention and whet the curiosity of the prospect. For example, when calling on jewelry retailers, Mary Collins, a salesperson for a watchband manufacturer, starts each call by handing the prospect a sample with the request, "Tie a tight knot in it." She has found that this gains the prospect's attention, and after a moment's hesitation the other person complies. She then asks the jeweler to untie it. The band snaps back immediately to its original form. In a few seconds she is able to show the ruggedness and flexibility of her product.

A successful display will gain the attention of the prospect more quickly than other methods are likely to do. A display also provides immediate participation for the other person and often provokes questions from prospects, thus providing an easy transition to your presentation of the product. On the other hand, it may be viewed as a stunt or gimmick and arouse unfavorable feelings from prospects. These negative feelings may then be applied to you and your company. Or if demonstrations are overdone, prospects may be so interested in the samples that you cannot regain their attention.

Compliment approach Another approach is to pay the prospect a compliment, providing you really mean it. Insincere compliments are quickly de-

tected and will hurt your credibility. But if you are sincere, you could begin
by saying, "This new building of yours is really impressive. It must be a pleasure to work in such nice surroundings." Or, "I just saw your new model
1200 on your display floor. That really is some machine. I'll bet it's a pleasure to run it." These compliments, if sincere, show that you take an interest
in prospects and their business and allow them to begin discussing their business.

Success stories approach A final approach is to tell prospects a success story
about a noncompeting customer. You must make sure, however, that the
company you choose for your story has some characteristic that is transfera-
ble to your prospects. For instance, you would not necessarily want to say to
prospects in a small CPA firm, "When General Motors bought this system
. . ." Even if they admire General Motors, they might not feel that a system
used by this large corporation will work for them. You should try to pick a
firm more similar to their own. For instance, you might say, "We installed a
word-processing system for a group of lawyers in town, and they doubled
their number of pages of output and cut their overtime in half." Success stories tell prospects how the product or service works in a real world and may
be a good way to get their attention.

EXAMPLES OF VARIOUS APPROACHES

APPROACH	EXAMPLE
Question	What are you looking for in a tractor?
Benefit	This product will cut your production cost in half.
New product	This is our new model. Isn't it compact?
Picture or sample	Here's a picture of our copier. Notice the collator?
Compliment	Your new offices are certainly pretty.
Success story	We tried this new industrial degreaser with ACME Manufacturers, and they now use it in all their plants.

SUMMARY

In this chapter the most important time in any sales call—the first few moments—was examined. The initial impression is generally a lasting one, or
one that is very difficult to change. The two methods of gaining entry are by
direct approach through a personal call, telephone call, or letter, and by
indirect approach, through a referral by a mutually respected person. The
advantages and pitfalls of each approach were discussed.

Just prior to your contact you should remember several basic assumptions: you are interrupting the prospect, so you must invest your time and the prospect's time wisely; you must also remember that the prospect is gathering information, that the prospect is at present satisfied, and that the prospect wants to buy profitably. Moreover, you should recognize the importance of first impressions and the possibility that a perceived similarity between you and the prospect may breed success. Finally, you must review your call objective and prepare your strategy.

After you have gained entry you must make the most of the opportunity. In each contact with a prospect you should state the customer's name, your name, your company's name, and the purpose of your call; be prepared to ask questions to get information and to verify precall information, and be sure to thank the prospect for the interview.

Next, you may engage in some preliminary conversation. As a good conversationalist, you must stay tuned to the prospect and adjust to his or her needs. You must also control the conversation without seeming to, or it will not be very useful. Then you can go into the specifics required to make the visit successful. A number of successful approaches for opening the selling part of the sales call were noted: you may begin with a question, a benefit, a new product or news, a picture or sample, a compliment, or a success story.

PROBLEMS

1. Attack or defend the statement, "Salespeople are at a tactical advantage with a prospect if they have made contact by indirect means."
2. Assume that you are a salesperson waiting in the reception lobby of a new prospect. You have an opportunity to talk to a noncompeting salesperson. What are some of the questions you would ask?
3. What are the advantages, limitations, and cautions in using each of the direct methods of making contact?
4. What are some questions a salesperson might use to get the attention of a cosmetics buyer?
5. In your own words, give an example of how you might begin if you are selling real estate to prospective home buyers.
6. What are the implications of the studies on similarity?

EXERCISE 8

Objectives: To illustrate a way of obtaining an appointment.

To illustrate "opening remarks."

PART A **Entrée by Letter**
You are a salesperson of women's apparel handling a well-known line of young ladies' fashions. You have learned that a large-volume suburban la-

dies' specialty store has changed ownership, and you hope to convince the new owner–manager to stock and sell your line. Your efforts with the previous management were unsuccessful. The store is an hour's drive from your headquarters. Write a letter requesting an appointment.

PART B Opening Remarks
Assume you have been granted an appointment. Outline your opening remarks.

Case 8-1 Acme Machinery Company (A)
Jim Johnson sells construction equipment for Acme Machinery Company, a distributor for Allis-Chalmers. He works out of Grand Rapids, Michigan. As he skims the week's accumulation of newspapers and magazines one Saturday, a note in the *Regional Contractor* catches his eye.

> **Mr. Atchison, president of Atchison Construction Company, has announced an expansion program for his firm that will include opening two new branches. One of the branches will be located in Grand Rapids.**

Jim is excited by this news. He knows of Atchison's reputation. It is based in Columbus, Ohio, and has been a major contractor in road building throughout Ohio, West Virginia, and the western part of Pennsylvania. Jim thinks of what steps to take in order to see Mr. Atchison and other members of company management—especially, the person who will head the Grand Rapids operation.

Jim jots down some things he will do Monday morning.

1. Check with boss and others to see whether anyone has any personal contacts within Atchison.
2. Look up Atchison in the national and Ohio directories of contractors to find out:
   a. "Who's who" in the firm.
   b. The size and structure of the firm.
   c. Information on brands of equipment used by the firm, if given.
3. Request a Dun and Bradstreet report on the financial condition of the firm and see what information is given; check for additional information either at the office or at the local library.
4. Phone the Allis-Chalmers sales representative to see whether he can find out anything, in the meantime, through the home office.
5. Depending on what is discovered, use either a direct or an indirect approach for obtaining the appointment.

Monday morning Jim is able to pull together a considerable amount of information. No one has a contact with Mr. Atchison, however, so Jim decides to write him a letter with the hope of seeing him in Columbus. Here are the bits and pieces he has for possible inclusion:

Full name and address: James R. Atchison, President
Atchison Construction Company
2100 Leland Avenue
Columbus, Ohio 43214

Vice-president, operations: Michael L. Murphy

Company founded: 1958

Dun and Bradstreet rating: Excellent

Number of branches (excluding the two new ones): four

Fleet: mixed; no known Allis-Chalmers equipment

He also sees his own company, Acme, as having the following points of competitive advantage.

In business for over 50 years.

Recognized as having a strong repair shop and reliable field service capable of handling all brands of equipment.

Small enough to give personal attention.

Strongest Allis-Chalmers distributor in western Michigan.

1. What tactics should Jim use to get to see Mr. Atchison?
2. Compose a letter from Jim to Mr. Atchison.

Case 8-2 Acme Machinery Company (B)[6]

Jim arrives in Cleveland elated. He has an appointment with Mr. Atchison. During the short plane trip Jim read and reread Mr. Atchison's letter.

Dear Mr. Johnson:

This is an answer to your letter of June 17. All of us in Atchison are eager to obtain any ideas that will help our business. I am circulating your letter and enclosures to appropriate members of my team.

I must advise you, however, that we are not now in the market for equipment. Initially, we expect to move existing units to any new jobs in Michigan.

If you still wish to visit us, we will be pleased to see you on June 26 at 9:00 A.M.

Sincerely,

James R. Atchison

James R. Atchison
President

[6]The reader should examine Acme Machinery Company (A) (case 8-1) before analyzing this case.

Jim asks himself: What kind of fellow is he? How shall I start off my meeting with him? He arrives at the Atchison offices at 8:50, presents his card to the receptionist, and tells her of his 9:00 A.M. appointment. Promptly at nine o'clock Mr. Atchison's secretary ushers Jim to a conference room and introduces him to Mr. Atchison. In turn, Mr. Atchison introduces him to "Mike Murphy, our number two; Jim Ellis, our controller; Sam Cohen, our chief engineer and the guy who helps us bid our jobs; and young Jim, my son, who's learning the ropes."

Inwardly, Jim is flabbergasted. He never expected this kind of reception. He tries not to show his surprise and uneasiness.

Mr. Atchison continues, "Jim, we don't stand on ceremony. Frankly, we've never really had a serious approach from an Allis-Chalmers distributor sales representative. We're impressed by your initiative and willingness to come to see us. Tell us about yourself."

What should Jim say?

Sending Messages

After studying this chapter, you should be able to

1. Develop a benefit matrix.
2. Determine factors to make your message understandable.
3. Specify ways to make your messages more interesting.
4. Understand factors that will make your message believable.
5. Identify ways to make your message more persuasive.
6. Describe different types and principles of suggestion.
7. Know various dimensions of the nonverbal messages you send in your presentation.

If your contact has been handled effectively, the prospect is now favorably oriented to hear what you have to offer. You have an assessment of the prospect's needs and wants, and you can relate your remarks to them. Thus, both parties are ready for the next step, the presentation.

In order to be effective in sending messages, you must stress benefits; make your message understandable, interesting, believable, and persuasive, and send positive nonverbal messages. An effective presentation consists of two-way communication; you send effective messages and involve customers in order to obtain feedback on their needs and reactions to your messages. This chapter covers sending of messages from the salesperson to the prospect, Chapter 11 deals with securing feedback from the prospect. The first step in sending messages is to place your firm's products or services in the best possible light from the standpoint of the customer or prospect.

PREPARATION FOR THE SALES PRESENTATION

As a sales representative, you face a key communication task in preparing effective presentations; you must translate your company's products, services, and people into benefits, uses, and want satisfiers for your customers. The more technical the product line, the more difficult this translation task becomes. The process consists of developing a benefit matrix and then customizing benefits for a specific presentation.

The Benefit Matrix: Development and Communication

Features of a product or service describe the item. For instance, you might say, that a table is 36 inches tall, made of formica, and brown in color. To give the benefits of a product or service, on the other hand, you must translate features into statements that show what these characteristics will do for the prospect. In our table example, because the table is 36 inches tall, it is a convenient work height; the formica means it will be easy to clean and is scratch-resistant. Finally, the brown color may enable it to blend with the customer's decor. It is important that your sales messages include benefits so customers will see the usefulness of your products. What customers really buy is benefits, what the product will do for them, not features.

A benefit matrix is a table that forces you to think through the prominent benefits of your offering, how they relate to your customers, and how they can be effectively communicated to your customers.

In preparing for a sales presentation, you should develop a set of benefit matrices that deal with (1) special benefits of your company, (2) the product group you hope to sell, (3) any associated services that accompany the product group, and (4) the special personnel talents that exist within your firm.

Table 9.1 provides a sample of the first type of benefit matrix. The prominent special features are size of the firm, number of years in business, and geographical location. Several customer benefits are listed for each feature, along with alternative ways of expressing these benefits to customers. Tables 9.2 through 9.4 provide examples of the three other types of benefit

TABLE 9.1
COMPANY BENEFIT MATRIX

FEATURES	CUSTOMER BENEFITS	ALTERNATE WAYS OF EXPRESSING
Large size	Can offer customer a spectrum of resources.	Has a wide variety of talents and equipment to service customers' needs.
	Enjoys benefit of economies of scale in production.	Produces at low cost because of large-scale operations.
Number of years in business	If old: Company is a stable source of supply. Reputation has been built over a number of years.	Has been providing the products for years. Not a fly-by-night operation.
	If new: Company is young and aggressive. Wants very much to attract new customers.	Willing to try new ideas. Hungry for business.
Geographical	Can give good service and quick delivery. Nearness to customer will reduce shipping costs.	Nearby location means good service. Transportation time and costs are less than competitors.

TABLE 9.2
PRODUCT GROUP BENEFIT MATRIX

FEATURES	CUSTOMER BENEFITS	ALTERNATE WAYS OF EXPRESSING
Assortment available	Wide variety from which to select.	Can meet most customer needs because a selection is available.
	As a fashion or style changes, will still have the right type to sell.	As colors, styles, and so on change (fads), can supply the right types of goods because a wide assortment is available.
Inventory supply	Can meet emergency needs of customers because a backup inventory is available.	When customers need quick delivery, can ship almost immediately from inventory.
	Production expenses reduced because product is made in large quantities.	Prices competitive because of economical production runs.
Available in alternate forms.	Better able to meet specific customer needs.	Can tailor product to customer desires because a variety of configurations is available.
	Not in direct competition with other sellers because several product variations are available.	Product differentiation created by selling different varieties.

DRABBLE ®

TABLE 9.3

ASSOCIATED SERVICES BENEFIT MATRIX

FEATURES	CUSTOMER BENEFITS	ALTERNATE WAYS OF EXPRESSING
Field service organization	Can provide customers with technical advice.	Producer's people are available to work on customer's problems.
	Can give qualified assistance for special problems.	When particular problems are encountered, will send people out to work on them.
Cooperative advertising	Will help promote the reselling of the product by paying a portion of the reseller's advertising expenses.	Will provide ad layouts or drawings to use in advertisements.
	Helps to develop an awareness of the reseller's existence.	Creates more business for resellers for specific product as well as for other products handled.
Company school	Ensures topflight training for customer's key personnel.	Customers gain competitive advantage through their people's expertise.
	Keeps employees from getting in a rut, as they exchange ideas with others in the industry.	Employees improve their attitude; they learn from others at the company school.

TABLE 9.4

TALENT RESOURCES BENEFIT MATRIX

FEATURES	CUSTOMER BENEFITS	ALTERNATE WAYS OF EXPRESSING
High caliber of management	Willing and able to work with customers on business problems.	Helps customers to make more profit by knowing about and working with them.
	Associating with a progressive supplier can keep customer on top of significant changes or trends.	Can keep customer informed of industry changes.
Qualified technical personnel	Best brains in industry guaranteed to tackle customer's problems.	In effect, each customer has the company's technical staff available.
	Assures continuing development and refinement of product line.	Can maintain technological leadership.
Customer-oriented salesperson	Each salesperson is an unpaid consultant for the customer.	Salesperson's availability is an important value added in each purchase.
	Provides direct personal linkage with supplier.	Makes supplier and customer "partners in profit."

matrices. Other situations may call for even more benefit entries for each matrix. The three sequential steps for developing and implementing these matrices are (1) determining the prominent features, (2) converting the features into benefits, and (3) expressing and demonstrating each benefit several different ways to the customer.

Determining the prominent features First you must list the prominent features for each benefit matrix. For instance, a feature for the firm would be number of years in business. A product feature would be that it is offered in different forms. An example of a service feature could be the availability of a corporate field-service organization staffed by engineers. Finally, talent features could include the size of the firm's research staff and the caliber of all company personnel.

Converting features into benefits Once each list of features has been drawn up, the next step is to convert the features into benefits, uses, and want satisfiers. This involves showing the significance of the features to the customers and prospects. If, for example, one company feature is its large size, the benefits for the customer might include the availability of a wide range of resources and cost savings through economies of scale. An example in the services matrix might be the availability of a company school, which would benefit customers by providing good training programs for their personnel plus an exposure to other people in their industry.

Expressing and demonstrating each benefit several different ways You must develop as many ways as possible of expressing and demonstrating each benefit for several reasons. First, there is no assurance that a benefit stated once will reach the conscious awareness of the customer. More likely, a given point that arouses interest will need to be made in many different ways before the prospect fully comprehends. A second application has to do with successive calls on the same customer. Often you must present essentially the same benefits during several visits. It is important that you have a fresh approach in such presentations to avoid boring the other person by repeating what you said previously. Third, you need to have different ways of handling a particular point if you are to reinforce your key points.

The time and effort invested in these three steps is applied to all the presentations you make. Essentially, these three steps are carried out only once, although a review and refinement of them is essential from time to time based on your accumulated experience, changes in customer behavior, shifts in competitive strategy, and, of course, any innovations your firm makes in the ways the product satisfies a customer's wants.

It is also helpful for you to analyze each of your competitors with benefit matrices in the same manner as you do your own firm, in order to anticipate the essentials of each competing salesperson's presentation. That is, for each competitor you would list their major features and benefits. This will allow you to work out ways of differentiating your claims from those your competitors are making. As a result, you will have a substantial advantage because you can emphasize your firm's relative advantages without attacking each competitor directly.

You are now equipped to prepare a specific presentation for a particular account. In view of your call objectives, you select elements from each relevant matrix for the presentation. For instance, with a current customer, the objective might be to acquaint the account with a new product your firm is introducing. You might first consider which products the customer is now buying and which of these give the customer greatest satisfaction. One element of this presentation might be to remind the person of these benefits and suggest the likelihood of getting similar benefits from the new product. The second and main element in the presentation might be the variety of benefits provided by the new product. If the customer is not familiar with this product, you might stress its many benefits. Then, you could expand on any points that arouse interest and a favorable reaction.

BENEFIT OR FEATURE QUIZ

Assume that a salesperson has made the following statements to a prospect. Indicate opposite each statement whether it is a benefit or a feature statement. Answers are at the bottom of the box, but don't look until you are finished.

BENEFIT	FEATURE	
_____	_____	1. "The hose on this vacuum cleaner stretches twice its normal length."
_____	_____	2. "This camera has a built-in self-timer."
_____	_____	3. "Our product, Mr. Dealer, is nationally advertised on television."
_____	_____	4. "The electrical parts of this blanket are insulated and sealed with waterproof plastic."
_____	_____	5. "You will receive five packs of Anscochrome 126 film free with every three 726 cameras."
_____	_____	6. "The protection from this deodorant lasts over twelve hours."
_____	_____	7. "This electric razor has specially ground shaving edges angled at eleven degrees."
_____	_____	8. "This automobile has a unitized crush-proof body."
_____	_____	9. "This machine makes clean, dry copies from an original in 4 seconds."
_____	_____	10. "One physical examination guarantees your insurability at standard rates to age 40."

SOURCE: Reprinted with permission of Sperry Vickers, a division of Sperry Corporation.

ANSWERS: All ten statements are features. They do not relate to how they will help the customer.

In contrast, if the contemplated call is on a prospect and the key objective is to establish goodwill, your preparation would be mainly a study and refinement of the matrix reflecting the benefits of the firm. In general, it is easier to prepare an individualized presentation for a customer than for a prospect. In fact, in the extreme case, when you know little about a new account, the general-purpose matrices are about all you can use as a basis for your presentation.

CRITERIA FOR AN EFFECTIVE MESSAGE

Whether the individual called on is a prospect or a customer, and whether the points to be covered are simple or complex, your messages must meet four basic criteria: they must be understandable, interesting, believable, and persuasive. These criteria are interactive in that each one is dependent on the others. It is difficult to conceive of a message's being interesting if it is not understood by the other person. If your message is to be believable, what is said must be understood and interesting. However, the acid test is that it must be persuasive.

Understandability

Five concepts combine to make a presentation understandable: (1) the customer's perception, (2) the customer's attention span, (3) the mind's attempt to make concepts concrete rather than abstract, (4) the customer's state of mind, and (5) the way the customer processes information.

Perception Perception is the way we take in stimuli and attach meanings to them. People perceive by hearing, seeing, touching, tasting, and smelling. The way a person perceives incoming stimuli depends greatly on past experience. Thus, if you learn more about the backgrounds of prospects and customers and present your ideas in terms of their backgrounds, they will be more likely to understand what you have to say. You can then use examples, illustrations, analogies, and comparisons in order to relate the presentation to the person's prior experience. It is easy to violate this principle by using technical terms, concepts, and examples beyond the understanding of the other person. In addition, you must avoid discussing points that are not relevant to the customer's needs and wants.

You must also realize that you may have to present your point several times and in several ways before you have really gained the customer's understanding. As an example, consider Mary Collins, a young salesperson who is very successful at selling stereo equipment in a retail store. After she has determined prospects' real needs, she presents the technical aspects of the equipment. Then she plays the stereo softly and reiterates the benefits of the equipment that is providing the music. Finally, she finds out what types of music prospects would like to hear, puts it on, and has them adjust the volume to the desired level. At this point she tries to answer any questions prospects have.

This salesperson recognizes two very important aspects of perception. First, she realizes that she needs to repeat her message several times if it is to be understood. Second, she recognizes the importance of visual and tactile stimuli to help the prospect understand her message. That is, by showing prospects the equipment (visual stimuli), having them listen to it (auditory stimuli), and asking them to set the volume at the level they wish (tactile stimuli), the prospects can understand the salesperson better.

Attention span You must consider your prospect's attention span if you are to achieve understanding. Research has shown that human beings can attend to only a limited number of stimuli at one time. The less familiar they are with the stimuli, the fewer the stimuli they can hold within their attention. Therefore, your presentation, to be understood, must consist of a sufficiently small number of points or concepts to allow the listener to grasp them. In addition, the very pace of your presentation will influence its understandability. The better informed you are, the more likely you are to move too quickly through your presentation for your listener to comprehend.

Concrete terms If you avoid abstract terms and use more concrete, tangible language, your listener will understand better. Technical terms that must be used should be defined adequately to avoid misunderstanding and confusion. This is particularly important for technically trained salespeople who call on purchasing agents who may not be technically trained. Often this type of salesperson uses technical language that the purchasing agent does not understand and thus does not communicate successfully. On the other hand, technical language may be fine when you are dealing with engineers. The important point is that most people do not like to admit that they do not understand a message; thus, you must use clear language and be attentive to the other person, to catch the cues that inform you how well your message is being received.

State of mind An individual's feelings or state of mind also influence understanding. If you establish a favorable feeling state in the other person during the beginning of a call, your presentation is more likely to be understood. Understanding may be blocked by the use of words and phrases that have emotional overtones for the other person. "Homemade" might cause a favorable feeling in one person because the expression is associated with an image of apple pie baked for Sunday dinner. To another person the term might mean less than adequate, or imperfect. Arousing some feelings or emotion will generally enhance understanding; it is difficult to communicate effectively to a person who has no feeling whatsoever for what you are saying. At the other extreme, a person whose emotions are too highly aroused may not perceive or think as clearly and thus may fail to understand the presentation.

Information processing Prospects differ in the way they process information. Generally, people process information in one of three ways, using a visual, an auditory, or a kinesthetic (feeling) system. The person who uses primarily the visual system will say things such as "I can see what you are saying." The person who uses primarily the auditory mode might say things such as "I hear what you are saying." Finally, a kinesthetic person might say, "I like the feel of this product." These sensory systems are called representational systems. In order to be understood, you should try to choose words and benefits that match the customer's representational system. Table 9.5 lists many words that may act as cues to the three representational systems. People use these different sensory modes as they do their thinking. Thus, if you note that prospects are very visually oriented, getting them to picture the product in their minds would be a good way to communicate. Similarly, letting them see the product would also be useful.

Understanding prospects' representational systems provides you with ideas of how best to communicate with them. For instance, a visual prospect will want to read a brochure and look at the product. An auditory prospect will want to hear about the product. Finally, a kinesthetic prospect will want to touch the product, try it out, and get a feel for it.[1]

You can determine prospects' representational systems by noting their verbal responses. A visual person will use words such as view, see, picture, and notice. An auditory person will use words such as listen, hear, respond, discuss, or mention. Finally, a kinesthetic person will use words such as feel, grip, and hold on to.[2] If you find that a prospect has a primarily visual orientation, you might say, "Mrs. Hawkins, as you can see, this product has very contemporary styling. Picture how nicely it would fit into your office." Notice that you can stress the same benefit differently, depending on the prospect's orientation. For instance, you could say, "Does it look as though this product will fill your needs?," or "Does it sound as though this product will fill your needs?" or, "Do you feel this product will fill your needs?" depending on whether the prospect is primarily visual, auditory, or kinesthetic.

Interest

The second criterion to ensure a successful presentation is obtaining the other person's interest. The best way to get prospects interested is to talk in terms of benefits that satisfy their needs. Relevant messages will hold their interest. Several sources of information, such as their personal background and professional role, can suggest the probable interests of prospects or customers.

Personal background The kind and extent of formal education customers or prospects have may provide some clues to their interests. With individuals who have substantial professional experience, you might draw inferences about their interests from knowing their work background. Peoples' life values, which affect their attitudes and interests and tell you what virtues they look for in the presentation, constitute a prime example of this kind of information. In addition, the more you know about their personality and motives,

---

[1]H. Stanley Connell III, "NLP Techniques for Salespeople," *Training and Development Journal* (November 1984), p. 45.

[2]William G. Nickels, Robert F. Everett, and Ronald Klein, "Rapport Building for Salespeople: A Neuro-Linguistic Approach," *Journal of Personal Selling and Sales Management*, Vol. 3, No. 2 (November 1983), p. 3.

TABLE 9.5

PREDICATE WORDS

VISUAL	AUDITORY	KINESTHETIC
analyze	announce	active
angle	articulate	affected
appear	audible	bearable
clarity	communicate	charge
cognizant	converse	concrete
conspicuous	discuss	emotional
demonstrate	dissonant	feel
dream	divulge	firm
examine	earshot	flow
focus	enunciate	foundation
foresee	gossip	grasp
glance	hear	grip
hindsight	hush	hanging
horizon	inquire	hassle
idea	interview	heated
illusion	listen	hold
image	mention	hustle
inspect	noise	intuition
look	oral	lukewarm
notice	proclaim	motion
obscure	pronounce	muddled
observe	remark	panicky
obvious	report	pressure
perception	roar	sensitive
perspective	rumor	set
picture	say	shallow
scene	shrill	softly
see	silence	solid
sight	squeal	structured
sketchy	state	support
survey	talk	tension
vague	tell	tied
view	tone	touch
vision	tutter	unbearable
watch	vocal	unsettled
witness	voice	whipped

[a]Predicates are the process words that customers use in their communication to represent their experience (visual, auditory, or kinesthetic). Listed are some of the more commonly used predicates in the business environment. The objective in "matching" predicates is to "match" the language in which the customer speaks, thus creating an atmosphere of rapport and understanding.

SOURCE: William G. Nickels, Robert F. Everett, and Ronald Klein, "Rapport Building for Salespeople: A Neuro-Linguistic Approach," *Journal of Personal Selling and Sales Management*, Vol. 3, No. 2 (November 1983), p. 2. Reprinted with permission by *Journal of Personal Selling and Sales Management*.

the better equipped you are to interest them. All the personal characteristics that make the other person unique are important considerations.

Professional role Another set of clues to likely interests stem from the position people hold in the firm and in particular the role they play in the decision-making "who's who." For instance, the purchasing manager and the controller are likely to have quite different interests. The purchasing manager is more likely to be interested in deliveries and availability and the controller in the terms of purchase or the tax implication of the purchase.

Fundamentally, of course, you must recognize that you need first to make prospects realize that the present supplier is not as satisfactory as they thought. In doing this, you face a dual task. You must meet not only the individual's needs and wants, but also the needs and wants of the firm as that individual interprets them. Your best assumption is that the prospect is satisfied with things as they are; therefore, you must disturb this complacency. Until this is done there will be little or no interest in your presentation. The exception, of course, is your own satisfied customers whose interests may be reinforced by encouraging them to describe the many benefits and advantages they see in the present selling–buying relationship.

Tactical considerations You must be able to sense diminishing interest as you continue with your presentation. The best single indicator you have of this is the degree of attention the customer or prospect pays to your presentation. Attention is a dimension of perception, and until incoming stimuli receive a substantial amount of attention, they do not reach the level of conscious awareness. Until they reach conscious awareness there can be no interest. If you sense diminishing interest, you must change your approach to try to regain the prospect's interests. This topic will be covered in much more detail in Chapter 12.

Because you must satisfy the personal needs and wants of the individual as well as those of the individual's firm (as the person interprets them), this suggests the importance of "you" appeal. You should avoid as much as possible referring to "I" or to "my" company. One of the weakest sales appeals is to seek an order on the basis of "I need the business." On the contrary, one of the strongest appeals is to the ego of the other person.

Believability

The third criterion for a successful presentation is believability. This is a function of several key variables, which include (1) your image, (2) your personal conviction, (3) overlearning the presentation, (4) your ability to reassure the customer, and (5) third-party selling.

Your image To a great extent, believability is not as much a function of the content of the presentation as it is a function of the personal image you convey. Your believability depends on how the receiver perceives it: it is not an objective evaluation, since it usually represents the subjective feelings of the receiver. A customer or prospect who approves of your conduct is likely to believe what you say. Conversely, a person who disapproves or feels threatened by your values is not likely to believe in your presentation.

In addition, your image and believability are a function of the firm you represent.[3] Take, for example, a salesperson for a well-known computer firm contrasted with a "Hot Shot Electric" salesperson. The salesperson for the well-known firm has an image of being honest, forthright, and an expert in computers. The salesperson who represents "Hot Shot" begins with the handicap that the buyer has never heard of "Hot Shot" before. Thus, the well-known salesperson has a positive image, whereas the other salesperson has either no image or a negative image in the mind of the buyer.

Your credibility is transferred to the product you sell, the company you represent, and the services you offer. It is very important, therefore, to verify the variables that influence source credibility. The level of expertise you display determines your credibility. It is important for the receiver to feel that you are knowledgeable about the subject matter. You must know the product you are trying to sell, you must know the most efficient use for the product, and you must convey your confidence in that knowledge to the prospect.

Your external characteristics are also important in conveying an image of credibility. Your mannerisms, appearance, language, dress, and age all provide bases for inferences about your credibility. Of course, appropriate dress and language depend on your audience; nevertheless they do influence credibility. Another determinant of source credibility is the extent to which you are able to give an unbiased opinion. If buyers perceive that you intend to change their attitudes toward a product, they may develop a defensive attitude. You should be able to show a balanced attitude toward the products and services you offer. You should show the advantages of your products over the competitor's, but you should not push for a sale when your product is not appropriate to satisfy the buyer's needs.

An image of prestige is also positively related to credibility. Because respected members of the community are perceived to be trustworthy, you can use them to obtain the confidence of prospective buyers. Furthermore, your local community activities are important to your credibility, and you should avoid any behavior that may jeopardize this credibility as perceived by buyers.

Your personal convictions You should feel that your offering represents a good value for the prospect or customer. You have to be sold on your offering if you are to sell it to another person. Belief or conviction on your part, by suggestion, encourages a similar reaction in the other person. You must be sincere if your presentation is to ring true. Your manner of presentation is more important than what you say in accomplishing this.

Overlearning the presentation A third factor influencing believability is the extent to which you have overlearned what you are presenting. When you have learned something until it is second nature to you, a part of yourself,

---

[3]See, for example, Theodore Levitt, *Industrial Purchasing Behavior: A Study in Communications Effects* (Boston: Division of Research, Harvard Business School, 1965).

you have succeeded in overlearning it. The importance of this process can be illustrated by what happens when a salesperson has not overlearned material. If a salesperson has only learned the presentation, but not overlearned it, some unanticipated reaction may cause the salesperson to stumble or hesitate to think through what to say or do next. This stumbling and hesitation may be interpreted by the prospect as a lack of expertise and conviction on the salesperson's part.

Of course, this need for overlearning does not mean that you memorize your presentation and make the presentation without thinking about it. It does mean, however, that you know your products and services so well that you don't have to stumble around to answer questions about them.

Reassuring the customer You can increase believability if you are able to reassure the other person. With a customer, this can be done by citing many favorable experiences and benefits that have been derived in the past from the selling–buying relationship. With a prospect, this may be accomplished by reminding the other person of the reputation of your firm and of your willingness personally to back up any purchase, and, if appropriate, by reference to any guarantees and warranties associated with the product.

TEN WAYS TO PROVE YOUR POINT

- Visual evidence—photographs, charts, diagrams.
- Demonstrations.
- The testimony of experts.
- Testimonial letters.
- Testimonial telephone calls.
- Statistics.
- Guarantees.
- Case histories.
- Published articles.
- Proof of analogy—cite a case from another field and make it applicable to your own.

SOURCE: Ted Pollock, "Ten Ways to Prove Your Point," *The American Salesman*, Vol. 26, No. 7 (July 1981), pp. 32–37. Reprinted with permission of *The American Salesman*, National Research Bureau, Inc., 424 North Third Street, Burlington, Iowa 52601.

Third-party selling The last method of instilling believability is through third-party selling. You give the customer or prospect testimonials of people who presumably have no vested interest in influencing the other person to buy.

Such statements are more believable than your claims. Testimonials may range from formal statements on the part of customers to evaluative data prepared by a testing laboratory, or to such endorsements as a Good Housekeeping Seal of Approval.

The issue of credibility cannot be overemphasized. In most instances, prospective purchasers are likely to be skeptical about claims made in ads, direct-mail pieces, and sales presentations. Unless you are believable, you will not make a sale.

Persuasiveness

Perhaps even more important than understandability, interest, and believability in a presentation is persuasiveness. Persuasion is a conscious attempt by one individual to change the attitudes, beliefs, or behavior of another individual through the transmission of some message.[4] You can persuade by some combination of suggestion and reasoning. When you suggest, you directly or indirectly get prospects to consider how they might satisfy certain needs; by adopting your suggestion, prospects purchase your product. For example, you might suggest that prospects buy a new product or that they order a certain quantity. In the second way to persuade prospects, through logical reasoning, you provide them with evidence and facts that show that your product or service will solve their needs. Generally, customers who are already deriving satisfaction from the selling–buying relationship are more amenable to suggestion than are prospects. Customers know you, your company, your products, and your services. They are convinced of your worth. Prospects, in contrast, are usually deriving satisfaction from competing offerings and consequently have to be reasoned with if they are to shift to other want satisfiers.

Strategic considerations You must weigh three strategic considerations in deciding whether the emphasis in your presentation should be on suggestion or reasoning. These include your personality and motivational analysis of the customer or prospect, your analysis of the situation within the account, and the nature of the products and services being sold.

You should begin by considering your personality and motivational analysis of the prospect or customer. As an example, an insecure person is more open to suggestions, but a self-confident person must often be provided with many logical reasons for taking a particular action. The extremely impulsive person may act immediately on suggestion, whereas an extremely deliberate person is likely to weigh any proposition with care. An individual with a relatively low level of intelligence and with little technical knowledge is likely to be more open to suggestion than a bright, technically able person.

A second strategic consideration in deciding whether suggestion or reasoning should be used is your analysis of the situation within the account. If there is a deadline by which the buying decision must be made, suggestion may be adequate. On the other hand, if there is no compelling reason to purchase immediately, the decision makers may want to weigh each detail of

[4]Erwin P. Bettinghaus, *Persuasive Communication*, fourth edition (New York: Holt, Rinehart and Winston, 1987), p. 3.

the presentation very carefully. The closer the proposal relates to the prior experience of the firm, the more you can rely on suggestion. In contrast, the more unprecedented the proposal, the more likely that you will have to supply sound reasons for accepting your offering. If you are dealing with only one decision maker, depending on the person's personality and motivational analysis, that person may be open to suggestion. In contrast, if the individual called on must become an internal salesperson within the decision-making group, it is important for you to provide the person with a comprehensive rationale for such a presentation.

A third strategic consideration that will influence your relative emphasis on suggestion or reasoning concerns the products and services being sold. If the products are relatively simple and nontechnical, suggestion may be sufficient. If they are complex and highly technical, the emphasis should be on reasoning. In addition, if the unit order represents a small outlay from the standpoint of the customer or prospect, the person may be open to suggestion, but if it represents a substantial investment, reasoning will be needed. Finally, the better known the products, services, and expertise of your company are, the more likely suggestion is to be effective, whereas if neither the product nor the company is known, reasoning will be necessary.

Tactical considerations Going beyond these strategic considerations, you must recognize that certain tactical factors also influence the choice between suggestion and reasoning. The prospect's mood and rapport with you are important, as is your assessment of the prospect's attention level.

If you find the customer or prospect in a pleasant mood, you can rely more heavily on suggestion and accomplish more than you had expected. In addition, if you are able to establish rapport and make a favorable impression, your suggestions are that much more likely to be acceptable.

As the call continues, your assessment of the attention level of the other person provides an additional tactical consideration. Usually if you have the full attention of prospects or customers, the accompanying thought processes are logical, analytical, and evaluative. These mental sets call for reasoning. You can gauge the level of attention by the type and number of questions asked. In contrast, if part of prospects' attention is diverted to other matters, they are likely to be more open to suggestion.

Strategic and tactical conditions often interact in influencing the choice between suggestion and reasoning, so you must be skilled in using both if your presentations are to be persuasive.

GUIDELINES FOR SUGGESTIONS

Since suggestions are so critical to the presentation, they will be considered in more detail. You may use several types of suggestions, and these can be based on several principles.

Types of Suggestions

Suggestions can be direct or indirect and positive or negative. These aspects, together with several other principles of suggestion, are analyzed here.

Direct versus indirect suggestions A direct suggestion usually leaves no doubt about what you want the customer or prospect to do. For example, you might bring a sample to a prospect and say, "Try this and you will see what I am talking about." In contrast, an indirect suggestion does not reveal the desire of the person making it, nor does it spell out the desired action. For example, you might say, "Dealing with the firm that has the lowest price may be very costly in the long run."

Indirect suggestion has two tactical advantages over direct suggestion. First, it puts the burden on the other person to decide what action to take. Therefore, the customer who decides to perform the desired act has the feeling of having generated the idea personally and thus is less likely to resist the sale. Second, in the event an indirect suggestion is unproductive, a more direct suggestion can be used. However, if you make a direct suggestion and it does not work, you have provided the opportunity for a negative reaction, and it will be difficult to regain a favorable position.

Positive versus negative suggestions A positive suggestion indicates an action to be taken or a decision to be made. In contrast, a negative suggestion indicates an action or decision to avoid. "Order now while we can still guarantee delivery" is positive. The same suggestion in negative form would be, "Don't postpone the decision or we may not be able to make delivery." The weakness of the negative suggestion is that two elements are present: what is to be avoided as well as what is to be acted upon. The difficulty is that the other person may react only to the negative element.

Principles of Suggestion
In addition to direct versus indirect suggestions and positive versus negative suggestions, other principles of suggestion that are applicable to the selling–buying process are analyzed.

The prestige of the suggestor The greater the prestige of the person making the suggestion, the greater the likelihood that the suggestion will be followed. Many factors contribute to prestige, such as the reputation of your company, or your social standing, financial resources, physical size, age, and educational attainment. The suggestion that a certain stock is a good investment is less likely to be questioned when coming from a person known to be a successful investor than when coming from a person with no comparable record of success. If you personally do not have this prestige, you may be able to use this type of suggestion by quoting persons of prestige such as executives in your company, persons well known in the trade, or community leaders.

The impact of numbers In a difficult sales situation, it may be effective to make calls with other company personnel. A joint call with a sales executive, a company engineer, or another person of authority will increase the likelihood of success from the standpoint of suggestion, especially if their suggestions are all compatible with yours.

Attention level One widespread idea is that a high level of attention to the subject at hand increases the likelihood that the suggestion will be acted upon. When people become concerned over a problem, their ability to be objective diminishes. Another idea indicates that a low level of attention also increases the likelihood of suggestions being acted upon. This conclusion is based on the idea of dissociation. Suppose you call on a prospect who is thinking about a problem unrelated to your presentation. You may present your proposition, but the prospect never really shifts attention to you. If you make the sale, you have done so without the prospect critically evaluating the proposition.

If these two ideas are correct, suggestion is likely to be more effective than reasoning when the customer is either barely attending or completely engrossed in your presentation. At the middle level of attention, the prospect is most likely to think critically about the proposition, and reasoning will be most effective.

Opposing ideas Psychology says that every idea that enters the mind will be acted upon unless there is an alternative item present. Thus, prospects are more likely to act upon a suggestion if they have not been exposed to ideas from competitors. If prospects have been exposed to ideas from competitors, your most effective approach may be the two-sided argument; that is, you mention the benefits of the competition as well as those you offer.[5]

Repetition of the suggestion When an idea is repeated often enough over a period of time, prospects may tend to forget its origin and may eventually adopt it as their own. This can aid you, because it is easier for buyers to act on their own ideas than on yours. Many times such an idea can be planted through company advertising, which is a good reason for coordination of advertising and selling. The advertising copy and your presentation should be couched in the same style as much as possible. This allows you to make maximum use of advertising as a preselling device.

Knowledge of the topic under discussion A prospect or customer may lack information to use in disagreeing. For example, someone having a house built might not know what material to use on the exterior. There is a wide choice of wood, concrete, and brick, and a variety of metals such as stainless steel and aluminum. If the contractor "suggests" a material and the person lacks knowledge of the materials, the person will usually adopt the ideas of the contractor. A greater knowledge about building would allow the person to weigh alternatives rather than accept a suggestion.

Your previous performance Any new purchase is likely to require a conscious effort and to engage critical thought processes. In selling, this means that you should not expect your first sale to a prospect to be achieved by suggestion. Initial contacts require undivided attention and a full presentation. Subsequent sales, however, may be accomplished by suggestion and without the customer's full attention. Of course, it takes more than suggestion

[5]For a discussion of one- versus two-sided messages, see Philip Kotler, *Marketing Management, Analyses, Planning and Control,* fourth edition (Englewood Cliffs, N. J.: Prentice-Hall, 1980), p. 482.

TABLE 9.6

APPROPRIATENESS OF SUGGESTION VERSUS LOGIC BASED ON PRINCIPLES OF SUGGESTION

PRINCIPLES OF SUGGESTION	SUGGESTION	LOGIC
Prestige of suggestor	High	Low
Number of people making suggestion	Many	Few
Attention level of prospect	High or low	Medium
Opposing ideas from competitors	None	Some
Repetition of suggestion	Yes	No
Prospect's knowledge of the topic	Low	High
Your previous performance	Good	No previous performance
Wording of the suggestion	Leading, definite, positive	Open-ended, indefinite, negative

to account for the ease of the second sale to a customer over the first one, such as satisfactory service from the first purchase and your increased knowledge of the customer's needs. But once you have gained a customer's trust, the customer will be more receptive to your suggestions.

Wording of the suggestion   There is evidence that leading questions, definite rather than indefinite articles, and positive rather than negative phrasing influence an individual's reply. For example, "Did you see the horse?" is more likely to produce a positive answer than "Did you see a horse?" You could suggest that a dog was dark-colored more readily by asking "Was the dog dark-colored?" than by asking, "What color was the dog?" Finally, "You liked the product, didn't you?" is more likely to get a positive response than "You didn't like the product, did you?" Although you do not want to make your suggestions sound pushy or manipulative, the wording you use is important. Thus, you must think through and plan the type of suggestion you want to use with a particular prospect. Table 9.6 provides a summary of the appropriateness of suggestion versus logic based on the principles of suggestion just discussed.

SENDING NONVERBAL MESSAGES

In addition to the verbal messages you send, you are also sending messages through your nonverbal behavior. As a rule, verbal communication sends your basic content, and nonverbal communication transmits your feelings, emotions, and personal meaning. You can have an effect on the way people react to you if you control your body language and other nonverbal communications. Your posture, the tone of your voice, your facial expressions, and body movements all convey information to your prospects. If you are slouching, not making eye contact, appear bored, and fumble with your fingers, then, no matter what you say, you will not convey the proper message. What you would like to convey with your nonverbal behavior is interest, enthusiasm, and sincerity. One reason nonverbal messages are so important is that you are always sending them. It has been estimated that as much as 93 percent of all communication takes place on a nonverbal level.[6] Thus, you must be constantly aware of the nonverbal messages you are sending. It is also important that your nonverbal communications not conflict with one another or with the verbal message you are sending. If there is an inconsistency in the messages you send, your prospects will sense this and be uneasy even if they do not know why. Thus, even though you are talking enthusiastically about your products, if you are frowning or slouching, your messages will contradict one another.

Entire books have been written on nonverbal communications, but this section is designed to acquaint you with the various signals you send to prospects.[7] Of course, you must also read your prospect's nonverbal communications. These are covered in Chapter 11, Securing Feedback. You send nonverbal messages through your dress, paralanguage, eye contact, facial expressions, gestures, handshake, posture, the space between you and the customer, and your respect for time. Each of these is reviewed.

Dress An important aspect of the message you send your customers and prospects is the way you dress.[8] Your dress has an impact on your image; this is why many companies have dress codes for their salespeople. It is important to dress for your audience—in this case, your customers. If you are calling on executives you should be dressed conservatively. On the other hand, if you are selling fashion merchandise to department stores, you would dress more fashionably. Appropriate attire has several benefits: it conveys an image of success, it makes you more likely to be accepted by customers, and it makes you more confident (see Figure 9.1).[9] Several guidelines for dressing and grooming are provided for men in Table 9.7 and for women in Table 9.8.

There are also regional guidelines for dressing. For instance, the casual business attire worn in southern California would be totally inappropriate in New York or Boston. It is important that you not violate these regional dress codes.[10]

---

[6]See Albert Mehrabian, "Communicating Without Words," *Psychology Today,* Vol. 2 (September 1968), p. 53.

[7]See Allan Pease, *Signals: How to Use Body Language for Power, Success and Love* (New York: Bantam Books, 1984).

[8]For a good discussion of a basic wardrobe for starting out, see Michael Korda, "A Wardrobe for Starting Out," *New York Times Magazine* (August 14, 1983), p. 44.

[9]For an in-depth discussion of dressing and grooming for men, see John T. Molloy, *Dress for Success* (New York: Warner Books, 1975); for women, see John T. Molloy, *The Woman's Dress for Success Book* (New York: Warner Books, 1977). For an interesting alternative opinion, see Mortimer Levitt, "Seeing Red about 'Never Wear Green,' " *Sales and Marketing Management,* Vol. 116, No. 5 (April 12, 1976), pp. 67–72.

[10]For more information on regional dress codes for men, see John T. Molloy, "Clothes: Your First and Last Salestool," *Marketing Times,* Vol. 28 (March 1981), pp. 28–34. For women, see John Molloy, "He Tells Women How to Dress for Sales," *Sales and Marketing Management,* Vol. 119, No. 8 (November 14, 1977), pp. 36–38.

FIGURE 9.1 The importance of dress. Which of these people would you feel more comfortable buying an expensive product from?

Although conservative clothing of good quality is a general rule, you should also be careful not to overdress to the point that your customers feel you are talking down to them. Again, appropriate dress depends on your audience.

Paralanguage Paralanguage is another dimension of the nonverbal messages you send. "Paralanguage consists of nonverbal vocal elements such as laughing, crying, throat clearing, inflection, volume, tone, rate, pitch, and enunciation. In short, any sound or variation in sound patterns is paralanguage because it communicates a nonverbal message."[11] Paralanguage reflects the way you speak—the emphasis, tone, and inflection of your voice. Notice how the meaning of the following sentences changes as you place the emphasis on the underlined word.

I want to buy an expensive stereo. (*not you but me*)

I <u>want</u> to buy an expensive stereo. (*I'm really serious*)

I want to <u>buy</u> an expensive stereo. (*not rent or be given*)

[11]Joel P. Bowman and Bernadine P. Branchow, *Understanding and Using Communication in Business* (New York: Harper and Row, 1977), p. 154.

TABLE 9.7
DRESS FOR SUCCESS FOR MEN

- If you have a choice, dress affluently.
- Always be clean.
- If you are not sure of the selling circumstances, dress more—rather than less— conservatively.
- Never wear school or masonic rings, ties connected with a particular area, political buttons, or religious symbols, unless you are absolutely certain that buyers share these beliefs.
- Always dress as well as the people to whom you are selling.
- Never put anything shiny or greasy on your hair.
- Pay special attention to the fit of your clothing.
- In general, wool or wool-blend suits are best.
- Do not wear short-sleeve shirts for business purposes.
- Ties are important as a symbol of respectability and responsibility.
- Clothes may be used to overcome liabilities of physical appearance.
- Never wear nonfunctional jewelry. Keep away from big rings and gaudy cuff links.
- Always carry a good attache case.
- If you have a choice, wear an expensive tie.
- Never take off your suit jacket unless you have to. It weakens your authority.
- Whenever possible, look in the mirror. You will be surprised at how many flaws you will catch—hair out of place, or a stain on your shirt.

SOURCE: Adapted from John T. Molloy, "Clothes: Your First and Last Salestool," *Marketing Times*, Vol. 28 (March 1981), pp. 28–34; and John T. Molloy, *Dress for Success* (New York: Warner Books, 1975).

I want to buy an <u>expensive</u> stereo. (*not a cheap one*)

I want to buy an expensive <u>stereo</u>. (*not a tape recorder*)

The tone of your voice and your emphasis are important in delivering your message. Your voice has an impact on the messages you send.[12] A number of different aspects of your voice will affect your messages. You must speak loudly enough to be heard but not so loudly that you overpower the prospect. You can also raise or lower your volume. For instance, raising your voice may indicate enthusiasm. The speed at which you talk can be very influential; you should vary your rate depending on the situation. You can slow down at important points or even pause after you have made an important point. Speeding up your presentation may also convey enthusiasm.

It is important to pronounce words correctly and enunciate clearly so that your message will be interpreted properly. Your voice should also vary in tone; a monotone delivery will only bore your prospects.[13]

[12]For more information, see Dorothy Sarnoff, *Speech Can Change Your Life* (New York: Doubleday, 1970).

[13]For some good exercises in improving your tone and speech, see Ralph Aiello, "Shape up Your Voice and Sharpen Your Presentations," *Specialty Salesman*, Vol. 71, No. 10 (October 1982), pp. 12–14.

TABLE 9.8

DRESS FOR SUCCESS FOR WOMEN

Always

- Wear a skirted suit for business.
- Tailor your clothing to the demands of your job and your company.
- Wear upper-middle-class clothing.
- Wear plain pumps in the office.
- Wear neutral-colored pantyhose to the office.
- Wear a coat that covers your skirt or dress.
- Carry an executive gold pen.
- Ask yourself whom you are going to meet and what you are going to do before you get dressed.

Never

- Be the first in your office to wear a fashion. Fashion fails.
- Wear anything sexy to the office.
- Wear a knit polyester pantsuit.
- Wear pants when you are dealing with men in business.
- Dress like an "imitation man."
- Carry a handbag when you could carry an attache case.
- Wear a midi unless it is a raincoat or a coat worn over a long dress.
- Buy a fad item.
- Let the fashion industry dictate skirt length in your businesswear.
- Take off your jacket in the office.
- Wear designer glasses.
- Wear a vest for business.
- Make an emotional decision about a piece of clothing when an intellectual decision is possible.

SOURCE: Adapted from John T. Molloy, *The Woman's Dress for Success Book.* (New York: Warner Books, 1977), pp. 185–186.

Mirroring is also an excellent skill for creating and maintaining rapport. You can use mirroring to match a customer's voice, tone, voice tempo, words, posture, gestures, and even breathing rate.[14] By matching the customer you will make them feel more comfortable. Keep this mirroring subtle enough to avoid creating the impression that you are mimicking the customer. Often you will find that simply adjusting your tone of voice or rate of speech to the customer's level, rather than trying to match the customer exactly, will create the desired rapport. For instance, if a customer talks at a very fast pace, you would speed up your delivery to match this pace.

Eye contact Eye contact is also an important and sensitive tool. Failure to maintain eye contact will make you seem cold and disinterested. On the

[14]H. Stanley Connell III "NLP Techniques for Salespeople," *Training and Development Journal* (November 1984), p. 44.

*"A word to the wise, Mr. Putnam. Mr. Dalrymple hates
salesmen who wear double knits."*

© Sales & Marketing Management

other hand, too much eye contact may make the prospect feel uncomfortable
or self-conscious. Good eye contact on your part conveys interest and sincerity; avoiding eye contact is associated with insincerity. Generally you should
have more eye contact when you are listening than when you are talking,
this indicates that you are interested in the prospect.

Facial expressions Your facial expressions are a key indicator of your attitudes and feelings. Sometimes it is necessary to hide your feelings, and in
these cases you need to control your facial expression. Although you can try
to hide your feelings by faking facial expressions, you must be careful because you may reveal your true feelings with even small expressions such as
a quick frown or smile.

Notice the meanings that are conveyed by the faces in Figure 9.2. What
is the person feeling in each of the four situations pictured? Even small
changes in your facial expressions can communicate. Raising or lowering
your eyebrows, heavy lines in your forehead, or glassy eyes can all convey

FIGURE 9.2 Facial expressions can tell you a lot about your prospect.

your feelings. Thus you must be aware of these signals and try to manage them.

Gestures The way you hold your hands, arms, and legs, and the way you sit all communicate. You must be aware of the messages you are sending by your gestures. John Malloy, after watching tapes of good and poor salespeople, noted that "good salespeople were calmer. Their body movements were smooth and unhurried. They made no jerky motions, particularly when they were handing a contract or a pen across the table."[15] Gestures such as clenched fists, wringing hands, or folded arms all communicate meaning to your prospects, no matter what you are saying. You must be aware of the gestures you are exhibiting, and you should try to make them seem as natural and compatible with what you are communicating as possible.

Handshake Your handshake also communicates part of your image. If your handshake is flimsy and limp, you will not be seen very positively. On the other hand, a bone-crushing handshake accompanied by a slap on the back may make the customer feel uncomfortable. Your handshake should be firm

[15]See John T. Molloy, *Live For Success* (New York: Perigord Press, 1981), p. 94.

but not too firm. In addition, when you shake hands, you should look the customer or prospect in the eye.[16]

Posture Your posture also communicates. If you slouch, you will convey that you are interested in neither your product nor what your prospect has to say. Alternatively, leaning forward and looking interested are important aspects of your believability. A stiff and rigid posture may make your prospects feel uneasy. Although posture is relatively simple to control, it is easy to forget and slouch, or to communicate an unintended meaning by posture. See, for example, Figure 9.3.

WHAT'S IN A HANDSHAKE?

The message you communicate with a handshake is a function of four factors.

1. Degree of firmness.	Generally speaking, a firm handshake will communicate a caring attitude, and a weak grip communicates indifference.
2. Depth of interlock.	A full, deep grip will communicate friendship to the other person.
3. Duration of grip.	There are no specific guidelines to tell you what the ideal duration of a grip should be. However, by extending the duration of the handshake, you can often communicate a greater degree of interest and concern for the other person.
4. Eye contact during handshake.	Visual communications can increase the positive impact of your handshake. Maintaining eye contact throughout the handshaking process is important when two people greet each other.

SOURCE: Reprinted with permission of Coop Farmland Industries, Inc.

Space Another dimension of nonverbal communications over which you may have some control is *proximetics*, or the study of space. If you get too close to prospects, you may make them feel uncomfortable and they may feel

---

[16]For a more in-depth discussion of the handshake as nonverbal communication, see Allan Pease, *Signals:* How to Use Body Language for Power, Success and Love (New York: Bantam Books, 1984), pp. 44–53.

FIGURE 9.3 What does this posture indicate about how interested this person is in what you are saying?

"Reprinted, by permission of the publisher, from LISTENING MADE EASY, by Robert L. Montgomery, pp. 36–37, © 1981 AMACOM, a division of American Management Association, New York. All rights reserved.

you are too aggressive. On the other hand, if you are too far away, you will seem cold and will find it difficult to communicate. According to Molloy, "good salespeople didn't come physically close to their clients until they could do it without offending. Sales to them was a process of getting closer, of breaking down barriers. Poor salespeople, on the other hand, invaded other people's territory, touched them in ways they found objectionable and turned them off completely."[17] To the extent possible, you need to conduct

[17]See John T. Molloy, *Live for Success* (New York: Perigord Press, 1981), p. 95.

the interview at a distance where you feel comfortable and, more importantly, where your prospects feel comfortable.

If you appear to be uneasy when you come into contact with an important prospect, you are indicating a lack of confidence in yourself or your product. The way you enter a prospect's office also indicates your confidence. The quicker you enter, the greater your perceived status. On the other hand, if you are timid about entering, or stop and wait to enter, your perceived status will be reduced. If you stop halfway to the desk, you indicate confidence, and if you stop in front of the desk, you indicate that you feel you have equal status with the executive.[18]

Your seating arrangement with the prospect is also important. Although you do not always have control of the seating arrangement, you must strive for the proper arrangement if possible. There are three common seating arrangements in a sales environment: across the table, corner to corner, and side by side.[19]

Across the table A seating arrangement in which you and the prospect sit across the table from each other provides the prospect with the security of a barrier and is generally used in more competitive situations or when you do not know the prospect well (see Figure 9.4a). Depending on your distance, you should still be able to pick up and send nonverbal messages.

Corner to corner In a corner-to-corner arrangement you sit beside the prospect's desk (see Figure 9.4b). This arrangement makes conversation easy, allows for eye contact, and enables you to pick up and send other nonverbal messages.

Side by side In the side-by-side arrangement you are seated beside the prospect (see Figure 9.4c). This arrangement is generally used for cooperative problem solving, such as when you are reviewing a proposal, working out the details of a contract, or examining a diagram. This situation tends to be a sign of trust, as you are typically closer than normal. However, reading nonverbal expressions is very difficult.

Time A final nonverbal message that you send is your respect for time. It is important to remember that someone is always in charge of time. In the buying–selling relationship this is usually the buyer. If you are late for a sales call, you may seriously hamper your chances for a successful sale. Similarly, at the end of a call you must respect prospects' time and show them that you respect it.

Putting it all together An important point is that all your nonverbal actions taken together will be interpreted to give the prospect a feeling for your true meaning. For example, Table 9.9 indicates several nonverbal behaviors that might be associated with warmth or coldness on your part.

[18]See Albert Mehrabian, *Silent Messages* (Belmont, Calif.: Wadsworth, 1971), pp. 24–39.
[19]Adapted from Phillip C. Hunsaker, "Communicating Better: There's No Proxy for Proxemics," *Business*, Vol. 30, No. 2 (March–April 1980), pp. 41–48.

A. Across the table

B. Corner to corner

C. Side by side

FIGURE 9.4 Seating Arrangements

TABLE 9.9

IMPRESSIONS CREATED BY NONVERBAL BEHAVIORS

	IMPRESSION	
BEHAVIOR	WARMTH	COLDNESS
Tone of voice	Soft	Hard
Facial expression	Smiling, interested	Poker-faced, frowning, disinterested
Posture	Lean toward others, relaxed	Lean away from others, tense
Eye contact	Look into others' eyes	Avoid looking into others' eyes
Touching	Friendly handshake	Avoid touching other person
Gestures	Open, welcome	Closed, guarding oneself and keeping others away
Spatial distance	Close	Distant

SOURCE: David W. Johnson, *Reaching Out: Interpersonal Effectiveness and Self Actualization*, second edition (Englewood Cliffs, N.J.: Prentice-Hall, 1981), p. 136. Copyright © 1981. Reprinted with permission by Prentice-Hall, Inc., Englewood Cliffs, N. J.

SUMMARY

Each part of a sales call is very important and is developed upon the basis already established in preceding sales call activity. If the initial impression conveyed in the approach is not favorable, the presentation will not be well received. Conversely, if a favorable set is established at the start, the presentation is likely to go well. The presentation, though not any more important than any other part, is perhaps the "core" of a sales call.

The first step for a good presentation is preparation. One way of being sure all the important points are covered and related to the prospect's or customer's needs is to develop four benefit matrices: one about your company, one about the product group, one about the available associated services, and one about your company's people. You can then use elements from these matrices as the basis for an individualized presentation.

The four criteria used to evaluate a presentation are understandability, interest, believability, and persuasiveness. An effective presentation must meet all four of these criteria. The key factors to consider in understandability include individual differences in perception and attention span, your ability to think concretely, the customer's state of mind, and the way the customer processes information.

The next criterion is interest. Relevant considerations here are the educational level of prospects, their life values, keeping their attention, and using "you" appeal. The third criterion is believability. Factors considered important in establishing believability are your image, your personal conviction and sincerity, overlearning the presentation, reassuring the prospect, and the use of testimonials. The final criterion, persuasiveness, is accomplished by suggestion and by reasoning. The decision of which to use in any specific sales call depends on strategic as well as tactical considerations. Strategic considerations include the customer's or prospect's personality and motivation, urgency of the buying decision, prior selling–buying relationships, products and services being offered, relative size of the proposed purchase, and prior knowledge of the goods being sold. Tactical considerations are the mood of the person, your rapport, and his or her attention level.

Your suggestions may be direct or indirect, and positive or negative. Generally it is better to make suggestions that are indirect and positive. The effectiveness of suggestions depends on the prestige of the suggestor, how many people make them, the prospect's degree of interest or disinterest, the absence of opposing ideas, repetition of suggestions, the prospect's lack of information, your successful previous performance, and the appropriate wording of the suggestion.

During your verbal presentation, you are also sending nonverbal messages by your dress, paralanguage, eye contact, facial expressions, gestures, handshake, posture, the space between you and the customer, and your respect for time. Each of these communicates messages to your prospects. If your verbal and nonverbal messages conflict or if your nonverbal communications are not viewed positively by your customers and prospects, no matter what you say, your presentations will not be effective.

PROBLEMS

1. You have been asked to address a group of high school seniors to influence them to enroll at your college or university. Prepare a benefit matrix as a basis for your presentation.
2. Prepare a checklist of principles, methods, and techniques peculiar to each of the four criteria of an effective presentation.
3. Give at least one example of each of the following kinds of suggestions: direct, indirect, positive, negative.
4. What traits of the customer would be influential in the salesperson's decision to use reasoning versus suggestion?
5. What nonverbal communications could salespeople send to increase the possibility of a sale?

EXERCISE 9

Objective: To apply the *matrix* method to a company offering.

Continue your role as a salesperson handling a well-known line of young ladies' fashions. (See Exercise 8.) Work out entries for each benefit matrix. (You may wish to peruse recent issues of such magazines as *Mademoiselle* and *Seventeen* for ideas.)

PART A Your Firm as a Source

FEATURE	BENEFITS	ALTERNATE WAYS OF EXPRESSING
1.	1a. _____	
	1b. _____	
2.	2a. _____	
	2b. _____	
3.	3a. _____	
	3b. _____	

PART B Your Product Line

FEATURE	BENEFITS	ALTERNATE WAYS OF EXPRESSING
1.	1a. _____	
	1b. _____	
2.	2a. _____	
	2b. _____	
3.	3a. _____	
	3b. _____	

PART C Your Associated Services

FEATURE	BENEFITS	ALTERNATE WAYS OF EXPRESSING
1.	1a. _____	
	1b. _____	
2.	2a. _____	
	2b. _____	
3.	3a. _____	
	3b. _____	

FEATURE	BENEFITS	ALTERNATE WAYS OF EXPRESSING
1.	1a. _____	
	1b. _____	
2.	2a. _____	
	2b. _____	
3.	3a. _____	
	3b. _____	

Case 9-1 Robinson's Carriage House

Marjorie Smith is a young college graduate on the sales staff of Robinson's Carriage House, one of the finest furniture stores in the greater Providence area. She has worked there for almost two years and has built up a following. In fact her principal source of leads is referral by satisfied customers.

A well-dressed, middle-aged woman enters the store and asks for Marge by name. Marge comes to the front of the store, greets the caller, and introduces herself.

MRS. JOHNSON: Mrs. Smith, I'm Mrs. Johnson and I've been recommended to you by my good friend and neighbor, Betty Jarrett. She sure thinks a lot of you.

MARGE: Mrs. Johnson, I'm delighted to meet you. Please call me Marge. Mrs. Jarrett is very kind. Doesn't she have a lovely home?

MRS. JOHNSON: She certainly does. She told me that you recommended several excellent pieces to her for her living room.

MARGE: Yes. One of the reasons her living room is so attractive is the mix of woods and fabrics.

MRS. JOHNSON: I certainly agree with you, Marge. I'm really here to see you and your store. Right now I'm not planning to buy. However, my husband and I are thinking of replacing our dining room set. It's been in use a long time. The years fly by. We have our twenty-fifth wedding anniversary coming up a few months from now.

MARGE: Congratulations. You certainly must have married very young. If you can spend a few minutes, I would like to show you through the store. We're very proud of Robinson's and the high-quality furniture we carry. You probably know that Jim Robinson is the third generation of his family to run the business. Every piece in the store has been approved by our interior decorator and Mr. Robinson, himself.

The two women stroll through room settings of dining room furniture.

MRS. JOHNSON: Marge, that certainly is an attractive dining room set.

MARGE: Yes, Mrs. Johnson, we just got that in. Mr. Robinson saw it at the last market and felt it was one of the best-designed sets he had seen in years.

MRS. JOHNSON: What's the price on it?

MARGE: Well, Mrs. Johnson, you have fine taste. It's the top set now in stock and a great value. It sells for $4400.

MRS. JOHNSON: My, that is a lot of money.

MARGE: Well, often the best is the least costly in the long run. It will give you the many years of service your present set has provided you. You'll be proud, too, knowing you have the very best.

MRS. JOHNSON: I certainly do like it, Marge.

MARGE: Mrs. Johnson, may I be presumptuous? I'd very much like to see your home before you buy anything, so that I may serve you better.

MRS. JOHNSON: Why, Marge, that surely is nice of you. Let's finish our tour, and we'll go now if that's all right. It will only take us a few minutes to drive out, and I'll be glad to bring you back.

MARGE: Oh, that's wonderful. Let me tell Mr. Robinson I'll be out of the store.

1. What has Marge accomplished so far?
2. What might have improved her efforts?

Case 9-2 WMSU (FM)

Bill Carr is a one-man sales force for WMSU. The station features classical and semiclassical music and provides a national and local news summary four times a day. It is on the air from 7 A.M. to 11 P.M. The city and suburban population is about 300,000. The urban area is heavily industrial; the suburbs are mainly "bedroom" communities. WMSU is one of three FM stations in the local market. The others feature country and rock, respectively. The reach of the signal is about 20 to 25 miles.

Bill keeps an active prospect file, and about two-thirds of his time is devoted to calling on them. He has obtained an appointment to see the head of a general insurance agency.

Set forth below are the notes he made for preparing his presentation.

WHAT I KNOW ABOUT THE PROSPECT?

Company:	Hughes Insurance
Head:	Mr. J. W. Hughes
Time in business:	18 years

Size: About 15 employees

Reputation: Excellent; Mr. Hughes well known and active in the community

Other: WMSU carries casualty policy with Hughes

WHY SHOULD HUGHES ADVERTISE ON WMSU?

Caters to people of substance and culture.

Has an excellent reputation.

Is independent, locally owned business.

Programs convey image of good taste.

At present no other insurance advertising.

Rates are competitive.

Will provide free assistance in preparing commercials.

One exclusive news sponsorship now available.

Prepare a benefit matrix for Bill, based on his notes.

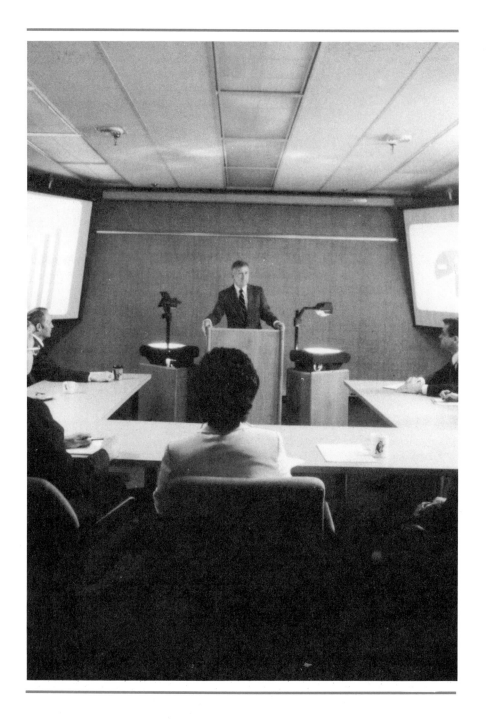

Supporting Your Message: Visual Aids and Demonstrations

After studying this chapter, you should be able to

1. Identify various kinds of visual aids.
2. Specify the considerations for using visuals.
3. Describe how to construct and use visuals.
4. Know the advantages of various demonstration sites.
5. Discuss when during the call a demonstration should be used.
6. Point out principles of learning that are applicable to the demonstration.
7. State various guidelines for using a demonstration.

VISUAL AIDS AND DEMONSTRATIONS

Regardless of how well you speak, you can increase your effectiveness by using visual aids to reinforce your message. This chapter examines various types of visual aids and offers suggestions for their use and development. It also examines demonstrations of the product, including location, timing, and suggestions for making demonstrations work for you. These sales aids can be a key factor in your sales presentation, but you must know when and how they can best be used and be aware of their relation to the rest of the presentation.[1]

VISUAL AIDS

Several considerations for the use of visual aids are presented in this section, along with different types of visuals, suggestions for their effective use, and guidelines for visuals using words.

Considerations for the Use of Visual Aids

The primary considerations for choosing visual aids are the individual differences that exist between auditory and visual learning, summation and selectivity of perception, memory, and professionalism.

Auditory versus visual learning As you plan your presentation to meet the basic criteria of understandability, interest, believability, and persuasiveness, you may ask, "Is there anything I can show the prospect that will enhance any of these criteria?" For instance, an equipment salesperson might decide that a diagram of a machine will help the prospect understand how the equipment is designed and why it is virtually maintenance-free. The same salesperson might use a miniaturized model of the equipment to arouse or maintain interest in the presentation. Then the salesperson might attempt to achieve believability by showing pictures of the equipment in operation in a situation similar to the prospect's. Finally, the salesperson might take the prospect to see the equipment in actual use. Visual aids not only supplement the oral presentation with additional information but also provide contrast that helps maintain the prospect's attention.

Summation and selectivity Sales aids capitalize on two aspects of perception—summation and selectivity. When you enable the prospect to see as well as to hear, you increase the likelihood of getting your message across; this is the summative nature of perception. Selectivity is utilized by deliberately designing the visual device to direct the prospect's attention to specified characteristics of the product. For example, the equipment salesperson might have a diagram of each component of the equipment; each diagram would be used to direct the prospect's attention to one or two ideas at a time.

---

[1]See, for example, Stephen C. Rafe, "Problems and Pitfalls of Using AV," *Public Relations Journal*, Vol. 35, No. 9 (September 1979), pp. 12–14.

Memory Forgetting is as much an active process as learning, and visuals can be very effective in helping people remember. When relying on spoken words alone, people retain only 10 percent of what they hear. Adding appropriate visual aids to accompany your speaking increases the retention rate to about 50 percent.[2]

Often there is a lapse between the time a salesperson conveys information and the time the other person uses it. This challenges you to reinforce your ideas so that prospects have no trouble remembering them. Because sales aids are an important means to accomplish this, many firms furnish their sales representatives with items they can leave with the customer or prospect. For example, one steel company provides its customers and prospects with one-foot rulers made of stainless steel. Imprinted on each ruler is the company's name, address, and phone number as well as similar information about the salesperson managing the account. Pharmaceutical salespersons often provide samples of their products to physicians, who can then prescribe them on a trial basis for patients who require such medication.

Added professionalism Effectively used visuals also show that you are prepared and organized, and they make your presentation more professional. However, visuals must be developed carefully and professionally. Visual aids also act as prompters for you during a presentation. They may serve to keep you organized and to ensure that you do not skip or forget important points. Thus, they make your delivery more professional.

Different Types of Visuals

A wide variety of audiovisual aids are available to you, ranging from very simple and inexpensive aids to very sophisticated and expensive devices. The audiovisual aids summarized in Table 10.1 are examined next.

Flip charts Flip charts are excellent for making presentations to small groups of customers or prospects. One advantage of the flip chart is that it is portable

TABLE 10.1
VARIOUS TYPES OF VISUALS

Flip chart	Diagrams
Sales portfolio	Mock-ups
Brochures	Miniaturized models
Overhead transparencies	Samples
Slides	Tests
Films	Demonstrations
Pictures	

[2]B. Y. Auger, "Use Visualization in Sales," *Specialty Salesman*, Vol. 70, No. 1 (January 1981), p. 8.

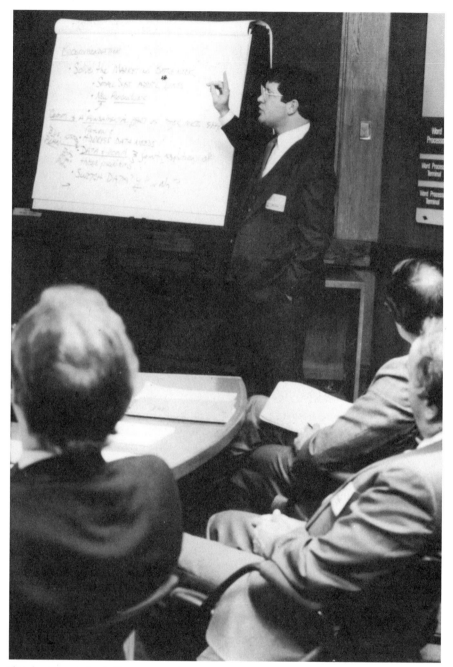

Flip charts can help clarify a presentation.

and requires no additional equipment.[3] Flip charts can be prepared prior to the call or can be used on the spot with a felt-tipped pen for making points during a presentation. Planned ahead, they can be artistic, colorful, and easy to read.

Sales portfolios A sales portfolio is a package of visual aids usually prepared by your firm to supplement your presentation. The portfolio could include pictures, product benefits, graphs, or charts. Often the visuals are arranged in a looseleaf binder that is easy to use and can be customized to the call being made.

Brochures Brochures can be a useful sales aid that can provide basic information about your firm and summarize technical aspects of your product. They may also have pictures, which can be useful in your presentation, and they are good items to leave with prospects to reinforce your information.[4] Brochures can also be used as a tool to make appointments, by securing the prospect's attention. A letter and accompanying brochure may briefly explain your company and say that you will call for an appointment.

SUGGESTIONS FOR HANDLING LITERATURE

■ Point.	This calls attention to the specific place where you want the customer to look.
■ Underline.	This is more dramatic than pointing. It makes a lasting impression.
■ Keep the literature out of sight.	Hold literature back until you are ready to use it. It is distracting to talk about one point while the literature is open to a different page.
■ Read upside down.	This allows you to refer to points without taking the piece from the customer.
■ Maintain control.	Don't let the customer take the literature from you. The customer will start leafing through it and stop listening.

SOURCE: Reprinted with permission of Davis-Geck, an American Cyanamid Company.

---

[3]Dean M. Wood, "Back to Basics Has Garlock O.E.M. Salesmen Flipping Over Flip Chart," *Industrial Marketing*, Vol. 59, No. 1 (January 1974), pp. 42–45.

[4]Louis Scott, "Is Your Literature a Real Sales Tool—or Just Another Leave-Behind?" *Industrial Marketing*, Vol. 62, No. 10 (October 1977), pp. 106–108.

Overhead transparencies Overheads are an inexpensive useful way to supplement a presentation. Portable overhead projectors are available, and transparencies can be made on copiers. Overheads can be utilized to show a wide variety of graphs, charts, tables, drawings, and diagrams.

Another advantage of overheads is flexibility in making your presentation. You can have backup overheads for anticipated objections, and you can skip an overhead if you are pressed for time.

In a study done at the Wharton Applied Research Center, people who used overhead projectors to make their presentations were perceived as significantly better prepared, more professional, more persuasive, more credible, and more interesting. Furthermore, decisions concerning the presentations were made faster and responses were more favorable than for those that did not use transparencies.[5]

When reproducing overheads, care should be taken to make sure that they are of high quality and that they are large enough to be seen. If very high quality is sought, you can have the masters typeset. Transparencies can also be reproduced in color to add interest to your presentation. Another useful technique is to frame your transparencies with cardboard frames so that you can jot down notes and figures on the sides. These can act as useful prompters for you.

Slides Slides are a good way to show previous jobs or a wide variety of ideas.[6] Slides can even be made on personal computers at a relatively low cost.[7] If you are going to use slides, make sure you have the proper equipment available and that the room can be darkened sufficiently. Although slides can enhance the presentation, once your slides are in the tray, you are literally locked into your presentation. Slides are the most useful when motion and flexibility are not important.

Films Some firms have developed films or videotapes to supplement their sales presentations.[8] Films are useful because they appeal to the prospect's sense of both sight and sound. Movies can show products in use and may also be used to show advertisements. Caterpillar, for instance, uses audiovisual presentations to show the "nuts and bolts," "facts and figures" about the company's product line.[9] A number of different types of portable projectors are available for you to use in your sales presentation.

---

[5]*How to Present More Effectively and Win More Favorable Responses from More People in Less Time* (St. Paul, Minn.: 3M Company).

[6]For a good description of how to put together a good slide show, see David Coleman, "On Your Own," *Real Estate Today*, Vol. 13, No. 1 (January 1980), pp. 49–54; or Sandra Kieckhafer, "How to Prepare a Successful Slide Presentation," *Public Relations Journal*, Vol. 39, No. 9 (September 1983), pp. 17–18.

[7]See, for example, Larry Riggs, "Computer-Generated Slides High-Tech, Low Cost," *Sales and Marketing Management*, Vol. 134, No. 1 (January 14, 1985), pp. 81–86.

[8]"American Saw goes to the Video Tape," *Sales and Marketing Management*, Vol. 126, No. 2 (February 2, 1981), pp. 46–50.

[9]"Video Becoming a Key Factor in Selling to Industry," *Industrial Marketing*, Vol. 63, No. 5 (May 1978), p. 21.

Pictures Photographs may be a useful way to supplement your message. Color pictures are preferable to black and white; they should be realistic and do the product justice. It is better to show the product in its normal use or setting rather than in isolation. Blowups or enlargements of parts may be used to show details.

Diagrams Diagrams are extremely useful for conveying ideas about highly technical products. Different colors may differentiate each component or system for clarity. These may be printed on transparent sheets and mounted in sequence. This method enables you to begin with the basic chassis of the equipment and build onto it the various systems and components, until you finally show the complete unit.

Mock-ups The advantage mock-ups have over pictures and diagrams is that they are three-dimensional portrayals of the product. People with limited space perception have difficulty visualizing in three dimensions from the two dimensions provided by pictures and diagrams. Although mock-ups should be realistic to be effective, they are normally oversimplified compared to the product itself, in that they are designed to reflect only the product's important features.

Miniaturized models Miniaturized models differ from mock-ups in that they are exact scaled-down replicas of the product. They have the obvious advantage of greater realism, but they may convey too much information all at once. The cost of such items may prevent their use in many situations.

Samples For the salesperson of small consumer and industrial goods, the best sales aid is the product itself. However, you must not distribute the samples so widely that they cut into your sales. If you are too generous with samples, small users may accept them instead of purchasing the product.

Tests In many fields of selling, especially industrial, your presentation can be reinforced by reports of product testing done by independent laboratories. A chemical salesperson may produce a copy of a report showing that a product exceeds government specifications of purity. Similarly, a pharmaceuticals salesperson may furnish a report from a medical journal indicating the effectiveness of a drug.

You can use testing in another way, by persuading the prospect's firm to use its facilities to test a sample of the product. If the firm does plan a test, you should be present to ensure that it is performed properly and fairly. You can also try to influence the decision makers who are present. On the basis of the favorable results, you can ask for an order immediately. If the results are unfavorable, however, you can take immediate steps to restore your position. If the prospect is reluctant to have you present, you should follow up and seek a report on the tests. It is easy for a firm to promise to test a product and then forget to do so.

Showing samples helps prospects to visualize.

Demonstrations A final visual sales aid is a full-scale demonstration in which you show the product in actual use. The demonstration will be covered later in a separate section.

Suggestions for Effective use of Visual Aids

Incorporating visuals into your presentation may be useful; however, you should observe the following suggestions in order to make them work for you.

Maintain eye contact When using visuals, you should maintain eye contact with your prospects and talk to them, not to the visual. Otherwise you will lose the prospects' attention and will be unable to pick up their nonverbal messages.

Practice You must also practice and become familiar with your visual aids and their use before you put them into your presentation. If you appear unsure of what you are doing and seem disorganized, you will lose your impact.[10] A classic situation in which poor planning and lack of practice can lead to disaster is a slide presentation. If done well, it can be extremely effective. However, if the slides are out of order and do not relate to what you are talking about, they will distract from your presentation and reduce your chances for a successful sale.

Keep possession One important point concerning sales aids is that they must not distract from your presentation. Although a brochure may be a good reminder of your product, if your prospect reads the brochure during your presentation, you have lost control and are in trouble. Generally speaking, the sales aid should remain in your possession so that you can use it to supplement or reinforce your presentation.

Guidelines for Visuals Using Words

One type of visual consists of textual material using words. Several guidelines should be observed in developing these types of visuals.

Emphasize benefits As with most other kinds of sales messages, it is important that visuals emphasize customer benefits as opposed to product features. They must convey to prospects how your product or service can help them.

Make visuals large and legible Visuals should be large enough to be seen by your customers or prospects. If you frequently make presentations to groups, your visuals must be large enough so that the entire group can see your message.

Use professional lettering If at all possible you should try to use professional lettering. Vinyl adhesive letters, large type, transfer letters, or other lettering systems are available at low cost. These lettering systems have the benefit of being very legible, looking professional, and adding to your credibility. It is important that your visuals be as high a quality as possible in order to reinforce your presentation.

Present one idea per visual Limiting each visual to one idea has two benefits. First, visuals are easy to understand because you do not mix various concepts. Second, you can customize your presentation by using various combinations of visuals to make the points you want to stress with each customer.

Use only eight lines When presenting textual materials, you should limit yourself to no more than eight lines per visual. More detail than this tends to get confusing and looks cluttered.

Keep them simple Another key idea when developing visuals is to keep them simple. Your visuals should show only the highlights you want to communi-

---

[10]Jack Falvey and Hervert Nagel, "Pointers for Effective Use of Visual Aids," *Successful Meetings* (September 1983), p. 49.

cate. Too much detail or too many ideas tends to confuse prospects rather than help them understand your presentation.

GRAPHS AND CHARTS

Often you need to introduce statistics into your presentation to make a point. Statistics can be effectively presented using graphs and charts.

Advantages of Graphs or Charts

Statistical relationships can be expressed verbally, in tables, or by means of graphs and charts. As can be seen from Table 10.2, the graphic form of presentation offers several distinct advantages over merely discussing statistics or showing tables. Graphs are more direct, reveal more, convey information more quickly, can be more convincing, and appeal to the prospect.

Graphic Aids Can Confuse the Audience

It is important to note, however, that if a message can be stated just as clearly and convincingly using text or tables, you should not turn to graphs or charts merely because "they look good" or "will help break the monotony." Graphic aids that are clever but are not really needed to clarify or to point up relationships distract from the continuity of your presentation. Moreover, precisely because of their strong dramatic impact, these graphic devices, if overused, may wind up stressing everything, but emphasizing nothing.

When you are deciding whether charts should be used and where, a good starting point is to ask, "Will this chart contribute appropriately to the effectiveness of my presentation?" "Will it communicate my message more quickly and more clearly than other means available?"

Key Elements of Effective Chart Design

Obviously, a salesperson making a presentation to an English-speaking prospect is not going to use visuals written in a foreign language. Such visuals would be self-defeating. For the customer or prospect to gain any benefit from them, you would have to take time out to translate each visual, simply to establish a common ground for understanding.

TABLE 10.2
ADVANTAGES OF THE GRAPHIC FORM OF PRESENTATION

Direct	The mind is presented with a ready-made image.
Revealing	When well designed, the main features of the data are shown at a glance.
Quick	When the key points are highlighted, the audience can focus immediately on what is truly significant.
Convincing	Instead of being merely stated or described, the relations between statistics are demonstrated.
Appealing	A graph attracts the attention of the viewer better than discussion or tables.

Yet, the charts used in many presentations might just as well be written in a foreign language for all their value as aids. Because they are poorly designed, such charts force the salesperson to waste valuable time translating and interpreting them. In such instances, audience impact—and often the message itself—are weakened.

Thus, proper design of charts is not a luxury, but a necessity. In the following discussion the four basic elements of chart designs are illustrated: simple visualization of relationships; clear, easy-to-understand titles; minimum detail; and eye appeal. When combined, these elements contribute substantially to making an effective chart.

Simple visualization of relationships Merely plotting lines on a piece of graph paper does not necessarily make a useful chart. The impact of the design must show the critical relationship borne out by the facts and figures, so that the image emphasizes a specific point. In Figure 10.1 the design does not concentrate on any specific idea. Rather the audience must wait for the speaker to translate the maze of lines into the intended message.

In contrast, Figure 10.2 clearly expresses the relation between the data and their significance. The visualization focuses attention on the specific point the chart is intended to convey. The dark "mountain caps" emphasize the critical elements, and the arrows add to the clarity of the message. Notice that the product unit scales have been omitted in this second exhibit. Quite simply, they were not needed because they did not contribute to the essential point being made with this chart. In short, a good presentation chart should make only one major point at a time. Less important ideas should not detract from the key point.

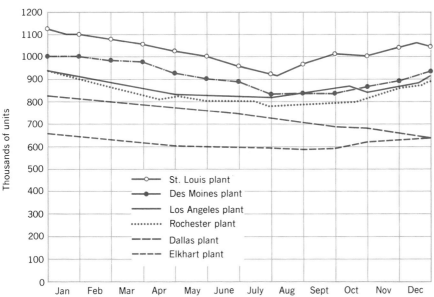

FIGURE 10.1 Unit production in six class "A" plants (January 1, 1987 through December 13, 1987).

Clear, easy-to-understand titles The surest way to make a chart understandable is to say in the title what the chart is trying to illustrate. This way, the message is conveyed quickly, leaving you free to develop details and to point out its significance. Newspaper headlines, which enable the reader to grasp quickly the meaning of a story before actually reading articles, are one familiar example of the value of clear titles.

The title of Figure 10.2 states exactly what the chart is intended to show. It serves to reinforce the impact of the oral message, since the listener reads it and simultaneously hears it from you. You can then proceed to concentrate your time constructively on relating the significance of this particular chart to the rest of your presentation.

Unless a great deal of thought is given to shaping the title, the chart itself can become misleading. Clearly, a title should avoid too much interpretation or editorializing; it should state what the chart has been designed to show. If based on objective facts, however, a degree of interpretation is permissible, and even desirable.

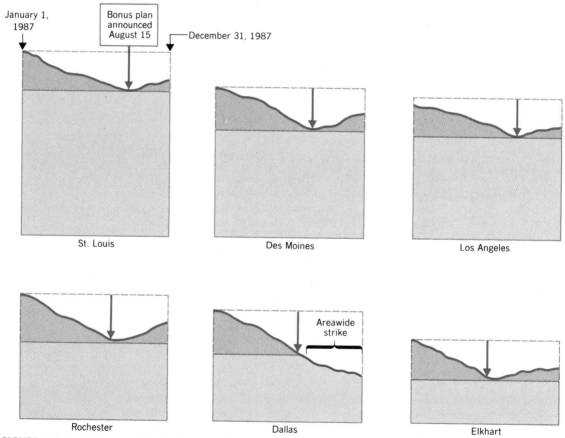

FIGURE 10.2 In all but one of the six class ''A'' plants, the new bonus plan reversed the dropoff in production.

Another important point about graphs or charts is that the axes or variables presented should be labeled clearly on the chart itself, not left up to the speaker to supply. Poorly labeled charts can be very confusing.

Minimum detail Unlike a reference chart, which is used time and again for different purposes, a presentation chart must get the message across quickly. Its function is to communicate in the brief time it is on display. For this reason, you should eliminate any material that does not constructively contribute to the message of the chart. Detailed statistics, excessive lines, lengthy labels, complex footnotes, and extensive sources should be minimized. Since any material included in a chart is open to discussion, excess detail might cause you to explain a point that is of no significance to the presentation.

The rough sketch is an important first step in the process of simplifying a chart design, and in deciding what to include and omit in the finished product. Figure 10.3 is an example of a rough sketch that includes all analytical details and is thus not effective. The figures are computed to decimals, and the source is mentioned. There is no grouping of the elements, and the title merely lists the elements. The intended message is not clear.

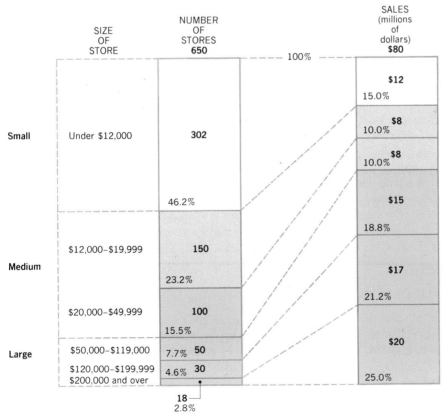

FIGURE 10.3 The number of stores and dollar sales for the United States. SOURCE: U.S. Department of Labor, 1973.

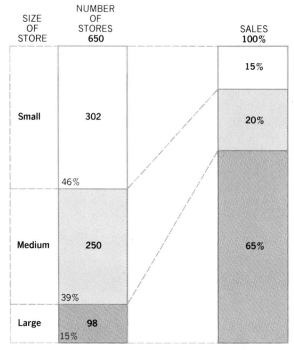

FIGURE 10.4 Only 15 percent of the stores account for 65 percent of the sales.

In contrast, Figure 10.4 is the finished product ready for presentation. The title spells out the critical relationship to be emphasized. All unnecessary elements have been removed. The groupings have been clearly indicated, and shading reinforces the critical segments.

Eye appeal For a chart to serve its purpose, it must attract the attention of the viewer and then hold it. Therefore, a certain amount of eye appeal is mandatory. However, a chart is primarily a medium of communication and not a work of art for art's sake. Its purpose is to convey a message clearly, quickly, and convincingly. It should reinforce the points you want to make rather than distracting from your presentation.

FULL-SCALE DEMONSTRATIONS

In a full-scale demonstration, you show the product in actual use. Several aspects of demonstrations are important, including where to hold them, when to hold them, how they relate to learning, and how to use demonstrations.

Where To Hold Demonstrations
A key consideration for a full-scale demonstration is where it is to be conducted. You may want to hold it on the premises of a satisfied customer, on your own premises, or at the prospect's place of business.

All things considered, the least costly arrangement is to take the prospect to a customer's place of business to see the equipment in use. A key advantage of this, in addition to economy, is the possibility of using testimony of the satisfied customer. On the other hand, there are advantages to conducting the demonstration on the premises of your own firm. This gives you the opportunity to provide VIP treatment and to control the situation fully. In addition, it is likely to cost less than if the demonstration is scheduled at the prospect's place of business. Holding the demonstration at the prospect's location also has advantages, however, because the prospect's people can see the product in use in their own work setting.

If the demonstration is brought to the prospect, you should, of course, check out the equipment to be used to be sure that it is in perfect running condition. If other people from your firm are going to accompany you on the call, you should brief each of them about all phases of the prospective account—what has occurred up until now, what applications are crucial for this account, and who are the decision makers. The demonstration will have greater impact if you can produce something of value to the account in the course of the demonstration. An office equipment salesperson, for example, might do a specified job for the prospect, such as duplicating a memorandum. You should also make sure that the decision-making group in the prospective account is present to observe the demonstration. In addition, if anyone in the account is to participate actively, you should instruct them in advance and give them an opportunity to practice what they are to do before the decision makers arrive.

When To Hold the Demonstration

Although the demonstration may be used at any stage in the selling–buying process, the most logical times are during the initial stage of the sale, at the time of the presentation, or when closing the sale.

The initial stage of the sale The demonstration may be used to begin the call as a dramatic way of gaining attention. If this strategy is used, you must be sure that what is shown is easy to understand and appropriate. If you know from previous calls what competing products are now being used, you may place the demonstration at the beginning of the call to show how favorably your products will contrast with presently used products. An additional consideration for using a demonstration initially may be the restricted amount of time you have for a call. It enables you to get down to business quickly. However, the great danger of placing the demonstration in the first phase of the selling–buying process is that if the other person rejects it, it is difficult to regain a position from which to continue the presentation. One of your major sales points has been used.

During the presentation The usual place for the demonstration is during the presentation itself. Well-conceived visual reinforcements are particularly important if you are to sustain the attention of the prospect for long periods of time. They are also invaluable in providing a change of pace. You must ensure that you synchronize your demonstration with your presentation. It is very easy, for example, for a visual aid to distract from, rather than reinforce, what is being said.

To close Occasionally, the demonstration may be used for closing. That is, you show the prospect the product in use and then ask for the order. In some fields of selling, the product may be left for trial use with a commitment to buy if it measures up to the claims made for it. If this is done, it is imperative that you make sure the personnel in the prospect company fully understand the product, and that any personnel using it are familiar with its operation. You must also avoid being exploited by prospects, who may use this means to obtain free service.

How Demonstrations Relate to Learning

When a demonstration is used, it adds realism and encourages learning on the part of the prospect or customer. Specifically, the demonstration capitalizes on four principles of learning: participation, association, transfer, and insight.

Participation Learning is an active process, and the more actively engaged in the situation prospects are, the more they will learn from it. In a demonstration in which the product in question is shown, prospects have an oppor-

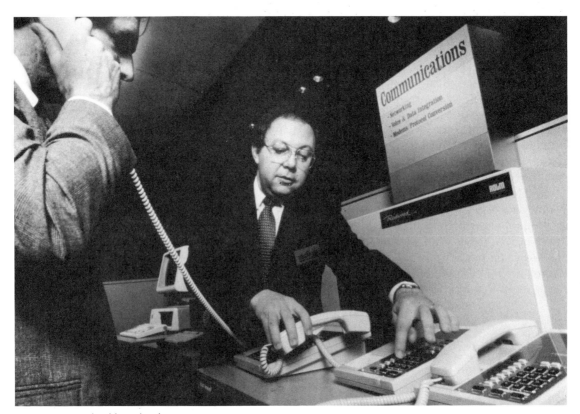

Demonstrations should involve the prospect.

tunity to see how the product performs. To illustrate this, a materials-handling salesperson might have a prospect stand on top of a certain shelving to demonstrate how strong it is. The important point is that involving customers with the product will encourage them to buy.

Association Engaging the prospect's senses in a presentation encourages learning by association. The two inputs for thought process are the past, through memory, and the present, through perception. By using a greater number of stimuli in the presentation, you encourage more ties or associations with the individual's past experience.

For this reason, it is critical that you be aware of the customer's background, so that your demonstrations can draw on the customer's past and facilitate the current sale. A good example of this might be a word-processing salesperson, who demonstrates the word processor by referring to the keyboard and the prospect's past association with the typewriter. Not only would learning be enhanced, but customers could also see how the word processor would make their jobs easier.

Transfer To the extent that demonstrations show the product in use, other people will find it easier to transfer their learning into their own use of the product. Thus, it may be useful for you to try to demonstrate your product under actual conditions in the customer's offices. If this is not possible, other alternatives are arranging for the prospect to view the product in question in another customer's facility, demonstrating the product's use in your firm's test facility, or simply outlining on paper the test results of the product. The first of these alternatives can be particularly effective if the customers are not competing with one another and if you have a very strong and positive relationship with the firm you visit. This transferability of learning from the sales call to on-the-job use is particularly pertinent to technical products and services.

Insight The demonstration also capitalizes on another learning principle—insight. The presentation alone may give the customer or prospect relevant details about the offering, but it may be necessary to use a demonstration to show the big picture—the total impact and use of the products and services. Thus you provide insight into how the product actually works. In this sense the demonstration acts as the "clincher" for the sale. It helps you put into focus all the important points about the product.

How To Use Demonstrations

Properly employed, the demonstration can significantly increase the presentation's effectiveness. Improperly used, it can seriously hurt the selling–buying process. If the following guidelines are observed, the demonstration can contribute much to your success.

Ensure involvement It is very important for your customers or prospects to be involved in the demonstration to ensure that they learn from it. How you involve the prospect is important. If you are demonstrating a word processor to a skilled secretary, you might have her type and correct something. On the other hand, if you are demonstrating the same machine to an executive, you might have her dictate a letter and make corrections. The key principle is to encourage prospects to become involved, but only in aspects of the demonstration that they can do well.

Check out and prepare materials You are responsible for checking out and preparing any materials that will be used in the demonstration. It is better not to use a demonstration than to use one that employs poorly working equipment.[11] Mechanical parts employed in a demonstration can fail to function through no fault of your own and may spoil an otherwise successful sales presentation. A dramatic example of this occurred several years ago at the Paris air show when the Russian Super Sonic Transport crashed while on a demonstration flight. This certainly did not help the Russians' efforts to sell their plane.

Organize materials You must organize the items in your demonstration so that they can be used effortlessly. If you have to fumble for materials, you may lose the attention and interest of the prospect. The smoothness of the presentation, including the demonstration, contributes to its credibility. If it does not go well, it will make you and the customer very nervous. This will give an atmosphere of tension to the selling–buying process, which will hurt your chances of success.

Determine the role of additional people If other personnel from your firm are on hand, you must see that they are briefed on the account and their roles in executing the demonstration. It is better not to have helpers if they are inept in their roles. In the same way, if the prospect's or customer's personnel are to take part in the demonstration, they must be properly instructed and briefed. Since the objective is to show that the product can be used effectively by the customer, advance instruction is imperative.

Synchronize the demonstration in the presentation If the demonstration is not synchronized with the presentation, it becomes a distraction rather than a reinforcement. Materials for the demonstration should not be in view until they are ready for use, and they should be put out of sight once they have served their purpose.

Appeal to several senses One major advantage of the demonstration is its ability to appeal to many senses. The prospect can see, hear, touch, smell, or maybe even taste the product as appropriate. Be sure you engage as many of the prospect's senses as you can. This will help the prospect learn and remember your product.

Practice A dry run of your demonstration is a good idea. The more familiar you are with your product's operation and how to use it, the better job you can do of demonstrating the product.

---

[11]Because of the difficulty of staging demonstrations, some firms have gone to videotape or filming of demonstrations. See, for example, Joseph W. Arwady, "Adding Video and Film to Your Presentation," *Business Marketing*, Vol. 69, No. 4 (April 1984), pp. 104–106.

Repeat the outstanding points Repetition is important. Key points should be reinforced in order to ensure that they are taken in by the prospect.

Tailor the demonstration Each demonstration should be tailored to the prospect's background, personality, motivation, interests, and vocabulary. Only by concentrating on the aspects of the product that the customer is interested in can you keep attention and have a successful demonstration.

Select an appropriate demonstration site The setting for the demonstration site should be as lifelike as possible. For this reason it is desirable (if feasible) to arrange for the demonstration to be made on the prospect's premises; otherwise, there may always be a nagging feeling on the part of the prospect that the demonstration went well but it was under "laboratory" conditions. These doubts about the product can be eliminated if the presentation is done at the prospect's place of business under actual working conditions.

Dramatize without distracting The demonstration should be as dramatic and vivid as possible without being distracting. Sometimes the demonstration becomes so compelling that it distracts from the primary message of the presentation. An example of this is the clever advertising used by a firm for its well-known stomach–headache remedy. Unfortunately, their research showed that prospects all too often become so interested in what was going on in the advertisement that they missed its point. As a result, the company's commercials won several advertising awards, but its sales did not increase.

HOW A DEMONSTRATION OVERCAME AN OBJECTION

A young couple, Bill and Marjory, was looking for a refrigerator. The wife, Marjory, asked the salesperson of a local appliance store for a model with glass shelves. After being shown such a model the husband, Bill, objected that the glass shelves might break when things were placed on them. The salesperson took out a glass shelf and placed it between two vegetable bins which he placed on the floor. He then stood on the glass shelf with all his weight, demonstrating how durable the shelves were. Bill and Marjory bought the refrigerator with the glass shelves.

Review the necessity of the demonstration If the presentation alone is enough to bring about a buying decision, a demonstration may not be necessary. An example of this situation was the attempted sale of a new home. Although the prospects were ready to buy, the salesperson volunteered to take them through the home one more time. Unfortunately, before the visit could take place, the prospects received a call from another realtor and bought another home. Thus, the sale was lost.

Keep the prospects informed If there is a lapse of time between the presentation and the demonstration, you should try to see that the prospect remembers the presentation. The usual way of accomplishing this is to give a prospect some "assignment" associated with the forthcoming demonstration. For example, the prospect may be asked to give to each of the people who will be present at the demonstration a descriptive brochure on the equipment and to instruct each of them to come prepared with questions.

SUMMARY

The importance of using visual aids and demonstrations to help reinforce an oral presentation is an accepted principle in selling, but far too often these auxiliary tools are not used at all or are used improperly. Care must be taken in planning, organizing, and using such techniques to help establish a sale. Several considerations when choosing visuals include auditory versus visual learning, the selective and summative nature of perception, the ability of the visual to enhance memory, and adding professionalism to your presentation.

A number of different visual aids were explored in this chapter, including flip charts, sales portfolios, brochures, overhead transparencies, slides, films, pictures, diagrams, mock-ups, miniaturized models, samples, tests, and full-scale demonstrations. Then suggestions for effective use of visuals were given: maintaining eye contact with the prospect, practicing beforehand, and keeping possession of the visual. Guidelines for developing word visuals were also given. Word visuals should emphasize benefits, be large and legible, utilize professional lettering, be limited to a single idea, have no more than eight lines, and be simple.

Graphs and charts are a good way to present statistics. They can be effective and dramatic but may also be confusing. Effectively designed charts give a simple visualization of critical relationships and have clear, easy-to-understand titles, minimum detail, and eye appeal.

Full-scale demonstrations may be held at the office of a satisfied customer, at your offices, or at your prospect's place of business; each location has advantages. Furthermore, demonstrations may be held at the initial stage of a call, during the presentation, or to close. Effective demonstrations will utilize principles of learning: participation, association, transfer to actual use, and insight. Finally, several guidelines for using demonstrations successfully were examined, including ensuring the prospect's participation, checking out and organizing materials, determining the role of additional parties, synchronizing the demonstration with the presentation, selecting the proper site, making the demonstration dramatic, reviewing the necessity of the demonstration, and keeping the prospect informed during a time lapse between presentation and demonstration.

The test for a good visual demonstration is whether it serves the needs of its intended user and audience. Using techniques suggested in this chapter will help you achieve this result. Such use of demonstrations and visuals will not only sharpen the focus and increase the impact of your message but will also facilitate the task of organizing the material and strengthening the delivery. Further, it will enable you to make full and proper use of your prospect's time.

PROBLEMS

1. In which of your college courses have you observed the most effective use of visuals for reinforcement? Describe them and be specific.
2. To appreciate the need for stimuli other than auditory in communication, sit on your hands and describe a circular staircase. What are your reactions?
3. Scan a current magazine and mark up or clip out ads that illustrate the principles of perception and learning described in this chapter.
4. Formulate a checklist of precautions for a full-scale demonstration. Justify each entry.
5. What type of visual or audiovisual aids would be most appropriate for meeting each of the four criteria of an effective presentation-understandability, interest, believability, and persuasion? Justify your choices.
6. For each of the different types of visuals covered in this chapter, describe a different sales situation for which this type of visual would be appropriate.

EXERCISE 10

Objective: To provide examples of how visuals can be used during a sales call.

Continue your role of selling young ladies' fashions (see Exercises 8 and 9). You have convinced the new owner–manager of the ladies' specialty store that your line has real potential. But, understandably, she does not want to make the decision unless her buyer is as convinced as she is. You are now scheduled to make a presentation to both of them. You have a big stake in this! The following are available as potential ways of reinforcing your sales message.

Indicate which ones you will use and how, why, and when you will use each.

1. Samples of next season's fashions.
2. Color photograph of the firm's display at a recent market.
3. Preprints of ads to be used in national media.
4. Statistical data in table form on company sales versus those of leading competitors.
5. Specimen point-of-sale display unit.

Case 10-1 Carter Chrysler–Plymouth

The Carter Chrysler–Plymouth dealership is located in a medium-sized southwestern community. It competes with three other dealers representing other major auto companies. Mr. Tom Carter is the owner–manager, Jim Harrison is sales manager. Ed Luckman is service and parts manager, and Viola Albertson handles financial and office matters.

Jim Harrison is conducting a sales meeting with Ed Luckman and the sales staff: Bill Baker, George Downing, Ben Lyons, and Pete Smith. "Fellows," says Jim Harrison, "we have a problem. New cars are moving pretty well considering business conditions. However, our used cars are almost standing still. In the past three months we've had to wholesale too many units. I think you know that when we do that we lose money."

Jim continues, "I want to try something different. Effective today, I'm naming you, George, used-car sales manager. You will have complete responsibility for this end of the sales effort. You can feel free to dress up the lot, change anything you like. Just keep 'em moving out."

After the sales meeting, George met briefly with Carter and Harrison. These are his thoughts about the new assignment.

> The attractiveness of our showroom, the company-furnished, multicolored displays, the brochures all help to sell our new cars. What steps can I take to make our used-car lot more attractive? How can I dress up the cars—perhaps feature a daily special?
>
> In selling a new car, the salesperson can negotiate from a known base, the window "sticker." Can I develop something comparable—perhaps a posted "retail book value"?
>
> The big problem is to generate traffic to the lot. What new steps can I take to do this?
>
> What about having each prospect fill out a simple rating sheet each time he takes a trial drive?
>
> What special tools can I provide the salespeople (and myself) for reinforcing our presentations?

1. How should George approach this problem?
2. What are some examples of effective ways he could use demonstrations?

Case 10-2 Selling Vacuum Cleaners Door To Door

Bill Zimmerman feels pretty good. He is ready to start selling in his own territory. He has completed his training with flying colors and is ready to make it big.

His company, Zenith, generates sales leads from inquiries in response to their national advertising. However, each sales representative is expected to prospect on his own.

With some apprehension Bill rings his first doorbell. A middle-aged, pleasant lady greets him.

BILL: Good morning, Ma'am, my name is Bill Zimmerman. May I show you our Zenith cleaner? It's the best in the world.

LADY: Mr. Zimmerman, I'm terribly busy, and besides, I don't need a new vacuum.

BILL: May I help you by cleaning one of your rugs?

LADY: None of my rugs is really dirty.

BILL: Well, Ma'am, our vacuum gets down deep and reaches dust and grit other cleaners miss.

LADY: If it will only take a few minutes you can demonstrate on the hall carpet. (*She shows Bill in.*)

BILL: Incidentally, Ma'am, what is your name?

LADY: I am Mrs. Underwood.

Bill shows Mrs. Underwood how a clean, disposable bag is inserted in the vacuum. He then plugs in the machine. He goes over the carpet very carefully and then stops the machine. He spreads a sheet of white paper on the floor and removes the bag and empties it. Very little dirt has accumulated.

1. What should Bill do next?
2. How might he have provided a more convincing demonstration?

Securing Feedback

After studying this chapter, you should be able to

1. Recognize the importance of feedback.
2. Specify guidelines for asking questions to get feedback.
3. Identify various types of questions.
4. Give reasons why it is important to be a good listener.
5. List guidelines for being a more effective listener.
6. Specify the dimensions of nonverbal feedback.

If you are to communicate effectively with your prospects, you must receive messages as well as send them. As you start to explain the advantages of your products, customers' reactions, questions, gestures, and other nonverbal messages, indicate how interested they are in the sales presentation. Your ability to make effective use of the ongoing interpersonal interaction is largely dependent on your adaptability. Adaptability, in this context, is defined as the ability to make accurate inferences about a potential customer during face-to-face interaction and to modify your behavior in response to these inferences. In addition to being able to enhance your own adaptability, there are three distinct advantages to getting feedback: (1) more accurate communication, (2) an opportunity for the customer to talk, and (3) an indication of which needs to stress.

More accurate communication Continuous feedback lets you know what progress you are making and which points in your presentation need amplification or amendment. As a result, communication is more accurate because you realize when you are getting your message across to the receiver.

An opportunity to talk When you seek feedback, the prospect has an opportunity to talk. The important psychological principle here is that the more prospects participate in a discussion, the more likely they are to agree with the discussion. Another advantage is that active participation tends to be ego-gratifying. As a result, if you ask the right questions, you may get customers to sell the product to themselves.

Which needs to stress A third advantage to getting feedback is that by allowing prospects to talk, you find out which needs to stress and how to stress them. If you listen carefully and watch prospects' nonverbal behaviors, these signals will often tell you what they are looking for or which benefits are important.

In Chapter 9 you saw how to develop your presentation around customer needs. Sending the proper message, however, depends on the specific needs of the buyer. It is important that you get feedback from your prospects in order to determine which benefits to stress and to determine their reaction to what you are saying. You can get feedback from your customers and prospects by asking questions, listening, and observing the prospect's nonverbal behavior, (see Figure 11.1)

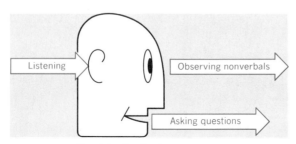

FIGURE 11.1 Receiving feedback.

When you ask questions to get feedback, you want prospects to open up and give you information about their needs or about their reaction to your offering. To be effective in getting prospects to share information with you, you must be sincere and empathic, and you must build rapport with them.

The way you ask questions is also important. Your tone and manner should be friendly and sincere, so that prospects are encouraged to express themselves. Your actions should encourage confidence and understanding. The tone of your voice is very important. If your tone suggests indifference, lack of confidence, distrust, sarcasm, or a know-it-all attitude, your questions will not be effective. On the other hand, a friendly, sincere tone, a pleasant expression, or a sparkle in your eyes can help ensure a good reception to your question.[1]

Guidelines for Feedback Questions
There are several guidelines for designing questions in such a way that you encourage prospects to give feedback.

Feedback questions should not be answerable by a yes or no Questions that can be answered by a yes or no do not give you enough information. For instance, if you ask, "Have you heard about our product?" and prospects respond "yes," you have not learned what they have heard or whether it is positive or negative. A much better question would be, "What have you heard about our product?" Notice that this question cannot be answered by a "yes" or "no.," Another disadvantage of asking questions that are answerable by a "yes" or a "no" is that you also have to ask many more questions, and this may annoy the prospect.

Feedback questions should not be leading Leading questions put words into the prospect's mind, do not encourage honest feedback, and may be perceived as high pressure. A leading question such as "You like our product, don't you?" has several potential negative outcomes. If the prospect disagrees with you and says so, you have an argument, which is not desirable. On the other hand, if the prospect disagrees with you and does not say so, you have a hidden objection, which must be detected in some way later and which is also not desirable. Finally, even if the prospect agrees with you, leading questions may be seen as high pressure and may discourage trust and feedback. A better question to get at the prospect's evaluation of your product would be, "What do you think of our product?"

Feedback questions should be short Long, involved questions tend to be difficult to answer and may cause prospects to lose interest. Questions such as the following are much better.

- What are you looking for in a copier?
- When are you planning to make a decision?

[1] See John S. Randal, "You and Effective Training—Parts 9 and 10: The Art of Questioning/Evaluation," *Training and Development Journal* (December 1978), p. 28.

275

- How do you feel about this color?
- Where do you plan to put this machine?

These short questions are easy to interpret, and they encourage prospects to open up and give you information.

Feedback questions should be limited to a single point Combining too many factors in a question can be confusing and may keep you from obtaining important information. Asking a question like "Do you like our product design, color, energy efficiency, and deliveries?" may confuse the prospect. Should they respond "Yes, no, yes, yes"?

Prospects may fail to answer one of the parts of the question, especially if there is a problem. Their objections to a product may be hidden in this way. If you really want information about these four dimensions, ask four separate questions.

Feedback questions should go from broad to specific When you are dealing with new prospects and you want information, you must start out with broad questions that are applicable to all prospects. For instance, you might say, "Tell me about your business" or "What kind of machinery do you have at present?" Asking these broad questions gives you important information about prospects and helps you avoid asking embarrassing questions or questions they cannot answer. Then, as you get to know prospects better, you can be more specific. Your questions should also lead from one to another or be conversational. For instance, you might say, "That sounds interesting; how does that machinery affect your quality control?" This natural sequencing of questions will make prospects feel comfortable and more likely to open up to you and give you information.

Types of Questions
Several types of questions can help you get information or feedback.

Probes Probes are used to pursue some aspect of a previous statement. For instance, if a prospect says, "I am unhappy with my present supplier," you might say, "Why are you unhappy?" or simply "Why?" Your objective with a probe is to get more information. Probes may be open encouraging discussion; or closed, encouraging a yes or no answer.

Mirror questions Another way to get more information about a prospect's statement is to use a mirror question, sometimes called a reflective question. In this type of question you repeat part of the prospect's statement and let your voice trail off at the end. For instance, if the prospect said, "What I'm really looking for is quality," you might respond "quality?" or "You are looking for quality?" The mirror question encourages the prospect to give you more information by expanding on the previous statements.

"W"-Word questions One way to get information is to use "W"-word questions—questions that begin with <u>who</u>, <u>what</u>, <u>when</u>, <u>where</u>, <u>why</u>, and <u>how</u>. If you ask a person, "Have you heard about our product?" the normal response will be a yes or no. However, if you ask a question such as "What have you heard about our product?" you will get a more complete response with more information. Table 11.1 gives several examples of W-word questions.

Other types of questions Besides getting feedback, questions may also help to verify information, to qualify prospects, to determine their most important needs, to clarify statements, or to close.

Verification Verifying questions are used to check the accuracy of information you have about a customer or prospect. For instance, if you have heard that a prospect is planning on introducing a new product, you might ask, "I understand you are planning on introducing a new product, is that correct?"

OPEN AND CLOSED PROBES

OPEN PROBES
Open probes are used to encourage customers or prospects to talk about their experiences and to uncover the customer's or prospect's attitudes. Here are some examples of open probes.

- What has been your experience?
- When was the last time this happened?
- Where do you turn when this problem comes up?
- Why is this a problem?
- How often do you experience this problem?
- Oh?
- Yes?
- Really?
- Tell me more.

CLOSED PROBES
Closed probes are used to direct attention to a problem that you can solve; they are also used to clarify doubt and to check whether your understanding is accurate. Here are some examples.

- Did you ever experience anything like that?
- Did you ever have this problem?
- Have you ever run into this situation?
- Has this ever happened to you?
- Do I understand you correctly . . . ?
- Are you saying that . . . ?

SOURCE: Reprinted with permission of Formica Corporation.

TABLE 11.1

EXAMPLES OF W-WORD QUESTIONS

- Who in your organization is responsible for ordering supplies?
- What factors do you consider when evaluating a copier?
- When does your current policy expire?
- Where would you put the machine?
- Why are you interested in term insurance?
- How will the machine be used?

Even though this question is generally phrased so that it is answerable by a yes or a no, it gives you valuable information because you do not have to assume you are correct.

Qualification Qualifying questions are used to determine whether you have a potential buyer. For instance, if you were selling copying machines, you might ask, "What type of copying equipment do you presently use?" or "How many copies do you need per month?" These questions are designed to determine whether prospects need the product you are selling.

Need development Need development questions are used to determine which benefits to stress to a prospect. In the copier example, you might ask "What do you look for in a copier?" or "What types of copies do you need?"

Clarification Clarification questions are used to make sure you understand what the prospect is saying. You might say, for example, "Let me see whether I understand what you are saying. Is eliminating downtime in this machine your most important concern?" These questions show that you are concerned about the prospect and may tend to overcome any misunderstanding you may have about what the prospect is saying.

Closing Closing questions are used to ask for an order or for a decision. These questions might be worded as follows: "May I have a purchase order number?" or "When would you like delivery?" In order to get a sale, you must either directly or indirectly ask for the business; these are closing questions. Without closing questions you will not make a sale.[2]

LISTENING

Your effectiveness in getting feedback from your customers and prospects depends on your listening to them. Most people feel that they are good listeners, but they confuse listening with hearing. You hear with your ears but you listen with your mind and body. Most of us hear fairly well; that is, we are able to pick up sounds with our ears. However, listening involves much more. It involves trying to understand what is really being said, conveying

---

[2]See Don Meisel, "Add Salespower! Ask Questions," *Industrial Distribution,* Vol. 65, No. 11 (November 1976), p. 64.

your understanding, and encouraging the other people to clarify their communications. Regardless of how well you hear, if you do not listen, the other person will lose interest and you will be left without anything to hear.

Reasons To Listen

There are several reasons for being a good listener: listening is polite, it helps clarify needs, it helps you identify prospects' personalities, it identifies objections, and if you listen, prospects may sell themselves.

Polite The first reason for listening to your customers or prospects is that it is polite. Conversely, if you do not listen, they will think you are rude and that you do not care about them. Thus, in order to build rapport you must show your prospects that you are listening. A closely related point is that if you are a good listener, prospects will tend to like you and feel you like them.

Dale Carnegie tells about meeting a distinguished botanist at a dinner party and listening carefully as the botanist told about himself and his career. Carnegie said little but encouraged the person to talk. The botanist was later overheard saying that Dale Carnegie was "most stimulating . . . and a most interesting conversationalist."[3]

Help identify needs If you listen to prospects, they will often tell you what they are looking for in a product or service. Information on the prospects' needs tells you what aspects of your offering to stress. Without this knowledge you are merely throwing out sales points and hoping they will hit a need. Given the information, you can proceed to show prospects how your product will satisfy their needs.

Reprinted with permission, Universal Press Syndicate.

[3]See Roland Sandell, "Listening Your Way into Sales Success," *The American Salesman*, Vol. 28, No. 11 (November 1983), p. 3.

Helps identify personality Another benefit of listening is that you can often get good information about prospects' personalities. People like to talk about themselves; they find the subject very interesting. Much of this information comes in parts of the sales call that are more sociable or rapport-building. You might find out a great deal about a prospect by carefully listening over lunch or at a social activity. This information is very useful to you in determining how to sell the prospect.

LISTENING MAKES THE SALE

Bill Jurgens called on the same prospect that several other data-processing marketers had called on. In the process, he had listened to the same reason for not buying at this time: Business wasn't very good. But by concentrated listening, he also heard that conditions to a sale might be different "if we can get a good contract." Five weeks later, Bill read that the firm he had called on had won a large private contract in their area of expertise. He immediately called on the prospect, reminded him of the previous interview, made an appointment for an objective practical demonstration, and closed the sale for seven new video computers. The key to the sale was that the other people calling on the same account swallowed the same old talk, while Bill listened for the clue that could make a future sales order.

SOURCE: See Roland Sandell, "Listening Your Way into Sales Success," *The American Salesman*, Vol. 28, No. 11 (November 1983), p. 4. Reprinted by permission of *The American Salesman*, National Research Bureau, Inc., 424 North Third Street, Burlington, Iowa 52601.

Uncover objections Another reason why listening is important is that you may uncover objections. Prospects may tell you they are not buying for reasons that are based on false or incomplete information. If you listen, you can pick up this information and correct the situation. On the other hand, if you fail to listen, you will face a hidden objection, which is difficult to handle because you do not know what information to provide.

Prospects may sell themselves Generally people like to hear themselves talk. Thus, if you are a good listener, prospects may talk themselves into buying your products. This is especially likely if you have asked questions designed to get them to evaluate their needs and your ability to solve their needs. Letting prospects sell themselves has the advantage of being low pressure. Prospects tend to be very convinced if they reach conclusions in this manner.

Guidelines for Effective Listening

Do not interrupt One common listening problem is to interrupt and finish the other person's sentences. If you do this, watch the other person's reaction. Usually it will be quite negative. Interrupting indicates that you do not value the other person's opinions or that you are impatient for them to finish. Interruption is permissible only when you need clarification. For example, as soon as you hear someone's name after an introduction, you might inquire how to spell it if it is difficult to pronounce. You might want to cushion your interruption with "Pardon me."[4]

Do not let your mind wander Another common listening problem is letting your mind wander. Because most people can listen at a rate about four times as fast as people normally talk, there is often a tendency to let your mind

COMPARING GOOD LISTENER TO BAD LISTENER

THE BAD LISTENER	THE GOOD LISTENER
▪ Tunes out dry subjects.	▪ Seeks opportunities, asks, "What's in it for me?"
▪ Tunes out if delivery is poor.	▪ Judges content, skips over delivery errors.
▪ Tends to enter into an argument.	▪ Withholds judgment until comprehension is complete.
▪ Listens for facts.	▪ Listens for central themes.
▪ Takes intensive notes using only one system.	▪ Takes fewer notes; uses four or five different systems, depending on speaker.
▪ Shows no energy output; attention is faked.	▪ Works hard, exhibits active body state.
▪ Is distracted easily.	▪ Fights or avoids distractions, tolerates bad habits, knows how to concentrate.
▪ Resists difficult expository material; seeks light, recreational material.	▪ Uses heavier material as exercise for the mind.
▪ Reacts to emotional words.	▪ Interprets color words; does not get hung up on them.
▪ Tends to daydream with slow speakers.	▪ Challenges, anticipates, mentally summarizes, weighs the evidence, listens between the lines to tone of voice.

SOURCE: John W. Richter, "Listening, An Art Essential to Success," *Success Unlimited* (September 1980), pp. 22–26.

[4]See Robert L. Montgomery, "Are You a Good Listener?" *Nation's Business,* Vol. 69 (October 1981), p. 68.

wander and to stop listening. Instead, you should use this excess capacity to organize the information you are getting and to understand exactly what the person is saying. You can do two things with your excess listening capacity: focus on the prospect's nonverbal activities to add more information to what you hear, and try to grasp the prospect's intended overall message.

Another thing you must do is resist distractions, such as a room that is too hot or too cold or an uncomfortable seat. Even the prospect's delivery and mannerisms can divert your attention. You might, for example, lose your concentration watching a person play with glasses or fidget with a pencil. Try to ignore mannerisms and instead pay attention to what the prospect is saying. It can be much more difficult to concentrate than to let distractions divert your attention. In this sense listening is hard work; it takes self-discipline.

Finally, there is also a tendency to let your mind wander if you become emotional, for example, when a prospect has an objection or when a close fails. Although the normal tendency in such situations is to stop listening, these are the times you should be listening even more closely.

Do not fake attention Often when you are not really paying attention, you may fake attention by nodding your head, looking at the other person, and responding positively with phrases such as "I see," or "Interesting" or similar responses. Such responses are part of good listening if they are genuine, because they let the prospect know you are paying attention. However, if you are faking, you may inadvertently give an inappropriate response and let the prospect know you were not paying attention. One salesperson who was faking attention had a prospect who said, "We've heard your products are overpriced." At the same time the salesperson was nodding approval. The salesperson quickly became alert and was embarrassed at not listening, but some credibility had been lost.

Listen for ideas Some people listen so closely for facts—perhaps often taking notes—that they miss a great deal of the meaning intended by the other person. The problem is that almost all of interpersonal communications has been estimated to be on the nonverbal level. The person who is busily taking notes may miss a great deal. It is all right to jot down a few key words or technical information, but your attention should be on the other person and the intended meaning rather than on the isolated facts.

Be interested Some salespeople are only interested in what they themselves have to say. They are so intent on making their presentation that they fail to listen to their prospects. These salespeople often miss closing signals, fail to capitalize on key benefits, or fail to recognize objections.[5] When you recognize the importance of what the prospect has to say, you will become more interested in the person and will be a more effective listener. Some salespeople listen only when they want to and thus miss key points, which are often made at the beginning of an interview or during the social portion of a call.

---

[5]For an interesting set of situations in which salespeople failed to listen, see B. Robert Anderson, "Good Selling Is Good Listening," *The American Salesman,* Vol. 20, No. 10 (October 1975), pp. 18–21.

If you are not listening during these times, you may miss information you
need to make the sale.

Show you are listening It is important that you convey to prospects that you are interested in what they are saying, that you encourage them to clarify points, and that you encourage them to give you more information. You can use body language to indicate your interest by nodding at appropriate times, leaning forward, keeping good eye contact, and not slouching or making other distracting movements. You can also show interest in others when you occasionally say "Um-mm" or "Uh-huh." These simple signs show that you are interested and encourage speaking. On the other hand, if you are slouching, daydreaming, or not maintaining good eye contact, you will convey to prospects that you are not interested in what they have to say. This will discourage them from continuing their conversation and will hurt your rapport with them.

Provide feedback An important aspect of providing feedback is to summarize what you think the prospect is trying to say. This shows that you are listening and gives an opportunity to clarify misunderstandings. You may also ask questions to clarify points of uncertainty. Questions can also be used to get information and to direct the conversation to areas in which you are interested.

Use silence Another good listening tool is silence. When you want prospects to talk, you simply stop talking and look them in the eye. This will generally encourage them to talk. It is best not to break every silence that occurs. Letting the prospect break the silence can usually give you more information,

---

SOME ADDITIONAL HINTS ON LISTENING

1. Be neutral. Let other people have their full say.
2. Give them complete attention . . . and reinforcement.
3. If appropriate, ask them to explain further.
4. Rephrase their main points and "play them back" to them . . . to help them see if they have said exactly what they want to say and to make sure you understand.
5. Put their "feelings" into words. This will help them evaluate and perhaps modify their statement . . . and it gives further evidence of your understanding.
6. At the appropriate time, get agreement. Summarize what you have both said as a preparation for the next step. If possible, have them suggest the course of action.

SOURCE: Selling Concepts produced by Vigortone AG Products. Reprinted by permission.

keep you both on the same topic, and even convey your own patience.[6] You must be careful not to make the prospect feel uneasy or manipulated when you use silence. However, people have a strong urge to talk when there is silence, and this feedback may be useful.

Silence has another benefit when dealing with prospects: "Silence is what keeps you from saying more than you need to—and makes the other person want to say more than he means to."[7]

Really understand Many times we fail to understand clearly what the other person is saying. There are several guidelines to help you clearly understand what is being said.

- Rephrase your understanding in your own words, and check with the prospect.
- When you disagree with the prospect but must accept a decision, take extra care to listen. Often your mind tends to wander when you disagree.
- If you find something you are told exciting, watch out for errors of exaggeration in your understanding of it.
- If you are bored by something you are told, watch out for errors. You may miss important facts or get only parts of messages, so you may misinterpret what is said.
- Concentrate on the information items in any message. Even if you have heard something before, continue to pay attention and look for new ideas or facts.[8]

A summary of guidelines for effective listening is provided in Table 11.2

TABLE 11.2
SUMMARY OF GUIDELINES FOR
EFFECTIVE LISTENING

- Do not interrupt.
- Do not let your mind wander.
- Do not fake attention.
- Listen for ideas.
- Be interested.
- Show you are listening.
- Use silence.
- Really understand.

---

[6]See Jane G. Bensahel, "Letting Silence Speak for Itself," *International Management,* Vol. 34 (July 1979), p. 52; or Jeremy Taylor and Alec Mackenzie, "The Power of Silence in Selling," *Business Quarterly,* Vol. 48, No. 1 (Spring 1983), pp. 38–41.

[7]See Mark H. McCormack, *What They Don't Teach You at Harvard Business School* (New York: Bantam Books, 1984), p. 108.

[8]Derived from Robert Froman, "Understand What You Hear," *Nation's Business,* Vol. 49 (October 1961), pp. 94–98.

Nonverbal messages are sent without words; they are communicated by using body gestures, posture, facial expressions, eye movements, paralanguage, and other gestures that add meaning to prospects' words. For instance, prospects who continually glance at their watches may be communicating a concern for time without saying so. One expert estimates that verbal messages account for 7 percent of message content, other vocal components account for 38 percent, and 55 percent of your meaning is communicated by your facial expressions.[9]

Thus, an understanding of nonverbal signals is critical to your sales success. Grikscheit found that high-performing salespeople took in significantly more nonverbal reactions in prospects than did low-performing salespeople.[10]

Most people read nonverbal signals accurately at the unconscious level; however, you can get more feedback if you become more conscious of the nonverbal signals your prospects are sending, then interpret them correctly, and alter your strategy according to the nonverbal signals. For instance, a frown from the prospect might mean that the prospect either has not understood your point or has a hidden objection. Because the meaning of nonverbal signals is very dependent on the situation, they must always be taken in context.

It is important to remember that almost no gesture has just one meaning for all occasions. For instance, a person with arms folded in front may be defensive or may simply feel cold. Thus, you must interpret nonverbal behavior cautiously. Patterns of nonverbal communication vary in different cultures and groups, so again caution must be exercised in evaluating nonverbal cues in another culture. For instance, in Japan, women will stick out their tongues to indicate embarrassment. And in much of the Middle East, raised eyebrows mean "yes."[11]

Sometimes the prospect's verbal and nonverbal messages are in conflict. This should alert you to examine the situation more closely, because the prospect may either have a hidden objection or may not be telling you the whole truth.

Dimensions of Nonverbal Feedback

You can get feedback from prospect's nonverbal behavior by watching several key dimensions, including body gestures, posture, and prospects' surroundings; the space they keep between you; prospects' facial expressions, eye movements, and paralanguage.

Whatever the importance of these various nonverbal actions, you should avoid looking for certain specific gestures and possibly missing others. Rather, you should be sensitive to the other person's patterns of nonverbal gestures and react to them.

[9]See Albert Mehrabian, "Communicating Without Words," *Psychology Today,* Vol. 2 (September 1968), p. 53.

[10]See Gary M. Grikscheit, "An Investigation of the Ability of Salesmen to Monitor Feedback" (unpublished doctoral dissertation, Michigan State University, East Lansing, 1971).

[11]See James C. Semmons, "A Matter of Interpretation," *American Way* (April 1983), p. 107.

Body gestures Body gestures can convey meaning, but you must be careful not to take any one gestures in isolation. Rubbing the chin may mean that prospects are evaluating your proposal, or it may simply mean their chin itches. Thus, attention to a single gesture may be misleading. What you must look for are patterns of gestures and consistency in these patterns.

One article proposed that infrequent use of gestures indicates either a negative attitude toward another person or disinterest in the subject matter. On the other hand, frequent use of gestures indicates positive attitudes toward another person or interest in the subject.[12] A number of body gestures and their nonverbal meanings are depicted in Table 11.3.

TABLE 11.3
SEVERAL BEHAVIORS AND THEIR NONVERBAL SIGNALS

BEHAVIOR	NONVERBAL SIGNAL	POSSIBLE INTERPRETATION
Openness	Opens hands, unbuttons coat, uncrosses legs, moves closer to you.	Is open to your proposal.
Defensiveness	Crosses arms on chest, clenches fists, crosses legs.	Feels defensive (or hostile?).
Evaluation	Brings a hand to the face, puts chin in the palm, extends index finger along the cheek; tilts the head, strokes the chin, pinches the bridge of the nose.	Is evaluating your proposal.
Suspension	Does not look at you, rubs nose, scratches head.	Is suspending attention, decision making.
Frustration	Breathes quickly, clenches hands lightly, places a hand on back of the neck.	Feels frustrated.
Nervousness	Clears throat, says "Whew" and breathes out air, fidgets in chair, jingles money in pocket, tugs at ears.	Feels nervous.
Boredom	Drums fingers on table, rests head in hand, doodles, stares at you blankly.	Is bored.
Acceptance	Puts a hand to the chest, touches you, moves closer to you.	Accepts your proposal or idea.

SOURCE: Adapted from Gerard I. Nierenberg and Henry H. Calero, *How to Read a Person Like a Book* (New York: Pocket Books, 1973), pp. 43–128.

[12] See Thomas V. Bonoma and Larry C. Felder, "Nonverbal Communication in Marketing: Toward a Communicational Analysis," *Journal of Marketing Research*, Vol. 14 (May 1977), pp. 169–180.

Posture Posture may indicate how receptive the prospect is. A rigid posture may indicate defensiveness, whereas slouching may indicate a lack of interest. Prospects' body angle can also give you information about their interest level. In general, if prospects are slouching in a chair, it indicates that they have no interest in what you are saying or are not evaluating it. On the other hand, prospects who are paying attention and leaning forward or sitting up straight are probably reacting positively to what you are saying.

Another aspect of posture is mirroring, which was discussed in Chapter 9. The prospect may assume partially or totally the same posture and position as you do. The more precise the mirroring, the more the prospect agrees with you.

The prospect's environment Decor, furnishings, pictures, trophies, diplomas, and awards can tell you about the prospect's interests, income level, and degree of responsibility. Status symbols such as size and location of an office and office furnishings are often keys to a prospect's influence and possibly the prospect's self-image.[13] Similarly, examining a prospect's home can tell you a great deal. The decor, furnishings, style, and possessions can often tell you about the person's background, interests, and personality.

Space Prospects may use space as a form of communication. For instance, if they feel uncomfortable around you, they may stay behind their desk; if standing, they may move away from you. On the other hand, if they feel comfortable, they may move closer or even come away from their desk and sit beside you. Noting prospects' reactions to distances between you and them is important, for you do not want to make them feel uncomfortable.

Facial expressions Facial expression takes many forms, including smiles, frowns, eye twitches, nose wrinkles, and eyebrow lifts, as well as facial color—either flushing or peakedness. A prospect who frowns may either not understand your message or disagree with it. Sometimes a prospect will fake an expression, thus looking interested while thinking of something else, or may smile even though upset. Prospects will also sometimes try to hide their emotions; this poker face makes it difficult for you to read them. However, most people are not very good at hiding their feelings, so you can get a great deal of information from studying their expressions.

Eye movements Eye movements can also give you a great deal of information. Prospects generally tend to have more eye contact with you and larger pupils when they are interested; lack of eye contact and smaller pupils tend to indicate lack of interest. Watching the prospect's pupils may be useful,

[13]For a review of some important concepts of space and other status symbols, see Phillip C. Hunsaker, "Communicating Better: There's No Proxy for Proxemics," *Business*, Vol. 30, No. 2 (March–April 1980), pp. 41–48.

SECURING FEEDBACK

I'm thinking about your offer.

I'm interested but tell me more.

What colors does it come in?

No way am I paying that much.

You still haven't convinced me.

because people are generally unable to control their pupils.[14] Excessive blinking is also associated with anxiety and may indicate that you need to put the prospect at ease. Watching the prospect's eye movements may also tell you something of their interests. For instance, a prospective car buyer whose visual attention is focused on the engine may be interested in the mechanical performance of the car. Finally, eye movements can convey meaning, as can be seen from Figure 11.2 Buyers can convey distaste, skepticism, lack of interest, or interest by their eye movements.

Paralanguage Paralanguage, as indicated in Chapter 9, consists of the vocal elements such as inflection, volume, tone, and rate of speech that convey a great deal of the meaning in words. Like other means of nonverbal communication, paralanguage communicates the prospect's attitude and emotions rather than concepts.[15] Just as the way you say things influences how the prospect will interpret your message, similarly, prospects' tone and inflections can give added meaning to what they say. If a prospect says, "Your product is wonderful," with enthusiasm and a smile right after a demonstration, it will have a very different meaning from a prospect's saying sarcastically, with a troubled look, "Your product is wonderful" after the product has been returned. You must learn to be alert for these voice inflections and changes in tone, so that you can understand the prospect's true meaning. Reading between the lines like this is very important and is a key skill for determining hidden objections.

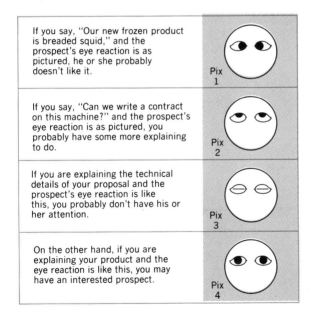

If you say, "Our new frozen product is breaded squid," and the prospect's eye reaction is as pictured, he or she probably doesn't like it.	Pix 1
If you say, "Can we write a contract on this machine?" and the prospect's eye reaction is as pictured, you probably have some more explaining to do.	Pix 2
If you are explaining the technical details of your proposal and the prospect's eye reaction is like this, you probably don't have his or her attention.	Pix 3
On the other hand, if you are explaining your product and the eye reaction is like this, you may have an interested prospect.	Pix 4

FIGURE 11.2 Several eye reactions and their nonverbal meaning.

[14]See M. Doctoroff, "Non-verbal Communication a Key to Executive Success," *International Management*, Vol. 32 (November 1977), p. 39.

[15]See Joel P. Bowman and Bernadine P. Branchow, *Understanding and Using Communication in Business* (New York: Harper and Row, 1977), p. 154.

The prospect's nonverbals can tell you a lot.

FIGURE 11.3 Interpreting your prospect's body language.

Paralanguage may also tell you something of prospect's moods. For instance, if prospects' voices crack, if their pitch is high, if they talk rapidly or continually clear their throat, they may be nervous. You must respond to these signals and adjust your presentation to make them feel at ease.

Reading the Prospect

How can you tell whether the prospect is evaluating your presentation positively or negatively? Research has shown that positive signs include prospects' moving closer, touching, maintaining eye contact, leaning forward, speaking more quickly, giving frequent verbal reinforcements (e.g., head nods and "uh-huh"), smiling, and opening their arms. These are all signs that prospects are regarding your proposal favorably. On the other hand, reclining, leaning backward, avoiding or cutting off eye contact, avoiding getting close to you, folding arms, and tapping fingers are all negative signs.[16]

Another author concludes that if prospects' eyes are downcast and their faces are turned away, you are being shut out. But if their mouths are relaxed, without a mechanical smile, if their chins are forward, they are probably considering your presentation. If their eyes engage yours for several seconds at a time with a slight, one-sided smile extending at least to nose level, your proposal is being weighed. Then, if their heads are shifted to the same level as yours, if they show a relaxed smile and appear enthusiastic, the sale is virtually made.[17]

One expert encourages salespeople to categorize buyers' total nonverbal behavior almost like a traffic light: green signals indicate you should proceed with the presentation; yellow signals indicate caution, that you are losing the prospect; and red signals warn you to stop and redirect your efforts, because the buyer has just about been lost.[18]

Figure 11.3 is a test to see how good you are in interpreting the prospect's body language. Try to classify each of the pictures as green, yellow, or red. The answers are below the test, but wait to look until after you have finished the test.

SUMMARY

Securing feedback is a very important aspect of selling. Opening up two-way channels of communication and getting feedback allows you to have more accurate communication, gives the prospect an opportunity to talk, and may tell you which need to stress.

Feedback is obtained by asking questions, listening, and reading nonverbal cues. Questions meant to elicit feedback should not be answerable by a yes or no, should not be leading, should be short and limited to a single

[16]See Albert Mehrabian, *Nonverbal Communication* (Chicago: Aldine, 1972).
[17]See Gerard I. Nierenberg and Henry H. Calero, *How to Read a Person Like a Book* (New York: Pocket Books, 1973) p. 29.
[18]See Gerald Gschwandtner, "How to Read Your Prospect's Body Language," *Industrial Marketing*, Vol. 66, No. 7 (July 1981), pp. 54–59.

point, and should go from broad to specific. Several types of questions can be used to stimulate feedback, including probing questions, mirror questions, and W-word questions. Questions also serve other functions in selling: verifying information, qualifying prospects, determining the most important needs of prospects, clarifying statements, and closing.

Listening, which is more than just hearing, is also essential. There are many good reasons for listening: not only is it polite, but it also helps you to identify the prospect's needs and personality, uncovers hidden objections, and allows receptive propects to sell themselves. To be a good listener, do not interrupt, do not let your mind wander, do not fake attention, listen for ideas, be interested, show you are listening, provide feedback, use silence, and really try to understand.

Nonverbal cues provide you with a great deal of feedback from prospects. Paying attention to nonverbal behavior consists of studying prospects' body gestures, posture, and surroundings, the space they put between you, as well as prospects' facial expressions, eye movements, and paralanguage. You must use all these factors together to read prospects and determine whether your presentaiton is going positively or negatively; then, adjust your behavior accordingly.

PROBLEMS

1. After describing the qualities of your product to a prospect, the prospect informs you that she is not sure her firm has the financial ability to acquire your product. Describe what your response would be, assuming you are capable of empathizing with the prospect's problem.
2. How can salespeople engage in two-way communication?
3. Describe in your own words the role that questions play in sales interviews.
4. What is meant by the statement, "Listening is more than hearing"?
5. Describe some important types of nonverbal feedback that could be effectively used by encyclopedia door-to-door salespeople.

EXERCISE 11

Objectives: To understand the difficulty of effectively listening.

To apply your knowledge of feedback questions.

PART A Listening
Listen to a five-minute tape of a newscast. Stop the tape. Then write down as much as you can about what you remember from the tape. Then play the tape back and see what you missed.

PART B Feedback Questions
Imagine that you are a salesperson for a firm that sells electric typewriters. Develop a list of feedback questions designed to (a) identify the prospect's needs and (b) qualify the prospect.

Julia Green had just received her master's degree in business administration from the University of South Carolina. She was very excited about her new career. Her father was a modest blue-collar worker, and she was the first one in her family to obtain a graduate degree.

There were considerable opportunities in the market for women graduates that year. Ms. Green wanted to be successful and to move up in her job.

Ms. Green felt that a sales job would give her a better opportunity to be promoted and to acquire "real-world" experience. She accepted the offer of a well-known chemical firm that sold fertilizers to large farm cooperatives in the Midwest. The firm offered a three-month course on the products they sold and, after that, two months of field training with a senior salesperson. The candidates, however, were given the choice of starting field sales immediately after the course, provided that they had shown adequate proficiency with company products.

Julia Green studied very hard during the initial three months and was offered the opportunity to start field sales immediately on her own. She considered the two alternatives and decided that she would rather start alone. She did not believe the two months of field training would help her very much, especially considering the fact that most of the senior salespeople were older men, without graduate degrees, and they might be intimidated by her.

Ms. Green knew that one of her major problems was to sound knowledgeable and credible to her prospective buyers. The purchasing agents of farm cooperatives were usually very conservative, hard-working men who were not used to trading with young, well-educated women. Julia felt that many of them would try to test her competence by asking her difficult and unusual questions, possibly not always relevant to the products she was selling.

After thinking very carefully about her problem, Ms. Green developed a well-structured sales presentation that covered all possible aspects of her products and offered a thorough description of their use. Her strategy would be to initiate the sales presentation and to continue on with it without giving the respondent a chance to interrupt her. In this way, she intended to eliminate the possibility of being put into an embarrassing position by her prospective buyers.

1. Considering the characteristics of the salesperson and of the prospects in this specific communication situation, do you agree with Ms. Green's strategy?
2. Is feedback needed in this sales relationship? If so, what kind?
3. Do you think Ms. Green will succeed in her new career? Why?
4. What advice would you give Ms. Green?

Case 11-2 New-Design Furniture Company

New-Design is a small manufacturer of office furniture. It was founded three years ago by three graduates in commercial design. The firm produced modern furniture of very luxurious design and materials. They built up a good reputation with decorators in town who worked with very wealthy professionals and corporate officers of major companies.

The three associates felt that they should expand their activities. Some informal market research done three months earlier had shown that there was a large market for office furniture within a more modest income bracket. This market was composed primarily of young doctors, lawyers, and businesspeople who were willing to spend $1000 to $5000 to furnish their offices.

At present, this market had a somewhat limited choice of office furniture, primarily restricted to traditional designs and materials. New-Design felt that more innovative and sophisticated furniture would appeal to the young, fast-growing market.

In designing and manufacturing furniture for a larger and less expensive bracket, New-Design had to start an aggressive sales policy, so that an increased volume in sales would make possible a drop in prices. In order to do this, Mrs. Betty Gettem was hired to select and train a force of twelve salespersons who would call on stores, decorators, and final customers.

Betty decided first of all to verify the actual demand structure, so that she could establish what sales appeals would be most effective. The results showed that the market was very concerned with such factors as price, durability, and design of the furniture. New graduates from law and medical schools were very anxious to establish their reputation. They were very ambitious and very hard workers. They tried to identify very closely with well-known, established practitioners. They were, however, more liberal, less pragmatic, and more cosmopolitan than their older counterparts.

New-Design offered four lines of their less expensive office furniture to this market—all modern and elegant. It was Mrs. Gettem's task to outline some important appeals that could be used and to design some feedback questions that salespeople could use to determine the young professionals' needs.

1. What are some important appeals that could be used by New-Design?
2. Make a list of some feedback questions the sales force could ask to determine the young professionals' needs.

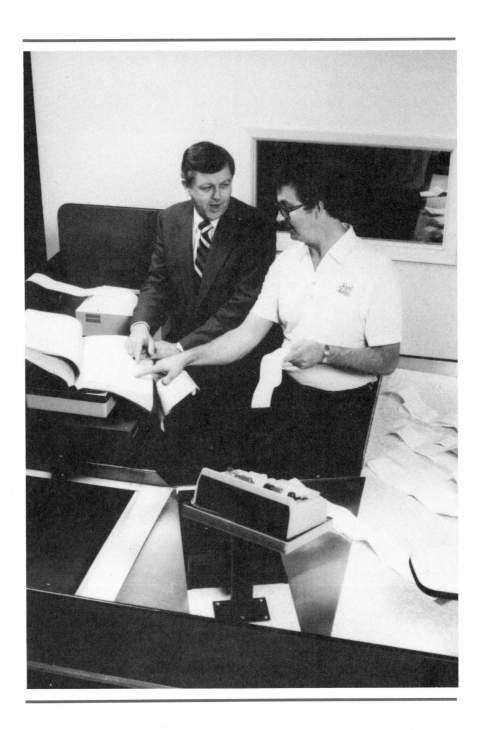

Adjusting to
the Prospect

After studying this chapter, you should be able to

1. Recognize the importance of adjusting to the prospect.
2. Differentiate between high- and low-pressure selling.
3. Understand differences between voluntary and involuntary and positive and negative reactions.
4. Identify ways to respond to positive–voluntary, positive–involuntary, negative–voluntary, and negative–involuntary reactions.
5. Specify other events that may require adjustments and appropriate changes in your tactics.
6. Understand elements of the customer's behavior that will be important in tactical adjustment.

As a salesperson, you are in a unique position to customize your firm's marketing program to each individual customer. This customizing process consists of adjusting tactics to the unique characteristics of the prospect and the prospect's situation. Like a military person, you can be good at tactics only if you have first developed a sound strategy, with clear objectives in mind and a plan for achieving them.

This chapter explores unexpected situations that you may encounter on a call and ways in which you can best respond to them. Before each call you should review what you know about individuals in the account, how your products and services meet their needs, who your competitors are, and what has occurred on previous visits. Even with such careful preparation, however, calls rarely go exactly as planned. An unanticipated problem, a change in the competitive situation, or a shift in the thinking of the prospect almost always occurs. You must be particularly aware of factors that will require on-the-spot tactical adjustments, such as the reactions of the customer or prospect, the mood the customer is in, unexpected time limitations, and interruptions.

TACTICS ARE ADJUSTIVE REACTIONS

Tactics are modifications of strategy and comprise the adjustments you make when you are face to face with the customer or prospect. The reactions of prospects are key indicators to you of what your tactics should be during the sales call. Reactions include not only *what* prospects do and say, but also *how* they do and say it. A hearty handshake, a pleasant greeting, a scowl, or a hesitant answer to a question are all signals to you to adjust. Sales tactics may be defined as *adjustive reactions* on your part to the actions and reactions you observe in the customer or prospect.[1]

Here is an example of a tactical adjustment. John White, a salesperson for a publishing company, is calling on Betty Williams, a professor at a major university, with the objective of trying to get her to adopt a new principles of marketing textbook for her large section. During the call he notices that she seems preoccupied while he is talking about the textbook. He questions her and finds out that her department chairperson has just asked her to teach a course in buyer behavior during the summer, a course she has never taught before. She is concerned about how to teach the course and what text to use.

John's tactical adjustment would be to stop describing his principles of marketing textbook and instead tell her about his firm's buyer behavior book, and relate how several other instructors in his territory approach the course. Failure to adjust in this manner would have seriously hampered his chances for a successful call, since the prospect's attention was on her problem rather than on his presentation. Furthermore, if John can help her with her buyer behavior course, he will be in a much better position to have her adopt his principles of marketing textbook. Thus, these tactical adjustments are critical to effective selling.

[1]For a good discussion of the importance and nature of adaptive behavior, see Barton A. Weitz, "Effectiveness in Sales Interactions: A Contingency Framework," *Journal of Marketing*, Vol. 45, No. 1 (Winter 1981), pp. 85–103.

To be effective at tactics, you must be both perceptive and able to adjust to the prospect. If you are not perceptive, you will miss cues in the other person's behavior. However, observing them is not enough; you must also be able to react appropriately to what you observe. Your perceptiveness is enhanced by your empathy with the prospect, and your ability to adjust is enhanced by your behavioral flexibility. Thus, two key qualities you must possess if you are to be effective at tactical adjustments are empathy and behavioral flexibility.

Empathy

Empathy consists of understanding the other person's thinking and feelings and letting them know that you understand. "People who are highly skilled in interpersonal communication are more empathic than those who are less skilled."[2] Empathy is essential in order to understand the prospect's position and to be sensitive to the person's needs and feelings. Merely understanding the other person, however, is not enough. You must also communicate to the

---

HOW A SHIFT IN TACTICS GOT THE ORDER

Bill Blake, former vice-president, sales planning and development, Sweetheart Cup, was selling paper napkins to supermarkets for Hudson Pulp and Paper at the time when the four big chains—A&P, Jewel, Kroger, and National Tea—controlled roughly 80 percent of the market. If you didn't get into these chains, you were out of business. Back then, paper napkins were not taken very seriously. They were thought of as a summer picnic item, and not for the winter months.

For two years he called on the buyer at Jewel in Chicago every week. But every time he went to see the buyer, he'd have something different to say about why he wouldn't buy from him. The buyer had a terrific mental block against napkins.

One day, he got an idea. His company ran manufacturer's coupons on every box of napkins they sold. People had to bring them to the store to redeem them for a free box, and the coupons eventually came back to his company. So he got hold of all the coupons, put them into big bags, and dumped hundreds of them on the buyer's desk one day in the middle of winter. Needless to say, the buyer was convinced.

Selling those napkins had to be the biggest sale of his life, because after selling to Jewel, his firm went from nothing to 50 percent of the market in Chicago.

SOURCE: "Strange Tales of Sales," *Sales and Marketing Management, Vol. 135, No. 8 (June 3, 1985), pp. 42–46.*

---

[2]William S. Howell, *The Empathic Communicator* (Belmont, Calif.: Wadsworth, 1982), p. 3.

person that you understand them. Communicating this interest and sensitivity to prospects will tend to establish trust and will help to build up your credibility. Empathy is the quality that will allow you to be perceptive.

Behavioral Flexibility

The other key concept in sales tactics, behavioral flexibility, is the ability to adjust appropriately to the personality of a customer or prospect.[3] That is, you must treat customers and prospects the way they want to be treated. This flexibility is essential.

You may be a very businesslike person who prefers to stress the facts when making a presentation. If, however, you are dealing with prospects who are reluctant to move too quickly and who seem uncertain, you may have to take the time to reassure them and make them feel comfortable. Even though this is not the treatment you would expect for yourself, you must be flexible and treat them the way they want to be treated.

NEED TO ADJUST TO DIFFERENT KINDS OF BUYERS

Buyers may exhibit several behavioral styles when interacting with industrial salespeople. They have been classified into the following categories.

- "Hard bargainers" obtain several price quotations or use several sources of supply for the same item; salespeople may find it difficult to make a sale.
- "Sales job facilitators" are amenable to salepeople's solicitations and even attempt to make the transaction go smoothly.
- "Straight shooters" behave with integrity and propriety; they rarely use their buying power to attain concessions.
- "Socializers" enjoy the personal interaction of the buyer–seller relationship.
- "Persuaders" attempt to market their own company to salespeople to stimulate a favorable impression of the buying firm.
- "Considerate buyers" show compassion and concern for salespeople; these buyers may be willing to accept substitute products.

Salespeople will be more likely to be successful if they tailor their selling strategy to the buyer's behavior style.

SOURCE: Alan J. Dubinsky and Thomas N. Ingram, "A Classification of Industrial Buyers; Implications for Sales Training," *Journal of Personal Selling and Sales Management*, Vol. 1, No. 2, Issue 1 (Fall–Winter 1981–1982), pp. 46–51. Reprinted by permission from *Journal of Personal Selling and Sales Management*.

---

[3]Anthony J. Alessandra and Phillip S. Wexler, *Non-Manipulative Selling* (San Diego, Calif.: Courseware Publishers, 1979), p. 25.

As a salesperson, it is your task to adjust to the person called upon rather than expect the customer or prospect to adjust to you. Obviously, though, each of you is influencing the reactions of the other.

THE KEY TACTICAL OBJECTIVE IN SELLING IS SUBTLE CONTROL

The tactical objective in selling is to *be in control without seeming to be*. Subtle influence is crucial. Customers and prospects react negatively to being pushed. How, then, can you be in control without seeming to be? One approach is to utilize low pressure. The other is to ask questions that will engage the buyer in two-way communication.

Utilize Low Pressure

Sales pressure can be defined in two ways: in terms of the salesperson's behavior or in terms of the customer's feelings. The preferred definition is in terms of the customer's feelings.

Salesperson's behavior Writers and salespeople frequently use the term *sales pressure* to refer to the saleperson's behavior toward the other person. From this perspective, a high-pressure salesperson is seen as a pushy, aggressive, fast-talking individual who forces action and will not take "no" for an answer. A low-pressure salesperson in this sort of definition would be friendly, courteous, let the product sell itself, and let the prospect take as much time as possible. There are two problems with these definitions. First, they are salesperson-oriented rather than customer-oriented, since they fail to consider how the customer feels. Second, they are really examples of high-pressure selling and zero-pressure or no-pressure selling, as can be seen from the top of Figure 12.1. The opposite behavior from high-pressure selling in this

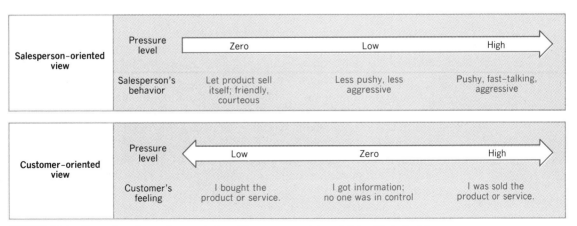

FIGURE 12.1 Alternative views of pressure in selling. SOURCE: Adapted from W. J. E. Crissy and Harold Cash, "A Point of View for Salesmen," in *The Psychology of Selling*, Vol.1 (Flushing, N.Y.: Personnel Development Associates, 1966), pp. 42–43.

context is to do nothing, be friendly and courteous, and let the product sell itself. This is not low-pressure but no-pressure selling, and it really is not effective selling.

Customer feelings Pressure is more appropriately considered in terms of the customer's feelings after the sales call. As can be seen in the bottom of Figure 12.1, if the customer's reaction is "I was sold; I was pushed into ordering," this selling represents high pressure. No one likes to be pushed into purchasing something. It makes us feel uncomfortable. Even the common term, "I was sold a bill of goods," implies that someone was forced to do something and is not happy with the results. No one likes to be sold something. In this situation customers feel that the salesperson was in control and that something was pushed on them against their will. As a salesperson, you cannot afford to create a high-pressure feeling in customers. This feeling may cause them to cancel orders and makes future business unlikely.

On the other hand, if the customer's reaction is "I got information from the salesperson," this represents no pressure. In this situation the customer would feel that information was exchanged, but that no one was in control.

Finally, according to this preferred definition, pressure is low when the customer's reaction is "I bought the product or service." Although people do not like to be sold something, they do like to buy things. Buying indicates that the customer was in control and made the decision. Customers like to buy and like to share information about their purchases with others. A customer might say, "Look at the new stereo I just bought. Isn't it beautiful?" An enthusiastic customer would be unlikely to say, "Look at the new stereo I was just sold." Thus, the distinction between high pressure and low pressure is more than just the semantics between being sold and buying. It is the total feeling the customer has after the call is completed. A good salesperson can be very involved and persistent and still leave the customer feeling that he or she was in control and bought the product. This should be your objective in every tactical situation.

Utilize Questions

A second way to be in subtle control is to utilize questions to get information and involve the prospect. In order to be in subtle control, you must direct the course of the sales call without seeming to be pushy. When you are talking, you are not necessarily in control since you are not certain what customers or prospects are thinking. You may be talking about the benefits of your product while they are thinking about their vacation. Similarly, when the customers or prospects are talking, you are not necessarily in control since they may be discussing things that do not help you to reach your objective.

One good way to stay in control is to ask questions. Questions allow you to obtain needed information, control the direction of the interview, encourage prospects to talk about what you want them to talk about, and get prospects involved. Finally, they give you feedback from the prospect. This two-way communication is a useful way for you to maintain control without monopolizing the conversation and being pushy.

In order to be effective at adjusting to prospects, you must be attentive to them. That is, you must pay attention to their behavior, to what they say, and to how they say and do things. Buyers may have a number of different types of reactions; there are several ways in which you can adjust to these reactions.

Different Types of Reactions

As one of the several different types of reactions to your presentation, the prospect may agree with you or disagree with you. Additionally, the prospect's reaction may take the form of conscious statements about your presentation or of unconscious reactions usually evident in nonverbal behavior. These reactions may be classified as positive versus negative reactions or as voluntary versus involuntary reactions. Each of these will be discussed.

Positive versus negative reactions The prospect's reaction is *positive* from a tactical standpoint if, as you see it, there is an increased likelihood of achieving your call objective. Positive reactions might include questions such as, "When can we expect delivery?" and "What kind of terms are available?"

Positive versus negative reactions.

Positive reactions might also be statements such as, "I like the texture," or "This seems to be an attractive package." Movements and gestures may also indicate positive reactions. For example, the prospect might pick up a sample, move forward in his or her chair, smile, or use the intercom to hold incoming calls.

In contrast, *negative* reactions, from your point of view, indicate a decreased likelihood of achieving your call objectives. Statements such as, "Your price is too high," or "I am satisfied with my present sources of supply," or "Don't take up my time with that," are examples. Others are gestures and movements by the prospect, such as moving the head from side to side, squirming in the chair, looking out the window, or engaging in other activities such as signing mail. Many times your judgment of whether prospects' reactions are positive or negative will be based on their nonverbal reactions or the tone of their voice. Thus you must use the feedback skills learned in Chapter 11 to size up the other person's reactions.

Your aim is to get positive reactions—those that indicate you are making progress. Each time a positive reaction follows another positive reaction, there is less likelihood of a negative reaction occurring. The tactical principle is that when you get a positive reaction, you ought to continue doing what you are doing or attempt to close the sale. On the other hand, if you get a negative reaction, you must shift and do something else. Furthermore, each time a negative reaction follows a negative reaction, it becomes more difficult to bring about a positive reaction. Figure 12.2 illustrates these points.

Voluntary versus involuntary reaction Voluntary reactions, those made consciously, include thoughtful statements and questions and deliberate movements and actions such as shaking the head. Involuntary reactions occur un-

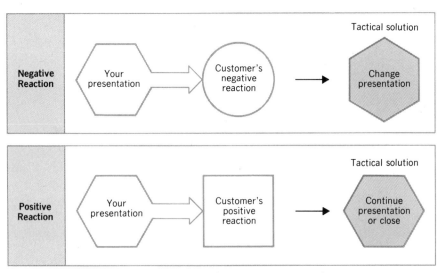

FIGURE 12.2 Tactical solutions to perceived customer-positive and customer-negative reactions.

consciously. They are usually accompanied by nonverbal actions such as a smile, a head nod, a spontaneous statement, or a symbolic rejection of a proposal, such as pushing the sample away from where you placed it. The customer or prospect is aware of voluntary reactions, and consequently, you must use more careful and deliberate tactics with these reactions than you would for involuntary ones. For example, if a customer or prospect asks a thoughtful question, it is a sound tactic for you to stop your presentation to answer it. If you ignore the question and continue with your own remarks, you are likely to lose the attention of the other person. The prospect or customer is likely to be thinking about the point raised rather than what you are saying. As another example, if a prospect says, "I would like to try this product," it is a sound tactic and common sense for you to stop your presentation, write up the order, and thank the customer. You should not talk your way out of the sale by continuing your presentation after you have an offer to buy.

Involuntary reactions are subtle, and the tactics used with them should be equally subtle. For example, if you see that you are losing the attention of the other person—the prospect may look away and start to wind his or her watch—you may regain the prospect's attention by passing a sample to examine, making it virtually impossible not to pay attention. The objective is to convert the involuntary reaction into a positive voluntary one.

Tactical Adjustments

If you combine the two types of reactions into a four-way classification, *any* reaction during a call will fit into one of the four categories: negative–voluntary, negative–involuntary, positive–involuntary, and positive–voluntary. Figure 12.3 shows this classification and the tactics you should employ with each of these reactions.

Negative–voluntary reactions Negative–voluntary reactions are consciously made and indicate little likelihood of achieving your call objectives. Often negative–voluntary reactions are objections, which are covered in Chapter 13. Objections might take the form of statements such as "Your price is too high," or "I'm not in the market right now." Other ways in which the prospect might object would be to stand up and show you to the door or to

	Positive	Negative
Involuntary	Tactic: No shift— reinforce.	Tactic: Subtle shift.
Voluntary	Tactic: Go to the next point or close.	Tactic: Substantial shift.

FIGURE 12.3 Reactions as a basis for sales tactics.

interrupt you and use the intercom to call a secretary. Here the prospect is clearly disagreeing with you and letting you know it; thus you must either overcome an objection or shift your tactics substantially to gain a positive reaction.

A good tactic for a negative–voluntary reaction is to ask a question that encourages the prospect to respond in a positive manner. For example, suppose you are selling copying machines and are showing a prospect a medium-sized model. If the prospect responds with the negative–voluntary comment, "We don't have nearly enough space for the model in our office," you might answer the prospect with the following question, designed to get a positive response: "We have decided that you need letter-quality copies, haven't we?" Then, if the prospect responds "yes," you can make a substantial shift in tactics and say, "Well, then, let me show you this portable high-quality copier. It makes very high-quality copies and doesn't take up much space at all."

Negative–involuntary reactions Negative–involuntary reactions of the prospect are not made consciously, and they also indicate little likelihood of achieving your call objectives. There are two subcategories of these reactions: beginning disagreement or disbelief and loss of attention. Examples of

---

HANDLING NEGATIVE VOLUNTARY RESPONSES

REACTION	TACTIC
▪ Openly hostile	▪ Be friendly. Don't back down. Stress benefits. Keep your cool.
▪ Chronic complainer	▪ Listen. Show honest concern. Don't ignore. Don't argue.
▪ Indecisive	▪ Don't offer too many choices. Help them make up their mind. Use testimonials.
▪ Unresponsive	▪ Involve them. Have them handle product. Use silence.

SOURCE: Emory Ward, "How to Sell 'Problem Prospects,'" *The American Salesman*, Vol. 22, No. 1 (January 1977), pp. 8–12. Reprinted with permission of *The American Salesman*, National Research Bureau, Inc., 424 North Third Street, Burlington, Iowa 52601.

beginning disagreement or disbelief by a prospect are a frown, head turning instead of nodding, leaning back in the chair, and pushing away a sample. In each instance a *subtle shift* is called for. Obviously, you do not wish the other person to repeat such reactions. However, if you act too deliberately yourself, you may bring about a shift to a negative–voluntary reaction on the part of the prospect. Your objective is to do or say something in a subtle fashion that will bring a positive reaction from the prospect. With loss of attention, a pause may be all that is needed. Few people can stand silence. Another useful tactic is to have the customer or prospect examine a sample or examine a visual aid, being careful not to lose control. A third tactic, if you can do it comfortably, is to use humor to get back the person's attention. Finally, you may simply wish to ask a question designed to find out the prospect's needs, or change your conversation to a topic of more interest to the prospect.

In the event of beginning disbelief or disagreement, the rhetorical question is a powerful tactic. Jim Jones, a road-building equipment salesperson calling on a contractor, observed a slight turning of the head and a frown to a remark he made. He countered by saying, "Mr. Contractor, you may be wondering whether your people are going to be able to operate this new equipment effectively? I wouldn't even want you to buy this equipment unless you would permit me to explain the operation thoroughly to all your people and train them." After that, the customer paid much more attention. A key consideration here is to direct the other person's attention to a positive point before what is bothering the prospect reaches conscious awareness.

Positive–involuntary reactions Positive–involuntary reactions of the prospect are not made consciously but indicate greater likelihood of achieving your call objectives. Examples include smiling and nodding, moving closer, examining a sample furnished by you, spontaneous "uh-huh's," and other affirmative verbal signals. From your standpoint, *no shift* in tactics is called for. Rather, you should do everything possible to reinforce the point that caused this kind of reaction. You will be successful if you have several different ways of making the same point or expanding on the point. Equipped with these different explanations, you can reinforce the favorable reaction and hopefully convert it to a positive–voluntary reaction. Some caution is needed here, however, because sometimes you can mistake a positive–involuntary reaction for agreement and move away from a point before it has reached the conscious awareness of the other person.

Positive–voluntary reactions These reactions are consciously made by the prospect and indicate a greater likelihood of achieving your call objectives. Examples include remarks such as: "When can I get delivery?" "I'll ask our engineering department to test this sample." "You can write up this order." In response to such a reaction, you must either *close* the sale or move to the next point, as appropriate. It is not a sound tactic for you to continue stressing a point once conscious agreement has been achieved with the prospect. Continuing to stress a point may raise questions and doubts in the prospect's

WHEN IS HUMOR APPROPRIATE?

SALES STEP	SELLING TASK	USE OF HUMOR
Contact	Seller meets prospective buyer; goals include gaining interest and attention of the prospect.	Gain attention, interest, and a favorable impression of the salesperson, and reduce hostility through humor.
Sales presentation	Salesperson presents the potential benefits of the product or service and the product—service characteristics.	Humor used to develop rapport and group solidarity. Humor should be based on the type of buying situation, the buying problem, and the goals of the sales presentation.
Meeting objections	Salesperson determines prospect's objections and allays them.	Humor used to reduce anxiety, hostility, and maintain attention, soften the meeting of objections, or distract the buyer from the objection.
Closing the sale	Salesperson's goal is to obtain action, either a sale or a future commitment to continue product—service consideration.	Humor inappropriate.
Follow-up	Uncovering problems that have occurred postsale, encouraging new purchases, and maintaining support.	Humor used to maintain rapport and group solidarity, and to regain attention.

SOURCE: Reprinted by permission of publisher from John S. Wagle, "Using Humor in the Industrial Selling Process," *Industrial Marketing Management*, Vol. 14, No. 4 (November 1985), p. 222. Copyright, 1985, by Elsevier Science Publishing Co., Inc.

mind. Unfortunately, some salespeople become so impressed with what they are saying that they talk their way out of sales.

In summary, negative reactions call for a tactical shift, substantial when the reaction is voluntary, subtle when it is involuntary. Positive–involuntary reactions call for staying on the point and reinforcing it; positive–voluntary reactions are signals for you to close or to proceed to the next point.

Your tactical objective is always to be in control without seeming to be. The key to achieving this control lies in responding appropriately to all reactions, especially the involuntary ones. You will make the correct response only if you are well prepared for each call and can focus your full attention on the other person and not miss any cues. Missed cues lead to lost control; lost control leads to lost sales.

OTHER TACTICAL CONSIDERATIONS

Your sales tactics include not only all your adjustive reactions, but also large-scale changes and modifications that you make in your call plan as you proceed with the call. It would be difficult to make a list of all the factors or conditions that can cause such tactical adjustments. However, some of those that you are most likely to face at some time in the course of your work will be examined. Each of these situations calls for tactical adjustments on your part.

The Prospect's Mood

The prospect's mood may be defined as the particular emotions or state of mind that colors his or her perceptions and thoughts. In the first few seconds of each sales call, it is important for you to gauge the mood of the customer or prospect. The bad mood of a prospect may call for a departure from your initial call plan.

The best single tactic to use with a person whose feelings are upset is *to be an attentive listener.* If you show concern and let the other person talk about any upset feelings, the negative feelings are likely to lessen and the prospect will respect your concern. On the other hand, if you are insensitive to the feelings of an upset or unhappy prospect and attempt to carry on your sales presentation, you are not likely to be successful at reaching your objectives.

A prospect who is in a bad mood will often react negatively to your proposal or to you. If this happens you may have to exercise *tension binding.* Tension binding is the ability to inhibit a natural response once the stimulus for that response has been received.[4] For instance, a prospect in a bad mood may say, "Your proposal just doesn't make sense, it couldn't work that well." Your natural response might be to be defensive and snap back at the prospect, "What makes you say that?" This emotional outburst on your part would seriously injure your relationship with the prospect. Instead, by using

[4]Joseph W. Thompson, *Selling: A Managerial and Behavioral Science Analysis* (New York: McGraw-Hill, 1973), p. 297.

*"Mr. Stewart is out of his gourd at the moment.
May I take a message?"*

Drawing by H. Martin. © 1976, The New Yorker Magazine.

tension binding you can control your emotions and perhaps say, "I thought I had done a good job of justifying our position. What could I explain better?" This degree of maturity and control will be an invaluable asset to you in handling customers and prospects.

Many times, of course, you will find the prospect in a good mood, which presents an opportunity to accomplish more than you initially planned. The person feeling "up" may take a favorable view of you and your proposal and agree to purchase rather quickly.

Preoccupied Prospect

Often the person called upon is too polite not to see you, particularly if you arranged an appointment in advance. Yet when you come face to face, you recognize that although the prospect is physically present, psychologically the prospect's mind is on a task that has been interrupted or on another subject. When you sense this, the best tactic may be to offer to wait or return at another time. Alternatively, you may take advantage of the situation to see other people in the account whom you might not be able to see under normal circumstances. The insensitive salesperson in this situation may carry on a presentation, only to find that the other person has paid little or no attention.

Limited Time

You may have counted on far more time than you find available once you begin the interview. For instance, you may have planned on an hour for an interview but find that you have only fifteen minutes to make your presentation. Several tactical alternatives are available to you. First, you may attempt to streamline the presentation and get the essential ideas across in the limited time. This has several disadvantages, one being that you may set too fast a pace for the customer or prospect to understand. Moreover, in your rush to cover everything, you may not give the other person a chance to participate actively in the interview, thus causing you to miss valuable feedback. Another danger is that you may not give full importance to your product by the very rapid pace of your presentation under the pressure of a deadline.

Alternatively, you may stress the importance of what you have to offer and try to set up another appointment when you will have enough time to make your presentation. Fortunately, when this tactic is employed, the other person's curiosity is often aroused and he allots more time for the presentation. This tactic also has the advantage of emphasizing the importance of your product, but it has the disadvantage of delaying the buying decision. During the time between your present visit and the next call, a competitor may move in and get the order. A third alternative is to take advantage of the situation as a way of reaching someone else in the account. In order to determine which of these tactics is preferable, you must be sensitive to the prospect and consider the situation from the prospect's perspective.

WORKING LIKE A DOG GOT THIS CUSTOMER

Ken Olson, a saleperson for a dog food company, was calling on one of his customers, a man who owned a large store in a small town in his territory. The customer had been very suspicious of Ken because he was working on a master's degree and was much younger than the customer. On making a call one day, Ken found that the roof in the customer's storeroom had leaked and the storeroom had flooded badly. There were many bags of wet dog food, which weighed a ton. Instead of making his call, Ken rolled up his sleeves and helped the customer clean up the storeroom and salvage some of the inventory. The customer is now one of Ken's most loyal and profitable accounts.

Unexpected Problems and Difficulties

In the first few minutes of a call, you may discover that the prospect has one or more problems you had not planned on. These may range from delay in delivery of an order to defective merchandise; on the other hand, the problems may be totally unrelated to your products and services. It is up to you to adjust to the situation as you find it; you must depart from your planned presentation to assist in any way possible with the problems encountered. If you are unable to help directly, you may enhance your position by just being a good listener. If you are helpful in solving the prospect's problem, you are likely to strengthen the selling–buying relationship more effectively than if you had been able to follow your original plan for the visit.

Another Person Present

On some occasions the individual you call on may have another person present and make no effort to dismiss that person. The soundest tactic may be to remain silent and wait for the customer or prospect to fill you in on who the other person is and what the person's potential interest may be in the presentation. If the prospect does not do this, you may have to question either the person you are calling on or the guest in order to have a basis for relating your presentation to both parties. The key difficulty is likely to be the relative unfamiliarity of the third party with what has occurred on previous calls. You may have to brief the third party or you may encourage a summary from the customer or prospect of what has happened thus far. The briefing or the summary will serve to reinforce what has been accomplished to date, as well as giving you an opportunity to correct any misinformation.

Unanticipated Competitive Activity

Some sales tactics are countermeasures to tactics employed by competitors. For example, you might encounter an unanticipated price decrease by a competitor, causing you to change the planned presentation. In this situation you may ask the prospect what she is actually looking for in the offering. In fact, you may be able to turn this price concession of the competitor into an indication that the competitor is not able to sell on a quality basis. As another example, you might discover that a competitor has offered extensive technical assistance on a speculative basis, with a view toward making an inroad in one of your accounts. You may not be able to match the offer because of your firm's policy on such matters. Even if it were feasible to meet the offer, such a maneuver may be tactically dangerous, because it gives an impression of having held back legitimate assistance. A better course of action is to come up with a countermeasure. For instance, you may raise the question whether you ever get something for nothing. Even when the competitor makes a questionable move to obtain the business, however, it is unwise to criticize the competitor. Criticism is likely to arouse an unfavorable reaction in the prospect.

"Brain Picking"

In selling–buying situations in which technical advice and service make up a considerable part of what is purchased, you must be wary of the professional "brain picker." Some buyers, fortunately few in number, attempt to generate needed technical information, advice, and service from sources that are competent to provide it. Once these have been obtained, they turn to less competent firms for the actual products needed, often at a lower price. When this situation is encountered, you are challenged to try to maintain a relationship without overcommitting the requested advice and service. Sometimes you can offset providing advice and service by arriving at a dollar value for such help through astute questioning of the person who is seeking to get it free. For instance, you might ask the prospect to place a dollar value on the time it took you to provide drawings of a new project and to cost out the system. Then you can ask the buyer to deduct this amount mentally from your bid.

Interrupted Interview

It happens quite frequently that your interview with a prospect is interrupted by a visitor, such as a subordinate or a secretary, or by a telephone call. If the interruption is of a longer or more personal nature, you should offer to excuse yourself. If you are encouraged to stay, you should not appear to be listening to the call, nor should you inquire about it after the interruption. This would be impolite.

When interruptions such as these occur, they will disturb the prospect's train of thought. Thus, your first objective is to guide the prospect's attention back to what you are discussing. There are several ways of accomplishing this.

Repeat the last statement If the interruption was short and impersonal, you should merely repeat your last statement and pick up where you left off, being careful to monitor the nonverbal cues to make sure you have the prospect's attention.

Review high points If the interruption was involved or lengthy, you should review the high points and summarize the material you have covered. For instance, you might say, "Let's see, where were we. We had covered the size of the unit you are interested in, the 2300; and the type of financing you wanted . . ." This gets the prospect back into the presentation and ensures that key points have not been forgotten.

Ask questions Another tactic is to ask questions designed to get the prospect involved in the discussion. For instance, you might ask, "Tell me again what qualities you look for in a broker?" These questions should be broad enough to get involvement but not so specific that the prospect cannot answer them or is embarrassed because he or she cannot remember the answer.

Discuss a subject of mutual interest Sometimes in order to get the prospect's mind off the interruption, you will want to introduce some light conversation on a topic of mutual interest. If you know that the prospect is interested in tennis, you might say, "Did you see that tennis match on television the other night? Wasn't that great?" After a brief discussion of tennis, you can pick up where you left off, review high points, or ask questions. Hopefully you can divert the prospect's attention from the interruption. Another tactic is humor, if you feel comfortable with it and if it is appropriate with the prospect. It is also a good way to clear the air after an interruption.

Use visuals or samples Getting something such as a visual or a sample into the prospect's hands is also a good way to shift the prospect's attention back to the subject. When any sort of visual is used, it is important that you remain in control. You do not want the prospect reading the visual and not listening to you. Therefore, you are better off leading the prospect through the visual so that you are still in control.

Silence A very useful tactic after an interruption is simply to look prospects in the eye and remain silent.[5] This gives prospects time to gather their thoughts and will shift attention back to you and your presentation.

BEHAVIORAL INPUTS TO TACTICAL ADJUSTMENT

A major problem in tactical adjustment is that the saleperson fails to look at the world from the perspective of the customer. All the other factors in the process of tactical adjustment are secondary to the importance of being customer-oriented.

Instead of really concentrating on the prospect, some salespeople keep planning what they are going to say next. If they are concentrating on themselves, it is impossible to pay attention to the prospect and to adjust to the prospect's behavior. During the call, as you find out more about the prospect's background, personality, and motivation (discussed in Chapter 6), you must adjust your strategy to incorporate this new information.

In order to adjust your tactics effectively to the prospect's behavior it is useful to understand several behavioral factors that affect how the prospect interprets your presentation. Especially important are the prospects' perception of your presentation and their level of knowledge.

Perception

Perception is the process by which people take in information and attach meaning to this information. Prospects perceive by seeing, hearing, touching, smelling, and tasting inputs from their environment. The process of perception is subjective, selective, and summative in nature. It is also influenced by personal factors, present needs, and past experience. Each of these characteristics of perception will be discussed.

Subjective perception Perception is subjective because no two individuals perceive the same object or event in the same way. If a Republican and a Democrat attend a political rally to hear a Republican senator discuss a clean-air bill he introduced into Congress, each of them is likely to perceive

---

[5]See, for example, Jeremy Taylor and Alec MacKenzie, "The Power of Silence in Selling," *Business Quarterly* Vol. 48, No. 1 (Spring 1983), pp. 38–41.

the presentation differently. The Republican might very likely perceive the bill to be "far reaching" and certain to help cure the nation's air pollution problems. In contrast, the Democrat might perceive the proposal as limited in scope and nothing more than political propaganda.

Why would the two views vary so dramatically? Although both people may see themselves as having an objective opinion concerning the proposed legislation, their political biases are likely to influence what they perceive the actual message to be. Each may walk away from the meeting wondering how the other could be so ignorant not to understand the true meaning of the senator's speech.

This same situation occurs in selling. You can feel that you have made a logical sales presentation of a product that really does represent a good value for the customer. However, the customer's background, including such factors as previous experience with your company, will influence perception of the entire presentation. Thus, the prospect may come away from the presentation with an entirely different meaning from the one you intended. Think, for example, of all the various meanings for the word "strike." When you mention this word, the prospect could think you are referring to a baseball term, something you do with a match, labor unrest, a bowling term, or various other meanings. It is important that you understand the meaning the prospect actually attaches to what you say. You can determine this meaning by questioning the prospect; the answers will provide feedback on how he or she subjectively perceives your statements. For instance, you might say, "What application of this idea do you see for your firm?" Then listen carefully to see how the prospect explains the idea.

Selective perception Only a few of the messages you are exposed to each day are converted into conscious awareness. For instance, you are exposed to approximately 10,000 advertising messages per day through exposure to billboards, store signs, and other forms of mass media. Because it is impossible to deal with 10,000 advertising messages, your mind takes in only a few. Thus, your perception acts as a filter; it is selective in the information it lets in.

In personal selling, perception is selective when the prospect or customer perceives only some of the appeals and reasons for buying the product from your sales presentation. This phenomenon occurs for a variety of reasons. The prospect may have some psychological reason for not wanting to perceive some of the sales appeals or be preoccupied and not want to listen to a particular sales presentation.

Whatever the reason for selective perception on the part of the prospect or customer, you must detect it and make sure that your presentation is fully accepted and heard. The concept of selective perception means that merely sending messages to prospects is not sufficient. You must make sure that the messages are taken in.

One useful recommendation for overcoming this phenomenon of selective perception is to limit the number of points made during any single presentation. Excessive information that cannot be easily handled by customers will cause them to perceive selectively only parts of the total message. You should therefore concentrate on items that appear to be the most relevant and necessary to the prospect or customer to whom you are making the presentation.

Another suggestion is to note carefully the prospect's nonverbal reactions to your presentation. If you see that the prospect's attention is wandering, you probably are witnessing selective perception. Take this as a signal to adjust tactically.

Summative perception Perception is summative because the reception of a message frequently depends on the cumulative effects of the message over time. The more often the message is received, the more likely is a customer to take it in. Often a message must be repeated several times before it reaches a prospect's conscious awareness. Furthermore, the probability that a customer will correctly interpret a signal is enhanced if it is sent through two or more channels. Thus, choosing visuals to reinforce your key points is a good way to utilize the summative characteristics of perception.

Repetition over time is another way to ensure that the message is interpreted. As an example, if you want to make sure a customer is aware of the qualities and availability of a new product, you may send the customer a direct-mail promotion, but you will also pay the customer a personal visit and demonstrate the uses of the product. You should not be upset if you have to make several calls to convey your message. In the same way, if the customer is able to see a demonstration of the product in question, it may increase the chances of this communication being received.

Personal factors Personal factors that influence perception include the individual's self-image, needs, and past experience. The manner in which individuals perceive themselves will influence how they perceive an object. People who see themselves as cosmopolitan are more likely to notice a sports car than a four-door sedan. People's needs also determine their perceptual selectivity. An advertisement for a new home is less likely to be perceived by persons who are extremely happy in their present home than by those who have been transferred to a new location. Prospects who have a need for a product will have a tendency to attend *selectively* to messages about this type of product. Have you ever noticed that when you are ready to buy a product, such as a stereo, there are suddenly many advertisements and discussions of stereos? These messages were there all along; you simply selectively filtered them out until you had a need for the stereo.

People's needs also affect their memories. They tend selectively to forget information in which they are not interested. On the other hand, they will tend to remember information in which they are interested and which has benefits for them. For instance, although students sometimes forget an examination, they rarely forget spring break. Similarly, prospects will tend to remember information if it is linked to their needs, whereas they forget other information.

People's past experiences also influence their perceptions. A person who has had a favorable experience with a product will tend to attach favorable meanings to information about the product and will selectively screen out negative information. Thus, prospects have a tendency to distort information selectively on the basis of their past experiences.

Knowledge Level

The more customers or prospects know about the subject of your message, the easier it will be for them to comprehend the message. Therefore, you must make a conscious effort to determine how much knowledge customers or prospects have concerning the subject of discussion. A prospect with only a limited background in your area of expertise may choose not to admit ignorance by asking questions. As a result, you may think that you are doing a fine job of communicating when, in reality, the prospect does not understand you. In selling, you must continually be on guard so that you do not talk over the customer's head. If customers really do not understand what is going on, the chances are very slim that they will purchase the product. You must also use vocabulary that is familiar to the prospect. If you use unfamiliar jargon, the prospect will either stop listening or guess at the meaning.[6]

In a buying–selling situation, you must aim your message at the correct level for the persons you talk to, keeping in mind their knowledge level. As an example, you may begin your call on a particular account with a purchasing agent who has very little technical expertise with the product. For this person your presentation must be kept on a rather nontechnical basis. You may then call on an engineer in the same firm's production facility. Here you must switch gears and be prepared to talk in very technical terms about your product in order to communicate effectively with the engineer.

SUMMARY

Throughout this chapter the need to adjust to the unknown during a sales call was stressed. In order to do this well, you need to be empathic and flexible in your behavior. Your tactical objective in face-to-face contact with a prospect is to be in control without seeming to be. There are two methods of accomplishing this: employing low pressure and asking questions. In low-pressure selling you leave prospects feeling that they bought the product rather than being sold the product—that is, that they were in control of the purchase and that they made up their own mind. You should also ask questions to get prospects involved while still controlling the direction of the call.

Reactions of the prospect were classified into four categories: negative–voluntary, negative–involuntary, positive–voluntary, and positive–involuntary. For each of these reactions, an appropriate tactic is required to help move the interview closer to a completed sale. Among the many factors that may require you to maneuver tactically are the prospect's mood, preoccupations, limited time, and unexpected problems and difficulties, another person's presence, competitive activity, brain picking, and interrupted interviews. On-the-spot adjustments must be made for each unanticipated situation.

[6]William S. Howell, *The Empathic Communicator* (Belmont, Calif.: Wadsworth, 1982), p. 49.

If you are to adjust effectively to buyers' reactions, you need to understand how they perceive your presentation. The perceptual process is subjective, selective, and summative. Furthermore, perception is influenced by a person's self-image, needs, and past experience. You also need to be aware of the person's level of knowledge about your presentations so that you do not talk over or under the knowledge level of the other person.

PROBLEMS

1. The text suggests that to be effective at adjusting, a salesperson must be both perceptive and flexible. Explain.
2. What additional traits would help a salesperson to adjust?
3. Explain and illustrate the four kinds of prospect reactions cited in the text.
4. What are some circumstances that might limit the time a customer or prospect makes available to salespeople?
5. Suppose that an interview with a customer is interrupted by a short telephone call that does not seem very important. How would you handle the interruption? How would your adjustment differ if the call is long and involved?

EXERCISE 12

Objections: To illustrate reactions and tactics as they occur in selling.

To apply basic tactical concepts to personal experience.

PART A Reactions and Tactics

In the designated spaces, classify each reaction as positive–voluntary, negative–voluntary, positive–involuntary, or negative–involuntary; then, indicate an appropriate tactic.

REACTION	CLASSIFICATION	TACTIC
1. Smiles.		
2. "When can I get delivery?"		
3. Shuffles papers on desk.		
4. "Your price is too high."		
5. Looks out window.		
6. "I have too large an inventory now."		
7. Winds watch.		
8. "That sounds good."		
9. Frowns.		
10. "What company did you say you represent?"		

PART B **Examples of Reactions and Tactics**
The text suggested that any reaction observed during face-to-face communications may be classified as positive–voluntary, negative–voluntary, positive–involuntary, or negative–involuntary. Provide three examples of each.
For each example, provide an appropriate tactic.

	POSITIVE REACTION	TACTIC	NEGATIVE REACTION	TACTIC
Voluntary	1.		1.	
	2.		2.	
	3.		3.	
Involuntary	1.		1.	
	2.		2.	
	3.		3.	

PART C **Applications of Other Concepts**
All of us have tried to engage the attention of persons who were in a bad
mood, were preoccupied, had limited time, faced an unexpected problem,
had another person with them, or were interrupted by a visitor or telephone
call. Set forth your own experiences, indicating how you handled each situation. Be specific.

1. Bad mood.
2. Preoccupied.
3. Limited time.
4. Unexpected problem.
5. Another person present.
6. Interrupted.

Case 12-1 The Inconsistent Prospect

Dale Werner prided himself on being a pretty good salesperson. Yet Jim
McManus baffled him. Dale has been trying to get business from Jim for over
two years and has learned two things for sure about Jim. He is a man of many
moods and he seems impossible to pin down to a buying situation. As today's
call opens, here is the conversation.

JIM: Hi, Dale. You don't give up easily, do you?

DALE: Good morning, Jim. I sure don't. Not when I know how useful and
profitable you'd find our product line.

JIM: Yea. That's what every salesperson tells me. What did you think of the
ball game last Saturday?

DALE: It certainly was a cliff-hanger. The folks that started leaving in the last
few minutes missed the best part.

JIM: Well, Dale, go into your spiel. I always like to listen.

DALE: Well, Jim, I think you know our products as well as I do. You've heard me talk about them and you've seen our literature. I'm sure, if you try them, they'll sell themselves.

JIM: Dale, every salesperson thinks that way about his products. If he didn't, he would be in the wrong field.

DALE: Well, the real proof of such claims is profitable use. However, today my purpose is to ask your advice.

JIM: That's a switch. What about?

DALE: In analyzing my twelve calls on you, I've been trying to find out where I've gone wrong. You see many sales representatives. What mistakes have I made in calling on you? Why haven't I obtained an order?

1. Was it sound tactics for Dale to avoid another presentation of his product line?
2. What do you think of the tactic of asking for advice?

Case 12-2 Morrison's Jewelry Store

Morrison's is an independent firm serving a middle-class clientele. It enjoys a good reputation in the community. Engagement and wedding rings make up a significant share of total business. Vera King is a salesperson at Morrison's. She is straightening up the stock when a young man enters the store. He is hesitant and looks around at the dazzling display cases. Then he slowly approaches the display of engagement and wedding rings. Vera moves behind the counter and greets him as he moves toward her.

VERA: Good evening, I'm Vera King. May I assist you?

YOUNG MAN: Err . . . Well, I want to look at engagement rings. *(Vera judges his age at about twenty-five. She notices that he is neatly dressed and that his clothes are of good quality.)*

VERA: A lucky girl. Let me show you some of our popular styles. By the way, may I ask your name?

YOUNG MAN: I'm Tom Gorman.

VERA: Mr. Gorman, all the rings on this display tray are Keepsake. Your fiancée will know that name. It's famous for quality.

TOM: They are beautiful. Can you give me an idea of the prices?

VERA: Well, they range considerably. You'll notice that in the lower two rows we have ensembles of engagement and wedding rings.

TOM: Yes, I see. Of course, our wedding is still a long way off.

VERA: The advantage of the ensemble is that the rings are designed to go with one another.

TOM: I hadn't thought of that. If I were to select an ensemble, could the wedding rings be put on layaway?

VERA: Yes. The advantage of Keepsake is that models are numbered and kept in stock.

TOM: What is the price of this ensemble?

VERA: You certainly have excellent taste. The engagement ring is a full carat and the wedding band has individually cut diamonds in it. The price for the set is $1990. The groom's band is $210.

TOM: Whew. That's a lot of money.

VERA: Of course, you're really making a lifetime investment. When you look at it that way, price is unimportant. Besides, many of our customers finance their purchases.

1. Criticize Vera's tactics.
2. As the call proceeds, should Vera suggest that Tom bring his fiancée to the store before making a final decision?

Handling Objections

After studying this chapter, you should be able to

1. Identify various classifications of objections.
2. Recognize logical objections.
3. Know how to approach logical objections.
4. Describe various types of psychological objections and ways to handle them.
5. Specify ways to handle true and false objections.
6. Provide some insight on how to handle objections.

Sales resistance is anything the other person says or does to prevent you from achieving your call objectives. Objections are one common form of sales resistance. Whenever objections are raised, it is evident that a conflict exists between acceptance and rejection of your offering. Thus, objections can provide a potentially desirable situation, and if you handle them effectively a sale may result. Objections let you know that some interest is present but that a perceived problem must be overcome before a sale can be made.

If a particular objection to your product comes up frequently, you may want to do your best to answer the objection before the prospect can raise it. Handling objections in this manner ensures that you can make a more orderly presentation and maintain better control.[1]

Some salespeople fear that if they encounter an objection, they will lose a sale. Yet, in fact, the opposite is true. As can be seen from Figure 13.1, there is a greater likelihood of a successful call when prospects raise objections than when they do not. Sixty-four percent of calls during which an objection was raised had a successful outcome, whereas only 54 percent of those that proceeded without one were successful. Thus, you should not be afraid of objections.

Objections may occur at any point in the call. For instance, a prospect may object when a salesperson tries to set up an appointment, set up a demonstration, asks to see other people in the account, or after the presentation has been made. Thus, you must develop expertise for dealing with all types of objections.

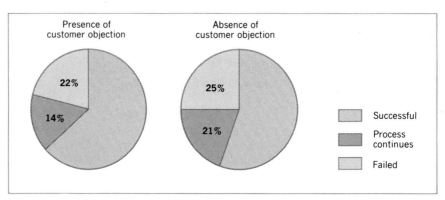

FIGURE 13.1 Outcome of sales calls by presence or absence of customer objection. Criteria for outcome: *successful calls*, prospect agrees to take some action furthering the sale; *process continues calls*, prospect agrees to meet again at some specific time and place but takes no additional action to further the sale; *failed calls*, all other calls. SOURCE: John Franco, "Skills, Coaching, and the Three Questions Sales Managers Ask Most," *Business Marketing*, Vol. 69, No. 12 (December 1984), p. 97. Copyright © 1984, by Crain Communications, Inc. Reprinted with permission of *Business Marketing*.

[1]See Dan Weadock, "Your Troops Can Keep Control—and Close the Sale—by Anticipating Objections," *Sales and Marketing Management*, Vol. 124, No. 4 (March 17, 1980), pp. 102–106; or Ralph Aiello, "Anticipate Objections to Make More Sales," *Selling Direct* (February 1984), pp. 14–18.

**CLASSIFYING
OBJECTIONS**

This chapter explores several aspects of objections. First, they are classified as logical or psychological, stated or hidden, true or false. Next, logical and psychological objections are explored in depth. Finally, methods for handling true and false objections are examined, and some concluding tips for handling objections are given.

CLASSIFYING OBJECTIONS

Before deciding how to handle an objection, you must first classify it according to the six categories shown in Figure 13.2. Your approach should vary, depending on which type of objection you are facing.

Logical Versus Psychological Objections

Logical objections stem from aspects of the offering itself over which you have some control, such as the product or deliveries. In contrast, psychological sales resistance is an emotional reaction to such factors as being disturbed by a salesperson, having to give up money to receive a product, or feeling pressure to make a decision. Logical sales resistance is usually overcome by providing information about the product or by reasoning. No amount of product information, however, will overcome psychological sales resistance, since it is not based on an evaluation of your offering. When an objection is psychological, you must determine more about its nature and then try to lessen or remove it. For instance, if you sense that the prospect does not like to make decisions, you must make the decision easy and show how others have found the decision rewarding.

Stated Versus Hidden Objections

Another distinction between objections depends on whether they are stated or hidden. The customer comes out and tells you a stated objection. For instance, the prospect might say, "Your price is too high, I couldn't possibly afford that," or "I don't feel comfortable making a decision right now; maybe I should wait until the new models come out?" The key point is that the prospect voices the objection (see, for example Figure 13.3).

When an objection is hidden, the prospect either does not voice it or comes up with a stalling objection that is not the real one. A prospect who likes a car but feels it is too expensive might say "I don't like the color" or "I'm not in the market right now," even though these are not real objections. The prospect may be afraid or embarrassed to admit an inability to afford the automobile. Some frequently heard objections such as "I'll have to think

---

Logical versus psychological
Stated versus hidden
True versus false

FIGURE 13.2 Classifying objections.

FIGURE 13.3 The stated objection. SOURCE: *Sales and Marketing Management*, Vol. 136, No. 1 (January 31, 1986), p. 78.

about it'' or ''I'm not really in the market'' do not represent the real objection but are merely stalls.

Prospects often give a stalling objection when the real one is psychological, such as an unwillingness to make a decision or being embarrassed by an inability to afford the product. Prospects then stall, saying I'll have to think this over,'' or ''I must discuss this with my wife or manager,'' or ''I'm busy now'' or ''I'm not interested.'' Objections such as these may be the real reason, or they may be a stall to hide the real reason. You must determine through questioning, listening, observing nonverbal cues, and empathizing whether they are real objections or stalls. The stall form of hidden objection is very difficult to deal with since it is not the real objection but merely an alibi or excuse; thus, it often does not seem to make sense. To get at the real reason, you must encourage the prospect to be honest and open with you. If you suspect an objection is a stall, ask the prospect whether that is the real reason. In order to be effective, however, you must have established the proper trusting relationship with the prospect.

An important point is that you would *always* rather have a stated objection than a hidden or stall objection. A stated objection gives you a chance to deal with the real problem and offer evidence or other benefits to counter the objection. With a hidden objection, however, you do not know whether

TABLE 13.1

_____327

HANDLING HIDDEN OBJECTIONS

- _Ask questions._ Asking questions is a good way to get at hidden objections. Questions such as, "How do you like this model?" or "Was this what you were looking for?" are useful. You should encourage prospects to talk about the product.

- _Listen._ Another useful technique is to listen carefully. Sometimes prospects will voice an objection in a way that, unless you are listening carefully, the objection will seem unstated. Many times salespeople gloss over objections, thinking they are minor; then they do not understand why they cannot close the sale. It is important to listen to your prospects.

- _Note nonverbal cues._ Nonverbal reactions to your presentation are often clues to hidden objections. If you pay careful attention to prospects during your presentation, you may see them frown, shake their head, or offer a puzzled look. Even if they do not state an objection, their nonverbal behavior may suggest one. The key point is that you must carefully monitor their reactions to pick up the objection.

- _Bring it up yourself._ As a last resort, you may bring up an objection yourself. For instance, if you have presented your benefits and are not getting any objections but also no signals that the prospect is ready to buy, you might state "Many people are worried about the price of this machine; is that a concern of yours?" If the prospect replies that it is, you can deal with the price problem. This approach should be used cautiously to avoid raising an objection the prospect has not thought about, but as a last resort it may work.

to talk about price, quality, delivery, or style. Like a marksman shooting at an invisible target, you do not know what you are aiming at. To keep prospects from hiding objections, which are nearly impossible to deal with, you must develop an atmosphere of trust so that prospects feel they can be open and talk to you. Table 13.1 shows a number of ways to identify hidden objections and bring them out into the open.

True Versus False Objections

Another way of classifying objections is by whether they are true or false. True objections are those that are in fact present and are undeniable by you as a salesperson. If a prospect for a new top-of-the-line $200,000 computer says it is expensive and this is true, you would not want to deny this. Similarly, if a prospect notes that a house lacks a swimming pool, you would not want to argue that there is a pool. The best general approach to take with true objections is to acknowledge them and then try to provide prospects with offsetting benefits.

On the other hand, many objections are false; prospects believe something about the product or company that is not based on fact. It is important to note that many times prospects perceive false objections to be true. Thus, you must be careful when handling false objections not to embarrass prospects or talk down to them. For instance, prospects may believe that a small machine would not be powerful enough for their needs. If this is not the case, it would be a false objection. To handle false objections, provide prospects with information so they can see for themselves that the objection is not true. Various approaches for handling true and false objections are given later in this chapter.

Of course, these categories are not independent. An objection may be psychological and hidden, or logical and false, or stated and true. Consider, for example, a situation in which prospects with hidden objections they don't want to reveal consciously provide you with a false objection, such as "I'm not in the market right now" or "I'm just looking." Since these are not the real objections, they are difficult to handle. Even though these categories are often interdependent, they can help you to understand the objection better.

LOGICAL OBJECTIONS

Prospects raise logical objections when they perceive a discrepancy between their needs and wants and the want satisfier offered by the salesperson. In this section various reasons for logical sales resistance are examined, as well as types of logical resistance, and, finally, tactics that may be used to overcome logical resistance.

Reasons for Logical Objections

A main cause of logical objections is poor communication on the part of either the seller or the buyer. You may not have obtained a comprehensive picture of the needs and wants of the account, or you may have misunderstood or misinterpreted the information obtained. The resulting presentation in either instance is likely to be less than ideal. Poor communication might also occur when you use words and phrases that have one meaning for you and a different meaning for the prospect. Abstract words and phrases, and technical jargon, cause misunderstanding and therefore sales resistance. Another cause of logical sales resistance is poor qualifying of prospects, in which case you are facing prospects who either do not have a need for the product or are not able to pay for it. Thus, they will object to the offering. Although logical objections can occur throughout the selling–buying process, they are most likely to come up during the presentation, for it is at this point that prospects are considering your proposition on its merits.

Specific Types of Logical Sales Resistance

Seven different types of logical sales resistance are explored, along with techniques for effectively dealing with each of them. The seven logical objections

FUNKY WINKERBEAN   **Tom Batiuk**

have to do with price, direct factory price, product characteristics, no demand for the product, deliveries, the salesperson's company, and the age of the firm.

Price In many fields of selling, the most recurrent form of logical sales resistance centers around price.[2] Price is the value, in monetary terms, placed on the offering by the seller. Unless the prospect sees value in the proposal that is equal to or greater than the quoted price, no transaction will occur. This is why it is important for you to avoid mentioning price until you have thoroughly explored the needs and wants of prospects and determined as well as possible their values. Of course, sometimes price can be a major benefit and should be mentioned up front, in which case you are not likely to get a price objection unless it is, "How can you make it so inexpensively?"

Almost without exception, when it comes to value, the prospect centers on the product itself. The prospect does not take into account associated services, the source's reputation, or your problem-solving and creative-thinking ability. It is up to you to include these in your presentation and to try to get the prospect to place a value on them. Otherwise, you may not be able to offset a competitor's price on the basis of product alone. Finally, you must remember that an objection to a price may reflect the true state of affairs—your prices may indeed be higher than those of the competition. Or the objection may be a false one—that is, your prices are in line with those of the competition. If the objection to price is true, the trick, says one salesperson, "is to know your field so well that when your competitor's price is lower, you'll not only know why, but you'll bounce back with reasons why your deal is still better than the next person's.[3] Specific methods of handling the price objection are shown in Table 13.2.

A direct factory price When the same product is available either directly from the manufacturer or through a wholesaler, the wholesaler's salesperson often encounters a special type of price resistance. The prospect claims to be getting a direct deal at a price lower than the wholesaler can quote. However, buying direct usually requires purchase of large quantities. Questioning may reveal that the direct price of the larger quantity is more than offset by the materials-handling costs, inventory costs, and the cost of the capital tied up in the purchase. The Steel Service Center Institute, an association of steel resellers, conducted a highly successful marketing campaign on the theme, "Cost of Possession," to offset these kinds of objections.

Product characteristics Almost as frequently as you encounter the price objection, you face objections to one or more characteristics or properties of your product. Often the aspects of the product that are objected to are unfamiliar to the objector and hence not completely understood. This kind of

---

[2]Bess Ritter May, "Overcome Price Objections: Don't Lose Sales," *Specialty Salesman,* Vol. 71, No. 6 (June 1983), pp. 10–12.

[3]Ted Pollock, "Objections—How to Handle Them," *The American Salesman,* Vol. 30, No. 1 (January 1985), p. 25.

TABLE 13.2

HANDLING THE PRICE OBJECTION

- *Sell benefits.* Rather than talking about the price of your product or service, it is useful to talk about the customer benefits associated with the offering.
- *Never quote a price without a supporting benefit.* Whenever you quote a price, be sure to accompany it with a supporting benefit. For instance, you might say "The delivered cost of this copier is $2500. That includes a one-year warranty and a service contract, which means you will have no maintenance for the first year."
- *Do not postpone responding to a price objection.* Often salespeople will postpone addressing a price objection until the offering has been described enough to show its benefits. The problem is that if the price issue is not addressed, the prospect may mentally tune out the rest of the presentation, having decided the product or service is unaffordable. Thus, although it is nice to be able to describe your offering completely before you deal with price, if price does come up earlier, it is advisable to address it then or risk the danger of losing the prospect's attention.
- *Do not invite price comparisons.* Unless you know that your prices are lower than competitors', do not invite price comparisons. Instead you should sell the value delivered by your product, the benefits from owning it, and the product's unique aspects, all of which make it worth the price.
- *Describe price in terms of a profit or an investment.* For many products there is a profit or return on investment associated with using the product. For instance, a machine may save labor, eliminate waste, and speed production—all resulting in a positive return. Stressing return on investment rather than price is a good tactic. Similarly, some consumer purchases may be perceived as an investment. For instance, purchasing an expensive house may be justified in terms of the home's appreciation and profitable resale.
- *Break price into small units.* Often it is useful to break total price down into smaller units in order to show the value being given. An expensive life insurance policy might be shown to cost only dollars a day, a building could be described in terms of the cost per square foot, or a consumer purchase might be explained in terms of the monthly payment.
- *Make sure you are comparing the same packages.* Often buyers will receive a price quotation from a competitor and then quote you that price if your price is higher. When you get this type of objection, it is important to make sure you are comparing the same offering. For instance, does the quote include warranty, or installation? Is it the base price or list price, and does it include any accessories? You must also find out what model is being quoted, at what quantity, and whether delivery is included. Failure to do this can hurt your position. A competitor may be quoting a base price for a large quantity and excluding deliveries. If you were quoting a list price plus accessories, without quantity discounts but with deliveries, your price would be much higher.

objection can be minimized if you become thoroughly familiar with the products your prospects use at present and explain in your presentation what your product has in common with them as well as its unique features. These can be presented in "benefit" terms.

No demand for the product Sales representatives calling on retailers often encounter the objection, "We have had no call for that product." In most instances this is the problem of the chicken and the egg. Until the product is stocked, it will not be promoted, hence customers will not seek it. If you note the competing products in stock, you may offset this resistance by inquiring about the volume of turnover in the other items. You may then be able to show, using marketing research information, that in test markets your product line did better than the competitor's product. In some retail situations, it can be shown that offering alternative brands of a product increases the total volume being sold. Finally, you may wish to stress the potential campaign your firm will use to stimulate demand for the product.

SELL QUALITY NOT PRICE

One John Deere salesperson relates the following story about selling benefits rather than just price. He was going after a sale and it came down to two final contenders. The buyer called the Deere salesman in to give him one last chance. He said, "You're just too high on the price side. No hard feelings, and we hope we can do business with you again in the future." The Deere salesperson was about to walk out the door, unhappy to say the least. Then he had an inspiration. He turned around and said, "Those are nice-looking boots you've got on." The buyer was a bit surprised but said, "Thanks" and went on to talk for a minute or so about those fine boots, how unique the leather was, and why they were practical as well as fine. Then the salesperson said to him, "How come you buy those boots and not just a pair off the shelf in an Army–Navy surplus store?" It must have taken twenty seconds for the grin to spread all the way across the buyer's face. "The sale is yours," he said, and he got up and came around the desk and gave the Deere salesman a hearty handshake.

SOURCE: Thomas J. Peters and Nancy K. Austin, *A Passion for Excellence* (New York: Random House, 1985). Copyright © 1985, by Thomas J. Peters and Nancy K. Austin. Reprinted by permission of Random House, Inc.

Deliveries In many fields of selling, deliveries provide a basis for objection. If you have been able to work with the account previously, you should have a fairly accurate idea of delivery needs. With manufacturing firms, these needs often relate directly to the production schedule. With resellers, the needs are a function of the volume of turnover of the item being sold. Sometimes purchasing executives do not have the full picture of their firm's delivery needs and hence insist on immediate delivery as a precautionary measure. Your understanding of the true delivery requirements of the prospect puts you in a good position to ensure that your company will be able to meet the prospect's needs.

Salesperson's company An objection to your company may take this form: "You are a giant firm; we are just a small business. We prefer to do business with companies our own size." Faced with this objection, you can show the advantages that can be gained from a big supplier; for example, certainty of a source of supply and a variety of technical resources to assist with problems. Or you may be able to demonstrate that, by virtue of the divisionalized structure of the firm and its decentralized sales organization, your firm is really no bigger than the prospect's.

In contrast, large prospects may indicate that your firm is too small to meet their needs. You may answer by indicating that the prospect will be considered a key account and given all the care and individual treatment that such a situation implies. You may also show that a small firm provides considerably more flexibility in meeting the needs and wants of the prospect than a large organization would.

Age of the firm Sometimes the age of your firm constitutes the basis for an objection. There may be a reluctance to deal with a new firm that is in the course of getting under way and establishing a reputation. If you represent such a firm, you might indicate the years of cumulative experience offered by the personnel of your firm. You may also show that, because it is new, the firm is far more innovative than many of its older competitors. In addition,

ICE WATER FOR BREAKFAST OVERCOMES AN OBJECTION

Joseph Schmelzer III, president of Equipment, Inc., a Jackson, Mississippi construction and materials-handling equipment dealer, relates that his most rewarding sale was at fifteen years of age. He was selling Black & Decker industrial tools, construction equipment, and Igloo water coolers to builders at job sites.

Being the son of the owner of the company, he drove the delivery truck. One day, his dad told him to go ahead and try to sell some equipment. He called on one builder and tried to sell him some tools. Unfortunately, the builder didn't need them. Next, he tried to sell him some steel scaffolding. The builder didn't need that either. Then he tried to sell him some concrete pins— no sale. By this time, he could see the builder was trying to get rid of him. The last thing he could think of to sell him were the portable water coolers, and the builder told him that they were no good without ice water in them. This gave him an idea.

The next morning, he got up at 5:30 and went to get ice to put in the coolers. He showed up at the job site at 7:00 A.M. with the ice still intact. Well, to make a long story short, the builder ended up buying two coolers—as well as all his other supplies—from him.

This was the first and definitely the most rewarding sale of his career, even though recently he closed a deal for some automated guided-vehicle systems and other materials-handling equipment. In twenty-five years, he went from $15 water coolers to $850,000 worth of equipment in a single sale.

SOURCE: "Strange Tales of Sales," *Sales and Marketing Management,* Vol. 134, No. 8 (June 3, 1985), pp. 42–46.

you may imply that, being new, the firm is going to have to try much harder to please each account than would a firm that is older and that has grown complacent. Rarely is there an objection to a firm on the basis of its being too old. Most people equate time in business with stability and reliability. If, however, you do encounter this objection you might show how innovative and progressive your firm really is and point out its proven track record in good and bad times.

One Way To Handle Logical Objections

Tactics for combating logical resistance are quite different from those used to reduce psychologically founded resistance. They are based on the premise that people place more credence in what they say themselves than in what others tell them. Thus, your task is to get prospects to answer their own objections. Logically founded objections are negative–voluntary reactions. A radical shift is called for to counter them; you must do or say something that will elicit a positive reaction.

Four steps designed to help you deal with logical sales resistance are to establish a positive set, clarify and define objections, select the best answer, and question the prospect. These steps are shown in Figure 13.4.

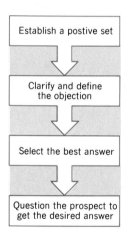

FIGURE 13.4 Steps in handling a logical objection.

Establish a positive set The first step is to establish a receptivity or positive mind set in the other person by doing two things: (1) show an appreciation of the prospect's point of view, and (2) give the prospect the deserved status as the prospective purchaser. You might say, for example, "I see what you mean" or "That's a good point, many people feel that way."

Clarify and define the objection The second step is to clarify and define the actual objection. Through questioning, you must get the prospect to be as specific as possible about the objection. After such questioning, you may state the objection as you understand it and see whether your statement is in agreement with the thinking of the prospect. For example, if the prospect objects to the price, you would want to clarify points such as these.

1. Is this a general objection not only to my offering but to the offerings of competitors as well?
2. If this objection is to my offering, is it based on a comparison with competitive offerings? If so, which ones?
3. If the objection is based on the judgment of the prospect, how was the judgment arrived at?
4. What would be a fair price? In other words, how much money is standing between us?
5. If price varies with quantity purchased, what quantity of the product is the prospect referring to?

Select the best answer Your third step is to formulate in your own mind the best possible answer to the objection as it has been clarified. You should not, however, furnish the prospect with the answer directly. Rather, it is important that customers be given the opportunity to take an active role in the process and thereby help sell themselves the product.

Question the prospect The fourth and last step is to question the prospect in a way that allows the prospect to answer his or her own objections. The dialogue as set forth in Table 13.3 illustrates this four-step method of handling logically based resistance.

TABLE 13.3
AN EXAMPLE OF THE FOUR-STEP METHOD OF HANDLING SALES RESISTANCE

Step 1 – Establishing Readiness

PROSPECT: That price is far too high.

SALESPERSON: Everything seems to cost more today, doesn't it?

PROSPECT: You're sure right about that.

SALESPERSON: Your firm expects you to make profitable purchases?

PROSPECT: Yes, I do my best.

SALESPERSON: This means you have to analyze carefully the full value in any offering, doesn't it?

PROSPECT: Yes, but I still say that your price is out of line.

Step 2 – Clarifying the Objection

SALESPERSON: Might I ask what you consider a fair price based on your value analysis?

PROSPECT: Well, I don't have exact figures, but I'd say about 30 cents a unit less than you quote.

SALESPERSON: What unit value would you place on our guarantee of uniform quality from batch to batch?

PROSPECT: I don't know, but that doesn't amount to much. We test a sample out of each delivery ourselves.

SALESPERSON: That sounds like a good precaution if you are not certain of quality. What does that cost?

PROSPECT: I'd say about 5 cents prorated over the normal order.

SALESPERSON: From a cost standpoint, what is your optimum order quantity?

PROSPECT: About 1000 units.

SALESPERSON: Would it increase your unit cost very much to order 4000 at a time?

PROSPECT: There would be some dollars tied up on inventory, but I can't think of much beyond that. However, with our plant expansion, storage space is at a premium.

Step 3 – Mentally Formulating the Answer

SALESPERSON: *(Our price breaks 30 cents a unit at 4000 quantity. The prospect's own estimate of testing cost is 5 cents. I can meet his price if I can get an order for 4,000 with delivery in modules of 1000 as the prospect needs them.)*

Step 4 – Questioning To Have Prospects Answer Their Own Questions

SALESPERSON: If you could eliminate testing incoming purchases, it would save at least 5 cents a unit, wouldn't it?

PROSPECT: This is right, but we'd need to be certain of quality if we did.

SALESPERSON: Would a guarantee covering replacement of goods plus any and all costs or damages incurred through faulty quality be attractive?

PROSPECT: Yes.

SALESPERSON: Would you place an order if you could save 5 cents under your own unit value estimate?

PROSPECT: I certainly would.

SALESPERSON: By ordering 4000 units, you gain the advantage of our volume price, which is 30 cents less per unit than when purchases are in smaller quantities. We will deliver your order in modules of 1000 on dates you specify. We will guarantee quality as I've just outlined so you can save the 5 cents unit cost of testing.

PSYCHOLOGICAL OBJECTIONS

Even if there were a perfect match between the benefits you offer and the needs and wants of the account, and thus there were no logical basis for failure to purchase, psychologically founded objections might still exist. In this section reasons for psychological objections, their timing, and seven particular types of psychological objections are examined.

Reasons for Psychological Objections

One of the most important causes of psychological objections is the availability of competitive offerings. The prospect may be concerned that all alternatives have not been explored. The greater the number of available options, the more difficult decision making becomes. A second reason is the interactive nature of the prospect's perceptions and feelings. Rarely is a buying decision, even in the industrial marketplace, made exclusively by logical thought processes; the prospect's perceptions and feelings are also influential. A prospective buyer may balk because of a vague feeling of uneasiness and uncertainty. A third reason is that human beings tend to engage in rationalization—that is, after-the-fact justification of decisions and actions. A prospect may think the proposal is satisfactory, yet hesitate to buy for lack of a sufficient number of reasons to justify it as a good idea. Thus they are not able to rationalize the purchase. Finally, psychological objections may come from attitudes and feelings present in interpersonal relationships. In these instances, resistance might stem from customer's lack of attention during the presentation or customer's unwillingness to admit ignorance of a specific aspect of the product.

Timing of Psychological Objections

Psychologically founded objections may occur at any time, but they generally surface during the beginning or end of the selling–buying process. Psychological sales resistance may occur at the beginning of a sales call since it is more comfortable not to need anything than to have one's needs disturbed. The more pleasant people find the status quo, the more likely they are to resist any disturbance of it. After all, there is always some risk in making a change.

Psychological resistance may build up as the presentation proceeds and you attempt to close. Many people find the decision to buy painful, either because they are parting with money or because they are uncertain of the purchase. This, incidentally, is why you should use the word value rather than price in talking with customers and prospects. Most people associate price with laying out money; they view value as what they are receiving.

Specific Types of Psychological Objections

Psychological sales resistance presents a more complex problem than logical resistance. To handle it, you must first determine the psychological or social needs the other person is satisfying by engaging in it. Once this is done, you must find some way to meet these needs and still achieve your call objective. Seven specific types of psychological sales resistance and techniques for handling each type are considered.

Resistance to interference Some prospects are content with their present situation and resist any interference that tries to change what they are doing.

There are several suggestions for reducing resistance to interference. First, you should try to set up interviews in advance through correspondence or over the telephone. In some instances, regular calls, such as those by route salespeople, can be made without a prior appointment. Second, you should be attentive to your physical appearance and personal manner so that your appearance is appealing. This will tend to overcome the initial impulse to deny an interview. Although it is unlikely that you can eliminate this type of psychological resistance, you can hold it to a minimum by a little forethought and planning.

Preference for established habits Habits are a stabilizing influence on society and on the individual. If it were not for habits, behavior would be less predictable than it is now. Habits can both aid and hinder the selling process. When you can get information about a prospect's habits, you feel you have a better chance of selling to the prospect; yet the very nature of selling is such that a sale almost invariably calls for a change of habits before the sale can be made. It becomes obvious, then, that anticipated change is a potent source of sales resistance.

To the salesperson who is aware of this resistance to change, there is no substitute for the knowledge of how the prospect will use the goods. Part of your job is to demonstrate how products fit into the buyer's living pattern. A change of habits that can be shown to increase satisfaction is more attractive than one in which no increase in satisfaction is apparent. For example, a prospect interested in an automatic lawn sprinkler may be shown the great amount of time saved by having the sprinklers on timers, which means that they do not have to be watched. If you know that the prospect enjoys tennis, you can point out how this extra time could be used for tennis.

Another way of reducing the resistance to changing habits is to reduce the gap or apparent difference between the old habit and the new one. This can be done by talking in language and terms familiar to the customer, by referring to people known to the customer, and by minimizing the novel aspects of using the new product.

Resistance is as likely to be focused on the dislike of giving up old ideas as it is on the dislike of adopting new ones. You should not make the mistake of repeatedly stressing the product benefits when they have already been accepted by the customer. Rather, you should concentrate on minimizing the change in habits made necessary for adopting a new product.

Apathy or lack of desire for new products It is natural for a customer to resist a proposition for which no need is felt. To supply product information and customer benefits convincingly is the best way to overcome this type of sales resistance. If you take the time to develop a presentation that stresses the quality of merchandise in relation to its price and ways it can help solve the customer's specific problems, you will have a good chance of overcoming this type of resistance.

Traditional unpleasant associations triggered by sales representatives Many persons react with resentment to a salesperson's approach. You cannot ignore this form of resistance, but you can reduce it by conducting yourself in a businesslike and dignified manner. In this instance you must first sell yourself. You can also try to counter such suspicions by referring the prospect to customers who will speak well of you. If appropriate, you can appeal to the fairness of the prospect by asking whether all salespersons should be condemned on the basis of experience with one who was unpleasant.

Tendency to resist domination by others The nature of the sales process is such that some salespeople encountered earlier may have tried to dominiate the prospect. Thus the prospect may be uncomfortable in dealing with salespeople. In fact, a prospect may anticipate domination and show resistance from the beginning of the sales contact. Even though a prospect wants the product, the person may be inhibited from purchasing it until a face-saving mechanism is found to make it appear to others that the product was bought by, rather than sold to, the prospect.

You should recognize the customer's need to feel in control of the interview. Your satisfaction should be derived from getting an order, not from dominating the interview. If you look for opportunities to make the customer feel important, you will eliminate this source of resistance. The technique by which this is accomplished is low-pressure selling.

Predetermined ideas about products or services Often a prospect's preconceived ideas about a product, though unwarranted, may close the prospect's mind to the purchase. If you question the prospect's belief or try to change the prospect's mind with logic, you will probably intensify the prejudice.

The first step in dealing with a prejudice is to accept the fact that it is held as firmly by the prospect as though it were based on truth. Show that you can appreciate the point of view expressed, and do not try to dispose of the prejudice on the basis of logic or your own belief. It should be recognized that the problem may be deep-seated and may represent emotional resistance. Solving such problems may be beyond your capabilities, so it may be necessary to ignore the prejudice and try to make the sale on some other basis.

Dislike of making decisions Making a decision is a painful process for some people. They fear the consequences of their actions and do not want to disturb the status quo. Yet, before an order is obtained, a decision must be made—namely, a decision to buy. Many sales are carried to the point at which the order is ready for signature, but the salesperson cannot overcome the resistance of the customer to this final act.

Nevertheless, things are not as bad as they seem. Obviously a strong tendency to buy exists or this point of conflict would never have been reached. The barrier may be a lack of self-confidence on the part of the customer. One way of handling this situation is to refer to customers who have bought and are satisfied. The greater the prestige of such references, the more effective they will be for this purpose. The important thing to remember is that where the motive to buy is strong, the problem is not so much one of talking about the product as of thinking about the customer and searching for ways to reduce apprehension about making a decision. There are several ways you can make it easier for buyers who do not like to make decisions. First, you can try to offer some protection against risks. You can stress to the buyer guarantees, warranties, and the ability to return a product if not satisfied. You can also point to satisfied customers as testimonials to the minimal amount of risk. Finally, you might offer some special bonus for making a decision now, such as additional merchandising, advertising, or a special discount. Often these will induce a decision.

ADDITIONAL METHODS OF HANDLING OBJECTIONS

Your approach to handling objections will differ depending on whether you are handling a true or a false objection. Specific approaches for handling each type of objection are presented here, as are some overall tips for handling objections.

Handling True Objections

True objections come up when a prospect identifies a real limitation of your product. Almost all products have some potential disadvantages. The product with the highest quality will generally be higher priced, and the low-cost alternative may suffer on some other dimension. When a true objection is raised, do not deny it but instead counter with all the advantages of your offering. You can handle the true objection by a number of different methods: agree and counter, list advantages and disadvantages, positive conversion, compare or constrast, and compare to alternatives.

Agree and counter The agree-and-counter technique consists of agreeing with the customer's objection and then giving more information to support your point of view. This technique is based on the premise that agreeing with prospects shows them that you respect their opinion, avoids an argument, and disarms them so that they will be more responsive to your point of view. This technique is also sometimes called the "yes, but" technique.[4] For example, if you are told that your firm's price is too high, you might counter by stating, "Yes, our prices do seem higher than those of the competition, but when you consider the free service that we provide at the time of the installation and our two-year guarantee, I feel you will conclude that our prices are very competitive."

Sometimes you do not want to agree with the objection itself, especially if it is false, but you still want to use the "yes, but" technique. In these situations you may want to agree that the prospect has raised an important point.

List advantages and disadvantages Another approach for handling the true objection is to list the advantages and disadvantages of your offering. The true objection would be the disadvantage, and you can counter with all the advantages of your product. One version of this listing would be a "T"-account close, as discussed in the next chapter. Using this method, you write a T on a piece of paper; then, on one side put "reasons to buy" and on the

---

[4]For an interesting alternative viewpoint, see Dan Weadock, "Saying 'Yes . . . But' Is Really No Way to Overcome a Buyer's Objection," *Sales and Marketing Management,* Vol. 123, No. 5 (October 15, 1979), pp. 94–96.

other put "reasons not to buy." Then list all the advantages of your product on one side and the true objection on the other.

Positive conversion Turning an objection into a reason for buying is a method called the positive conversion or boomerang. A typical example is to answer a statement such as, "Although the proposition seems very desirable, I have no money," with "The reason I brought this to your attention is that it will save you money." Another objection, "Your organization is too small to provide the service we need," can be boomeranged by replying, "Our small size is one of our assets: it permits us to give personal service."

Compare or contrast Comparing or contrasting are special ways of offsetting or minimizing an objection. Rather than offering a counterargument or playing down the importance of the objection, you contrast or compare it with something that is quite acceptable. A sophisticated machine that is designed for many years of service might appear expensive in terms of its list price. Pointing out that the cost is about that of a quart of milk or a pack of cigarettes a day, however, can make the amount seem inconsequential. Such a comparison may have the effect of neutralizing the objection.

Compare to alternatives Although your offering may have a certain limitation, you can often compare it to the other alternative products or to not buying; it may be better than anything else available. In response to a price objection, you might respond, "It's true our price is higher, but look at the features you get that no one else has." Then list the unique features of your machine.

Handling False Objections

False objections are easier to handle than true objections, because you can counter them with facts. However, such objections pose a specific problem in that it is important not to countradict the prospect, even if the person is wrong. You will be tempted to jump in and show where the prospect is wrong; however, rather than providing prospects with the correct information, you must allow them to accept the facts without losing face.[5] That is, you don't want to make them embarrassed or uneasy. Several approaches are available for doing this in a professional manner. You can take the blame for the misunderstanding by saying something like "Maybe I didn't explain the situation well enough" and then provide the correct information. You might also indicate that the incorrect information is held by others. You might say, for instance, "Many people believe that this product is not very efficient. However, let me show you the test results from an independent lab . . ."

Another tactic is to use a third party to soften the misunderstanding. You might say, for example, "I had another customer who felt the same way. She

---

[5]See George Reinfeld, "Objections: What are They? Their Cause and Cure," *Inland Printer/American Lithographer* (January 1975), p. 73.

tried the product and she has been very satisfied." You might even use the customer for a testimonial. Again, this allows the buyer to save face and makes a change of mind easier.

There are a number of different methods for handling the false objection, including direct denial, testimonials, tests, warranties and guarantees.

Direct denial Sometimes customers offer an objection that is not valid; perhaps they are misinformed, or perhaps they want to harass you. In either case, a direct denial of the objection together with a statement of the facts may be in order. Caution must be used, however, for such an outright contradiction may cause the customer to take offense.

Your manner is also important when you deny the objection. You should remain cool and calm and show that you respect the prospect's position. You might even indicate that you would probably feel the same way were you in that position. The important point is that your denial of the objection does not disrupt your relationship with the prospect.[6]

Testimonials Another way to counter the false objection is to use testimonials. Rather than talking about the offering yourself, you let a satisfied customer overcome the objection. For example, a prospect might not agree that a product would cut energy bills. Rather than trying to convince the prospect yourself, you could arrange calls that would allow satisfied customers to report what they feel about cost savings. Use of testimonials has the advantage of using a very credible source as spokespersons for your offering. You must, however, be careful to prescreen the customers you use to make sure they are satisfied.

Tests Using test results such as those of independent laboratories and *Consumer Reports* to support your claim is another approach. The objectivity of these sources makes them especially useful in countering false objections. For example, salespeople for a pharmaceutical company might quote a research study done at a prestigious medical school to overcome an objection on a new drug they are selling. Quoting unbiased outside sources tends to add credibility to your statement.

Warranties and guarantees Warranties and guarantees are another good means for handling false objections. If a prospect is worried about quality and the product has a money-back guarantee or is under warranty for the first year, you can mention such safeguards. These are direct indications that the customer is protected and that your firm will stand behind its products.

Tips for Handling Objections
Here are several specific tips you can use to handle any type of objection.

---

[6]See Herman Harrow, "You Can Disagree Without Being Disagreeable," *Sales and Marketing Management,* Vol. 123, No. 8 (December 10, 1979), p. 67.

Listen. Don't interrupt When prospects raise objections, even if you have heard them many times and even if they are false, you must remember that they are important to the prospects. Therefore, be sure to listen carefully and hear prospects out rather than interrupting.

Ask questions Before you answer an objection, ask questions to make sure you understand the objections. Asked in a pleasant, sincere, nondefensive manner, such questions can give you valuable insights into the prospect's thought process and the real objection. Questions such as ''What don't you like about the style?'' ''How much too high is the price?'' and ''Why do you see this as a problem?'' can be asked to gain valuable information.

Don't argue The first reaction when hearing an objection, especially a false one, is to argue. This defensive reaction is not the appropriate response, however. As the old saying goes, ''You may win the argument and lose the sale.'' The preferred response should be concern for the prospect, respect for the person's opinions and feelings, and a mutual problem-solving orientation. These are the reactions that build a long-term buying–selling relationship.

Don't evade or minimize If you fail to respond to or gloss over an objection, your prospect may feel slighted, decide you are a high-pressure salesperson, and lose respect for you. Remember that although the objection may seem small to you, it may be perceived as important by the prospect.

Make a list of common objections Many of the same objections will come up from time to time, and it is useful for you to make a list of them. Then, with the help of others in your firm, such as your manager, other successful salespeople, technical people, decide on several methods for handling each. Writing them down gives you a convenient way of remembering such objections and gives you something to refer to when you meet with these individ-

BEING PREPARED TO
HANDLE OBJECTIONS

Before entering a prospect's office, Mike De Rogatis, a salesperson for Hertz, reviews a card file he keeps in his briefcase in which all possible objections he has encountered have been listed, along with suggestions for overcoming them. The objections have been classified according to topics such as price, delivery, and service. This allows him to begin each call freshly fortified with the facts.

SOURCE: Raymond Dreyfack, ''How to Be One-up on Customer Objections,'' *The American Salesman,* Vol. 29, No. 1 (January 1984), p. 47. Reprinted by permission of *The American Salesman,* National Research Bureau, Inc., 424 North Third Street, Burlington, Iowa 52601.

uals. Many times these issures come up in sales meetings or other informal discussions.

Offer benefits When you are faced with an objection, especially a true objection, the best tactic is to counter with benefits of your product. For instance, suppose a certain tractor cost 15 percent more than the competition. When faced with a price objection on this tractor, Jim Schutz responded "Yes, it's true our price is 15 percent higher than our competitors, but look at what we offer. We have 20 percent more power, which will help you with heavy loads. We have guaranteed a 24-hour service contract so you will not experience downtime. And our machine has these four accessories not available on anyone else's machine to help you with your unique needs. Now, isn't that worth the price?"

Empathize It will be much easier for you to identify objections if you exercise empathy when trying to understand the objection. If you can see the customer's point of view and communicate that empathy, the person will be much more open with you.

SUMMARY

Sales resistance includes anything the prospect or customer says or does that prevents you from achieving your call objectives. There are six categories of objections: logical versus psychological, stated versus hidden, and true versus false. One important distinction is between logical and psychological objections.

Logical objections come up for the most part during the sales presentation and are directly related to your offering. Several frequently encountered, logically founded objections were examined in the text. Handling such resistance effectively hinges on the premise that people place more credence in what they say themselves than in what others tell them. Four specific steps must be taken to overcome logical resistance: (1) establish a positive mind set; (2) clarify and define the actual objection; (3) formulate, but do not reveal, a "best" answer; and (4) through questioning, obtain the answer from the other person.

Psychological resistance is more recurrent and difficult to counteract. You handle it by identifying the underlying psychological and social needs of the prospect and finding ways to help the other person fulfill them. Various types of psychological sales resistance were explored in the text.

An important distinction is made between true and false objections. You must never deny true objections but instead offer additional evidence to overcome them. On the other hand, when handling false objections, you need to provide information that will correct false impressions, but you must be careful not to embarrass the prospect. Several methods for handling true and false objections were presented in the chapter.

Finally, some tips for handling objections include listening and not interrupting, asking questions, not arguing, not evading or minimizing objections, making a list of common objections and getting help in answering them, responding to objections with benefits, and empathizing with prospects.

PROBLEMS

1. Differentiate, in your own words, between logically founded and psychologically founded resistance. Then differentiate between stated versus hidden objections and between true and false objections.
2. Which of the seven forms of psychological resistance would you consider easiest to overcome? Which ones would be most difficult?
3. Select one form of psychological resistance and list as many tactics as possible for coping with it.
4. Differentiate between price and value.
5. What examples of devious reasoning have you encountered?
6. Who are "they" in the expression "They say . . .

EXERCISE 13

Objectives: To illustrate various kinds of psychological resistance.

To illustrate logical resistance.

PART A **Psychological Resistance**
Many of the seven types of psychological resistance occur in everyday interpersonal relationships, especially in situations in which one person is seeking to influence another to do something. For each type, indicate from your personal experience its frequency of occurrence; and, for each one you have encountered, indicate how it was handled.

1. Resistance to interference.
2. Preference for established habits.
3. Apathy or lack of desire for new products.
4. Traditional unpleasant associations triggered by sales representatives.
5. Tendency to resist domination by others
6. Predetermined ideas about products or services.
7. Dislike of making decisions.

PART B **Logical Resistance**
Assume your role as fashion salesperson. Prepare a hypothetical dialogue that might occur between the buyer and yourself. Try to structure the dialogue around the four-step approach for handling logical objections outlined in the test.

BUYER: We are successful with our present brand-name line.

YOU:

BUYER:

YOU:

etc.

Case 13-1 Bonne Bell Cosmetics (A)

Maria Alameda is an account manager for Bonne Bell and has a territory covering the Phoenix–Tempe–Scottsdale area. The Bonne Bell product line includes skin care lotions and creams, lipsticks, eye makeup, etc. The company has received many awards for its products and has served as cosmetician to the U.S. ski team. Bonne Bell is retailed through cosmetics departments in leading department stores, specialty stores, and better drugstores. In large outlets, Bonne Bell contributes to the salary of a salesperson. Such firms are designated "demonstration accounts." In lower-volume accounts, Bonne Bell pays a commission to a sales representative. These are called "PM accounts" (preferred merchandise; this is also called "push money").

Maria is calling on Mrs. Walker, cosmetics buyer for a new luxury department store, which has recently opened a large branch in Scottsdale.

MARIA: Mrs. Walker, I can understand why you haven't had calls for Bonne Bell. Many of your shoppers rely on what they see displayed, and they are greatly influenced by the recommendations of your salespeople.

MRS. WALKER: That's true, I guess, but as you know we carry only the best labels, and these are well known.

MARIA: Yes. The brands you display are well known and of high quality. However, our Bonne Bell products are specialty items that will not compete directly with your other labels. For example, our "TEN O'SIX" is a skin cleanser and stimulator for women of all ages. It has been approved for skin care by the American Medical Association. Our lipsticks keep the lips moist and prevent chapping.

MRS. WALKER: Well, I don't question the quality of your products. However, our department can carry just so many labels.

MARIA: I can certainly appreciate that. You have to be highly selective, considering the number of brands available.

MRS. WALKER: You're certainly right about that.

MARIA: Here are our markup and turnover figures for stores comparable to yours. (She shows Mrs. Walker a table of such information.) May I ask what profit performance you set for any brand you carry?

MRS. WALKER: Well, I don't have an exact norm, but these Bonne Bell figures are impressive.

1. If you were Maria, what would you have done differently?
2. Is there a basic objection that Mrs. Walker seems to have to Bonne Bell cosmetics?

Case 13-2 Province Realty (A)

Donna Stark is one of six salespeople who make up the sales force of Providence Realty. The company has a policy of sharing advertising expenses with any of its personnel who choose to generate leads by this means. Donna decides to run the following ad in the *Sunday Examiner:*

NEW LISTING—7 rooms, 3 bedrooms, located at 429 Hillcrest Ave. Large lot, fireplace in living room, close to schools. Immediate possession. Call Donna Stark, Providence Realty, 332-3534, evenings 332-3253.

She receives a call at her home from a Mrs. Leonard.

MRS. LEONARD: Miss Stark, or is it Mrs. . . . ?

DONNA: Mrs. But please call me Donna.

MRS. LEONARD: We are interested in that home you have listed, provided it isn't too expensive. What's the price?

DONNA: It's a real bargain, Mrs. Leonard. You'll have to see it to appreciate it. I'll be glad to show it to you anytime tomorrow. Can we make a definite appointment?

MRS. LEONARD: Well, my husband and I don't want to waste time looking at homes we can't afford.

DONNA: I can certainly understand that. However, I think you're going to like it. If by chance you don't, I can show you other listings. By the way, how big is your family?

MRS. LEONARD: We have two children, a boy and a girl. Our son is almost six and our daughter is almost four. That's why we'd like to find a home with three bedrooms. We only have two now, and besides we are not very close to a school.

DONNA: How lucky you are to have two youngsters. They're going to like the big backyard. Mrs. Leonard, may I jot down your full name, address, and phone number? *(She does.)* It may be easier for you to have me drop by for you and your husband. Is 6:30 tomorrow evening convenient for him?

MRS. LEONARD: Let me check. Yes, we'll be ready at 6:30. I have a nice neighbor who will mind the youngsters.

Has Donna done a good job of handling the call? Explain.

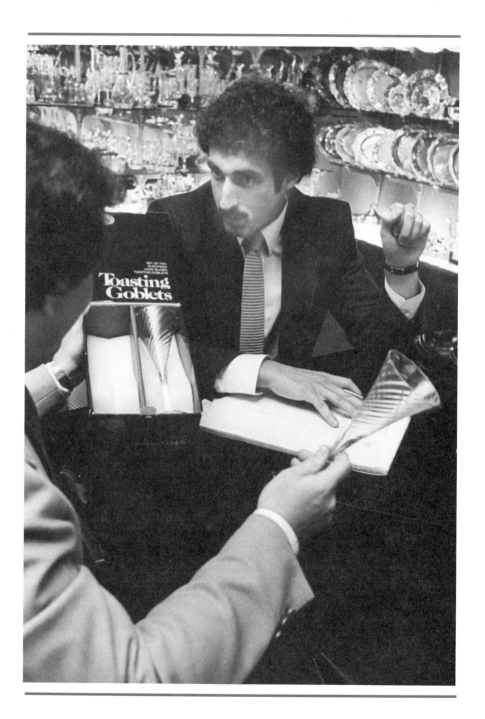

Closing and Postsale Activities

After studying this chapter, you should be able to

1. Understand why some individuals fail to close.
2. Recognize different closing signals.
3. Appreciate the values and uses of the trial close.
4. Determine different times when it would be appropriate to close.
5. Differentiate between closing methods and strategies.
6. Identify different types of closes for different people and situations.
7. Know what to do when a sale cannot be made.
8. Understand the importance of follow-up and other postsale activities.

PURCHASING

*"I've decided to give you that $50,000 order. . . .
All right, control yourself!"*

© Copyright, *Sales & Marketing Management.*

The close may be defined as the process used by the salesperson to induce a purchase or to obtain acceptance of a proposal. In a general way, everything the salesperson does is directed toward facilitating the close. Looking at this another way, you could do everything well that has been described thus far and still not be successful if a sale is not made.

For example, Bill Johnston, a salesperson for a large machine tools company, felt that after several calls he was not yet ready to ask for the order for machinery to go in the new fabricating plant being built by Fabricators Inc. Bill felt he needed one more call to make sure everything was tied down before he asked for the order. When he came back, he found that one of his competitors had gotten the order even though Bill had made numerous calls and invested many hours in trying to get Fabricators' business. Later discussions with the management of Fabricators Inc. indicated that they would have given the order to Bill, but that between the last two calls a competitor came in with an offer and they accepted it. What are some reasons why Bill or other salespeople may fail to close?

WHY SOME SALESPEOPLE FAIL TO CLOSE

Closing is one of the most important aspects of selling; without a close and an accompanying order, no sale is made. As can be seen from Table 14.1, the average cost to close a sale varies by industry but is still quite high. The more calls it takes for the salesperson to close, the more expensive and the

TABLE 14.1
DIFFERENT COST OF SALES CALLS AND NUMBER OF CALLS TO CLOSE A SALE
ACROSS INDUSTRIES

INDUSTRY/SERVICE	AVERAGE NUMBER OF CALLS TO CLOSE A SALE	AVERAGE COST PER SALES CALL	AVERAGE COST[a] TO CLOSE A SALE
Food and kindred products	2.6	$88.14	$229.16
Lumber and wood products	3.8	89.30	339.34
Furniture and fixtures	3.8	102.16	388.20
Paper and allied products	4.7	127.07	597.22
Chemicals and allied products	4.3	136.93	586.79
Petroleum, refining, and related industries	4.0	90.14	360.56
Rubber and miscellaneous plastic products	3.7	85.14	315.01
Stone, clay, glass, and concrete products	3.7	99.51	368.18
Primary metal industries	3.9	119.46	465.89
Fabricated metal products	3.9	116.66	454.97
Machinery except electrical	4.7	167.17	785.69
Electrical and electronic machinery equipment and supplies	4.2	154.33	648.18
Transportation equipment	4.9	229.78	1121.02
Measuring, analyzing and controlling instruments; photographic, medical and optical goods; watches and clocks	4.2	116.85	490.77
Miscellaneous manufacturing industries	3.8	103.36	392.76
Transportation by air	4.1	64.80	265.68
Credit agencies other than banks	3.0	57.60	202.50
Hotels, rooming houses, camps, and other lodging places	3.8	50.40	191.52
Business services	5.6	142.86	800.01
Automotive repair, services, and garages	5.0	97.60	488.00

[a]This is determined by multiplying the average number of calls to close a sale by the average cost per sales call for each industry.

SOURCE: "Industrial Sales Call Tops $137, But New 'Cost to Close' Hits $589," *Marketing News*, Vol. 15, No. 10 (May 1, 1981), p. 1.

less profitable the sale will be for the salesperson and the company.[1] Yet despite the importance of closing, one estimate is that, in 60 percent of all customer–salesperson contacts, the salesperson did not make an effort to close and the sale was not made.[2] Even though a close is not the objective of every call, these figures seem rather out of proportion and are costing a considerable amount of money.

There seem to be four basic reasons why salespeople fail to close sales: (1) they do not have the required confidence in themselves, their company, or their product; (2) they feel guilty about asking people for an order; (3) they prospect poorly or have poor presentations; and (4) they fear they will not be successful, and therefore they postpone asking for the order.

Lack of Confidence

Some people find it difficult to attempt any form of close. They do not have the confidence to look the customer in the eye and ask for an order. However, you must remember that if you represent a company that sells a product of value, most of your prospects need to see you. When the sale has been completed, not only have you and your company profited, but the customer also is better off than before the product was purchased.

If you lack confidence in a product you are promoting, you should communicate this feeling to your superiors. Perhaps your manager can relieve your misgivings by providing you with information or training. Then you will be in a stronger position to sell the product because you understand it better. If, however, your doubts cannot be alleviated, you may have to find employment with another firm.

Guilt Feelings

Some individuals fail to close sales because they feel guilty about asking for any kind of commitment. Think how uncomfortable you might feel asking for charitable contributions or asking a friend to repay a debt owed you. Even though these are legitimate requests, it is uncomfortable to ask other people for their commitments. A more positive image is to think of selling as a way of helping prospects to fill their needs. When you realize that you are providing a service to the prospect, you should be able to overcome any guilt feelings.

Poor Prospecting or Presentations

Probably the predominant reasons that salespeople fail to close are poor prospecting and poor presentations. If you are making presentations to prospects who have no need for your products, they will not be sending out any signals indicating a willingness to buy. In these situations, it is difficult or uncomfortable to close because prospects just do not seem ready.

Similarly, if your presentation is not geared to the needs of prospects, they will not appear ready to buy. Salespeople may become too wrapped up

[1]F. E. Poole, "First Call Closings Vital as Sales Costs Soar," *The American Salesman,* Vol. 26; No. 9 (August 1981), pp. 5–8.
[2]"The Ingredients and Timing of the Perfect Close," *Sales Management,* Vol. 106, No. 12 (June 1, 1971), p. 30.

in themselves or their products and therefore do not look for feedback from prospects: thus they do not know where they stand and whether they are addressing the right needs.

Fear of Failure

Another reason for not closing is fear of failure. A salesperson spends time working with a prospect and is afraid to ask for the order for fear that the prospect will say "no" and that all the work on the prospect will be lost. It is often psychologically easier to rationalize the need to provide information or to make another call than to risk asking for the order. It is important for you to realize that no salesperson is 100 percent effective, and that an expected part of selling is having prospects decide not to buy or to buy competitors' products or services. Providing that you have done your job, failing to ask for the order merely postpones the inevitable and leaves you in the same situation you would be had the prospect said "no"—without an order. For examples of other mistakes in closing, see Table 14.2.

ON HANDLING REJECTION

Bernice H. Hansen, one of the top Amway distributors, tells about handling rejection.

"The trouble with most people in the sales field is that they let other people's reactions upset them. For example, they take it too personally when a prospect rejects them or gives them a hassle. I never let a rejection upset me. I always believed that if I did my best job in presenting my products to a customer, and he or she still didn't buy, then at least I was able to educate that individual, and so I performed a service. If I could teach them something about food supplements—and believe me, I'm not a fanatic on the subject—then my visit with the prospect was valuable even though it didn't result in a sale! And the same thing was true when I presented any of our household or personal-care products.

SOURCE: Robert L. Shook, *Ten Greatest Salespersons: What They Say about Selling* (New York: Harper and Row, 1978), pp. 41–53. Copyright © 1978, by Robert L. Shook and Roberta W. Shook, Trustees. Reprinted by permission of Harper and Row Publishers, Inc.

CLOSING SIGNALS

Closing signals are actions, statements, or questions from the prospect that indicate a willingness to buy. They are signs to the salesperson that a favorable climate exists and that a close may be appropriate.[3]

---

[3]See, for example, John Nemac, "Signal for Closing Time," *The American Salesman*, Vol. 26, No. 11 (November 1981), pp. 11–13.

TABLE 14.2

THE TEN MOST COMMON MISTAKES IN CLOSING SALES

1. **Waiting too long to close.**   Recognize that your customers are all different, and many don't need or want a full presentation. It is foolish to keep on "selling" when your prospect has already mentally "bought."

2. **Having the wrong attitude.**   You must have faith in yourself and believe in what you are selling. If you have any doubts about yourself or your product, customers will sense that and will be reluctant to buy from you.

3. **Not closing on every call.**   Successful salespeople realize quickly that they are paid to sell, not to be social workers or professional visitors. You should commit yourself to making every call a selling call.

4. **Growing stale with the same old close.**   Challenge yourself to learn and use new closing techniques. Keep in mind that closing is a technique you can improve. The changes you make in your closing will be refreshing and will help you grow.

5. **Inadequate presentation.**   Build up to a successful close by being sure the customer understands the benefits of your offering. Ask questions, listen to the customer, and present specific benefits. Then close the sale.

6. **Failure to keep trying.**   If you stop your closing effort with the first no, you are limiting your success. Ask your customers to discuss the reasons they said no, aim your sales presentation to these points, and bring the sale to a successful close.

7. **Remaining too long after the close.**   All experienced salespeople have heard stories about the salesperson who made the sale and then bought it back. When you close the sale, thank the prospect for the order and leave.

8. **Failure to practice closing.**   Dry-run closings with fellow salespeople is one way to improve your closing skills. Practicing on smaller accounts is another way to limit losses and gain valuable experience.

9. **Not having an alternative closing plan.**   Always have one or more alternative closing strategies in mind. Different people respond to different approaches.

10. **Failure to see the need to close.**   Take each sales presentation through to the close. Remember, you don't accomplish anything in selling until you get the order.

SOURCE: Adapted from Archie Jordon, "The Ten Most Common Mistakes in Closing Sales," *The American Salesman*, Vol. 27, No. 2 (February 1982), pp. 22–25. Reprinted by permission of *The American Salesman* by the National Research Bureau, Inc., 424 North Third Street, Burlington, Iowa 52601.

Weak or Strong Closing Signals

Closing signals may be weak or strong. The salesperson must continually monitor the prospect to determine whether the prospect is showing any signals that could be interpreted to mean a readiness to have the sale closed. As discussed in Chapter 12, prospects have two types of reactions: positive or negative and voluntary or involuntary. If you see that the customer is acting in a positive–involuntary manner, such as nodding or picking up the product and examining it as you talk, you may wish to try to close the sale at this time or you may prefer to continue with the points you are emphasizing. Positive–involuntary reactions may indicate a weak closing signal. However, only experience will enable you to separate positive–involuntary reactions that are closing signals from those that are merely indications of interest.

Strong positive closing signals.

No closing signals here.

In contrast, positive–voluntary reactions such as, "When can I get delivery," or "I'll ask our engineering department to test this product," require that you close the sale or move to the next item on your agenda. Positive–voluntary reactions are generally stronger closing signals than positive–involuntary reactions. When evaluating the strength of a closing signal, you must take into account the buyer's personality and style. Thus, a positive–involuntary closing signal from a shy, timid buyer may be as strong a signal as a positive–voluntary response from a more outgoing buyer.

Specific Closing Signals
There are three specific types of closing signals a salesperson should watch for: physical actions, statements or comments, and questions. Although there is no way to be absolutely sure you are correctly interpreting a situation, you should be alert to these signals. If you focus on the prospect rather than on your presentation, you will catch most of them.

Physical actions The physical actions of prospects may provide nonverbal clues that they are ready to buy.[4] For example, a prospect might closely ex-

---

[4]See, for example, Gerhard Gschwandtner, "Closing Signals via Body Signals," *Marketing Times*, Vol. 29, No. 5 (September–October, 1982), pp. 12–13.

amine a product or might indicate with nonverbal enthusiasm that he or she is sold. These are clear indications that the prospect is responding favorably and that a close may be successful.

Statements or comments Often the prospect will make statements or comments that indicate a close would be appropriate. These would include very favorable comments about the product such as "That sure would look nice in our living room," or, "That word processor would really help our clerical people." These statements indicate a positive attitude toward the product and again signal that attempts to close may be appropriate.

Questions A third type of prospect response that would be viewed as a closing signal consists of questions that indicate a readiness to buy. These questions are usually about the terms of ownership or the steps the prospect would have to go through in order to purchase the product or service. For example, a prospect might ask, "Would you be able to have the product installed before the first of the month?" or "Can I charge this on my bank card?" These questions show a favorable reaction to the product and indicate that you should answer the questions, solve the problem if you can, and ask for the

TABLE 14.3
EXAMPLES OF CLOSING SIGNALS

TYPE OF SIGNAL	EXAMPLES
Physical actions	Reexamining the product carefully. Taking possession of the item (e.g., picking it up). Beginning to read the order form. Nodding in agreement as you summarize. Pointing at the samples on display.
Statements and comments	"That would fit right into our production schedule." "I always wanted a hi-fi set." "These new machines should reduce the number of breakdowns we've been having." "The letters typed on your electric machine are attractive." "I've always liked dealing with your company."
Questions	"Can we open a joint account?" "When must you have the full down payment?" "When can you make delivery?" "In what colors is it available?" "How long did you say the warranty lasted?"

SOURCE: Adapted and expanded from Albert W. Frey, *Marketing Handbook* (New York: Ronald Press, 1965), pp. 9–26.

order. Examples of these three types of closing signals are illustrated in Table 14.3.

TRIAL CLOSE

Once specific closing signals have been identified, the next step may be the trial close. The *trial close* is a question designed to determine whether the prospect is willing to make a decision about some aspect of the purchase without forcing the prospect to make a final buying decision on the total offer. Such a question could be, "What size order would you like?" or "Which color do you prefer?"

The Advantage of the Trial Close
The advantage of the trial close is that it avoids an overall yes-or-no decision, especially early in the interview, yet it allows you to gauge interest and sometimes commitment. Avoiding a yes-or-no decision is important since, once a person has expressed an opinion, it is natural for the person to defend or justify that opinion. Thus, the trial close allows you to take the prospect's temperature.[5] A trial close can be tried sooner and more frequently, because a failure on a trail close is not as detrimental as a failure on a regular close. If the prospect's response is positive, you can move toward a close. If the response indicates that the prospect does not like something, you can learn why without putting the prospect on the defensive.

Examples of a Trial Close
As an example of a trial close, here is a typical sales situation in a retail appliance store.

PROSPECT: Do you carry the Super Clean washing machine that sells for $329?

SALESPERSON: We certainly do. It is an excellent machine, and it is right over here in the corner.

PROSPECT: Can you show me how it works?

SALESPERSON: Yes. You put the soap in here, the bleach here. You set this dial for the type of washing you do and this dial for the size of load, and then you push this button.

PROSPECT: That sounds interesting.

SALESPERSON: The machine comes in white, rust, and harvest gold. Which color do you like?

In the following trial close, if the prospect indicates a color and seems sold as in situation 1, the salesperson attempts to close. If there are other questions as in situation 2, the sale continues.

---

[5]"The Ingredients and Timing of the Perfect Close," *Sales Management,* Vol. 106, No. 12 (June 1, 1971), pp. 31–32.

SITUATION 1

PROSPECT: I really like the harvest gold, it would look good with my dryer.

SALESPERSON: Can I write this gold one up for you?

PROSPECT: Yes, please do.

SITUATION 2

PROSPECT: I like harvest gold, but do you have any others?

SALESPERSON: Yes, we do, right over here, but they are not on sale.

PROSPECT: Boy, those other machines sure are expensive.

SALESPERSON: Since the Super Clean is on sale, it offers an excellent buy for the money. Do you like the top loader or the front loader?

COMMENT: The salesperson has made another trial close, testing the buyer's readiness to buy

PROSPECT: I like the top loader model over there, and it is a bargain.

SALESPERSON: Can I write this one up for you?

PROSPECT: Yes, please do.

The important point in situation 2 is that the salesperson made two attempts to close the sale before being successful. When it became clear that the prospect was not ready to close, the salesperson continued the presentation until another attempt could be made to close the sale.

WHEN TO CLOSE

There is no special time in the selling process that is best for closing. The proper time to close will depend on the situation and the prospect. Some prospects learn faster and make decisions faster than others. The best time to close is when the prospect is ready to buy. Thus, it is important to monitor the prospect for closing signals that indicate a readiness to buy. Trying to close too early will create an atmosphere of tension, and waiting too long may cause a sale to be lost. There are several times during the process when prospects are likely to feel ready to buy and may send closing signals. These are outlined in this section.

Closing at the Beginning of a Presentation

Although closing at the beginning of a presentation is not the normal course of events, there are several situations in which this tactic may be appropriate.

One such situation is when several calls are necessary, as they are in selling machinery, computers, and consulting services. In these situations, after several calls your objective for the next one will be to close. You will start the call by summarizing the benefits of the product or service and then ask for the order. Another situation encountered frequently in retail selling is a customer who has already done considerable shopping and enters the store ready to buy. You should quickly note this and close the sale promptly.

Closing after a Benefit Is Recognized
As was pointed out, if you receive a positive strong agreement to a sales point, one of the appropriate responses is to close the sale. Thus, if the prospect agrees with the value of a benefit, this may be an appropriate time to close. For instance, you may suggest to a prospect that your company has a financing plan that will allow the prospect to pay for the products over an extended time period, thus lowering the payments. If the prospect's response to this is enthusiastic, you may wish to close by saying, "Can we sign you up for our extended-payment plan?"

Closing after Overcoming Objections
Often a prospect will raise an objection regarding a product. Overcoming this objection removes a barrier to the prospect's buying, providing a logical time to close. For instance, prospects may feel that a particular piece of machinery is too sophisticated for their business. Your response may be to show them how easy it is to operate the machine, explain the training program you will conduct for their employees, and give them an example of a noncompeting, similar-sized firm that is using the product successfully. If they become very interested in the product after these statements, you might want to ask for the order.

Closing after a Demonstration
Closing after a demonstration is another possibility. The demonstration allows the prospect to become involved with the product and to get a personal view of it. Because the demonstration may generate a greal deal of enthusiasm, its conclusion is often a very appropriate time to close. As an example, a salesperson for a heavy-equipment distributor may have just given a demonstration on a power shovel, in which the machine moved a large pile of dirt and filled a large truck in a very short time. If the mine representative was favorably impressed at this time, a close might be in order.

Closing after an Extended Pause
Frequently, there is a time in a sales call when the prospect has decided to purchase your product or service but has not yet told you. In these situations there is often an extended pause in the interview. This may be a clue to you to help the prospect make a decision by closing. For example, Mary Jones makes a presentation for a new specialty item, a brass business card holder. After she has described the product and its advantages as a public relations tool for the prospect's company, she notices that the prospect has been quiet for several seconds and is carefully examining her sample card holder. This could be a clue to Mary to ask for the order.

Closing at the End of a Presentation

Another logical time to close is at the end of a presentation. You have made all the points you deem appropriate, and it is now time to close. This may be true; however, too many salespeople feel they must make their entire presentation before the time is right to close, and they waste valuable time by missing closing signals earlier in the interview. Furthermore, many sales are lost because salespeople talk themselves out of sales. Thus, even though the end of a presentation may be a time to close, earlier points may also be appropriate.

CLOSING METHODS AND STRATEGIES

There are basically two *methods* of closing a sale: the *direct* method, in which salespeople ask for the order directly, and the *assumptive* method, in which the salespeople assume indirectly that the order has been made and ask prospects questions to indicate agreement that the sale has been made. These two closing methods are used with a number of closing strategies. *Closing strategies* are techniques that you can use to move the prospect to a point where you can use the direct or assumptive close. Closing strategies, however, do not actually ask for the order or assume that the order has been made. Thus, as can be seen from Figure 14.1, closing strategies are used in conjunction with closing methods. Strategies get the prospect ready and methods are used to consummate the sale. Strategies precede methods, so they will be covered first.

Closing Strategies

You can use a number of different closing strategies to put the prospect in the right frame of mind for you to ask, directly or indirectly, for the order. Your choice of closing strategy should be based on what you feel comfortable with and what fits a particular situation. The best or most appropriate strategy depends on the situation, on the prospect, and on the relationship between you and the prospect.

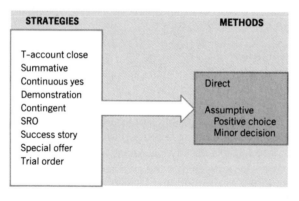

FIGURE 14.1 Closing strategies lead to closing methods

You are more likely to use a combination of closing strategies rather than a single one. The considerations that will dictate the actual choice of strategies are (1) your analysis of the other person's background, personality, and motivation, and (2) the amount and kind of resistance that you have encountered closing the sale. Thus, the strategy to be used is-a matter of judgment on your part and will depend on the prospect and the situation. Nine different closing strategies are outlined here.

"T"-account close strategy The "T" Account close consists of taking out a piece of paper and making a T similar to a balance sheet. On the left side write "Reasons not to act." On the right side write "Reasons to act." Then, with the help of your prospect, list all the positive benefits of your product or service on the right side, and have your prospect list any negative aspects on the left side (see Figure 14.2). Needless to say, the reasons to act should far exceed the reasons not to act. This method is especially useful for handling true objections and for dealing with industrial purchasers who are used to thinking in terms of balance sheets. Furthermore, this strategy can also be used to uncover hidden objections by saying, "Are there any problems standing in the way of your decision?" This may bring out hidden objections.

As an example of a T-account close, assume that you are selling a high-quality grinding machine that will be used by another manufacturer. The purchasing executive and the head engineer are listening to you talk about your machine, but they have also done their homework and have told you they know that your machine is more expensive than you competitor's machine. You might suggest, "Let's analyze this situation," then draw a T like the one in Figure 14.2. You might then proceed by saying, "We know that this grinder is 10 percent more expensive than our competitor. However, let's also look at these benefits we have covered. Our machinery is more efficient. It takes up less space, so you won't be crowded. It requires less maintenance,

Reasons not to act	Reasons to act
Machinery is 10% more expensive.	Machinery is more efficient.
	Takes up less space.
	Needs less maintenance.
	Uses less energy.
	Operators don't need as much training.
	Machine has two-year payback.

FIGURE 14.2 Example of a simple "T" account.

so you will save on those expensive costs. It uses less energy, which also saves you dollars in the long run. Your operator will not need as much training to operate this machine, because it is so simple to use. And finally, the machine has a two-year payback. So even though our machine is more expensive in the short run, it is a good investment and will save you time, space, and money in the long run.''

Summative strategy With the summative strategy, the salesperson reviews the points of agreement and thereby promotes a positive buying decision. It is a particularly appropriate method if negotiations have taken place over several calls and if many sales points have been covered. It has the additional advantage of offsetting the inevitable forgetting that may occur, particularly on points that were made early in the selling–buying relationship. The review also gives you the opportunity to reinforce points for which resistance was present and objections overcome.

With this strategy, you have a choice to make concerning the sequence of the summary. You may reaffirm points in the order in which they have been handled. This has the advantage of logic, and it is likely to be the best way of reminding the person of what has taken place. Or you may choose to review in inverse order, picking up the last point agreed on first, and working backward. This sequence has the advantage of starting with points more likely to be remembered by the other person.

The preferred method for summarizing major sales points applies three laws of learning: primacy, recency, and frequency. The law of *primacy* states that in order to be remembered, important points should be placed at the beginning of a message. The law of *recency* says that important points should be placed at the end of a message, and the law of *frequency* encourages the repeating of important points. Thus, you should place the most important points, the points in which the prospect is most interested, at the beginning of the summary (law of primacy), and at the end of the summary (law of recency). By repeating the most important points, you can also use the law of frequency. The critical thing is not to let your most important points be lost in the middle of your summary.

Continuous-yes strategy The continuous-yes strategy is used to put the prospect in a positive frame of mind by obtaining agreement on a number of different benefits from purchasing the product. For instance, consider the following dialogue.

SALESPERSON: You'll agree that the design of the new robot fits your needs, won't you?

PROSPECT: Yes.

SALESPERSON: And we've shown that the return on investment for the robot is attractive. Haven't we?

PROSPECT: Yes.

SALESPERSON: We've also agreed that the robot will improve your quality control. Haven't we?

PROSPECT: Yes.

Notice that the salesperson asked questions designed to get yes answers. These questions asked at the beginning of a sales interview would be pushy, leading, and high pressure. But after you have gotten agreement from the prospect, they are merely summaries of what the prospect has already agreed to or stated.

It is a good idea to sequence the points in this method in order of least likely resistance. Thus, you begin with the point of most likely continued agreement, follow this with the one of the next most likely continued agreement, and follow this with the one of the next most likely acceptance, until you have covered sufficient points to obtain the order. This ordering establishes a series of positive responses and builds a favorable attitude toward buying. Each time prospects agree with a point, they are less likely to disagree with the next point you make. This strategy also commits prospects to a number of minor points. Saying yes to a number of benefits makes it psychologically more difficult to say no to the purchase. The method also gets prospects involved. To the extent that they agree with the statements, prospects will put more credence in what they say than in what the salesperson says.

Demonstration strategy The salesperson may prepare for the close by demonstrating the product or equipment in use. A demonstration strategy is strictly low pressure because it allows prospects to seem to be in control and encourages them to make the buying decision. It has a unique advantage of providing prospects with a sample of the satisfaction that will accompany the purchase. In all other forms of close, such satisfaction is merely anticipated. This is a particularly appropriate close to use with cautious, skeptical prospects. Frequently applied in the sale of equipment and machinery, it affords an opportunity for the decision makers and other personnel who will be concerned with the equipment to see it firsthand.

If you use the demonstration, you should identify one or more decision makers who are fully convinced about the merits of the proposal, so that they can act as "internal sales representatives" to convince other decision makers. If the demonstration is shown to a group, you ask the satisfied persons for agreement first, with the hope that others will join in the positive reaction.

Contingent strategy With the contingent strategy the salesperson obtains a commitment that the prospect will buy, or at least be very interested, if certain conditions can be established. For example, you may respond to a price objection with, "If I could show you that this typewriter will pay for itself in two years through more productivity and smaller maintenance charges, would you buy it?" This "if . . . then" method of getting commitment is a very powerful sales tool and is especially effective when a prospect raises a false objection. However, it must be applied with caution because it can be viewed as high pressure if used improperly, and you must be able to prove to the prospect that you can establish the condition you suggest. Thus, if you could not show that the typewriter would pay for itself in two years, the sale would probably be lost.

SRO and impending-event strategies The standing room only (SRO) close stresses that there is only a limited supply of the product and that if the prospect does not buy, the opportunity will be lost. Similarly, the impending-event close stresses the need to buy now before some impending event happens: "Buy now or the prices will go up." "Buy now or interest rates will go up." "Buy now or this special offer will be withdrawn." With these closing strategies, you show the disadvantage and discomforts of failing to act. Implying that a general industrywide price increase is imminent, that inventories are low, or that delivery may be questionable later on are all examples. One paper products salesperson wished to sell the firm's line to a large chain of supermarkets. This individual closed by computing the opportunities that would be lost by not stocking the company's products during their special promotion. These strategies are particularly appropriate with prospects who are suggestible, complacent, and emotional.

These strategies, however, have the limitation of negative suggestion and should not be used except when more conventional methods fail. Care must also be exercised when using this strategy since the buyer may call your bluff and say, for example, "Well, I just can't buy this product for two weeks so I guess I'll have to miss out on this offer." You are then put in a position of possibly losing a sale because the prospect may give up and not come back in two weeks.

Although they may be effective, both of these strategies can be perceived as high pressure. When saved until the end of an interview, these two closing strategies tend to shock the prospect and appear to be manipulative. One way to minimize the high-pressure impact of these closes is to provide the information about the limited supply or impending event to the prospect very early in the interview. When you give this information at a time when no close is even remotely anticipated, the information content is present but the manipulative and shock impact is lessened. A good salesperson would be in error by not mentioning a short supply or an impending event, for such an omission would keep important information from the prospect. However, it is important to recognize that the time and the way the information is conveyed will affect credibility. If you convey the information early in the interview, you merely have to remind the prospect of the shortage or the event as a close.

Success story strategy With the success story strategy the salesperson tells the prospect about a noncompetitive customer in a similar situation who benefited from buying the product or service. Describing the customer's situation in detail allows prospects to project the situation to their own circumstances. For instance, you might say, "Bill Jones over at Acme Manufacturing was also worried about the noise level of this word-processing printer but he bought it, along with this noise cover, and he thinks it is terrific. He tells me his office has never been quieter."

A variation of this technique is to list some of the people who have already bought the product. This strategy is useful for timid or risk-adverse prospects. In these situations it is useful to mention important, prestigious people or accounts who have purchased the product. Testimonial letters from

satisfied customers may also help. But, as always, you must take care when
choosing past clients to use for testimonials. You need to do your homework
to ensure that clients are really happy and satisfied before you use them as a
reference.

Special-offer strategy In the special-offer strategy the salesperson makes the
prospect a special offer if the prospect will purchase now. This strategy is
often useful in dealing with prospects who do not like to make decisions. The
special offer often tips the balance toward a favorable decision. For instance,
you might say, "If you order this lettering machine now, we will give you
two printing wheels free." It is important to remember that, although this
technique may be effective, special offers may affect the profitability of a sale.
To achieve a high rate of close on nonprofit or low-profit products can be a
relatively worthless accomplishment at best.[6] Therefore, you should use this
technique carefully and only when it is in the long-run best interests for your
company's profits.

Trial order strategy The trial order closing strategy consists of getting the
prospect to try a smaller than normal order the first time the product is purchased, often at a reduced price. Sometimes your firm will need to make a
"special production run" to meet the prospect's needs. The rationale behind
this strategy is to get your foot in the prospect's door and secure part of the
business, hoping that the prospect is happy enough with the product to buy
more. Again you must use this strategy carefully, because trial orders are
often unprofitable and because the concessions that often go with a trial order
may be perceived as "normal business practices" by the prospect. Thus, getting subsequent business may be difficult.

Closing Methods

After using one or several of the closing strategies reviewed, you are ready to
take the critical step of closing the sale. All the preceding strategies get you
ready to close, but they do not really ask for the order; they just prepare the
prospect. As we indicated earlier, the two closing methods are the direct
method and the assumptive method.

Direct method With the direct method salespeople ask prospects to buy,
prescribe, recommend, or use a product. This method can be effective when
you have encountered little or no psychological resistance. Prospects have
been businesslike, and any objections have had logical foundations and have
been handled to the prospect's satisfaction. Self-confident buyers are likely to
appreciate this kind of approach on your part.

In contrast, directness may scare insecure people and actually *cause*
psychological resistance. You should ask for the order tactfully so as not to
seem high pressure. You wouldn't want to say to a prospect, for instance,
"Give me the order." Ideally a less direct, softer approach is preferable, such

[6]"The Close and Your Bottom Line," *Sales Management,* Vol. 106, No. 12 (June 1, 1971), p.
22.

as "Since this will fit right into your line, will you authorize us to deliver it to you immediately?" or "If you just sign here, Mr. Jones, you will begin to realize the savings from our product immediately."

Assumptive method In the assumptive close sales people behave as though there has been a meeting of the minds and prospects have decided to buy. You make a statement that presupposes buying, and if prospects agree with it, the sale is closed. The method is desirable because it helps prospects make a decision. Because prospects do not actually have to say yes or commit to the entire decision, the decision process is simplified. The method can be very effective and low pressure if it is used appropriately and if prospects are ready to buy. However, if prospects do not see a need for the product or if you use the technique too aggressively or too early in the call, the approach can be viewed as high pressure.

There are really two different kinds of assumptive closing methods, the positive-choice method and the minor-choice method. The *positive-choice method* consists of asking prospects to make a decision between two alternatives: "Would you like this product delivered Tuesday or Thursday?" or "Would you like to pay cash or would you like us to bill you?" Either response indicates that the buyer has decided to buy the product. An important principle relevant to this method is that as the number of alternatives or options increases, the decision making becomes more difficult and consequently less likely to occur. Thus, you should limit the alternatives to only a few. This method is particularly appropriate if you sense psychological sales resistance. This closing method minimizes the likelihood of such resistance by making the decision easy and simple. It is especially effective with indecisive people.

Similarly, in the *minor-point method,* prospects are asked to make a decision about a minor aspect of the product or service. For instance, you might ask, "When would you like delivery?" or "How would you like to pay for this?" If the prospect indicates in the first example a preference for delivery on Wednesday, the person has in effect bought the product.

With this method you seek a response on a small decision. This is often used in selling expensive consumer items. For example, if you are an automobile salesperson whose prospects are a husband and wife, you might ask the wife for a decision on the color of the paint or upholstery for the new car. Since any decision involving a large dollar outlay can be difficult, the effectiveness of this method is based on the principle that small decisions are made more easily than big ones. This method is also particularly appropriate when suggestion has been effective. During the presentation and demonstration, you may have noted favorable reactions to one or more aspects of the product. Obviously, these are the charcteristics you should use to present the minor decision to the other person. In the example just given, you may have noted the husband's interest in engine options. You might then ask the husband to indicate which engine he pefers. If you have encountered psychological resistance during negotiations, this is an additional reason for attempting to close on a minor point.

These methods are appropriate when you note that commitment and decision making are difficult for the buyer. If suggestion has been used effectively during the presentation, it is reasonable to expect that an assumptive close will be appropriate. Another factor that influences the effectiveness of this method of closing is the confidence the other person has in the salesperson. For example, if you have had an ongoing selling–buying relationship over a period of years, the customer is likely to accept your offering with little resistance.

As to personality and motivational factors, the submissive person who depends on the environment for security is more likely to accept this form of close than the strongly independent individual. Another advantage of this method is that it may bring hidden objections out into the open. If you assume the order and the prospect or customer is not ready to buy, you may learn why very quickly.

DIFFERENT TYPES OF CLOSES FOR DIFFERENT PEOPLE AND SITUATIONS

Each customer and prospect must be treated as a unique individual. By analyzing the person's background, personality, and motivation, you can decide how to customize your presentation to the prospect's level. Customizing is especially helpful for closing. You must adjust your closing technique to fit the prospect's personality. Trying an assumptive close with a very aggressive, dominant, self-confident prospect, for instance, could be a disaster, unless the person is really ready to buy. However, a minor-decision close may be very appropriate for an indecisive person, who may feel more comfortable with a minor decision.[7]

Similarly, different situations may prompt different closing strategies. A prospect who is rushed, for instance, may find a summative close too time-consuming, and a direct method may be better. The important point is this: you must "read" the prospect and the situation and choose the type of close that is most appropriate. No single close will work with all people or in all situations. You must be flexible and adapt to the person and the situation.

WHAT TO DO WHEN A SALE CANNOT BE MADE

Sometimes, despite all your efforts, a sale will be lost. The prospect will decide either not to buy or to buy from a competitor. There are two things you can do in these situations.

Leave the Door Open
It is important for you to leave the door open for future business with prospects. Although they did not buy this time, they may buy in the future. After losing a sale, your natural reaction is to be defensive and blame the prospect. This has the effect of creating hostility and blocking the possibility of future sales. It is much better to keep a cordial relationship with the prospect in hopes of gaining future business.

[7]Alan A. Schoonmaker and Douglas B. Lind, "One Custom-Made Close Coming Up," *Sales and Marketing Management*, Vol. 118, No. 8 (June 13, 1977), p. 63.

Use a "Postmortem"

Another tactic that can be used after a sale has gone to a competitor is a "postmortem." Ask the prospect why you did not get the business and what made the competitor succeed. If you do this sincerely and if you have established good rapport with the prospect, you are likely to get good feedback.

PRACTICAL SUGGESTIONS FOR CLOSING

Here are a number of practical suggestions that will help you to close.

Show appreciation. Make sure to let prospects know that you appreciate their business.

Don't talk past closing signals. When the prospect indicates a willingness to buy, don't continue talking. Close the sale. Many sales have been lost by salespeople who talk themselves out of business. Remember, the best time to close is when the prospect is ready to buy.

Reduce the number of buying alternatives. Through questioning and listening to the prospect's needs, try to reduce the number of buying alternatives to a manageable few. Too many alternatives merely confuse the prospect and make the purchase more difficult.

Don't be afraid to close. It is important to ask for the order. Failure to do this, no matter how well the rest of the call is conducted, will not result in a sale.

Avoid pressure. High-pressure closes are generally to be avoided. Orders made under high pressure may later be canceled and may impair your ability to do business with the prospect over the long run. You can be very persistent and still not be high pressure.

Avoid forcing premature decisions. Try not to force a decision until you are fairly sure that it will be favorable. Once the prospect makes a negative decision, not only do you have to change the person's mind, but you also have to allow the prospect to save face. Furthermore, the prospect may be defensive and try to justify the decision.

Avoid interruptions if possible. Preventing interruptions is not always under the salesperson's control, but they should be avoided if at all possible. Interruptions make it difficult to maintain continuity and may take the prospect's mind off of the sale. Interruptions can be minimized by scheduling calls for times when the prospect is not likely to be interrupted.

List and memorize closings. Although canned sales talks are generally to be avoided, you should list various ways to close and memorize them. It is good to have overlearned these closes to such an extent that they become second nature and you don't have to think about them. Having to think about how to close will make it difficult for you to monitor the prospect for nonverbal clues and closing signals.

This feedback is invaluable in obtaining future orders and in analyzing your position in relation to your competitors.

TWENTY-SIX TESTED WAYS TO LOSE A SALE

1. Get in to see your prospect under false pretenses.
2. Be overdressed.
3. Apologize for taking up the buyer's time.
4. Try to be funny at the wrong time.
5. Use precocious language.
6. Bring up controversial subjects.
7. Talk about your operation or other troubles.
8. Monopolize the interview.
9. Be belligerent.
10. Treat little prospects differently from big ones.
11. Talk your company down.
12. Knock your competitor.
13. Sell on the basis of friendship.
14. Sell them more than they can profitably use.
15. Leave in a huff if you don't make the sale on the first call.
16. Threaten to go over the buyer's head.
17. Expect special treatment.
18. Make promises you cannot fulfill.
19. Be an order taker.
20. Make extravagant claims.
21. Be pessimistic.
22. Fear your prospect.
23. Emphasize your low, low price.
24. Criticize the prospect's firm.
25. Be ashamed of your job.
26. Use high-pressure selling tactics.

SOURCE: Ted Pollack, "26 Tested Ways to Lose a Sale," *The American Salesman*, Vol. 28, No. 7 (July 1983), pp. 27–32. Reprinted by permission of *The American Salesman*, National Research Bureau, Inc., 424 North Third Street, Burlington, Iowa 52601.

POSTSALE ACTIVITY

Once the sale has been closed, your job is only partially completed. You must now follow up to make sure that the customer is satisfied. If you handle the postsale activity well, the next sale will be much easier; if you do not, you will face considerable resistance the next time you approach this particular customer. One of your key objectives in postsale activities is to build such a good relationship with your customers that they will perceive the costs of switching to a competitor as too high. Building this relationship is a key goal of postsale activities. Three areas of the postsale activity are analyzed here: the time immediately following the close, the long-term follow-up, and the handling of customer complaints.

Immediately after Closing

Salespeople are frequently told that once they close a sale, they should leave as quickly as possible in order to avoid further conversation that might raise doubts. In many instances, however, details must be worked out, such as delivery time and purchase terms. It is important that these details be easy to complete.

If the decision maker might have to defend the purchase with other people, you will want to provide additional ideas to serve as justification for the purchase. For example, when a wife buys a piece of furniture, she needs to be able to justify the purchase not only to herself but also to her husband. Thus, if a furniture salesperson senses that the points covered for the close are not sufficient for the wife to use in justifying her decision, additional points should be provided. It is also desirable to reassure the buyer by painting a vivid picture of the satisfactions that will come from owning the product.

Long-term Follow-up

Posttransactional satisfaction must be linked with the closing effort. You must never sell and forget. Effective follow-up has several advantages. First, it gives you an opportunity to see whether the customer has any problems with the offering. If there is any dissatisfaction, you handle it immediately. Second, if the customer is satisfied, this is possibly an opportunity to get referrals. Third, follow-up also shows that you care about the customer and helps to develop a long-term relationship. The follow-up does not always have to be done in person, however; often a telephone call or a thank-you letter or card will suffice. You will be more likely to follow up in person when the sale is large or when there is a high probability of repeat business. Here are a number of tips you can use to be more effective in your follow-up.

Check on the order Before the delivery of the order, you can check on it to see how it is progressing and when delivery might be expected. Customers are usually much more satisfied when they are informed about an order's progress than when they are surprised.

You initiate the contact It is important that you make the contact with the customer, rather than waiting for the person to contact you. If you wait for the customer to make contact, you will hear only from the very satisfied or the upset customers. Often you can solve little problems that can make a big difference in customer satisfaction. You can also act as a sounding board if there are any problems. In order to secure feedback, one travel agent had a plant delivered to each of her foreign travelers on their return. This encouraged them to call her and thank her for the plant, giving her an opportunity to inquire about their trip.

Provide services If appropriate, you may arrange for a follow-up call in order to provide necessary services, such as the start-up of equipment, instruction on using the product, and assistance in merchandising if the customer is a reseller. This service call has the advantage of being a logical bridge to the next call and ultimately to the next sale. You may need to train customer personnel in how to use the product. You may also need to ensure that the product is installed properly, which may require that you be present or that you assist in the installation. Finally, if you are present, you may find that the customer has not ordered enough of the product, and you may be given a follow-up order immediately.

THE IMPORTANCE OF FOLLOW-UP

Joe Gerard set many records for automobile sales. He was a wonderful salesperson but he didn't stop there. He recalls,

One thing that I do that a lot of salesmen don't, and that's believe the sale really begins *after* the sale—not before! Most salesmen just figure, now that I got ya, who needs ya. With me, I consider a sale a sacred thing. I consider you *my* customer and belonging to me, not to the dealership or General Motors. The customer is my private business and I let them know constantly.

When he comes back for service, I fight for him all the way to get him the best. You won't believe the way I fight for him! I show people that I really care for them. And people see that and they appreciate it.

Joe's customers won't forget him once they buy a car from him: he won't let them! Every month throughout the year they get a letter from him. It arrives in a plain envelope, always a different size or color. He sends out 13,000 cards every month.

SOURCE: Robert L. Shook, *Ten Greatest Salespersons: What They Say about Selling* (New York: Harper and Row, 1978), pp. 19–24. Copyright © 1978, by Robert L. Shook and Roberta W. Shook, Trustees. Reprinted by permission of Harper and Row Publishers, Inc.

Continue assurance A key psychological reason for follow-up is that it may help relieve the buyer's cognitive dissonance. In varying degrees, each time a substantial purchase is made, the person making it experiences doubt, wondering whether it has been the right purchase. As a final step following the close, you should try to make sure the buyer can rationalize the purchase. The follow-up visit contributes further to the buyer's conviction that the right decision has been made.

You can do several things to reduce the possibility of dissonance. You can provide customers with new information that reinforces their purchase, for example, by providing them with additional benefits that they did not know about. You can also send a letter telling them how pleased you are to have their business and what a good decision they made. Such reassurance shows customers that you really care and paves the way for your next sale. Salespeople who keep in touch with their customers are likely to get more repeat business and more referrals.[8]

Allow the customer to talk objectively In a follow-up call, you should allow the customer to talk objectively about the product or service. This serves two functions. First, talking about any problems tends to clear the air and will make the customer feel better. Second, if you know about problems, you may be able to solve them.

Update your records Another good follow-up procedure is to update your customer file, taking note of any new developments or changes in the account. This paves the way for your next call and removes the strain of trying to remember details.

Be dependable An important aspect of follow-up is being dependable. You must keep your promises to get back to the customer, do what you said you would do during the sales call, and carefully make sure all details are taken care of. This step is the difference between a really successful salesperson and an average one. Dependability is an important trait which encourages repeat business. Customers know that you will keep your promises and take care of them.

Handling Complaints

A third important aspect of postsale activities is handling customer complaints. Sometimes, despite your best efforts, customers will not be satisfied. Their level of expectations for the product or service may have been too high, they may be using it improperly, or the product may have not been delivered as promised. You should welcome complaints as an opportunity to soothe hurt feelings before more serious problems develop. At 3M, for example, a substantial number of new-product ideas come in response to the complaints of users. They use the complaint as an opportunity.[9] Conversely, poor complaint handling can give customers negative feelings about you or your firm. Here are some suggested guidelines for handling customer complaints in a way that they do not turn into major problems.[10]

Be informed Customers want their problems solved quickly, and they want their questions answered promptly. Thus, you must know your firm and its policies and be able to locate information to deal with the problem. This

---

[8]For an interesting discussion of follow-up in real estate, see Bonnie L. Lugger, "Follow-Up and Follow-Through," *Real Estate Today,* Vol. 12, No. 3 (March 1979), pp. 38–41.

[9]Tom Peters and Nancy Austin, *A Passion for Excellence* (New York: Random House, 1985), p. 25.

[10]The following section is adapted from Donald W. Jackson, Jr. and Janet E. Keith, "Rx for Member Complaints," *Credit Union Management,* Vol. 5, No. 6 (June 1982), p. 23.

knowledge will allow you to offer clear, concise suggestions or solutions rather than vague, ambiguous double-talk.

Anticipate complaints If a complaint is anticipated, inform the customer as soon as the error is recognized. This will let the customer know you are giving individual attention and will reduce the potential for a complaint.

Thank the customer Be sure to thank the customer for bringing the complaint to your attention. Also apologize for any inconvenience caused by the problem and make a genuine effort to help the customer.

Encourage the customer to talk Often when customers complain, they are angry or confused. In order to reduce tension and get information, you should encourage the customer to talk about the problem. This may provide you with sources of misinformation and will show the customer that you are concerned.

DON'T COMPLAIN ABOUT COMPLAINTS

In a study prepared for Coca-Cola, it was shown that when a company fails to deal successfully with a complaint, the person will tell, on average, ten people about the bad experience. On the other hand, satisfied customers tell only four or five people about their positive experience. The author of the same study estimates that for every dissatisfied person who complains, there are fifty who simply stop buying the product.

SOURCE: "Don't Complain about Complaints," *Sales and Marketing Management,* Vol. 129, No. 4 (September 13, 1982), p. 158.

Listen, listen, listen It is important to listen carefully to the complaint. Regardless of how small or trivial a complaint may seem to you, all complaints are important to your customers. Thus, you must listen attentively to show that you are concerned and to get all the facts.

Never take a customer's complaint personally Often customers become angry when they complain and may overstate their case or make cutting remarks. It is easy to interrupt, stop listening, or become defensive in such circumstances. However, a better approach is to remain calm and listen.[11]

Establish the facts Always try to establish the facts first. Ask questions to clarify the complaint and obtain all the information possible before trying to solve the problem. Strive to resolve the complaint fairly once you have the facts. The customer must be told precisely what can and cannot be done to correct the problem, and why. You must convince the customer that the action is fair.

Resell and educate When you handle complaints, it is important to resell customers and educate them to use the product properly. Failure to do this may result in a repeat of the problem and additional complaints or dissatisfaction. Often when customers complain there is an excellent opportunity to sell them something.[12] A bank customer who complains about a check bouncing is a prime prospect for a service that provides an automatic line of credit to cover overdrafts. The important thing when handling these customers is to show them how the new service can satisfy their needs and keep the problem from happening again.

Follow up Once an appropriate solution is derived, you must follow through with immediate action. Customers expect their complaints to be resolved promptly. You will also want to keep the customers informed of what you are doing.

Keep records of complaints It is important to keep records of complaints and feed the information back to your company so that the problems can be eliminated or at least kept to a minimum. Only if complaints are recognized can steps be taken to resolve the problems that cause them.

SUMMARY

In a general way, everything you do is directed toward the close. You could perform superlatively in all aspects of work but fail if you are unable to close.

Four reasons why salespeople fail to close sales were discussed. Some people lack confidence in themselves, their product, or their company; some

---

[11]See, for example: Darlene Bari, "How to Keep Your Cool with Hot Customers (and Sell More, Too)," *The American Salesman,* Vol. 28, No. 3 (March 1983), pp. 3–7.

[12]Jim Thompson, "Turn Complaints into Sales," *Selling Direct,* Vol. 72, No. 11 (November 1983), pp. 16–18.

fear failure, and others have guilt feelings about selling. Another reason some salespeople fail to close is that they have not made the necessary preparations and do not prospect or present properly.

Various closing signals the salesperson should watch for were also examined. Closing signals may take the form of physical actions, comments, or questions. Although there is no guarantee that a specific gesture, comment, or question means that the prospect is ready for the close, the salesperson who pays careful attention to the prospect will have a better feel for when to close the sale.

The trial close is designed to determine the prospect's reaction without forcing a final buying decision on the total offer. This is a way "to take the prospect's temperature." Although there is no single best time to close, several situations were suggested as points in the process when buying signals would be sent and when a close might be appropriate.

The two closing methods, direct and assumptive, along with nine closing strategies were explained. Closing strategies are used to persuade or put the prospect into a favorable mind set so that one of the two closing methods can be employed. The salesperson can either ask for the order, the direct method, or assume that the sale has been made, the assumptive method, and act accordingly.

Choosing the most appropriate closing method or strategy depends on the situation and on the prospect; thus your ability to "read" the prospect and the situation is vital to your effectiveness.

Some practical suggestions for making the close of the sale easier and more effective and some major mistakes in closing were listed.

If a sale cannot be made to a prospect, you should leave the door open for future business and use a "postmortem" to determine what led to the competitor's success and why your firm did not get the order.

Postsale activities are an important part of selling. Immediately after closing you must make sure to work out the details of the sale and provide the customer with ample justification for the purchase decision. Long-term follow-up is also important to eliminate cognitive dissonance and to ensure satisfaction. In order to follow up effectively, you check on the order, initiate the postsale contact, provide services, continue to assure the customer, allow the customer to talk objectively, update your records, and be dependable. Handling customer complaints is also important to keeping customers satisfied; to do a good job of handling complaints, you must be informed, anticipate complaints, thank your customers, encourage them to talk, listen, not take complaints personally, establish the facts when there are complaints, resell and educate customers, follow up on solutions to their problems, and keep records of complaints.

PROBLEMS

1. Describe closing in your own words.
2. Which of these sales representatives would have the greatest percentage of sales calls become closes for actual orders?
   a. Furniture manufacturer's salesperson

      b. Machine tools wholesaler's salesperson

      c. Cosmetics retailer's salesperson

      Justify your answers.

3. Which of the closing strategies and methods described would you respond to if you were considering buying a personal computer? If you were considering buying an unusual gift for a friend?

4. As a salesperson, which closing strategy or method would appeal to you most if you were selling life insurance? If you were selling typewriters? Why?

5. What traits in salespeople would predispose them to misinterpret closing signals?

6. Scan a current magazine and mark up or clip out ads that illustrate any of the closing methods or strategies described in this chapter.

EXERCISE 14

Objectives: To reinforce knowledge of closing methods and strategies by case analysis.

             To illustrate ways of ensuring postsale satisfaction.

PART A **Closing Methods and Strategies**

An industrial salesperson used the following closing methods and strategies during the course of her work. Identify these methods and strategies and indicate what factors may have influenced the choice she made—for example, earlier events, characteristics of the other person or persons, and the kind of sales resistance encountered. Remember that often combinations of methods are used. Don't miss any.

1. Presentation to a purchasing agent in a prospect account.

    SALESPERSON: . . . I certainly appreciate your willingness to have your technical people test our product. It's bound to look good against anything in the field. May we set a time for my next visit? You indicated the lab might need a week for the test. What day next week would be better for you? Wednesday or Thursday?

2. Presentation at a conference attended by three people in a customer account: Ed McDonald, the chief design engineer; Betty Parker, the director of purchasing; and Don Johnston, the production manager.

    SALESPERSON: May I summarize where we are in this new project? Incidentally, I'm sure our firm will be able to do as fine a job for you this time as was done on the last project.

       First of all, the specifications as revised are now firm. Second, our #201 switches and #342 transducers meet your specifications without modification. Believe me, this was good news to our plant people.

       Third, purchasing is about ready to receive final bids on specified quantities. Mrs. Parker, when do you anticipate having the quantity schedule drawn up?

3. Presentation to a vice-president of manufacturing in a customer account.

   SALESPERSON: I can understand your hesitation about making this change. As you indicate, there have been no major headaches using the XYZ component, and your personnel are used to handling it. On the other hand, have you considered how much you would save in labor alone if you switched to our unit? You've said yourself that the other products you have bought from us have been excellent in every respect. However, we would like you to try our product for one production run. We are sure that the savings will be substantial.

PART B Postsale Satisfaction

1. List as many ways as you can think of that this industrial salesperson might use to provide postsale satisfaction to each of her accounts.
2. Again assuming the role of the fashion salesperson, list as many ways as you can to provide postsale satisfaction to your customers.

Case 14-1 Bonne Bell Cosmetics (B)[13]
Maria Alameda's call on Mrs. Walker continues.

MARIA: All our products are profit makers. I'd like to demonstrate how they can make money for you.

MRS. WALKER: Well, as I indicated, we've had no calls for Bonne Bell, and we may have too many brands in stock now.

MARIA: Mrs. Walker, if you are willing, I'd be glad to work with your assistant in compiling your turnover and profit figures for the items you now carry. This will enable you to evaluate how Bonne Bell can fit in.

MRS. WALKER: I don't think I should open up our records to an outsider. I'm sure the other salespeople who call on us would be upset if they found out.

MARIA: I am sorry. I was only trying to be of service. By the way, you're free to share these Bonne Bell figures with anybody. We're proud of our acceptance and record.

MRS. WALKER: Well, thanks for stopping by.

MARIA: Mrs. Walker, will you do me a favor? Accept these Bonne Bell samples and try them yourself. I think you'll be convinced that you should stock them.
A week later Maria phones Mrs. Walker.

MARIA: Mrs. Walker, this is Maria Alameda, the Bonne Bell representative. What did you think of our TEN O'SIX?

MRS. WALKER: It certainly is a fine product. I enjoyed the tingly feeling it gave me.

[13]Examine Case 13-1, Bonne Bell Cosmetics (A), before analyzing this case.

MARIA: Might I see you this afternoon or tomorrow morning? I have a proposal I'm sure you'll like.

MRS. WALKER: Well, I'm very busy, but I can give you fifteen minutes at about four o'clock today.

MARIA: Thanks very much. I'll see you then.

Maria plans to get an order with the stipulation that she will work behind the counter training the salespeople in handling Bonne Bell.

1. How should Maria try to accomplish her objective?
2. What closing approach should she use?

CASE 14-2 Providence Realty (B)[14]

Donna Stark drives up to a modest, well-kept home and rings the bell. Mrs. Leonard greets her and introduces her husband. Donna notices an older-model station wagon in the carport as the three of them set out to see the listing. After exchanging initial pleasantries, Donna and Mr. and Mrs. Leonard leave to see the house in Donna's car. The following conversation takes place.

MR. LEONARD: Mrs. Stark, I must tell you we don't want to bite off more than we can chew. We pride ourselves on paying as we go. Our only debt is the mortgage on our present home.

DONNA: That's certainly the way to live. I guess if more people lived that way we'd all benefit.

MR. LEONARD: I told my wife specifically to ask the price, and I find she doesn't know it yet.

DONNA: Mr. Leonard, I must apologize for that. This house you are going to see is such a buy I didn't want either of you to miss seeing it. Here we are. (Donna pulls into the drive.)

MRS. LEONARD: Isn't this a nice neighborhood. The lawn and shrubbery are well cared for.

DONNA: Wait until you see the inside and the backyard. You'll love it. (Donna unlocks the door and ushers them in. She turns on lights as they proceed through the house.)

DONNA: (As they look at the basement) Mrs. Leonard, think of the space the children have down here to play on rainy days.

MRS. LEONARD: Will the washer and dryer be included? They are much newer than mine.

DONNA: Not as a rule. However, I can find out. Perhaps we can strike a bargain.

MR. LEONARD: Before we go any farther, just what is the asking price?

DONNA: It's listed at $69,900.

---

[14]Examine Case 13-2, Providence Realty (A), before analyzing this case.

MR. LEONARD: Wow. That's over my head.

DONNA: Well, it is a lot of money. However, I think you'll both agree that this is a lot of house.

MRS. LEONARD: It certainly is. And it's such a nice neighborhood.

MR. LEONARD: What's wrong with our neighborhood?

MRS. LEONARD: Nothing at all, dear, but you'll agree this is more residential and nearer to the school.

DONNA: You know, it occurs to me that you may wish to trade in your present home. My firm can handle such an arrangement.

MR. LEONARD: Well, that sounds okay, but I've got to know what it's going to cost if we go ahead.

DONNA: I'm sure we can work things out to your satisfaction. Our assessor can give me a price on your home tomorrow. He'll need to know such details as status of the mortgage, your tax rate, things like that. This home has an assumable mortage with a face value of $50,000, Mr. Leonard. That tells you something about the value of this property.

MR. LEONARD: $69,900 still sounds too high to me. However, since my wife likes the home, I'm willing to look at some figures.

DONNA: Our assessor, Mr. Ed Jones, will come by tomorow, and tomorrow evening I'll come to the house with a definite proposal. It's been a pleasure to meet you.

In preparing for her meeting the next evening, Donna finds that the Leonards' current monthly payments are $350, whereas the monthly payments on the new mortgage would be $566.

She muses. Any way you figure it, the Leonards will be paying an additional $216 per month. Our office has found that the Leonards are an A-1 credit risk and that Mr. Leonard's salary is such that the payments are not out of reach.

How should Donna proceed?

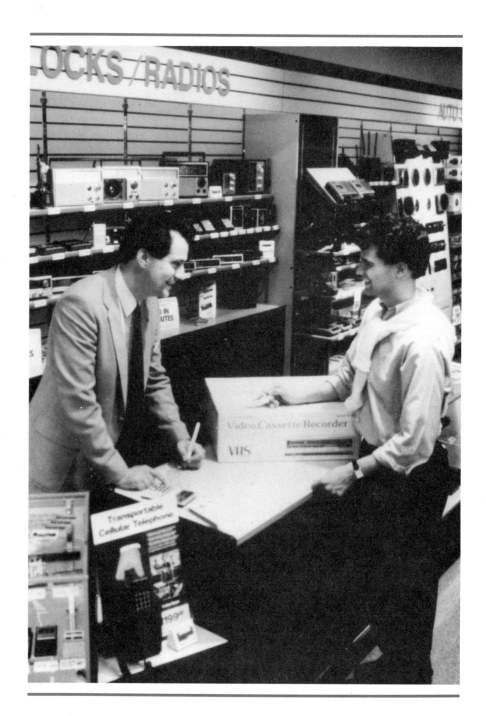

Different Types
of Selling
Situations

After studying this chapter, you should be able to

1. Identify the knowledge needed by retail salespeople.
2. Specify the steps in the retail sales process.
3. Understand selling strategies for increasing retail sales.
4. Recognize the unique aspects of selling services.
5. Describe various suggestions for selling services.
6. Understand how industrial purchasing is done.
7. Identify tools and approaches used by the industrial buyer.
8. Specify unique aspects of industrial selling.

Although the general principles of selling outlined in this book are applicable to virtually all types of selling, some distinctive aspects of selling are unique to particular situations. This chapter explores retail selling, selling of services, and industrial selling as selling situations that require special approaches or knowledge.

RETAIL SELLING

Retail establishments range from small, independent grocery stores to national supermarket chains, from automobile dealerships and used-car lots to real estate firms and banks, from beauty parlors to health clinics. Retail establishments deal directly with the public as customers rather than with businesses as customers.[1] In spite of the great differences in these various retail establishments, they all have some aspects of selling in common that are unique to the retail market. These are described in this section, followed by the knowledge needed by retail salespeople, the retail sales process, some strategies for increasing sales, and some recurring retail selling problems.

Unique Aspects of Retail Selling

Several aspects of retail selling make it unique from other types of selling. Often prospects come to you rather than your having to seek out prospects. Thus, it is generally not possible to do any "homework" before the interaction to find out prospects' needs or to qualify them. Furthermore, retail transactions are generally concluded during a relatively short time period, so you must establish rapport and size up the other person relatively quickly. Therefore, during the short call you must determine customers' needs and qualify them in order to show them the proper merchandise.

Because retail prospects are often part-time purchasers and not as well informed as their industrial counterparts who are often professional buyers, they will need basic information on the product, its operation, the major alternatives, and the producer. Generally speaking, the terms of sale are not negotiated in retail selling, although when the product is an automobile or a major appliance, there may be some negotiation concerning price and terms.

Many times the retail salesperson has a wide variety of products from a wide variety of sources to sell. Industrial or reseller salespeople may also have broad product lines, but they generally receive much more formal product training than the typical retail salesperson. Thus, retail salespeople must often get this information on their own.[2]

---

[1]For our purposes we will deal mainly with in-store selling. Technically speaking, door-to-door selling and catalog selling are also retail sales; however, door-to-door selling is different from retail selling since you seek out customers rather than having them come to you. Catalog selling does not normally require salespeople except for telephone work.

[2]For an interesting discussion of the values of retail sales training, see "Retailers Discover an Old Tool: Sales Training." *Business Week* (December 22, 1980), pp. 51–52.

To give adequate counseling to your customers, you must have knowledge about the store, the merchandise, and the customers you serve.

The store Retail organizations frequently differentiate themselves from competitors by selling particular lines of merchandise and offering special services. You should be aware of these policies so that you can pass the information on to the customer. Price, quality, or guarantees may be crucial factors in the purchasing decision. Store services, special promotions, delivery, and availability of credit should also be pointed out whenever they may favorably influence the purchase. It is important for salespeople to be knowledgeable about their store's local advertising so that they will be able to respond with the correct information when asked questions.

The merchandise Thorough knowledge of the merchandise handled by the store is very important information. Most buyers are anxious to learn more about the products under consideration, and they often judge salespeople to be experts on the merchandise. You should be able to answer at least the most common questions about your products.

Consider the following situation. A customer enters a store to purchase a color television set. The customer asks the salesperson, "What is the difference between these two brands? Why is this one more expensive?" It is very important, at this point, to give the customer a thorough explanation of the technical differences between the two products, in order to justify the price differential. If you cannot answer customer questions, you will lose credibility.

WAYS FOR RETAIL SALESPEOPLE TO GET PRODUCT INFORMATION

- Talk to buyers.
- Talk to buyers who own product.
- Talk to other salespeople.
- Talk to supplier's salespeople.
- Talk to your management.
- Read merchandise labels and tags.
- Read advertisements.
- Read brochures.
- Read instructions.
- Read trade journals.
- Read reports from testing bureaus.
- Use the product yourself.

Understanding merchandise helps retail salespeople sell.

The customer As a good retail salesperson, you should also know your customers. People like to have you remember their name, their product preference, and particular merchandise they have been looking for, so you should keep records to refer to when appropriate. When new merchandise reaches the store, you may want to call some of your regular customers and let them know about particular products. In addition, when you approach new customers, your general knowledge about the store's clientele will help you to ask pertinent questions and suggest possible choices.

Retail Sales Process
Retail selling consists of eight selling steps plus some additional nonselling duties. These eight steps form a logical sequence of events when a consumer enters a store; (1) greet the customer, (2) determine the person's needs, (3) select the merchandise that would satisfy these needs, (4) describe and demonstrate the product, (5) narrow the choices, (6) handle any objections, (7) attempt to close the sale, and (8) if appropriate, follow up.

Greet the customer It is essential that a customer feel welcome when enter-ing the store. Salespeople who ignore customers and continue with their busywork or talk to other salespeople will give a negative impression and may eventually lose the customer altogether.

The initial greeting should encourage the customer to stay in the store, look around, and ask questions about the merchandise. It is important to encourage customers to share ideas about the product they want, and questions such as "May I help you?" often elicit an automatic response: "No, thank you, I'm just browsing." Thus, this approach should be avoided. More pointed approaches that might encourage a dialogue are preferred: "We are featuring Brand C this week at a special price," or "This is a product that has pleased many of our customers."

Many of the approaches discussed in Chapter 8 may be adapted for retail selling. For instance, the following may be appropriate in various situations.

- **Question approach** "Hello, how may I help you?"
- **Benefit approach** "I see you are looking at this new sweater. Did you know that it is completely washable? You will save a considerable amount of money in dry-cleaning charges."
- **New-product approach** "Have you seen the new sweaters we just got in? They are really a good value."
- **Product approach** "Here, touch this new sweater. Isn't it soft?" or "Why don't you try it on?"
- **Compliment approach** "That is a lovely coat you have on, Mrs. Green."

Embarrassing questions—for example "Can you tell me exactly how you would use this product?"—should be avoided. The customer must feel free to browse and ask for information without being pressured into buying.

Determine the customer's needs You should observe and listen to customers so that you can properly assess their needs. By encouraging customers to share ideas and feelings about a product, you can determine their preferences and tastes and thereby suggest specific alternatives to them. Screening questions are especially useful. For example, a person selling furniture might ask, "Is your home modern or traditional?" "What rooms are you furnishing?" "What pieces are you looking for?" "What price range are you considering?"

If you were selling in a men's clothing department, you would note what shoppers examine as well as how they are dressed. If the customer is looking at slacks, you might ask such questions as, "Do you prefer a plain front or pleats?" "Are they for business or leisure?" "What colors do you prefer?" "What is your waist size?"

Another method for determining a customer's needs is to mention several key benefits and then watch carefully and listen for the prospect's reactions. Often this method will tell you what the prospect is interested in or will bring out objections.

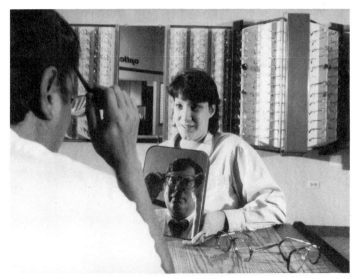

Selecting the right merchandise makes selection easier.

Select merchandise Taking into account customer's responses to questions about needs, you can then make an initial selection of merchandise. Variables such as the model, size, price range, and color of the product may be the initial selection criteria, but it is rare to find a customer who has already made all product decisions before entering the store. A common mistake, however, is for the salesperson to show a multitude of products without attempting to determine the customer's needs. This method is confusing and tiring, and it certainly does not help the customer.

Describe and demonstrate the product Even though most American consumers are relatively knowledgeable about products and services, it is still important to present them with all aspects of the purchase. Actual demonstration of product uses, in addition to verbal description, may be crucial to the buying decision. Actively involving prospects and stimulating several of their senses also tends to increase your chances of making a sale. For instance, you might want the customer to touch a cashmere sweater, or smell a new fragrance, or listen to a stereo, or drive a new car.

With some items, demonstration or trial use is an effective strategy. Consider the following examples.

- A supermarket demonstrator offers a sample of a new sandwich meat to a shopper.
- A videotape showing the uses of power tools attracts a customer.
- A local automobile dealer encourages a prospect to take a test drive.
- A vacuum cleaner salesperson cleans a rug for a homeowner.
- A professional model wears a new dress style.

The customer's reactions suggest what points should be reiterated or strengthened, and also encourage you to show additional products to the customer.

Narrow choice alternatives Still another strategy, applicable where a wide range of choices are possible, is to show only a limited number of items at a time. For example, a salesperson might select three ties from among hundreds in stock. If one is rejected, the salesperson immediately puts it aside. If the choice narrows to one of the three ties but there is still uncertainty, the salesperson brings out an additional tie that might appeal to the customer. The strategic principles behind this example are simple. First, avoid providing too many choices; a buying decision becomes more difficult as the number of options increases. Second, offer a limited number of positive alternatives; it minimizes a "no purchase" response as one of the options.

Handle objections Frequently customers object to particular features of the product, such as color or size. You can then respond easily by showing more desirable alternatives.

A more serious type of objection may reflect deep-seated feelings that customers are not willing to state clearly, such as financial constraints. In this situation customers may voice vague objections, such as "Well, we are not really sure . . .," or "I will talk to my wife abut this." Here you would add comments concerning special purchase plans, or ask customers general questions that may bring out their real feelings. And, of course, there will always be times when you cannot satisfy the customer's objections.

Close the sale A good salesperson should be able to recognize closing signals promptly and should then stop showing merchandise to the customer. At this point, you should ask for the customer's agreement in order to eliminate any possible indecision. You should not, however, rush the customer into buying. Some frequently used closes are, "Should I charge this to your account?" or "Would you like us to deliver this to your home?" "Will that be cash or charge?"

Follow up As a retail salesperson you have two major ways to follow up: by a letter or by telephone. In a study comparing the two methods, it was found that the customer receiving a letter experienced less doubt, had more favorable attitudes toward the store, and had more definite intentions of shopping at the store again.[3] Customers receiving telephone calls seemed to question the salesperson's motives and viewed the telephone call as an interruption.

Another study found that postpurchase communication by means of a follow-up letter increased satisfaction with the purchase and encouraged a greater number of recommendations of the retailer.[4] Thus, effective follow-up on high-priced items may be a good strategy and may increase your sales.

[3]See Shelby D. Hunt, "Post Transaction Communication and Dissonance Reduction," *Journal of Marketing,* Vol. 34, No. 3 (July 1970), p. 50.

[4]See Eldon M. Wirtz and Kenneth E. Miller, "The Effect of Postpurchase Communication on Consumer Satisfaction and on Consumer Recommendations of the Retailer, *Journal of Purchasing,* Vol. 53, No. 2 (Summer 1977), pp. 39–46.

Strategies for Increasing Sales

Several strategies that may be used to increase your sales include trading up, suggestive selling, and developing a personal trade.

ADDITIONAL DUTIES OF THE RETAIL SALESPERSON

- Serve as a source of information about different products.
- Provide adequate service to customers before and after purchase.
- Handle customers' complaints.
- Inform management of trends in customer needs.
- Provide assistance when products are returned or exchanged.
- Help maintain store seurity by watching for shoplifting.
- Help customers through the store.
- Help keep stock by checking and marking incoming merchandise, maintaining adequate shelf inventory, building displays, taking inventory, and keeping stock neat.

Trading up Trading up consists of selling customers more expensive merchandise than they might have originally considered and pointing out the advantage of *quality* buying. Prospects who come in looking for a radio might be shown an AM–FM clock radio if it fits their needs. Nevertheless, if customers come in and ask for a specific product, you should always show them that product first. You must be careful not to be insensitive to customers' real needs and not to oversell the higher-quality merchandise to the point that you talk yourself out of a sale. On the other hand, customers will often be even more satisfied with merchandise that is higher in quality and has more features.

Suggestive selling Another strategy is suggestive selling, which may take the form of selling customers related merchandise such as a shirt and tie to go with a suit, or a belt to go with slacks. The salesperson may also suggest that the customer examine new merchandise. You might say, for example, "Have you seen our new line of shirts; they're very popular." Suggestive selling would also include showing customers the advantage of *quantity* buying and telling them about specials or sale items. The more the suggestion seems to be spontaneous and directly related to the customers' needs, the more likely it will result in a tie-in sale. However, just saying "Will there be anything else today?" is not of much use.

Personal trade A third strategy for increasing your sales is to develop a personal trade. These are customers who come into the store and ask for you. You can develop this type of loyalty by keeping cards on customers, personally notifying them of sales or other merchandise they would be interested in, remembering their names, and giving them special attention. Another way to build up a personal trade is to give customers good service, then hand them your business card, and encourage them to ask for you the next time they come into the store. One car salesperson always took care of the servicing of his customers' automobiles. They would bring the car in to him; he would then arrange for their transportation back home or to work and would notify them when their cars were ready. This service helped him develop a strong following of personal trade.

Recurring Retail Selling Problems

Several recurring problems face retail salespeople, including customers who are "just looking," handling several customers at once, selling to groups of customers, and handling out-of-stock merchandise.

"Just looking" Many times people will say they are "just looking." Sometimes this is true and persistence will only make them uncomfortable. On the other hand, sometimes customers are looking for an item but may wish to look over the merchandise themselves or to check prices.

There are several ways of dealing with prospects who are "just looking." You can, of course, leave them alone but keep an eye on them from a distance to see whether they need help; or you can try to point them in the direction of the general merchandise they are seeking. You might say, for example, "Is there anything special I can direct you toward?" and then assure them that they are welcome to browse.

It is important when dealing with browsers, to be sensitive to their needs and not make them feel pressured, yet at the same time to be available if they need assistance.

Selling to groups Sometimes a retail salesperson will be approached by several prospects at once, such as family members or friends. When this happens, it is important to pick out the influential person and direct your attention to this person's concerns and needs. If a man and wife are shopping for a suit for him and the woman is obviously playing an important role, you might note her reaction and say something like, "Doesn't that suit look nice on him?" When appropriate, you should also allow the people to talk over their purchase in private. If you suspect that they are holding back, you may excuse yourself and allow them to talk.

One study showed that when retail purchasers were accompanied by another person, the probability of their making purchases was higher.[5] Thus, selling to several people can be an advantage.

Handling several customers at once Often there will be more customers in the store than there are salespeople. This poses a ticklish problem for the retail salesperson. Should you stay with the customers you are serving and risk having the unattended customers leave because they cannot find the mer-

[5]See Arch G. Woodside and J. Taylor Sims, "Retail Sales Transactions and 'Purchase Pal' Effects on Buying Behavior," *Journal of Retailing*, Vol. 52, No. 3 (Fall 1976), pp. 57–64.

chandise, or should you leave the customers you are with and risk hurting their feelings or having them leave? Although there is no universally correct answer to this problem, there are several considerations. First, there are times during a sale when customers may easily be left alone, such as when they are trying on clothes or looking at various types of merchandise. You can then excuse yourself, greet the other customers, and point them in the right direction. You must, however, be aware of your original customers should they need help. Second, as a general rule you should wait on people on a first-come, first-serve basis. An exception is handling small purchases, should the timing be right, while continuing to help customers with a large sale. Third, it is extremely important that you be sensitive to the buyer's needs and that you have a sense of timing. Leaving potential customers—even for a moment—when they need you or before they have seen the merchandise they are interested in may lose a sale. Fourth, you must be polite and excuse yourself. Your sincerity and politeness will make you much more effective.

Handling out-of-stock merchandise Another problem faced by retail sales-people is how to handle the situation when you are out of stock on the item customers want. There are several considerations. First, you must make sure that you are actually out of stock on the item—that is, that it is not in back stock or in a storeroom. Many sales have been lost by salespeople who failed to check. If you are working for a chain, you might call another of your stores to see whether they have the item. Second, if you are out of stock, you should find out when you can expect deliveries. Often people are willing to wait a few days when necessary. If it is a high-ticket item, you may even take the customer's name and number and agree to call when the item comes in. Third, you may be able to switch them to another comparable brand if they are willing to accept a substitute and if you have one available. But you should be careful not to be too persistent, to watch their reaction, and never to push something on them that they do not want or need. Even if you make a sale under these circumstances, you may lose goodwill and perhaps future purchases. Finally, as a last resort you might suggest somewhere else the customer could buy the product. Even though you lose a sale, you may build goodwill and the customer will probably appreciate your efforts.

SELLING SERVICES

Services are an important part of our economy and account for many jobs. Growth in the service sector has been phenomenal: service sector jobs currently account for 72 percent of all employment in the United States.[6] Many of these jobs consist of selling services or require direct customer contact. There are some unique aspects of services that require you to sell differently. Finally, some specific suggestions for selling services are offered.[7]

[6]James L. Heskett, *Managing in the Service Economy* (Boston: Harvard Business School Press, 1986), p. 3.

[7]For a good overview of selling services, see William R. George, J. Patrick Kelly, and Claudia E. Marshall, "The Selling of Services: A Comprehensive Model," *Journal of Personal Selling and Sales Management,* Vol. 6, No. 2 (August 1986), pp. 29–37.

There are several categories of salespeople in the service sector. Some services, such as insurance, airline travel, and lodging, are sold by independent agents who are compensated by service providers on a commission basis. Other services, such as communications, transportation, financial services, and public utilities, have their own sales forces, often called customer representatives or account representatives. A third type of services salesperson is an employee such as a bus driver or an auto mechanic who comes into personal contact with the customer. Even though these people may not be trained as sales people, their people skills and the human relations aspects of their jobs are crucial to the success of the service.[8]

A similar situation is prevalent in professional services, where partners or principles sell professional services. This is what accounting firms, market researchers, and consultants do. Although the people making the contact may not actually perform the service, they do get actively involved in selling the capabilities of their firms.

Finally, there is the situation in which the provider of the services must also do the selling, such as doctors, dentists, barbers, and independent financial planners. Here clients evaluate not only technical skills but also people skills.

Table 15.1 presents a number of different types of services that require selling.

Unique Aspects of Services

Unique aspects of services that require different approaches from product selling include the intangibility of services, the participation of the buyer and simultaneous production and consumption of services. In addition, the way people view services may require different sales approaches. Services may be viewed as riskier than products, people may rely on word of mouth for information, and postpurchase doubt may be more prevalent.

Intangibility When you are dealing with intangibles, most of the general principles of selling are applicable. The one characteristic that makes selling intangibles different is that prospects cannot use their senses to examine them.[9]

Products for sale can be touched, examined, operated, demonstrated, and may even be listened to, smelled, or tasted. When services are for sale, on the other hand, there may be no product; therefore, you cannot physically demonstrate the service. The advice that you must first sell yourself is particularly appropriate in this situation; where you have no product to sell, you must win the prospect's trust and confidence.

Some services such as real estate, restaurants, and hotels are accompanied by a tangible product—a house, a meal, or a hotel room—but others

[8]See John M. Rathmell, *Marketing in the Service Sector* (Cambridge, Mass.: Winthrop Publishers, 1974), p. 101.

[9]For an interesting discussion of trying to make intangibles more tangible, see Kathleen A. Krentler and Joseph P. Guiltinan, "Strategies for Tangibilizing Retail Services: An Assessment," *Journal of the Academy of Marketing Sciences*, Vol. 12, No. 4 (Fall 1984), pp. 77–92.

TABLE 15.1

A SELECTED LIST OF SERVICES THAT REQUIRE SELLING

Advertising agencies

Private employment agencies

Consulting services

Temporary help

Accounting, auditing, and bookkeeping services

Universities, colleges, and other schools

Banks

Savings and loan associations

Security brokers

Credit institutions

Commodity brokers

Health care services

Household services

Apartment rentals

Hotels

Insurance

Legal services

Funeral services

Jewelry repair

Museums and art galleries

Transportation

Professional organizations

Religious organizations

SOURCE: Adapted from John M. Rathmell, *Marketing in the Service Sector* (Cambridge, Mass.: Winthrop Publishers, 1974), pp. 217–220.

such as insurance and consulting are almost purely intangible. When the service has a tangible product, you may display it or sell it almost as you would sell a regular product.[10] With intangible services such as life insurance or stocks, you are selling pieces of paper that have no value in and of themselves but only in what they represent; thus, you must convince the prospect that you can deliver what you say you will.

The relative intangibility of services requires you to stress customer benefits. For instance, in selling mangement consulting you might want to stress customer benefits like increased productivity or decreased costs. Moreover, since a service cannot be experienced in advance, you have to appeal to the prospect's imagination in decribing benefits. For instance, when selling a tour

[10]For an interesting classification of various types of services offerings, see Christopher H. Lovelock, "Classifying Services to Gain Strategic Marketing Insights," *Journal of Marketing*, Vol. 47 No. 3 (Summer 1983), pp. 9–20.

This real estate salesperson has developed a strong relationship with her client.

to the Greek Islands, a travel agent must help clients visualize the fun, romance, intrigue, and excitement of a trip.[11]

One study suggested the following strategies for dealing with intangibility. First, you can stress tangible cues of your offering, as Prudential does with "Buy a piece of the rock." Second, you can try to stimulate word-of-mouth communications, and third, you can follow up with post purchase communciations.[12]

Participation of buyer In many services, such as life insurance and financial planning, customers are actually involved in the creation of the service. In these situations the salesperson must customize the service to the unique needs of the customer. To do this you must be empathic, ask questions, get the customer involved, listen, and be flexible. Furthermore, in this situation you must act almost as a consultant in putting together unique configurations of services to meet the personal needs of the buyer.

Simultaneous production and consumption Whereas products are produced at one point in time and consumed later, many services are produced and

[11]See John T. Mentzer and David J. Schwartz, *Marketing Today,* fourth edition (New York: Harcourt Brace Jovanovich, 1985), p. 325.
[12]See Valarie A. Zeithaml, A. Parasuraman, and Leonard L. Berry, "Problems and Strategies in Services Marketing," *Journal of Marketing,* Vol. 49, No. 2 (Spring 1985), p. 35.

consumed almost simultaneously. As a result, the salesperson and the consumer must interact in order to deliver the service effectively, and the service salesperson is also a production worker.[13] An accountant assisting people with tax returns, for example, provides them with a customized service in which they are buying the accountant's expertise. To the extent to which there is simultaneous production and consumption, you must also sell as you go and adapt the service to the needs of the prospect.

Consumer risk Since it is difficult to judge the quality of a service, consumers may perceive service purchases as riskier than goods purchases.[14] Thus, one of the key aspects of selling services is to reduce this perceived risk. To accomplish this you can reassure the prospect, use testimonials, sell yourself and the capabilities of your firm, and be sure to follow up.

Importance of word of mouth It is important to remember that customers rely heavily on the influence of others when purchasing services.[15] Thus, when you are selling services, it is important to develop a strategy that emphasizes referrals and testimonials.[16] Using satisfied customers as part of your selling strategy also reduces the risk on the part of the prospect. In order to capitalize on this unpaid sales force, you will have to build a strong positive relationship with your customers. You will have to be very professional and low pressure, and you will have to be dependable.

Likelihood of postpurchase doubt Customers may also experience postpurchase doubt for several reasons. First, the perception that services are riskier increases the likelihood of postpurchase doubt. Second, because they often have no tangible product to back up their purchase, customers may tend to question the wisdom of their choice . Thus, it is important to reassure customers on the wisdom of their choice and to encourage them to tell their friends about the purchase.[17]

Suggestions for Selling Services

Several techniques for selling services include using extrinsic and intrinsic appeals, being knowledgeable, managing your appearance, building personal relationships, and stressing benefits.

---

[13]See W. Earl Sasser and Stephen P. Arbeit, "Selling Jobs in the Service Sector," *Business Horizons,* Vol. 19, No. 3 (June 1976); pp. 61–65.

[14]See William R. George and Thomas A. Myers, "Life Underwriters' Perceptions of Differences in Selling Goods and Services," *CLU Journal* (April 1981); p. 45.

[15]See Martin R. Schlissel, "The Marketing of Services: Observation and Opportunities," *Proceedings Southern Marketing Association* (1978), p. 471.

[16]See William R. George and Thomas A. Myers, "Life Underwriters' Perceptions of Differences in Selling Goods and Services," *CLU Journal* (April 1981), p.48.

[17]See Richard M. Bessom, "Unique Aspects of Marketing Services," *Arizona Business* (November 1973), p. 14.

Extrinsic and intrinsic appeals Selling services can be approached in two ways: the *extrinsic* approach consists of selling the capabilities, abilities, and qualifications of your firm, the *intrinsic* approach consists of providing the customer with the specific benefits of the service.[18] Using the extrinsic approach, you would stress past accomplishments, the qualifications of your employees, and the satisfaction of previous clients. Given the intangible nature of some services such as consulting, this may be an important part of your selling. On the other hand, using intrinsic appeals, you would show the prospect how your service would benefit them. For example, a CPA selling the intrinsic value of her firm's auditing services might stress the benefits derived from her firm's objectivity, which would give credibility to her client's financial statements, and the efficiency of her efforts, which would mean lower fees to the client.

Be knowledgeable People who are involved in selling services must be very knowledgeable about their offerings to be successful. In product sales, the product itself can do some of the selling. When shopping for a new car, people can examine various models, colors, and styles themselves and can even test-drive the car. On the other hand, with many services all the salesperson has is knowledge. When a customer buys an insurance program, for example, the policy is custom-tailored according to income, needs, and other investments. The point is, since it is difficult for prospects to shop for themselves, the salesperson must be knowledgeable in order to match the right policy to their needs.

Manage your appearance Words are not the only factors in selling a service; buyers also give weight to the salesperson's manner and appearance, even though they may have no connection to the quality of the service.[19] Since there is often no physical product, customers may also judge the quality of the service by such factors as the office, the waiting room, brochures, and other visual cues. Thus, all these factors must be managed to create a positive image of the service.

Build personal relationships If customers are not satisfied with the personal aspects of dealing with a service, they may become dissatisfied with the entire service.[20] To the purchaser of a service the salesperson is an integral part of the purchase decision. Consumers choose a supplier of a service because of their image or impression of the people who will supply the service.[21]

---

[18]See Aubrey Wilson, *The Marketing of Professional Services* (London: McGraw-Hill, 1972), p. 30.

[19]See G. Lynn Shostack, "Every Word Counts When Selling Complex Services," *American Banker* (March 10, 1982), p. 14.

[20]See Eugene M. Johnson, "Are Goods and Services Different? An Exercise on Marketing Theory" (doctoral dissertation, Washington University, 1969), p. 98.

[21]See Richard M. Bessom and Donald W. Jackson, Jr., "Service Retailing: A Strategic Marketing Approach," *Journal of Retailing*, Vol. 51, No. 2 (Summer 1975), p. 82.

Thus, you must concentrate on the interpersonal aspects of the sale, on being conscientious and on follow-up.

Stress benefits Although you should always stress benefits when you sell, it is even more important when selling services. You should stress what your service can do for the prospect. The features of many services, such as the interest on an investment, are intangible   d thus difficult to envision. However, customer benefits are much more   ncrete and you can paint the prospect into the benefit. When selling life insurance, for instance, you might say, "Having $250,000 available on your death would ensure your children's education, and it would make your wife feel a lot more comfortable."

Because many services are intangible, you have to choose your words carefully in describing the service and its benefits so that the customer can actually visualize the sale.[22]

Encourage customer involvement Given the nonstandardization of many services, it is important to customize the service offered to the unique needs of prospects. You will need to involve prospects by questioning them about their needs. For instance when selling life insurance, you would need to know prospects' ages, incomes, family situations, and health in order to customize the insurance coverage to their needs.[23]

INDUSTRIAL SELLING

Industrial selling offers many lucrative opportunities.[24] Industrial salespeople sell goods and services to organizations, such as industrial firms and the government, and to institutions, such as hospitals, universities, and utilities, both profit and nonprofit. Although most of what you have learned about selling in this book is directly applicable to industrial selling, some unique aspects of industrial buying make the buying–selling relationship different. Several aspects of industrial buying–selling are examined in this section, including how the purchasing department is organized and how the buying is done, using the Buygrid framework. Then additional aspects of the buying process are explored, and tools used by industrial buyers are reviewed.

Unique Aspects of Industrial Buying and Selling
In general, industrial buying behavior is more complex than consumer buyer behavior, because additional elements intervene and interact. Industrial pur-

[22]See G. Lynn Shostack, "Every Word Counts When Selling Complex Services," *American Banker* (March 10, 1982), p. 4.

[23]William R. George, J. Patrick Kelly, and Claudia E. Marshall, "The Selling of Services: A Comprehensive Model," *Journal of Personal Selling and Sales Management,* Vol. 6, No. 2 (August 1986), p. 33.

[24]For an interesting discussion of industrial selling, see Thomas R. Wotruba, "The Changing Character of Industrial Selling," *European Journal of Marketing,* Vol. 14, No. 5/6 (1980), pp. 293–302; see also Clifton J. Reichard, "Industrial Selling: Beyond Price and Persistence," *Harvard Business Review,* Vol. 63, No. 2 (March–April 1985), pp. 127–133.

"Wait a minute—maybe I could give you a small order..."

chases involve individual needs and also the individual's needs as an employee of an organization. This means that you have to consider human factors and organizational objectives alike when attempting to make a sale to a business firm. Several of the unique aspects of the industrial buying–selling relationship are shown in Table 15.2

Who Does the Buying?

Even in the smallest firm, it is likely that more than one person influences the buying decision. The people involved in the purchasing decision are called the buying center, and in larger firms the number can range up to seven or more. Although the term buying center is seldom used in the business world, it is a useful, descriptive phrase for the people concerned with purchasing a product or service. These people might include representatives from purchasing, engineering, and production, users of the product, and even top management. The members of this decision-making group, both individually and as a group, generally have greater sophistication with respect to sales representatives' offerings than, say, the family buying unit considering a large expenditure in the consumer sector.

The members of the buying center may change with different types of decisions and products purchased. Furthermore, the relative influence of the members of the buying center shifts with the decision.[25] Finding out who the key buying influencers are and learning what criteria they use for making a purchasing decision are key factors in making a complex sale.

---

[25]See, for example, Donald W. Jackson, Jr., Janet E. Keith, and Richard K. Burdick, "Purchasing Agents' Perceptions of Industrial Buying Center Influence: A Situational Approach," *Journal of Marketing,* Vol. 48, No. 4 (Fall 1984), pp. 75–83.

TABLE 15.2
UNIQUE ASPECTS OF THE INDUSTRIAL BUYING–SELLING RELATIONSHIP

- Buying is generally done by a group of people called the buying center.
- The composition of the buying center changes for different types of products.[a]
- Different members of the buying center will have different needs and motives that must be addressed in making a sale.
- Often a group of people from the selling firm take part in making a sale. One of the key roles of marketing in such a situation is to orchestrate the interaction of the selling team with the buying team.[b]
- Since many industrial goods are used as components for other products, or are machines that produce consumer goods, the demand for industrial goods is derived from demand for consumer goods and tends to fluctuate more.
- Buyers of industrial goods tend to be sophisticated. Perhaps no other business group, with the exception of accountants, has moved as far as purchasing agents in establishing a professional status.[c] Industrial purchasers help to formulate certification programs, attend continuing education programs, and are very committed professionals.
- Generally, industrial purchasing requires more negotiations on elements such as the terms of sale, deliveries, prices, and postsale activities than consumer purchases do.[d]
- Industrial purchases are usually larger than consumer purchases because capital acquisitions are generally larger and because quantities are also usually larger.
- Because of the relatively large purchases and the relatively few customers, more emphasis is placed on personal selling as a component of the communications mix in industrial marketing, whereas advertising is more likely to have a key role in consumer marketing.

[a]See Donald W. Jackson, Jr., Janet E. Keith, and Richard K. Burdick, "Purchasing Agents' Perceptions of Industrial Buying Center Influence: A Situational Approach," *Journal of Marketing,* (Vol. 48), No. 4 (Fall 1984), pp. 75–83.

[b]See Michael D. Hutt and Thomas W. Speh, "The Marketing Strategy Center: Diagnosing the Industrial Marketer's Interdisciplinary Role," *Journal of Marketing,* Vol. 48, No. 4 (Fall 1984), pp. 53–61.

[c]See Gregory P. Upah and Monroe M. Bird. "Changes in Industrial Buying: Implications for Industrial Marketers," *Industrial Marketing Management,* Vol. 9, No. 2 (April 1980), p. 118.

[d]For a discussion of negotiations from the purchaser's point of view, see Michael R. Leanders, Harold E. Fearon, and Wilbur B. England, *Purchasing and Materials Management,* eighth edition (Homewood, Ill.: Richard D. Irwin, 1985), pp. 303–308.

Organization of the Purchasing Department

Some purchasing departments have complete authority and responsibility for buying products and services. At the other extreme, some departments function strictly in a staff capacity and merely fill requisitions and specifications set by others. In firms that must purchase a great diversity of relatively technical products and services, there is likely to be specialization within the purchasing department—with specific buyers for each category of goods and services required. In many firms purchasing is combined with inventory control, transportation, and traffic into a materials management department.[26]

[26]See Gregory D. Upah and Monroe M. Bird, "Changes in Industrial Buying: Implications for Industrial Marketers," *Industrial Marketing Managment,* Vol. 9, No. 2 (April 1980); p. 118.

It is not unusual for purchasing executives to face an "internal selling job" within their firm in the course of their work, and the salesperson must be prepared to give the executive the proper information to be passed on.[27] For example, purchasers may learn about a new product that, in their judgment, is far superior to the one now being used by one of the operating units of their own company. Their task is to convince the department concerned.

How Is the Buying Done?

A framework is required for analyzing the various buying situations and how they emerge from the continuous process of problem solving and decision making within the buying offices of a corporation. One system that takes into consideration the particular selling techniques required for each phase of the buying process is the Buygrid framework (see Figure 15.1). The Buygrid framework divides each situation into buyclasses and buyphases.

Buyclasses All buying situations may be divided into buyclasses according to the newness of the problem to the decision maker. Thus, the "new task" situation is one that has never occurred before and consequently requires buyers to learn much about an area in which they had had little experience. In contrast, the "straight rebuy" pertains to a recurring requirement that is filled by the same supplier as a matter of routine. In a "modified rebuy" a company decides to consider other suppliers for a product that it has previ-

Buyphases	Buyclasses		
	New task	Modified rebuy	Straight rebuy
1. Anticipation or recognition of a problem (need) and a general solution			
2. Determination of characteristics and quantity of needed item			
3. Description of characteristics and quantity of needed item			
4. Search for and qualification of potential sources			
5. Acquisition and analysis of proposals			
6. Evaluation of proposals and selection of supplier(s)			
7. Selection of an order routine			
8. Performance feedback and evaluation			

FIGURE 15.1 Buygrid framework. SOURCE: From Patrick J. Robinson, Charles W. Faris, and Yoram Wind, *Industrial Buying and Creative Marketing* (Rockleigh, N.J.: Allyn and Bacon, 1967). Copyright © 1967, by Allyn and Bacon, Inc. Used with permission.

[27]See W. J. E. Crissy and Donald W. Jackson, Jr., "Dynamics of the Purchase Interview," *Journal of Purchasing and Materials Management*, Vol. 10, No. 1 (February 1974); pp. 55–67.

ously bought on a straight-rebuy basis. Your sales tactics must be tailored to each situation, especially in the amount and type of information you provide to the purchasing decision makers. They are likely to want much information in a new-task situation and very little when considering a straight rebuy. You should also recognize that because there is considerably more risk in a new buy, you should use strategies such as warranties, testimonials, and demonstrations to help reduce that risk.

Buyphases The procurement process itself may be broken down into eight buyphases, as shown on the left side of the Buygrid framework. Taken together, these buyphases show the process that organizations go through when purchasing a product. The first step is the recognition of a need. A need may originally be recognized internally or may become operational because you or your firm's advertisements make the prospect aware of it. In the second and third steps the buying center tries to specify the characteristics and general quantity of the needed item and then describes these characteristics. The fourth step is the search for and qualification of potential vendors. The fifth step involves proposals, which may be received in written form or heard as presentations.[28] In the sixth step the proposal is evaluated, and a supplier or suppliers are selected. Next an order routine is established to determine how often orders should be shipped and, if appropriate, how often the vendor should call on the account. Finally, the last step consists of performance feedback and evaluation. Many industrial buyers have formal evaluation procedures for rating vendors.

Once the process gets underway, it will move from one phase to the next until the purchase is made or the deal is called off. Depicting the process as eight decision points underlines the importance of directing the sales effort toward the entire chain of events, instead of treating the sale as an isolated moment that happens independently of the other events. As the process unfolds, a "creeping commitment" is made by the buyer, gradually narrowing the field of potential suppliers. Thus, in most situations it is difficult for a vendor to enter the selling–buying process during the late phases with any hope of success.

It becomes apparent from studying the Buygrid matrix that the most intricate selling–buying situations fall in the upper left-hand corner of the chart—that is, in the early stages of a new-task assignment. It is here that management makes its most difficult decisions and, in many instances, welcomes the advice of suppliers. But this stage is by no means the first at which an alert salesperson can influence the selling–buying process. Something must set off the chain reaction to begin with and, although this stimulus may come from within the buying organization, it frequently comes from a member of the selling team who anticipates a need for a product or service within the purchasing company.

---

[28]For information on writing proposals, see Timothy J. Conner, "Writing Sales Letters and Proposals," *The American Salesman*, Vol. 29, No. 3 (March 1984), pp. 10–15; and *The American Salesman*, Vol. 29, No. 4 (April 1984), pp. 10–11, 41–42.

There are several facets in the industrial purchasing decision, the most basic of which is whether to make or to buy. That is, is it wiser for the company to produce the needed item itself or to purchase it from an outside supplier? Other facets of the process are evaluating sources and follow-up. It is important to understand these aspects of buyer decision making if you are to sell industrial goods.

Make or buy? The selling–buying process begins with needs. For some needs in an industrial firm, an immediate decision must be made whether to make or to buy an item, and the solution is not often simple. Because the buying firm has the capability of making the product themselves, you as an industrial salesperson must constantly show that you are offering value and that you are willing to work with the customer.[29]

Evaluating sources Another important function for purchasing agents in the industrial selling–buying process is the continuing evaluation of sources.[30] Purchasing departments are responsible for knowing where the various goods and services may be produced. Appropriate criteria must then be applied in evaluating the merits of each source. Most firms are reluctant to depend on a sole source for any product or service essential to their continuing operation, because it would place them in a vulnerable position. In addition, having several sources of supply encourages competition among the suppliers to improve quality, reduce price, and add services. Some large firms even set quotas on the percentage of business allocated to each supplier.

Follow-Up Just as you cannot afford to sell and forget, neither can purchasing agents buy and forget. Follow-up by purchasing agents is an important step in the industrial buying process. It is their responsibility to follow up on their purchases to see that deliveries are made as promised, that the quality of the product is as specified, and that any other commitments by the vendor are fulfilled. Just as you enhance your relationship with purchasing agents by a follow-up once orders are placed, so purchasing agents enhance their position with their own company's personnel by showing this interest. Furthermore, purchasing agents learn by doing this. It provides them with information that will help them to refine their evaluation of sources and of products and services. It is good business to favor sources that have been checked out as dependable and able to fulfill all commitments as promised at the time of the purchase. Thus, as a salesperson you need to recognize the importance of this activity and to follow up carefully and dependably.

[29]For a good discussion of make or buy, see Robert W. Haas and Thomas R. Wotruba, "Marketing Strategy in a Make or Buy Situation," *Industrial Marketing Management,* Vol. 5, No. 2, 3 (June 1976), pp. 65–76.

[30]See, for example, David Bonneville, "Vendor Analysis Packs a Punch in Negotiations," *Purchasing World,* Vol. 27 (March 1983), pp. 32–34; or C. David Wieters, "Influence in the Design and User of Vendor Performance Ratings," *Journal of Purchasing and Materials Management,* Vol. 12, No. 4 (Winter 1976), pp. 31–35.

Tools Used by Purchasing

Many techniques and tools are used by purchasing to help them make better decisions, including annual buying, inventory management, value analysis, materials requirement planning (MRP), and life cycle costing. Although these are only a few of the tools available, they will give you a perspective on how industrial purchasers may make decisions and how you should go about presenting your offering.

Annual buying If an item is used in large quantity and on a continuing basis, the actual buying may consist of annual or semiannual contract negotiations. In such instances, specifications are usually given to several selected sources and bids are evaluated. It is not unusual for the buyer to specify an annual level for efficiency improvement of, say, 3 percent—the rationale being that the manufacturer must improve efficiency in order to remain competitive. The firm then passes this requirement on to its key vendors as a condition of the selling–buying relationship.

Inventory management Relatively standard items, used on a continuing basis, are generally kept in inventory with a maximum inventory level and a specified reorder point. The purchasing department is responsible for seeing that adequate quantities of these items are kept in stock. On many items, the optimization of inventory may contribute favorably or adversely to a firm's profit picture and may markedly affect the smoothness of the production process.[31]

In one new technique for inventory management, called just-in-time, components and raw materials arrive at the factory at the exact time that they are needed, greatly reducing the inventories that must be held. This system is ideal for firms that manufacture large amounts of the same product with a reasonably predictable production schedule.[32] Understanding these inventory management systems is important to understanding purchasers' needs and to keeping them satisfied in the buying–selling relationship.

Value analysis "Value analysis is the organized systematic study of every element of cost in a material, part, or service to ensure that it fulfills its function at the lowest total cost," and the salesperson can play a critical role in implementing value analyses.[33] For example, one salesperson recommended that one of his customers switch from a metal to a plastic connector, saving the customer $10,000.[34] Value analysis is widely used by many firms today and

[31]For a discussion of various inventory management tools, see Michael R. Leanders, Harold E. Fearon, and Wilbur B. England, *Purchasing and Materials Management,* eighth edition (Homewood, Ill.: Richard D. Irwin, 1985), pp. 164–171.

[32]For more information on this technique, see ibid., pp. 182–189.

[33]See Harold E. Fearon, William A. Ruch, Ross P. Reck, Vincent G. Reuter, and C. David Wieters, *Fundamentals of Production/Operations Management,* second edition (St. Paul, Minn.: West Publishing Company, 1983), p. 195.

[34]See Somerby Dowst, "This Year's Winners: All Around Performers," *Purchasing,* Vol. 87, No. 2 (August 22, 1979), p. 43.

is seen as an important way to control costs while continuing to monitor quality.[35]

Materials requirement planning (MRP) Material requirement planning (MRP) is a computerized system that links a buying company's materials needs with vendors. Vendors thus hold the materials longer. MRP cuts costs on the buying firm by lowering inventory-holding costs, eliminating shortages, and improving on time deliveries.[36] As an industrial salesperson you may have to understand MRP. You should try to get your firm specified as one of the key suppliers to be linked by computer to the buyers' materials needs.[37]

Life cycle costing Life cycle costing consists of identify, qualifying, and evaluating all costs associated with owning a product. These costs include initial purchase price; operating, maintenance, service, and overhaul costs; and the costs of disposing of the product. Life cycle costing allows the purchaser to evaluate the total cost of a purchase rather than just the purchase price. For instance, if two machines were being evaluated as in Table 15.3, machine A would be chosen if only the initial purchase price was considered. However, machine B would be chosen if life cycle costing was utilized. Life cycle costing is often used when firms buy captial equipment or purchases with substantial operating costs. When dealing with firms that use life cycle costing, you must be able to provide them with the costs of your product. Furthermore, you may also use the life cycle concept to justify your product when it has a higher purchase price but offers operating efficiencies.[38]

TABLE 15.3
EXAMPLE OF LIFE CYCLE COSTING

	INITIAL COST	MAINTENANCE COST	ENERGY COST	TRADE-IN VALUE	LIFE CYCLE COST
Machine A	$20,000	$6000	$4000	+ $4000	$26,000
Machine B	25,000	2000	2000	+ 8000	$21,000

[35]For a good discussion of value analysis and many examples, see " Value Analysis 1984: A Status Report," *Purchasing*, Vol. 96, No. 3 (March 29, 1984), pp. 79–158.

[36]See Terri Thompson, "MRP: A Good Idea, But Can You Make It Work," *Purchasing*, Vol. 88, No. 2 *(February 1980), pp. 71–75.*

[37]*For an interesting dicussion of the effect MRP has on suppliers, see Joseph R. Biggs, Donald C. Bopp, Jr., and William M. Campion, "Material Requirements Planning and Purchasing: A Case Study," Journal of Purchasing and Materials Management, Vol. 20, No. 2 (Spring 1984), pp. 15–22.*

[38]For a discussion of life cycle costing, see Donald W. Jackson, Jr., and Lonnie L. Ostrom, "LIfe Cycle Costing in Industrial Purchasing," *Journal of Purchasing and Materials Management*, Vol. 16, No. 4 (Winter 1980); pp. 8–12.

SUMMARY

Several different types of selling situations were explored in this chapter, including retail, services, and industrial selling.

Retail selling has several unique aspects: customers generally come to you, the time of the call is relatively short, prospects are not as well informed as in other sales situations, generally less negotiation takes place, and retail salespeople are usually not as well trained as their industrial counterparts. In order to be successful in retail selling, you need knowledge about the store, about merchandise, and about your customers.

The retail sales process consists of greeting customers, determining their needs, selecting merchandise, describing and demonstrating the product, narrowing choices, handling objections, closing, and following up. Additional nonselling duties were also discussed. If you want to increase your sales, you should encourage customers to trade up; in addition, you should practice suggestive selling and develop a personal trade. Finally, several problems of retail selling were examined—customers who are just looking, selling to groups, handling several customers at once, and out-of-stock merchandise.

Many opportunites are available for selling services since they are so vital to our economy. Several unique aspects of services were explored, such as their intangibility, the fact that buyers may participate in the service encounters, the simultaneous production and consumption of services, the possibility that services may be viewed as riskier than products, the importance of word of mouth, and the likelihood of postpurchase doubt. When selling services you should use both extrinsic and intrinsic approaches. You must also be knowledgeable, be mindful of your appearance, build personal relationships, stress benefits, and encourage customer involvement.

Industrial selling is a source of many job opportunities. Becoming adept at industrial selling requires that you understand clearly the unique aspects of the buying–selling process, who does the buying, and the organization of the prospect's purchasing department. One way to understand the buying process is to utilize the Buygrid framework. In this model, purchases are divided into (1) buyclasses, consisting of new buys, modified rebuys, and straight rebuys; and (2) eight buyphases, which are steps in the buying process. Various additional aspects of the buying process include make-or-buy decisions, evaluation of sources, and follow-up. Buyers often use various tools to make decisions, including annual buying, inventory management, value analysis, materials requirement planning, and life cycle costing. You must know about these tools to deal successfully with industrial purchasers.

PROBLEMS

1. Describe, in your own words, the scope of retail selling.
2. What are some examples of suggestive selling, that you have experienced while shopping?
3. List as many types of services sales positions as you can that a college graduate with a marketing degree might qualify for.

4. Describe in your own words the unique aspects of selling services.

5. What aspects of selling to manufacturers do you consider the most challenging? Why?
6. Summarize the differences in assignment between (a) the retail salesperson in an open-stock department; (b) the industrial salesperson calling on manufacturers.

EXERCISE 15

Objectives: To appreciate the problems and challenges faced by a retail salesperson.

To understand better the unique aspects of selling a service.

To consider selling from the industrial purchasing executive's point of view.

PART A Retail Selling
Interview a salesperson in an open-stock department in a local store. Obtain answers to the following questions.

1. What do you like best about your job?
2. What do you like least?
3. How do you handle the situation when a number of customers are seeking your attention?
4. What talents are needed to succeed in your kind of selling?
5. How would you describe a typical day's work?

PART B Selling Services
Interview a salesperson who sells a service such as insurance or financial services. Obtain answers to the following questions.

1. What do you like best about your job?
2. What do you like least?
3. What makes selling services different from selling products?
4. What special approach, if any, do you use for selling services?
5. What talents are needed to succeed in your kind of selling?
6. How would you decribe a typical day's work?

PART C Industrial Selling–Buying
Complete this exercise either by interviewing a purchasing executive or by putting yourself in his or her place. (You may want to consult a text such as the *Handbook of Purchasing*.)

1. What are the key qualifications of a purchasing executive?
2. What are the key challenges and problems in the job?
3. How much working time is devoted to interviewing salespersons?
4. How much working time is devoted to interviews establishing needs within the company?

5. What criteria should be applied in establishing a source?
6. What are some common errors on the part of sales representatives?
7. What qualities are most essential in industrial salespeople?

Summarize what you have learned from the interview. What new insights did you get that were not covered in the textbook or in class?

Case 15-1 Campus Toggery

The Toggery, owned and operated by Mr. and Mrs. Owen, is one of several shops catering to the fashion needs of coeds at Central Michigan University. It has a choice location, opposite the Student Union. The store is a regular advertiser in the *Central Daily*. This ad appeared, late fall, in the Monday edition.

SPECIAL! SAVE 25 PERCENT

SHIRTS, Long-sleeve classics in soft, washable material. Choose from delicate pales, richer tones, pretty patterns. Available in sizes 10 to 18.	$17.99	regular $24
PANTS, Color-compatible pants. With smooth-fitting elastic waistbands. Proportioned for Tiny, Typical, and Tall.	$23.99	regular $32

About thirty female students were waiting for the store to open. There was a rush for the clothing on sale. More students continued to arrive.

Mrs. Owen and one salesperson, Sue Hartley, were the only ones available to handle the mob. They dashed about trying to help and to answer questions. Everyone seemed to be talking at once. Confusion and delay occurred in making sales. The small dressing room area was soon crowded. Mrs. Owen noticed that some of the students were leaving, and their facial expressions showed their displeasure.

1. What should be done?

Case 15-2 Integrity Life Insurance

Integrity is a medium-size company now in its fourteenth year. It is cleared to do business in four midwestern states. It sells mainly through independent agents although it is building its own sales force in southern Illinois where it has its headquarters. It relies heavily on advertising with coupon returns to generate leads. These, in turn, are furnished to the appropriate company salesperson or agent, depending on the address of the prospect. The company processes each lead by a letter telling the individual to expect a personal call. This processing costs Integrity roughly $8 per coupon, so salespeople and agents are reminded to handle the leads with care.

Bob Williams, a salesperson for a general agent in Indiana, receives a coupon lead filled out as follows.

```
┌─────────────────────────────────────────────────────────┐
│                                                          │
│     NAME:        M. C. Marston                           │
│     ADDRESS:     31 Oakland Rd.                          │
│                  Greenville, IN 47124                    │
│                                                          │
│   __ SINGLE      _✓_ MARRIED                             │
│     OCCUPATION:  Carpenter                               │
│   _✓_ YES. I want to hear more about the double-benefit life policy. │
│                                                          │
└─────────────────────────────────────────────────────────┘
```

Bob notes that Mr. Marston lives about thirty miles away. He has only one customer near Marston's address, so he decides to phone Mr. Marston and screen him as a prospect before he makes a trip to see him. After the telephone conversation, Bob decides it is worth a trip and makes a date to see Mr. Marston at 7:30 P.M. on Thursday. He is greeted pleasantly.

MR. MARSTON: You must be Mr. Williams. Come right in. This is Mrs. Marston.

BOB: Good evening, folks. Thank you both for seeing me.

MR. MARSTON: Pull up a chair. We generally do our business right here at the table.

(After a brief discussion about the weather and what a pleasant community Greenville is, the following conversation takes place.)

BOB: Before I talk about insurance, I'd like to know about you. Your answers to my questions will help me help you. First of all, Mr. Marston, as a carpenter, do you work for yourself, or are you on a company payroll?

MR. MARSTON: On my own all my life and proud of it.

BOB: I would be too. Might I ask you what your approximate income is?

MR. MARSTON: Well, work is seasonal but I'd say overall, about $25,000 a year.

BOB: How much life insurance do you now have in force on yourself and on Mrs. Marston?

MR. MARSTON: We have an old policy for $1000 on Mrs. Marston. Dates back to before we got married. Her parents took it out and transferred it to us. I have my veteran's policy for $10,000.

BOB: The way things are today a $10,000 coverage isn't very much.

MR. MARSTON: That's why we sent in the coupon. Your company has insurance that provides protection for a husband and wife and builds a retirement income, too, isn't that right? See, I've saved the ad.

MRS. MARSTON: Actually, Mr. Williams, I think we've talked about having more insurance for years. Now that our boy is on his own, maybe we can afford it.

BOB: Oh. How old is your son?

MRS. MARSTON: Nineteen. He joined the navy a year ago and he's doing just fine. My husband was a navy man.

MR. MARSTON: I'm still navy in spirit. Great outfit.

BOB: You both look young, but if your son is nineteen you both must be in your late thirties.

MR. MARSTON: Nope. I'm forty-four and my wife is just past forty.

BOB: Our double-benefit policy is just what you need. As you mentioned a few minutes ago, it protect both husband and wife and builds up a retirement income. Here's how it works. *(He spreads a folder on the table.)* Let's use forty-two as an entry, the average of your ages. Now, notice at the top of each column is the amount of protection needed. Let's say $20,000 in the event of the husband's death. Notice that under this number is $2000, which covers the wife's death. Notice that there are two numbers where the age and coverage come together. The upper one, $161.50, is the monthly retirement payment, which commences when the wage earner reaches age sixty-five. The lower one, $46.20, is the montly cost if payments are made annually.

MR. MARSTON: Just a minute. I have some questions. If I should die at any time, Mrs. Marston would get a lump sum of $20,000. Is that right?

BOB: Yes, unless we arranged the policy for monthly payments to her over a time period, say twenty years.

MR. MARSTON: Here's my next question. If Mrs Marston were to die, I'd receive $2000, but then what happens to the policy?

BOB: It remains in force and you are still covered. We have found that the most sought-after coverage on the wife is 10 percent of the face value for the husband.

MR. MARSTON: Well, we already have $1000 on my wife's life. If we wanted only $1000 additional coverage, could that be arranged?

BOB: It would be difficult since we have developed our double-benefit insurance based on the 10 percent formula.

1. Critique what has occurred so far.
2. What should Bob do next?

Mr. Baker is attempting to design a strategy that will increase the sale of Madison Glove's products to the Claymore Steel Company. Four individuals play a role in purchasing at Claymore: Waxley, the company's purchasing agent; Fitzgerald, the plant foreman; Cardoza, a senior blue-collar worker; and Claymore, the owner of the steel service center.

Baker feels that Waxley is generally interested in buying a quality product. Waxley is proud of stating, "I always feel that a few extra dollars buy a great deal of value." From his own experience, Baker knows that Waxley has been willing to trade up in the products he buys from Madison when Baker was able to make a reasonable case for a better product. Finally, Baker feels that although Waxley has full authority to make purchasing commitments for Madison, he is reluctant to buy merchandise that has not been requested and "tested" by the part of the service center that will use the merchandise.

Mr. Fitzgerald wants a high-quality product, but he is also very concerned with price. He wants his employees well protected, yet his unit is charged with the product. Therefore, if Waxley buys more costly products than the employees really need, it comes out of Fitzgerald's budget, not Waxley's.

Fitzgerald is also critically interested in delivery and inventory maintenance and control. Twice last year his people lost half a day's work because they ran out of heavy-duty steel-reinforced work gloves. This occurred because the supplier does not have a warehouse in the same town as Claymore. In addition, had Claymore kept better records and control over its own inventory of work gloves, this situation would not have developed. Finally, Baker knows that Fitzgerald is a real detail man. Whenever Baker needs to talk with Fitzgerald, he sets up a lunch date, because there are so many interruptions in Fitzgerald's office. These lunch dates present at least a minor problem, for it is well known that Waxley does not approve of operations people being entertained by salespeople.

Mr. Cardoza is a well-respected long-term employee of Claymore. He is also Fitzgerald's son-in-law. Although he does not have any direct management responsibilities, it is generally felt that when Fitzgerald retires in three years, Cardoza stands better than an even chance of becoming foreman. Cardoza is frequently consulted informally by Fitzgerald about operations problems, and he would be the one who would oversee any tests on Madison's gloves.

Mr. Claymore is the owner and manager of the service center. He is not involved in these types of purchasing decisions as long as there are several suppliers of merchandise. Claymore feels that multiple sourcing is bound to keep the situation more competitive and assures the firm the most for its money. If a product is to be single-sourced, he wants to know precisely what his firm will gain from such a deviation from company policy.

The company is currently purchasing its gloves from four different glove firms. The standard gloves that Madison sells to Claymore cover direct ex-

[39]The reader should examine the Madison Glove Company (A), Case 6-1, before analyzing this case.

penses but do not contribute to profits or overhead. The competitors are good companies that manufacture quality products. The Burke glove company is the one that had the two delivery problems with Claymore. Baker thinks that this was really Claymore's fault, but it might give the other competitors a better chance to get Burke's portion of the business. Neither of the other two competitors has had any problem with Claymore that Baker knows about.

Claymore buys four basic types of gloves—one from each of its suppliers. The standard work glove is purchased from Madison. Burke supplies the thermal insulated glove. The two other gloves are heavy-duty gloves with steel fiber running through them to help protect the hands from sharp objects. All the gloves that Claymore buys could be purchased from any of its suppliers at approximately the same price. Madison's thermal glove is slightly better than Burke's.

Baker has considered several alternative strategies for obtaining a larger share of Claymore's business. Two years ago he gave Claymore two free samples of Madison's $65 per pair thermal gloves. He knows that they were never tested; in fact, he is aware that Fitzgerald and Cardoza each took a pair to use at home for working on their cars.

1. How much added business should Baker try to get from Claymore?
2. Why did Baker's attempt to get Claymore to test Madison's gloves fail?
3. What strategy should Baker employ to increase his sales to Claymore?

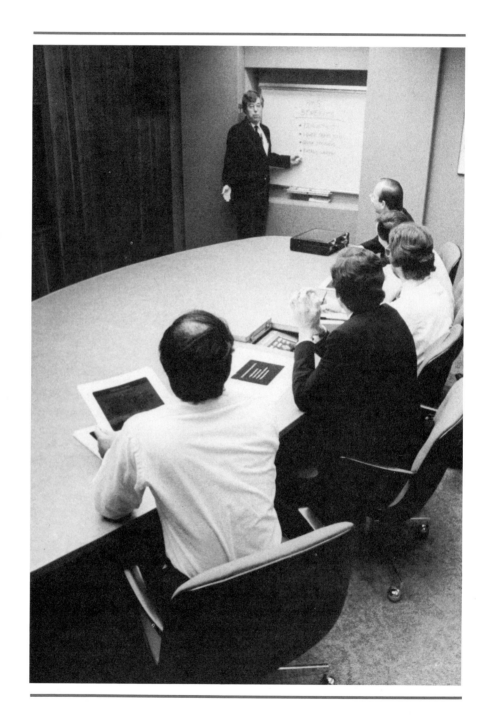

Using the Telephone in Selling

16

After studying this chapter, you should be able to

1. Understand the unique aspects of telephone selling.
2. Describe the steps in planning for a telephone call.
3. Specify the uses of the telephone by outside salespeople.
4. Discuss the uses of the telephone by inside salespeople.
5. Appreciate mistakes and cautions in using the telephone.
6. Point out various guidelines for using the telephone.
7. Recognize various telephone services useful in selling.

Effective use of the telephone in business, especially in selling, is vital to the firm's success. Salespeople can make more calls on the telephone in an hour than they can make in a day in person. The field salesperson, who is responsible for maintaining personal contact with the prospect or customer, relies on the telephone to follow up on earlier visits, to make appointments, and, in some situations, to close the sale. Thus the telephone is an integral part of these salespeople's sales strategies. In-house salespeople—those in retail sales or others who handle their responsibilities from within the firm—use the phone to generate new business. In addition, inside salespeople play an important intelligence and expediting role for the firm by maintaining telephone contact with customers and prospects between visits by field sales representatives.

This chapter examines the effective use of telephone selling, with special attention to precall planning and the unique applications of the telephone sales call for field sales representatives and in-house salespeople. The differences between incoming calls and outgoing calls are also discussed. Several cautions in using the telephone are offered. Next, guidelines are provided for using the telephone. Finally, several services that might make use of the telephone easier or more productive are also described.

PRECALL PLANNING

It is just as important to plan a telephone sales call as it is to plan a personal sales visit, and all the principles of actual call planning apply. A carefully outlined plan can be used as an agenda while the actual telephone conversation is taking place.

Unique Aspects of Telephone Selling

There are four aspects unique to telephone selling that should be taken into consideration when planning the call: (1) most telephone calls are an interruption to the party being called; (2) only the auditory channel can be used in telephone selling; (3) timing is important; and (4) courtesy on the telephone is necessary at all times.

The telephone call as an interruption A telephone call almost always constitutes an interruption for the other person. For this reason what is said in the first few moments of the call can mean success or failure. The opening remark must immediately grab the attention and arouse the interest of the other person. It must have "you," not "I," appeal. Here is an example.

> "Mr. Jones, this is Bill Smith at Hill's Clothing Store. We've just received some new sportcoats that I know you'll like . . ."

The other person's initial reactions are the best guide for determining whether an order can be completed on the phone or whether a personal visit will be required. In most types of business, a visit is necessary. Thus, the objective is to get a commitment for a follow-up in person. It is important that you not use all your ammunition, only to receive a turndown. Assuming a favorable initial reaction to the foregoing example, you might continue:

"Mr. Jones, you'll really have to see these jackets to appreciate their style and quality. Would it be convenient for you to come in today? I'll be here ready to show them to you."

Auditory channel In telephone selling, only the auditory channel is available. From a perceptual standpoint, this puts a premium on your manner of speaking as well as on what you say. Your enthusiasm and conviction must be reflected in how you convey your sales message. Image-provoking language, examples, and illustrations are necessary. You must paint a picture in the mind of the prospect or customer. Contrast the impact of these statements:

The dimensions are two by three inches.

It's small enough to fit in your pocket.

Over the telephone you cannot obtain feedback, other than by full attention to what is said and how it is said. As a result, you must pay close attention to any innuendos, changes in pitch, side comments, or other cues the prospect may be conveying between the lines.

The importance of timing Time is of the essence. Rarely does a telephone sales call last longer than a few minutes, so the call must be well planned; every word must count. Far more can be sold by asking the right questions than by a lengthy statement. A questioning approach also ensures active participation on the part of the prospect or customer, whereas a monologue is usually ineffective.

It is easier to follow a call plan when you are on the telephone than when you are in a face-to-face situation, because you can write down your plan and use it as an agenda. As each point is made, it can be checked off, and if the customer provides any relevant information, you can make a note of it.

The importance of courtesy Courtesy is often overlooked when people talk on the telephone. For some unknown and unjustifiable reason, many people are not as courteous on the telephone as they are in person. Examples of discourteous behavior are interrupting the other person, using an abrupt tone of voice, and hanging up before the other person is completely finished. This behavior may be easy to slip into because the two parties who are communicating with each other do not have eye-to-eye contact. Yet it is critical to remember that the individual you are talking with could represent a substantial potential profit for your firm, and therefore deserves to be treated respectfully.

The telephone conversation is sometimes the only contact you and the customer have. In this situation, the customer must be made to trust your judgment, and if you are not respectful to begin with, there is little chance that a positive seller–buyer relationship will develop.

Southern Bell Telephone Company suggests the test shown in Figure 16.1 as a good measure of telephone courtesy. Courtesy really costs you nothing except the few minutes it takes to think of others. If you follow this

DO YOU?

		Yes	Sometimes	No
1.	Answer promptly.	___	___	___
2.	Greet the caller pleasantly.	___	___	___
3.	Identify yourself properly.	___	___	___
4.	Speak in a natural tone.	___	___	___
5.	Say "Thank you" and "You're Welcome".	___	___	___
6.	Explain waits.	___	___	___
7.	Leave word where you're going.	___	___	___
8.	Check the number.	___	___	___
9.	Apologize for mistakes.	___	___	___
10.	Keep a pad near.	___	___	___
11.	Stay on the line.	___	___	___
12.	Take the message.	___	___	___
13.	Signal the company operator slowly.	___	___	___
14.	Allow time to answer.	___	___	___
15.	Ask whether it is convenient to talk.	___	___	___
16.	Help the company operator.	___	___	___
17.	End the call properly.	___	___	___
18.	Replace receiver gently.	___	___	___
19.	Listen attentively.	___	___	___
20.	Ask questions tactfully.	___	___	___
21.	"Space" your calls.	___	___	___
22.	Make your call brief.	___	___	___
23.	Listen for the dial tone.	___	___	___
24.	Keep the cord free of kinks.	___	___	___
25.	Plan the conversation.	___	___	___

FIGURE 16.1 The telephone courtesy test. For each "yes" you receive four points, for each "sometimes" you receive two points, and no points are given for a "no" answer. If you score over 85, you are a very courteous telephone user.

philosophy, you will probably find that you are treated much better by your customers in all aspects of your business relationship, and these few minutes will pay high dividends.

Steps in Planning the Call

If you are going to use the telephone as a sales tool, it is important to plan. "The phone is not the best vehicle to win sales if your approach is to 'wing' it or to literally try to 'play it by ear.' "[1]

[1] See Robert W. Chevrow, "Phone Selling Is No Time to 'Play It by Ear,' Techniques Call for Discipline, Preparation, Script Writing, Tact, and Good Listening," *Marketing News,* Vol. 10, No. 18 (October 8, 1976), p. 9.

Three steps in planning the telephone approach are (1) develop a call objective, (2) prepare an effective opening statement, and (3) prepare your sales message.[2]

Call objective To use the telephone effectively, you must have a clearly defined call objective. Are you following up, setting appointments, or getting fill-in orders? Without a clearly defined objective, you will waste time and your calls will not have a direction.

Opening statement The opening of your telephone call is crucial. You must identify yourself and your company, establish rapport, and create interest.

Several suggestions for your opening statement are useful. First, identify yourself and your company. You might say "Hello, Mr. Jones, this is Mary Smith from Bayless Silk Flowers Company." Second, use the buyer's name in the introduction. This is polite practice and conveys your interest in the customer or prospect. Third, establish rapport.

Throughout the text the need to focus on the other person has been emphasized. This rule certainly applies to selling by telephone—a "you" attitude is a must. Focusing on the person called is particularly important when the person reached has no advance knowledge of the call. Rapport must be established in the first few seconds.

One method of establishing rapport is to *praise* prospects or their company. All of us react to praise when it is appropriate and sincere. For example, opening a call by saying, "Mr. Jones, in view of your firm's number one position in the industry . . ." is very likely to be favorably received. In contrast, praise that is phony and is perceived as such by the customer will be very poorly received. If you cannot think of any genuine praise to use, you should try other ways to gain acceptance.

Another technique takes into consideration the fact that few people can resist the opportunity to give advice. This nearly universal trait might be capitalized on by saying, "Miss Black, we need your help and advice in evaluating a new publication on miniaturization. May we send you a copy for review?" With customer calls, establishing rapport is easy since you already know your client and their business, and you can comment on a previous call. This personalization is useful. If you have an account card listing background, key interests, and previous calls, it is even easier. With prospect accounts, establishing rapport is more difficult.

You should also create a statement that will create interest in your offering. For example, you might say "Mr. Silverman, we have just come out with a new security program that has been developed for small businesses such as yours. I have just talked with several other small businesses, and they are very interested in the program."

There are two techniques that you can use to get the customer's attention: an initial-benefit statement and the hinge technique.

---

[2]This general approach was adapted from *Telephone Techniques for Account Coverage*, a pamphlet developed by the Bell System (1980).

Many successful salespeople use an initial-benefit statement to interest the prospect. This tells the prospect what you are selling and what's in it for the prospect if they listen to your presentation. It also mentions the product or service by name. If you were trying to get a wholesaler to stock your firm's line of paneling, you might say, for example,

> "Mr. Smith, Acme Permawell Paneling will increase your paneling business because of the wide variety of designs and textures we offer."

Notice that the statement includes a feature, variety of designs and textures; a benefit, increase your business; and the name of the product, Acme Permawell Paneling.[3]

In the hinge technique, a second way to gain the customer's attention, your call is "hinged" or linked to a previous occurrence in the selling–buying relationship.[4] As an example, you might telephone customers to say that the merchandise they ordered is being packed today and that if they place additional orders at this time, they would be eligible for quantity discounts. Another example would be the retail salesperson in a woman's clothing store who calls a customer to tell her that the coat she looked at during the previous month is now on sale. With the hinge technique, you try to tie yourself and your product back to the customer. Twelve recurrent hinges are presented in Figure 16.2.

Sales message Selling over the phone requires a much higher degree of structure since you do not have access to many of the aids that help in person-to-person selling, such as visuals, diagrams, or samples. Therefore, you may want to have a script, or at least an outline and some key questions in front of you to keep you on track.[5]

Your sales message should stress the benefits of your offering rather than the features. That is, it should stress what your offering can do for the prospect. Your message should also stress words that include "colorful adjectives, dynamic words, personal words, and phrases that paint word pictures."[6] Because prospects cannot see your offering over the telephone, you must help them visualize it and "see" how the product or service will be of use or benefit them. When preparing your message, you may wish to write out several key benefits, several key objections and how you might overcome them, and several closes that you might use. This precall planning will make you much more confident and will make your telephone conversation flow much more smoothly.

---

[3]See "Lead-Ins: The Snappy Hookers," *Sales and Marketing Management*, Vol. 119, No. 3 (August 29, 1977), p. 62.

[4]See William A. Garrett, *Phonemanship—The Newest Concept of Marketing* (New York: Farrar, Strauss, 1959), pp. 139–142.

[5]See Stan Billue, "20 Shortcuts to Success in Telemarketing," *Telemarketing* (November 1984), p. 30.

[6]See *Telephone Techniques for Account Coverage*, a pamphlet developed by the Bell System (1980).

Reprinted with permission from *Sales & Marketing Management* magazine: © 1977.

USES OF THE TELEPHONE

No matter what type of selling you pursue, the telephone can be a useful asset. The telephone may be used by outside and inside salespeople alike, and it may be used to handle incoming requests for information.

Uses of the Telephone by Outside Salespeople

Outside salespeople use telephone calls to complement and increase the effectiveness of personal visits. The key psychological impact of a telephone call is that it helps to keep you, your company, and your products and services in the *conscious awareness* of the prospect or customer. The longer the time span between field calls, the more necessary it is to fill in the gaps. Otherwise, a competitor might move in.[7]

_____
[7]For an interesting discussion of the uses of the telephone in industrial selling, see Jeffrey Pope, "What Industrial Telemarketers Have That Consumer Telemarketers Don't," *Industrial Marketing*, Vol. 66, No. 8 (August 1981), p. 80.

1. Thank-you approach.

SALESPERSON: Mr. Customer, this is Mrs. Telephone Salesperson of the Alpha Company. We received your order in the mail this morning and wish to thank you for it. Shipment will be made immediately. You should have it Wednesday. Will that meet your needs?

CUSTOMER: Yes. Thank you.

SALESPERSON: Mr. Customer, while I have you on the phone, I was wondering whether you knew we could give you a quantity discount if your order was increased to . . .

2. Inactive-account approach.

SALESPERSON: Good morning, Mr. Customer. This is Mrs. Telephone Salesperson of the Alpha Company. Our records show we haven't done business with you for two months, and I thought I'd call you to find out why . . . . *(Settle any complaints at once before trying to sell.)*

3. After-mailing approach.

SALESPERSON: Good morning, Mr. Customer. This is Mrs. Telephone Salesperson of the Alpha Lumber Company. We mailed you a letter a few days ago telling you about a special offer we had in house siding . . . .

4. Advertising tie-in approach.

SALESPERSON: Good morning, Mr. Customer. This is Mrs. Telephone Salesperson of the Alpha Machinery Company. Did you see our ad in the *Trade Journal* about cutting down stitching time? I would like the opportunity to discuss this new machine with you . . . .

5. Saving freight cost (railroad and truck).

SALESPERSON: Good morning, Mr. Customer. This is Mrs. Telephone Salesperson of the Alpha Can Company. We are loading your order and noticed that it is just short of a carload lot; we were wondering whether you might not wish to increase your order to take advantage of this savings . . . .

6. The service approach.

SALESPERSON: Mr. Customer, this is Mrs. Telephone Salesperson of The Alpha Company. Our truck is leaving to deliver the order you placed last week. Because several days have elapsed since then, I was wondering whether there are any last-minute items you may need . . . .

FIGURE 16.2 Twelve recurrent "hinges."

7. Special-sales or bargain approach.

SALESPERSON: Good morning, Mr. Customer. This is Mrs. Telephone Salesperson of the Alpha Auto Tire Store. We just received a new shipment of Wear-Better Tires, which we were able to obtain at a very low price. As a result, we are giving our better customers an opportunity to purchase before we start our big sales offering to the general public on Monday . . . .

8. Special-occasion approach.

SALESPERSON: Good morning, Mr. Customer. This is Mrs. Salesperson of the Alpha Jewelry Company. Congratulations on your approaching first wedding anniversary. I was looking over my sale of wedding rings of a year ago and saw your name. I suppose you are thinking of some sort of anniversary present for your wife . . . .

9. Birthday approach.

SALESPERSON: Good morning, Mrs. Customer. This is Mrs. Telephone Salesperson of the Alpha Boy's Store. I just happened to think that Johnny was having a birthday next Thursday (three days hence), and I was wondering whether you had in mind buying any clothing as a present. I recall the nice overcoat you bought for him here last September, and he seemed to like it very much. Incidentally, if you can drop by, we have a present for Johnny . . . .

10. Demonstration approach.

SALESPERSON: Good morning, Mr. Customer. This is Mrs. Telephone Salesperson of Alpha Automobile Company. We are calling some of our better customers to let them know we are having a special showing of the new model next Thursday . . . .

11. Inventory approach.

SALESPERSON: Good morning, Mr. Customer. This is Mrs. Telephone Salesperson of the Alpha Oil Company. We are taking annual inventory beginning next week and are offering the following items at a special price to cut down on inventory cost. . . .

12. Inventory control approach.

SALESPERSON: Good morning, Mr. Customer. This is Mrs. Telephone Salesperson of the Alpha Wholesale Company. My purpose for calling this morning is to make sure that you are not running short of _____. Now that the (weather, demand, price, etc.) has changed we felt you might need an additional shipment . . . .

A telephone call may be made to achieve one or more of five recurrent objectives: to prospect or qualify, to make an appointment, to call on out-of-the-way accounts, to close the sale, and to follow up.

Prospect or qualify The telephone may be an effective way of finding out whether a company or an individual has a need for your products or services. The telephone may also be used to identify who the decision makers in the organization are. Sometimes the receptionist can direct you to the proper decision maker; however, you may at times be directed to the wrong person. Thus, when you are prospecting over the telephone, it is important to make certain that you are talking to the proper decision maker. A person who is not a decision maker for your products or services may not even recognize a need for your offering. One possibility is to start off as high in the organization as you can and have them identify who the decision makers are. This has a dual benefit of carefully identifying the person or people and giving you the ability to say you were referred by the higher office.

One caution in using the telephone for contacting prospects is that it is easier for them to say "no" to you over the telephone than it would be in person. Thus, you have a trade-off between the time you save over the telephone and the greater effectiveness of a personal visit. Only experience will tell you which approach is best and with which types of prospects.

Make an appointment If the primary objective is to set a time for the next visit, it is important to provide sufficient information to whet the interest of the prospect, but not so much that you render the visit unnecessary. It is better to offer a choice of two dates than to ask, "When may I see you?" If you wish to see other people in the account, you should indicate this and, if appropriate, ask the customer to help make such arrangements; but you should always be careful not to make the customer feel used. However, if a group meeting is to take place and you and the buyer have built up a solid relationship, it may make sense to ask the buyer to help with the arrangements.

There are two ways to get through to the decision maker or to make an appointment. One tactic—the direct approach—may be used when you face no interference, such as when the prospect has initiated the call or has written to ask for information. In these situations you may only have to identify yourself and ask for the appointment. For instance, you might say "Hello, this is Heather Brown, with Acme Communications. I would like to set up an appointment with Mr. Jones to discuss his communications needs. Mr. Jones called me last week to inquire about our services."

You should counter any resistance with the benefit approach. Here you show the person the benefit they will receive from making an appointment with you. The prospect—not you—must appear to be the beneficiary of the meeting.[8]

---

[8]See "Phone Power: Qualifying Prospects and Making Appointments" (provided courtesy of Mountain Bell), p. 15.

If you have done a good job of precall planning, you should have identified the benefits of your offering. In trying to match the proper benefit to the
prospect, you may find it useful to ask open-ended questions. Again, remember to avoid giving so much information over the phone that a visit from you
becomes unnecessary. Because it is easier for the prospect to say "no" over
the phone and more difficult for you to keep the prospect's attention, say
only what is required to get to see the prospect. Finally, it may be useful to
set aside a block of time for making appointments. Try to use time that is not
prime selling time but during which the prospect or customer is normally in.

Call on out-of-the-way accounts The telephone may be used to call on marginal or out-of-the-way accounts. This keeps you in contact with these accounts but takes much less time and effort and may greatly increase your
productivity. Using the telephone to handle these out-of-the-way accounts
can, in effect, increase the size of your territory. Although you may not get
as much business over the telephone as you might in person, given the high
cost of personal visits, this business may be much more profitable. One salesperson for a golf equipment firm in Arizona used the telephone as a primary
means of contacting golf professionals in out-of-the-way communities. He
could then spend most of his time on the Phoenix and Tucson areas where
there was much more business. By carefully following up on the telephone
business and keeping frequent contact, he was able to build a strong business
in the outlying areas that he could never have served in person.

Close the sale A phone call to an established customer is more likely to close
a sale than a phone call to a prospect. The firm that has no earlier buying
experience with you will be understandably reluctant to place an order on
the basis of a telephone call. Generally speaking, low-volume and distant
accounts are handled in this manner because of the high costs of personal
calls. Of course, it sometimes happens that such a call is actually a contin-
uation of a personal visit. For example, you may have been unable to close
during the face-to-face discussions because the prospect wanted time to consider the proposal. The major use of the phone for getting orders initiated by
you will be for repeat business, routine orders, or fill-in orders.[9]

Follow up Follow-up calls may cover many matters, depending on conditions in the account. It is always appropriate to thank the person for seeing
you. Often you may call to furnish information that was not available at the
time of your personal call, or you may call to make sure delivery was received. There is an effective takeoff on this technique. When the shipping
department notifies you that the customer's order should have been received,
you can call the account to inquire about the status of the shipment. When
the purchasing agent checks and finds that the order was received on time,
the call serves as positive reinforcement for the buyer–seller relationship.
This technique works particularly well if the buyer has requested that the

[9]See Charles N. Waldo, "Using the Telephone Intelligently and Effectively," *The American Salesman,* Vol. 24, No. 6 (June 1979), p. 41.

order be expedited because of some particular problem. The telephone call then serves to drive home the point that you and your company have been helpful to the buyer.

Uses of the Telephone by In-House Sales Representatives

The telephone can be used effectively by two types of in-house salespersons: retail salespeople, who sell their merchandise to the final consumer, and inside industrial salespeople, who sell their merchandise to other organizations.

Retail salespersons Retail salespeople have frequent opportunities to increase business by effective use of the telephone. Periods of low store traffic can be used for phoning regular customers. The following circumstances might prompt such outgoing calls.

- Arrival of a special order.
- Advance announcement of a sale.
- Addition of a new line.
- Clearance of overstocked items.
- Setting a date and hour for delivery of goods already purchased.
- Arrival of new models.
- Invitation to a fashion show or other special event.
- Verification of delivery of goods previously ordered.
- Goodwill (e.g., calling a person who has not shopped in the store for a long time).

As an alert retail salesperson, you should keep a card file on each customer containing the dates of personal contacts, telephone calls, and other pertinent

Phone calls may be made during slow periods.

1. Customer's Name _____

2. Telephone Number _____

3. Address _____

4. Occupation _____

5. Marital status _____

6. Suit _____
   Size
   Color preference
   Quality preference

7. Sport jacket _____
   Size
   Color preference
   Quality preference

8. Dress shirts _____
   Neck size
   Sleeve size
   Quality preference
   Color preference

9. Sport shirts _____
   Size
   Quality preference
   Color preference

10. Slacks _____
    Waist size
    Inseam size
    Quality preference

11. Hat size _____

12. Shoe _____
    Size
    Quality preference

13. Formal wear _____

FIGURE 16.3 Men's store account card.

information. Figure 16.3 illustrates a card that a salesperson in a men's cloth-ing store keeps on each established customer. When a suit or sport coat ar-rives that the salesperson thinks the customer might like, measurements can be checked against the data on the card, and the customer can be called.

Inside sales representatives An inside salesperson for an industrial firm sells some of the same products that the outside salesperson sells. The major dif-ference is that the inside person does most of the work from behind a tele-phone or a computer terminal.

The inside salesperson is not just a passive order taker but a full member of the sales team whose work it is to distribute the firm's product.[10] These inside salespeople keep prospects aware of their firm and provide and obtain information of mutual interest to the customer and prospect accounts.

Inside and outside sales representatives will frequently "team-sell" an account. That is, the outside salesperson may call on an account once each month to demonstrate new products and try to sell as many of these and other products as the customer needs. Then, the inside salesperson follows up by telephone during the month to try to complete the sale or make new sales.

Inside salespeople serve in two valuable capacities. First, they are a source of information for the firm. They have substantial day-to-day contact with customers and thus can provide information regarding new customers, changes in the order patterns of old customers, and special requests for items not carried in stock. This information may call for immediate tactical adjustments that could not have been accomplished had the same facts appeared only later in a monthly sales analysis report. The inside salesperson may be able to sense when certain customers are dissatisfied with specific aspects of the field salesperson; in such a situation, behavioral adjustments can be made and a potential crisis averted. The inside person can also make note of any potential customer leads that the outside person should follow up.

Second, the inside salesperson is also an expediter. More than any other single individual, inside salespeople translate their firm's commitments to the customer into tangible products delivered on time. In so doing, inside salespeople have a unique opportunity to develop customer loyalty, and the repeat business developed from that loyalty assures the long-range success of the firm and its product offerings.

Uses of the Telephone for Incoming Requests for Information

If the selling effort is to be effective, incoming calls must be handled courteously and competently. Some companies have full-time inside sales representatives to whom such calls can be channeled. In many companies, however, such inquiries are handled on a "who's available" basis. In this case, any and all employees who are likely to answer should be trained in telephone courtesy and should be able to switch each inquiry to the person best able to handle it. Often it is simply a matter of getting the caller's name, company, and telephone number so that a salesperson can call back. Customers or prospects often use the telephone to make inquiries or to handle complaints. Such action furnishes prime evidence of their interest; effective handling of such calls is likely to result in sales. Attentive listening and skillful questioning can be used to help callers define their needs and wants. In the course of the conversation, additional requirements may be developed beyond those that prompted the inquiry. Five categories of positive outcomes are possible from an inquiry.

---

[10]For an interesting discussion of the inside salesperson, see Ben M. Enis, "Role Gap Narrows Between Inside and Outside Industrial Salespersons," *Marketing News*, Vol. 13, No. 8 (April 4, 1980), pp. 3, 7.

- An order may be taken as specified by the caller.
- A "trade-up" may be achieved—that is, the caller may buy higher quality, or greater quantity.
- A "tie-in" may be made and additional items sold.
- An inquiry may be converted into a "follow-up."
- A substitute product may be sold, if the specified items are unavailable.

It is important to verify all details, so that order processing or follow-up can be handled promptly and efficiently. Firms handling a large number of incoming calls often use a form to ensure that full and accurate information is obtained and recorded.

Several guidelines that can be used for handling incoming calls are summarized in Figure 16.4. These are applicable to all types of sales situations.

Handling complaints Every business, despite its best efforts, is likely to receive calls airing complaints. If goodwill and repeat business are to be sustained, such calls must be handled promptly and effectively. Switchboard operators must know where to channel each problem. They must quickly connect the person with someone capable of handling the complaint. Ineptness and delay only aggravate the situation.

The people handling the complaint should start by identifying themselves by name and title; for example, "This is Joyce Vanfleet in the shipping

---

1. Answer on the second ring:
   First ring—compose yourself.
   Second ring—answer the phone.
2. Give your complete attention to the phone call.
3. Identify yourself (name and department title if appropriate).
4. Ask for the customer's name, telephone number, and other data immediately.
5. Make sure you have a good connection. Call back if necessary.
6. Determine the purpose of the call; who is the right person to be handling it?
7. If the call is to be transferred, notify both caller and callee, telling both whom they'll be talking to.
8. Follow through; make sure the connection is made.
9. Use a standard format; start by gaining control.
10. If the customer is disturbed, angry, or downright rude, do NOT respond in kind. Keep your cool!
11. Listen
12. Restate all information, changing the pattern to verify.

FIGURE 16.4 Guidelines for handling incoming calls. SOURCE: Adapted from Warren Blanding, *Customer Service: A Profit Center Through Telemarketing* (Denver, Colo.: Mountain Bell).

department. May I help you?" Next, they should allow the other person to talk. This is a prime application of *catharsis,* the relieving of upset feelings by telling someone else the problem. Warm and attentive listening is called for.

Even if the complaint seems trivial or unwarranted, it should be handled with care. The matter is real and important in *customers'* minds, or they would not have called. Phrases that may reflect on the validity of the complaint, such as "You claim," should be avoided.

There is no substitute for honesty and openness. It is generally better to make what seems an unjustified settlement than to have a dissatisfied customer. A generous settlement may create a satisfied customer; if you make a grudging settlement, you may lose repeat business from the account as well as potential business from those who are influenced by the unhappy customer.

An agreement should be reached before the customer hangs up. If it is not feasible to handle the matter immediately, a commitment should be made about the steps to be taken and when they will occur. The longer the delay, the more aggravated customers will become. For more information on handling complaints, see Chapter 14.

CAUTIONS IN USING THE TELEPHONE

Some cautions should be observed in using the telephone as a sales tool. First, sometimes the person called is interrupted *during* your conversation. If this happens, you must quickly recap the points that were covered prior to the interruption. It is unrealistic to expect the other person to remember what was said. This is critically important if a call back is necessary. Second, just as in face-to-face selling, the pace and tempo of coverage should be slow enough for comprehension but not too slow. However, the lack of nonverbal feedback makes it more difficult to determine whether the other person understands you. Third, the other person must be a participant, not a passive listener; questions can help ensure this. Fourth, in large organizations it is important to determine that the right person is on the phone. Here, too, judicious use of questions can make sure of the proper contact. Fifth, it is easier to say "no" over the telephone, so you must be careful to use the telephone for the right purposes and to stop talking once you have reached your call objective. Sixth, because you are not there in person and cannot use multisensory appeals, you cannot hold the person's attention as long; therefore, you must be brief but concise. Finally, there are many errors you can make when using the telephone. Figure 16.5 lists the ten biggest mistakes people make when using the telephone.

GUIDELINES FOR USING THE TELEPHONE

Several factors are important when using the telephone, including your oral skills, telephone vocabulary, listening, and adjusting to the other person's communication style.

- Using the wrong tone of voice.
- Talking too fast or too slow.
- Not getting through to the right person.
- Failing to check the prospect's availability to talk.
- Using the telephone for the wrong purpose—that is, for calls that should have been made in person.
- Giving too much information, thus undermining your face-to-face presentation.
- Not offering the buyer a provocative reason for listening.
- Not probing for needs.
- Assuming that you understand the buyer correctly.
- Assuming that the buyer heard you correctly.

FIGURE 16.5 The ten biggest mistakes you can make in using the telephone. SOURCE: Adapted from John M. Rosenheim, "The 10 Biggest Mistakes in Telephone Selling," *Sales Management*, Vol. 108, No. 11 (May 29, 1972), pp. 24–25.

Oral Skills

In the absence of visual communication, oral skills become even more important on the telephone. Your voice reflects your personality. You should try to vary your voice tone to stress the particular points you want to make. You should also try to avoid talking too fast. Since you are very familiar with your offering, you may tend to speak too rapidly, which can cause misunderstandings and may create mistrust.[11]

Two qualities useful for your voice are enthusiasm and a positive attitude.[12] Enthusiasm gives you vibrance; you sound upbeat without seeming phony or making rash statements about your offering. A positive attitude helps you to assume that good things will come from the call. You will not sound to the callee as though you are just going through the motions. You must be confident, and you must be sold on yourself in order to have a positive attitude.

An effective telephone speaking voice is not something you acquire by accident; you must practice. You can improve your oral presentation in several ways. First, if you smile it will tend to be translated into what you are saying. Second, you can use body language to emphasize your points. Although the prospect cannot see you, the emotions expressed by body language will be conveyed in your voice. One good idea for self-improvement of verbal skills is to tape-record yourself and critique your calls. You can use

[11]See Darryl M. Smith, "What Do You Say after You've Said Hello?" *Sales and Marketing Management*, Vol. 119, No. 3 (August 29, 1977), p. 52.

[12]See Gary S. Goodman, *You Can Sell Anything by Telephone* (Englewood Cliffs, N.J.: Prentice-Hall, 1984), p. 25.

the tapes to listen for good delivery and to catch any annoying mannerisms you may have acquired.

Telephone Vocabulary

Telephone selling precludes demonstrating the product; therefore, you must develop a sales vocabulary that will enable your customer or prospect to "see the product over the phone." In order to accomplish this, you should use the following types of language.

- Expressive and highly descriptive words, such as luxurious, foolproof, velvety, detectable, and flawless.
- Dynamic words, such as breakthrough, power, and trust.
- Personal pronouns, such as you, your, I, me, my, we, us, and our.[13]
- Colorful adjectives that arouse feelings of pleasure, such as cool, fragrant, elegant.
- Phrases that paint word pictures, such as "lush, velvety crimson upholstery."[14]

Several guidelines will help you decide on your telephone vocabulary. Your telephone sales message must be worded without too much formality because it is person to person, and it should make no vague claims that might raise questions in the other person's mind. The message should encourage the prospect to respond and to feel comfortable.[15] Finally, it is especially important that you avoid technical terms when using the telephone, since you cannot evaluate your listener's understanding by observing nonverbal reactions.

Listening Skills

Listening is critical for using the telephone effectively, for it is your only means of acquiring feedback. Yet many telephone users fail to listen because they are so preoccupied with what they are going to say next. This is why your precall preparation is so important; it allows you to listen without losing the sense of your presentation—as well as to hear objections and closing signals.[16]

Listening is also your means of determining whether the timing of your call is appropriate. When you are face to face, it is easy to see when the prospect is busy or is being interrupted. However, in using the telephone you cannot see prospects, so you must listen carefully to be sure your prospect has time for your call.

To listen effectively you must make your calls in a distraction-free environment. Be sure to control your emotions, and seek feedback by saying

[13]"Phone Power: Qualifying Prospects and Making Appointments" (provided courtesy of Mountain Bell), p. 12.

[14]*Telephone Selling Skills* (Phoenix, Ariz.: Mountain Bell), p. 15.

[15]See Murray Roman, *Telephone Marketing* (New York: McGraw-Hill, 1976), p. 46.

[16]See Martin D. Shafiroff and Robert L. Shook, *Successful Telephone Selling in the '80s* (New York: Barnes and Noble, 1982), p. 138.

things such as "Ah ha . . . Oh . . . I see . . . Is that right." Finally, you must be careful not to interrupt the other person.[17]

Listening on the telephone is different from listening in person.[18] In person you can use eye contact and nod your head to let the other person know you are paying attention. Over the telephone you need to make comments such as, "Yes, I agree," "I understand," or "That's interesting," without interrupting the other person's flow. Thus, although the other person cannot see you listening, they can *hear* you listening.[19] Furthermore, because you do not have to worry about sending or receiving nonverbal cues, you may want to take notes on the telephone conversation.

Another common courtesy and listening tip is to let the other person hang up first. This helps you catch any last thoughts that the prospect has and will be regarded as polite.

Adjusting Communication Style

It is important to understand that people have different communication styles when using the telephone. You must be a good listener to identify the other person's communication style and then adjust your style to that of the other person.[20] For instance, some people like to be very brief in their telephone conversations, getting right down to business and having very factual discussions. Others like small talk and enjoy spending much more time on the telephone. You can detect people's preferences for short and long phone conversations from the tone of their voices or from their responses to questions. The most important thing is that you adjust your rate of speech and the things you cover to correspond with their style. When you deal with people for the first time over the phone, a key objective should be to determine what their communication styles are and adjust to them. Similarly, it is important in dealing with customers to find out their phoning preferences; adjusting to them will be easier because you probably already have considerable information about customers' personalities.

TELEPHONE SERVICES USEFUL IN SELLING

There are a number of telephone services that you can use. Some of the most important ones are WATS lines, 800 numbers, answering services, mobile telecommunications services, conference calls, amplification, and teleconferencing.

---

[17]Adapted from Don Christman and Bert Holtje, "Telephone Body Language, or, How to Sell 'By Ear,' " *Industrial Distribution*, Vol. 72, No. 5 (May 1982), pp. 76–78.

[18]See, for example, Don Christman and Bert Holtje, "Telephone Body Language, or How to Sell 'By Ear,' " *Industrial Distribution*, Vol. 72, No. 5 (May 1982), pp. 76–78.

[19]See Martin D. Shafiroff and Robert L. Shook, *Successful Telephone Selling in the '80s* (New York: Barnes & Noble, 1982, pp. 142–143).

[20]See Gary S. Goodman, *You Can Sell Anything by Telephone* (Englewood Cliffs, N.J.: Prentice-Hall, 1984), p. 29.

WATS Lines

The purchase of a WATS line (Wide Area Telecommunications Service) permits the caller to make an unlimited number of long-distance calls within a specified geographical area. The area may be as small as a state or as large as the entire continental United States. WATS lines can be purchased for as short a period of time as ten hours spread over thirty days or for as long as eight hours per day. Companies that do a considerable amount of telephone selling may save thousands of dollars in toll charges by converting to WATS. In addition, the fixed charge makes feasible more frequent contacts, which might not be affordable on a toll charge basis.[21]

Long-distance calls tend to have greater impact than local calls. Switchboard operators and secretaries are more reluctant to screen out such calls than those from local callers. Some sales representatives take advantage of this by setting up appointments by long distance.

800 Numbers

Complementary to an outgoing WATS line is the payment for incoming calls by the firm through an 800 service. With this system, customers or prospects may call in without incurring toll charges. These calls can be useful for taking orders, handling inquiries, handling complaints, and handling service or repairs; in addition, they are useful in building goodwill. The G.E. Answer Center is a good example of how an 800 toll-free number enables a company to respond rapidly to customer inquiries. The calls range from questions about the location of the nearest G.E. dealer to requests for information about products that will allow customers to make minor repairs.[22] Perhaps the widest use of this method is by motel chains. Firms whose incoming sales volume does not warrant such service may increase sales by encouraging incoming collect calls.[23]

Answering Services

Field sales representatives working without backup office personnel may increase their effectiveness by using an answering service—either live or electronic. The live service has the advantage of enabling you to call in for messages. Many salespeople, however, use electronic answering devices to receive incoming calls placed after business hours. Some national firms even use 800 numbers for accepting messages.[24] You can also install a telephone-answering machine if you cannot afford an answering service. Some machines have remote capacity, which enables you to call the machine and pick up incoming messages over the telephone.[25]

---

[21]For an interesting discussion of WATS uses in selling, see Mark G. Gilbert, "WATS My Line," *The American Salesman,* Vol. 27, No. 3 (March 1982), pp. 3–7.

[22]John I. Coppett and Roy Dale Voorhees, "Telemarketing: Supplement to Field Sales," *Industrial Marketing Management,* Vol. 14, No. 3 (August 1985), p. 215.

[23]For a discussion of 800 numbers, see Joani Nelson-Horchler, "Consumer Feedback? The Magic Number is 800," *Industry Week,* Vol. 111, No. 6 (November 2, 1981), pp. 63–66.

[24]See, for example, "Making Sure Salespeople Get the Call," *Sales and Marketing Management,* Vol. 123, No. 5 (October 15, 1979), p. 24.

[25]Richard Ensman, "Keeping in Touch . . . The Sales Rep and Modern Communication," *The American Salesman,* Vol. 29, No. 7 (July 1984), p. 39.

Mobile Telecommunications Services

To eliminate time lag in receiving calls as well as in answering them, some sales representatives use mobile telecommunications service (MTS). There are three basic categories of these services: (1) mobile telephones (e.g., cellular telephones) for two-way communication with telephones anywhere—even overseas, (2) two-way radios for communication with other two-way radios, and (3) pagers—commonly called beepers because of the sound they emit—which are one-way devices that alert you to telephone a prearranged person or location.[26] Pagers are normally equipped to tell you to call your office, although some sophisticated systems are able to print out electronically the number you are to call. Pagers enable you to receive messages almost immediately and allow you to stay in close touch with your office or with customers.

Conference Calls

You may use a conference call to confer with several persons in various locations. For example, you may wish to talk to your district sales manager, the credit manager at headquarters, and the plant that makes shipments to your customers. You may also use a conference call to facilitate decision making in one of your accounts by having members of the buying center, who may be scattered geographically, confer together simultaneously. Another use of conference calls is for testimonials. Here potential customers can talk to current customers in conference calls initiated by the salesperson or by groups that offer this service.[27]

Teleconferencing can be an effective way to communicate with customers.

[26]See Steven Mintz, "Jeepers, Beepers!" *Sales and Marketing Management,* Vol. 128, No. 4 (March 15, 1982), p. 50.

[27]See Margaret Price, "Getting Customers to See Each Other," *Industry Week,* Vol. 107, No. 6 (November 10, 1980), pp. 32–34.

Amplification

You may have an occasion to use telephone amplifying equipment. For example, you may assemble several people in your organization before calling a customer and have them all talk into a special speaker. In this way, all members of the group can back up your efforts without the time and expense of making a joint call in the field.

Teleconferencing

Firms are using teleconferencing to introduce new products to their customers. For example, Zimmer Inc. demonstrated new medical instruments to surgeons throughout the country through teleconferencing.[28] This enables customers actually to see the product, greatly speeds up the communication process, and may greatly increase productivity.

SUMMARY

The telephone is an invaluable selling tool, but it must be used properly to be effective. Telephone sales calls must be planned with the same care as field calls. As a guide to planning, remember that the telephone call is usually an interruption to the person you are calling; it uses only the auditory channel, and timing and courtesy are important. In order to plan, you should have a call objective; then, prepare an opening statement and a sales message. The call plan, once formulated, can be used as an agenda for note taking and questions.

Outside salespeople may use the telephone to prospect or qualify, to make appointments, to call on out-of-the-way accounts, to close the sale, or to follow up. In-house sales representatives may use the telephone to keep in touch with customers, to follow up, or to generate additional sales. Two types of in-house salespeople are retail salespeople and inside sales representatives. In many firms, they coordinate their efforts with the field sales representatives and often play an important role in the total sales effort.

The telephone may also be used for incoming inquiries with many positive results. There are several guidelines for handling incoming calls effectively, especially when answering complaints.

Several cautions to be aware of when using the telephone are handling the break when the callee is interrupted, adjusting your pace, involving the other person, getting to the right person, using the telephone for the right purpose, and keeping the attention of the callee.

Given the relatively unique problem of verbal communications without visual backup, you must devise special approaches when using the telephone. First, you must sharpen your oral skills and develop a telephone vocabulary so you can transmit a clear, powerful message to the prospect. Listening is also important, since it is the only way you receive feedback. Finally, you must adjust to the communication style of the other person. When calling a prospect, this is a key objective.

[28]See Paul E. Gillette, "Picture This Presentation," *Sales and Marketing Management,* Vol. 132, No. 8 (June 4, 1984), p. 37.

A variety of telephone services—WATS lines, 800 numbers, answering services, mobile telecommunications services (MTS), conference calls, amplification, and teleconferencing—are useful in selling.

_____435

EXERCISE 16

PROBLEMS

1. Which items on the test of telephone manners (Figure 16.1) do you think are violated most often? Which ones are most likely to "turn off" the other person?
2. Assume you are a salesperson in a local stereo store and have a special on a component system that could be attractive to upper-income consumers. Outline a plan for a telephone sales call.
3. Why are sales calls by telephone more effective with a customer than with a prospect? How would the salesperson's call plans differ for each?
4. How can a complaint call be made into a sales opportunity?
5. Which of the "hinges" have you experienced as the prospect or customer being called?

EXERCISE 16

Objective: To learn more about using the telephone in selling.

1. Phone a local store requesting information of some kind. Note the manner in which your inquiry is handled by the salesperson.
2. Resume the role of a fashion salesperson, phoning ahead for an appointment. What do you say?
3. Use the test of telephone manners as a checklist, and note how many violations occur on calls you make or receive in the course of a week.

Case 16-1 Les Deux Soeurs

Les Deux Soeurs is an exclusive dress shop in West Palm Beach located on a shopping promenade. It is owned and operated by two sisters, Marie and Antoinette Bourjois, now in their sixties. The store carries the most expensive clothes in the area, many of the selections being one-of-a-kind imports by name designers. Whenever the store is open one of the sisters is likely to be present. The sales force varies in size, from six during the height of the winter season to two or three during the summer.

Customers include year-round residents, many of whom are retired, and affluent winter vacationers. Each sister, as well as the more experienced salespeople, has a personal following. Word of mouth is the strongest promotional force, although display ads are run from time to time in the local paper. Each salesperson is encouraged to keep a card file on her customers and to make phone calls to let them know of new arrivals.

Susan Baxter has been with Les Deux Soeurs for ten years and has developed a good following. One of her customers is Mrs. Thomas L. Green, owner of an elegant winter home and acknowledged to be one of _the_ hostesses among the well-to-do.

Susan has selected a Christian Dior creation, a luscious, deep-green caftan that she feels Mrs. Green will like. It is set off at the neckline with tiny sequins and is priced at $575.

How can Susan use the telephone in this situation?

Case 16-2 Gulden's Department Store

Gulden's is the largest of three department stores in a metropolitan shopping area. It has two suburban branches in addition to the main store downtown. Intensive advertising and direct mail are used to generate traffic to the stores. Sales personnel are encouraged to remind shoppers of specials and possible tie-in purchases. Gulden's has a large number of charge customers who are viewed as the "backbone" of the business. All transactions and other records are computerized, and sales are analyzed on a continuing basis.

Jack Bolton has just graduated from college and has been employed by Gulden's as a trainee. Mr. Thompson, the vice-president of marketing, is addressing Jack and the other trainees on the importance of Gulden's maintaining a personal, "customer is right" image. He poses the following assignment to each of them.

"We have over 14,000 charge customers on the books. About 20 percent of them are inactive. We seldom hear from them. It costs Gulden's about $10 per year to maintain them in the files. How can we stimulate business from this group?"

Jack decides that a telephone campaign might be directed to the inactive group.

Outline a plan that Jack could utilize effectively.

The Legal and Ethical Dimensions of Selling

After studying this chapter you should be able to

1. Understand federal laws that have an impact on selling.
2. Identify aspects of the Uniform Commercial Code that affect selling.
3. Recognize the importance of state consumer protection legislation.
4. Specify what is meant by ethics.
5. Identify ethical problems facing salespeople with respect to the firm, customers, and competition.
6. Appreciate ethical dilemmas faced by salespeople.

THE LEGAL AND ETHICAL DIMENSIONS OF SELLING

This chapter examines the legal and ethical aspects of selling. In the United States, legal provisions affecting the field of sales are primarily concerned with maintaining competition and protecting consumers' rights from unfair trade practices. It is essential that you understand these provisions, since your relationship with customers, dealers, and your own firm are continually affected by the government's actions. The many laws that regulate selling are examined first, then the ethical aspects of the sales function.

LEGAL ASPECTS

It is important to know the legal aspects of selling, because salespeople are the ones who represent their firm's products and services to customers and they are the ones who negotiate contracts.[1]

The Sherman Antitrust Act

The Sherman Antitrust Act of 1890 was the first federal law designed to prevent restraint of trade in interstate and foreign commerce. It stated that "Every contract, combination in the form of trust or otherwise, or conspiracy, in restraint of trade or commerce, is illegal among the several states." Specific sales practices that are illegal in interstate commerce under the Sherman Act are (1) the dividing up of markets by agreement of competing firms; (2) the fixing of prices either horizontally, between competing firms, or vertically, between members of the same channel of distribution; and (3) refusal to deal with a current or former customer for other than good business reasons.[2]

A classic case of restraint of trade was the great electrical conspiracy of 1960, in which salespersons and executives of the electrical industry met regularly to decide on pricing and trade policies. The companies and individuals involved were found to be in violation of a number of laws, including the Sherman Act.

The Clayton Act

The Sherman Act was not sufficient to stop trade abuses, however. In order to strengthen and complement it, Congress passed the Clayton Act in 1914, which stated that it was no longer necessary to produce proof of conspiracy or actual monopoly as had been required under the Sherman Act. The Clayton Act states that certain practices are illegal, where the effects "may be to substantially lessen competition or tend to create a monopoly . . . ."The government did have to prove, however, that the acts of the defendant did indeed "substantially lessen competition." Sections 2 and 3 of the Clayton Act have provisions that apply directly to selling.

---

[1]For additional legal aspects of selling, see Steven Mitchell Sack and Howard Jay Steinberg, *The Salesperson's Legal Guide* (Englewood Cliffs, N.J.: Prentice-Hall 1981).

[2]See, for example, Mike Shatzkin, "Planning a Sales Itinerary: A How-To Guide for Today's Conditions, "*Publishers Weekly* (July 30, 1979), pp. 44 – 47.

Section 2 The second section of the Clayton Act states that it is generally illegal for a seller to offer the same merchandise to two different buyers at different prices. Price differences have to be based on different marketing and distribution costs or on variations in grade, quality, or quantity of the product. Differences in price could also be justified by the need to meet competitive practices. This section of the Clayton Act was subsequently amended by the Robinson–Patman Act, which will be discussed later.

Section 3 The third portion of the Clayton Act prohibits exclusive-dealing and tying contracts when they substantially lessen competition.[3] *Exclusive-dealing contracts* are agreements that force an intermediary to handle the products of only one manufacturer. *Tying contracts* force a buyer to purchase unwanted products in order to obtain a desired item. Only agreements that substantially affect competition are considered violations.[4] There is no definite general standard that can be applied to all firms, because several factors are considered, such as sales volume and the location of competitors. Defining "competition" and "substantially lessen" is the task of the enforcement agencies in each case.

The Federal Trade Commission Act
In 1914, the Federal Trade Commission (FTC) Act was passed, establishing a commission of specialists with power to investigate any business practices that might represent "unfair methods of competition."[5] If the commission feels that an improper act is being committed, it can issue a cease-and-desist order. If the firm in question refuses to accept the order, the FTC is empowered to take the firm to federal court to have its order enforced. The theory behind the FTC Act was to create a body that can investigate potentially monopolistic practices and stop them faster and on a more informal basis than the courts can.

The Wheeler–Lea Act In 1931, the courts determined that the FTC had power only over cases in which injury is done to one firm by another and not over cases in which a firm damages the final consumer. As a result, in 1938 Congress passed the Wheeler–Lea Act, which amended the FTC Act to declare unlawful, "unfair methods of competition in commerce and unfair or deceptive acts or practices . . . ." This extended the FTC's power to include the investigation and prohibition of unfair or deceptive practices involving the final consumer.

[3]For more on exclusive-dealing and tying arrangements, see Steven Mitchell Sack, "Treat the Customer Right—or Else," *Sales and Marketing Management* Vol. 136, No. 1 (January 13, 1986), pp. 63–64.

[4]See Russell Decker, "Supreme Court Puts Tie-in Sales to New Test," *Purchasing*, Vol. 83, No. 10 (November 1977) pp. 97–99.

[5]For an in-depth discussion of the Federal Trade Commission Act, see Steven Mitchell Sack, "The High Risk of Dirty Tricks," *Sales and Marketing Management*, Vol. 135, No. 6 (November 11, 1985), pp. 56–59.

The FTC investigates all selling practices that may be deemed unfair. Acts ranging from collusion in pricing between supposed competitors to false statements by a salesperson are legitimate concerns for the FTC. In addition, the FTC is concerned with all sales practices that attempt to deceive and mislead customers. Since the Wheeler–Lea Amendment does not specify the "unfair trade practices," the FTC can adapt to changes and determine what it may consider unfair according to each specific case. You must keep informed of court decisions in FTC cases, as well as the regulatory activities of the commission itself, in order to be aware of legal trends in this field.

The cooling-off rule The FTC adopted a Trade Regulation Rule in 1974 to deal directly with sales practices. This rule establishes a cooling-off period for door-to-door sales to allow consumers to review buying decisions made during a sales presentation or under the persuasive influences of a salesperson in their home. Under this rule, the consumer may cancel a business transaction during the three working days following the day on which the transaction was originally made.

The cooling-off rule specifies the form in which this information must be given to the buyer. Along with the requirement that the buyer be presented with a complete contract, a receipt of the transaction, or both, written in the same language as that principally used in the sales presentation, the seller must include on the first page of this contract or in the space next to the buyer's signature, the following statement

> **You, the buyer, may cancel this transaction at any time prior to midnight of the third business day after the date of this transaction. See the attached notice of cancellation form for an explanation of this right.**

In addition, the seller must furnish the buyer with a notice of cancellation as stated in Figure 17.1.

Failure to provide these two items is considered an unfair or deceptive practice. The cooling-off rule applies to any door-to-door transaction of goods with a price of $25 or more, whether this is done under single or multiple contracts.

The FTC rules does not annul or exempt any seller from complying with the laws of any state, or with municipal ordinances regulating door-to-door sales. An exemption is made, however, when such state laws or ordinances are considered directly inconsistent with the rule. State laws could be tougher, but not more lenient than the federal rule.

The FTC's concern with unfair or deceptive trade practices is shown by this rule. The federal government, through its agencies and other regulatory bodies, has had an increasingly important role in trading practices and activities, and this greater concern has been extended to most states. It is important, therefore, to examine the role of state legislation as it affects the selling–buying relationship. This will be done later in this chapter.

The Robinson–Patman Act

The Robinson–Patman Act (1936) which amended Section 2 of the Clayton Act, made unlawful in interstate commerce any price discrimination between

---

Notice of Cancellation

_____
(enter date of transaction)

You may cancel this transaction, without any penalty or obligation, within three business days from the above date.

If you cancel, any property traded in, any payments made by you under the contract or sale, and any negotiable instrument executed by you will be returned within 10 business days following receipt by the seller of your cancellation notice, any security interest arising out of the transaction will be canceled.

If you cancel, you must make available to the seller at your residence, in substantially as good condition as when received, any goods delivered to you under this contract or sale; or you may if you wish, comply with the instructions of the seller regarding the return shipment of the goods at the seller's expense and risk. If you do make the goods available to the seller and the seller does not pick them up within 20 days of the date of your notice of cancellation, you may retain or dispose of the goods without any further obligation. If you fail to make the goods available to the seller, or if you agree to return the goods to the seller and fail to do so, then you remain liable for performance of all obligations under the contract.

To cancel this transaction, mail or deliver a signed and dated copy of this cancellation notice or any other written notice, or send a telegram, to

_____, at _____ no
(name of seller)   (address of seller's place of business)

later than midnight of _____.
                              (date)

I hereby cancel this transaction.

_____
(date)

_____
(buyer's signature)

FIGURE 17.1 The notice of cancellation required for a sale made in the home.

different purchasers of goods of "like grade and quality" that may tend to "injure, destroy, or prevent competition." It was therefore no long necessary to show that competition had been *substantially lessened;* any injury to competition was sufficient cause to bring action. The Robinson–Patman Act also included regulation against discriminating practices, such as advertising allowances, that are not available to all customers on "proportionately equal terms." This means that if a manufacturer wishes to give a large chain store assistance in designing a full-page newspaper advertisement, it has to offer

TABLE 17.1

TEN DON'TS OF ANTITRUST

Companies most frequently issue the following warnings to employees to keep them in compliance with antitrust laws.

1. Don't discuss with customers the price your company will charge others.
2. Don't attend meetings with competitors (including trade association gatherings) at which pricing is discussed. If you find yourself in such a session, walk out.
3. Don't give favored treatment to your own subsidiaries and affiliates.
4. Don't enter into agreements or gentlemen's understandings on discounts, terms or conditions of sale, profits or profit margins, shares of the market, bids or the intent to bid, rejection or termination of customers, sales territories or markets.
5. Don't use one product as bait for selling another.
6. Don't require a customer to buy a product only from you.
7. Don't forget to consider state antitrust laws as well as the federal statutes.
8. Don't disparage a competitor's product unless you have specific proof that your statements are true. This is an unfair method of competition.
9. Don't make either sales or purchases conditional on the other party's making reciprocal purchases from or sales to your company.
10. Don't hesitate to consult with a company lawyer if you have any doubt about the legality of a practice. Antitrust laws are wide-ranging, complex, and subject to changing interpretations.

SOURCE: "How to Avoid Antitrust," *Business Week* (January 27, 1975), p. 84.

the same type of service to the small retailer in designing their smaller advertisement.

The Robinson–Patman Act and the subsequent court decisions make it very clear that you must be cautious in giving preferential treatment to any of your customers. If you grant a price break or extra cooperative advertising expenditures to one customer, you must be prepared to offer the same types of programs to each of your customers unless you can justify them by (1) the fact that it costs less to do business with one customer, or (2) the fact that you are meeting the practices of your competition. In addition, you must resist temptation to get speedier delivery or better service arrangements for your larger customers, for if you offer one customer these incentives and not others, you will find yourself in violation of the law.

The acts described constitute a body of law called antitrust legislation. Table 17.1 lists several guidelines you should follow when trying to comply with antitrust law.

Federal Consumer Protection Legislation

Since the early 1900s, several laws and regulations have been passed to protect consumers from trade abuses by overly aggressive merchants and salespersons. These abuses have led more recently to a movement called "consumerism," which attempts to achieve organized reaction to abuse, fraud, deception, and misrepresentation in marketing. The federal legislation protecting consumers covers a variety of specialized issues: product content, packaging, labeling, and several informational points about contractual agreements, such as credit and lending.

The consumer protection laws enable you to emphasize product quality
and reliability and to use compliance with federal regulation as a competitive
advantage, when your offer does comply. At the same time, since oral agreements between you and your customers are often a very important part of the
sales contract, you must be aware of the legal requirements and disclose the
appropriate information to your customers. This is a complicated area of the
law, but one that is critical if you deal with final consumers. (Later in the
chapter, state consumer protection laws will be discussed.) In order to understand better the contractual agreements between salespeople and buyers, you
must know about the Uniform Commercial Code.

The Uniform Commercial Code

The Uniform Commercial Code (UCC) and its chief predecessor, the Uniform
Sales Act, comprise the legal guide to commercial practice in the United
States (Louisiana excepted). The code was drafted by the National Conference
of Commissioners on Uniform State Laws and the American Law Institute over
a period of ten years. The initial draft was completed in 1952, and the final
edition, which has since been accepted by 49 states, appeared in 1958. The
provisions of the UCC bear directly on your relations with your customers. In
each, you face *must* and *must-not* actions and decisions. You are your firm's
agent under the law. Some of the implications of the UCC are considered
here.

The definition of a sale The UCC defines a sale as "the transfer of title to
goods by the seller to the buyer for a consideration known as the price."[6]
The code introduces a number of separate rules which apply to sales between
merchants to sales in which merchants are a party. Fifteen sections of the
UCC are concerned with sales between merchants and cover such items as
the need for written contracts, warranty of goods sold by merchants, delivery
agreements, commissions, and reimbursements.

Oral agreements between sellers and buyers are considered as binding
as written contracts. It is important that you be aware of such provisions,
since you are the spokesperson and legal representative of your company in
its relations with buyers and potential buyers.

You must be informed on all details of the contracts of sale that you
negotiate for your firm. This is a particularly important consideration if the
unit order is large, or if durable goods with warranties or guarantees covering
the purchase are involved, or if stipulated services are included in the sale.
You have the power legally to obligate the company you represent.

The salesperson and the reseller When you have resellers as customers and
prospects, you must know the details of the contractual relationships between
your firm and the reseller. In particular, you must note the *obligations of your
firm to the reseller* and the *expectations your employer has of the reseller*. A
recurrent problem is stipulating the marketing and sales performance of the

---

[6]See Len Young Smith and G. Gale Robertson, *Business Law—Uniform Commercial Code Edition,* third edition (St. Paul, Minn.: West Publishing, 1971), pp. 497–498.

intermediary with respect to the manufacturer's product line. For instance, how much should the reseller promote the product, and what types of discounts should the reseller give? A relationship stipulated between vendor and purchaser in which the reseller deliberately or inadvertently holds forth as agent for the manufacturer may also cause problems. The reseller's advertising, use of trademarks, and other promotional efforts may all feature a manufacturer.

Warranties and guarantees The UCC distinguishes between express warranties and implied warranties. Express warranties are those found only in the express language of the seller. Implied warranties are obligations imposed by law upon the seller that were not stated in express language.

Statements or promises made by the seller a long time before the sale or subsequent to the contract of sale may be express warranties. The code also states that manufacturers and sellers of goods may be liable to users and consumers on the basis of (1) negligence, (2) fraud or misrepresentation, and (3) express or implied warranty.[7] Recently there have been a number of product liability lawsuits. In situations giving you latitude to develop your own sales message, you must be careful to describe the product accurately or your company may be liable.[8]

Salespersons handling durable goods covered by warranties and guarantees must be aware of the extent of the coverage. The problems associated with this coverage become important when the goods move through indirect channels. The ultimate user complains to the reseller, and the reseller in turn attempts to shift the burden to the manufacturer. The manufacturer is one step removed from the situation and must rely on salespeople to be investigators and arbitrators.

Financing Another legal aspect of customer relations is financing. You often face situations in which your firm is directly involved in financing the items purchased or in arranging such financing from outside sources. Under the UCC, claims against products being financed are treated by reserving a security interest in the product for the seller referred to as a lien in earlier legislation). That is, you have the first right to the financed goods if they are in default. If repossession becomes necessary, you must know the legal restraints under which this action can be accomplished.

Consignment Another legal factor peculiar to some sales operations is the handling of goods on consignment, where title remains with the seller. This

---

[7]For more information on what you should or should not say about competitors or products, see Steven Mitchell Sack, "Watch the Words," *Sales and Marketing Management*, Vol. 135, No. 1 (July 1, 1985), pp. 56–58.

[8]For a complete discussion, see Fred W. Morgan and Karl A. Boedecker, "The Role of Personal Selling in Products Liability Litigation," *Journal of Personal Selling and Sales Management*, Vol. 1, No. 1 (Fall/Winter 1980–1981), pp. 34–40.

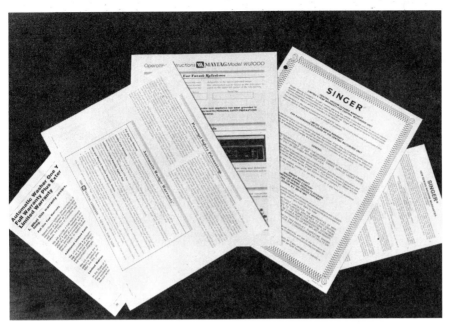

Salespeople must be aware of warranties.

becomes complicated if the goods have a limited shelf life and depreciate with time. In the event that repossession is necessary, you must know the legal restraints to repossession as well as your company's rights with respect to depreciated value. In most states, for example, it is a criminal offense for a reseller to sell consigned goods and not immediately pay the owner the money owed.

The provisions in the UCC regulate business transactions and cover in detail those involving the sale of goods and services. Because the UCC is so widely adopted, it is important that you be aware of its implications in regulating sales activity.

State Consumer Protection Laws

In addition to the federal laws and the UCC, there is now state legislation protecting consumers. These more recent laws were written when consumers became alarmed about deceptive trade practices. Several states passed consumer protection laws, also called "little FTC laws," which are aimed at preventing and prosecuting abuses by salespersons and merchants at the local level. The "little FTC laws" are very often more specific than their federal counterparts, and they are usually enforced through the attorney general's office at the state level.

An excellent example of a "little FTC law" is the Texas Deceptive Trade Practices and Consumer Protection Act. This law was passed to give the

TABLE 17.2

EXAMPLES OF DECEPTIVE ACTS AS PROVIDED BY THE TEXAS DECEPTIVE TRADE PRACTICES AND CONSUMER PROTECTION ACT

1. Passing off goods or services as those of another.
2. Causing confusion or misunderstandings about the source, sponsorship, approval, or certification of goods or services.
3. Using deceptive representations or designations of geographical origin in connection with goods or services.
4. Representing goods or services as having sponsorship, approval, characteristics, uses, or benefits that they do not have.
5. Representing goods as being original or new when they are deteriorated, reconditioned, reclaimed, used, or secondhand.
6. Representing goods as being of a particular standard, quality, or style when they are not.
7. Disparaging the goods, services, or business of another by a false or misleading representation of facts.
8. Making false or misleading statements concerning the reasons for the existence of, or the amount of, price reductions.

Texas attorney general the power to prosecute "false, misleading, or deceptive acts or practices in the conduct of trade or commerce." The law is relevant to all salespersons in Texas, whether they are dealing directly with the final consumer or with a firm. Several acts singled out as deceptive that apply to salespersons are shown in Table 17.2.

ETHICS

In addition to the legal aspects of selling, you must also comply with ethical expectations. Often some activity such as talking about a competitor may be legal, but you may not wish to do it for ethical reasons. Just as your firm must be socially responsible in dealing with its many publics, you must also be responsible in your dealings with others.[9] Several aspects of ethics are explored in this section, including ethics and the salesperson, and ethical considerations with customers, with your company, and with competition. Finally, several ethical dilemmas of salespeople are explored, and a code of ethics is provided.

Ethics and the Salesperson

To be effective in selling, you must first of all be trusted and respected by your customers. People evaluate others by comparing their behavior with a set of standards, but morality and ethics are abstract standards, and as such they will vary from individual to individual. Ethics are standards of right and wrong. Clearly, ethics are situational, and what is ethical may vary, depending on the situation. For example, certain business practices that are frowned upon in the United States such as bribes, are common in other countries.

[9]Ramon J. Aldag and Donald W. Jackson, Jr., "A Managerial Framework for Social Decision Making," *MSU Business Topics*, Vol. 23, No. 3 (Summer 1975), pp. 75–84.

"Where do I draw the line between good and evil?"

Despite the relative and situational nature of ethics, people's judgment of what is ethical behavior is usually based on two concepts: the generally accepted social standards and their personal ethical judgment. The question of what is ethical and moral for salespeople must conform to the generally accepted social standards, and because salespeople are exposed to many individuals, their action must be acceptable to the majority rather than the minority.

One definition of ethics states that they are "a set of moral principles or values." Companies do not have ethics; people do. However, each firm's policies, as written and as practiced, make up the ethical position of the company, just as your life values, as verbalized and shown in your behavior, constitute your ethical position. When plans, actions, and decisions of individuals and their companies reach the ethical level, they must be, at a minimum, defensible.

Some companies may require their employees to obey more rigid standards of behavior than those generally acceptable to society. When this is not the case, however, you must at least conform to general rules of ethics.

To the extent that you fulfill your obligations as a good citizen and actively participate in community groups, you assist your firm in operating at an ethical level. Often, because of the overlap among your firm's various publics, your conduct in the community as an individual citizen may contribute favorably or adversely to business. Since you deal with the public constantly, your reputation is important.

Ethical Conduct toward the Client

You are a key link between your organization and your customers. You may face ethical questions when you have to choose between making short-term sales quotas and your long-term goal of developing a positive relationship with your customer.[10] Your behavior directly affects your customers; it may influence customers' decisions to buy as well as their recommendations to other customers. For these reasons, you should establish standards of behavior to follow when in contact with your customers.

Your ethical conduct with customers covers several dimensions: truthfulness, pressure, misrepresentation, discretion, bribes, gifts and entertainment, business lunches, and reciprocity.

Truthfulness As you strive to gain your customers' confidence, your persuasive contact with them must always be realistic and truthful. The use of deceitful means to make a sale is not acceptable. When customers have needs that your company cannot satisfy, you should refer them to someone who can. You also have a responsibility to tell your customers about any negative aspects of your product. A salesperson for a pharmaceutical firm, for example, would have to tell a doctor about the side effects of a product. Failure to do so would be unethical and might endanger the lives of patients.

Pressure Another moral aspect of dealing with customers is how much pressure you should apply in getting them to buy. Throughout this book, low-pressure selling has been stressed as being more conducive to building long-term relationships. However, unscrupulous salespeople may push customers into making purchases they neither need nor want. This clearly raises some ethical issues.

Misrepresentation Another problem is misrepresenting your product or service. You could misrepresent your offering by overselling its benefits, by making promises about deliveries that you cannot keep, or by covering up limitations of your product. Besides the legal aspects of these misrepresentations, there are also ethical considerations.

Discretion Discretion is another important requirement of a sales relationship. Often you are exposed to confidential competitive information that has no bearing on your product or your firm. Such confidences must be kept private and should not be used in gossip with others. The greater knowledge of your customers and their problems must be used only to help you to serve them better, not as a conversation topic with other clients or colleagues. You should also use discretion with respect to proprietary information about your company. For instance, you would not want to leak information about a new product that might reach your competition, or to mention confidential marketing research that is important to your firm.

Bribes There are salespeople who try to gain a customer's business with bribes, and there are unscrupulous purchasers who ask for kickbacks or bribes in return for making a purchase. A kickback is a percentage payment

---

[10]See Alan J. Dubinsky, Eric N. Berkowitz, and William Rudelius, "Ethical Problems of Field Sales Personnel," *MSU Business Topics,* Vol. 28, No. 3 (Summer 1980), p. 12.

to the buyer in order to get the business. Thus, salespeople who offer buyers 10 percent of their commission would be offering a kickback. Purchasing agents also might indicate that their golf game would be improved with a new set of clubs. Fortunately, purchasing executives are as a rule very ethical, but there are always exceptions. There are no simple answers to the bribery issue. Some buyers and sellers will continue to engage in these activities and you may lose some short-term sales to them. However, you should guard against becoming involved in these types of situations; not only would your reputation suffer, but you might also face legal actions.

Bribes and kickbacks are normally illegal in the United States; however, bribes are considered a normal part of business in some other countries.[11] Because bribes and kickbacks are means of avoiding normal competitive practices, they may not be in the best interests of the buyer's firm. Recently, several firms have been caught giving kickbacks and have been prosecuted. In general, the process of bribery benefits neither the seller's nor the buyer's firm and may have some very detrimental consequences. Another factor to consider is the reaction of the purchasing executives' firm. Should management find out about the bribery, they will be upset and the purchasers may lose their jobs.

Gifts and entertainment One very delicate topic is offering gifts or other inducements to clients. Traditionally, some salespeople lavishly entertained clients in order to obtain orders from them. As can be seen from Table 17.3, some forms of entertainment are much more likely to be chosen than others. Although entertainment is considered more acceptable than gift giving, both activities could easily be exaggerated to the point where they may be considered a form of commerical bribery. At some point, providing entertainment

TABLE 17.3
PERCENTAGE OF INDUSTRIAL SALESPEOPLE CHOOSING VARIOUS ENTERTAINMENT ACTIVITIES

ACTIVITY	INFREQUENTLY OR NEVER, percent	OCCASIONALLY OR FREQUENTLY, percent
Take clients out for lunch.	14.3	87.7
Take clients out for an evening meal.	42.3	37.7
Take clients out for a drink.	61.2	38.8
Entertain clients with leisure activities like golf or fishing.	75.0	25.0
Give parties for clients.	92.5	7.5

SOURCE: Reprinted by permission of the publisher from David W. Finn and William C. Moncrief, "Sales-force Entertainment Activities," *Industrial Marketing Management*, Vol. 14, No. 4 (November 1985), p. 230. Copyright© 1985, by Elsevier Science Publishing Company, Inc.

[11]See, for example, Jack G. Kaikati and Wayne A. Label, "American Bribery Legislation: An Obstacle to International Marketing," *Journal of Marketing*, Vol. 44, No. 4 (Fall 1980), pp. 38–43.

Pepper... and Salt

THE WALL STREET JOURNAL

"I've got him softened up—now what is our product again?"

for customers crosses the line between just being in poor taste and actually trying to "buy" the customer.

Some businesses, as a matter of policy, prohibit acceptance of gifts of more than nominal value. Any person who does so—even when not forbidden by policy—is vulnerable to the accusation that their business is being bought. Some firms feel so strongly about this that they prohibit their personnel from accepting any kind of gift, even a luncheon. Other firms encourage vendors to make a donation at Christmas to a charity in lieu of providing gifts.[12] A small gift, such as an appointment book or a paperweight with your corporate logo on it, is clearly not unethical. However, a color television probably poses some problems. One way to judge the ethical aspects of a gift or entertainment is to ask whether an objective outside person would reasonably suspect that the gift or entertainment was aimed at blurring the buyer's independent judgment.[13] Another guideline is intent: even a small gift if given or received with the intent to compromise the buyer's objective decision making is wrong.

In a study of industrial purchasing managers, a majority of them felt that free trips, free meals, and other free entertainment were significant ethical issues. They did, however, make distinctions: a trip to Hawaii and a short fishing trip were clearly two different situations.[14]

Business lunches Discussing business at lunch or dinner may be a very wise sales practice, since the customer may be more attentive to the salesperson's considerations in a relaxed atmosphere than during a hectic business schedule. There are several arguments in favor of buyers and salespeople sharing a

---

[12]See, for example, Solom J. Cooper, "Set Strict Policy for Workers on Accepting Suppliers' Gifts," *Merchandising*, Vol. 9 (April 1984), pp. 80–85.

[13]See Vincent Barry, *Moral Issues in Business*, second edition (Belmont, Calif.: Wadsworth, 1983), p. 247.

[14]See William Rudelius and Rogene A. Buchholz, "Ethical Problems of Purchasing Managers," *Harvard Business Review*, Vol. 57, No. 2 (March–April 1979), p. 8.

business lunch, including the need to get to know each other, the opportunity lunches offer to get away from distractions, and the opportunity to extend your day by conducting business during the lunch hour. On the negative side, some people believe that a business lunch may actually waste time, and some fear that buyers will be influenced by lunches.[15] Clearly, the business lunch can be beneficial; however, it can be abused, and excessive wining and dining may pose some ethical problems.

WHEN SHOULD BUYERS PICK UP THE TAB?

A group of purchasing managers was asked when it was appropriate for purchasers to pick up the tab for a meal with a salesperson. Here are their answers.

- When the eating facilities are in-house at the buying firm.
- When a meal can help get rid of overly persistent salesperson.
- When the salesperson has just lost a big order.
- When the salesperson has just won a big order.
- When the supplier has done something outstanding for the buying firm.
- When the vendor needs a stern lecture about performance.
- When buying firm's personnel attending outnumbers supplier personnel.
- When chance meetings immediately precede or follow a main event at the buying firm.
- When it is a special day for the salesperson.
- When solving problems of the buying firm has already made a number of late-night meals necessary.
- When the buyer's needs have taken up most of the morning.
- When the salesperson is unfamiliar with the area.

SOURCE: Somerby Dowst, "When Should Buyers Pick up the Tab," *Purchasing,* Vol. 90, No. 7 (April 16, 1981), pp. 97–99.

Reciprocity Another ethical question concerns reciprocity, a restraint that is sometimes imposed on the purchasing department. In reciprocity, sources that are themselves customers of the purchasing agent's own firm must be favored. In general, this is an impediment to profitable purchasing because the department is precluded from investigating other sources of supply. In the extreme, this type of buying might even raise the company's purchasing costs. It can also cause complacency in the sellers if they know that they can count on the business.

[15]See Paul J. Halvorson and William Rudelius, "Is There a Free Lunch?" *Journal of Marketing,* Vol. 41, No. 1 (January 1977), pp. 44 – 45.

As a seller you must be careful in using reciprocity as a motive for buying, for it may indicate to buyers that your products or services cannot stand on their own merit. Reciprocity, if overemphasized, becomes a form of industrial blackmail and may actually cause you to lose business. Moreover, if reciprocity is used as a restraint of trade, it may not be legal. Even when

PURCHASING EXECUTIVES' ATTITUDES TOWARD CERTAIN PURCHASING PRACTICES

PRACTICES	PERCENT SEEING ACTIVITY AS AN ETHICAL PROBLEM
1. Acceptance from a supplier of gifts like sales promotion prizes and "purchase volume incentive bonuses."	83
2. Giving a vendor information on competitors' quotations, then allowing him to requote.	77
3. To a supplier, exaggerating the seriousness of a problem in order to get a better price or some other concession.	68
4. Preferential treatment of a supplier who is also a good customer.	65
5. According special treatment to a vendor who is preferred or recommended by higher management.	65
6. Allowing personalities—like of one sales representative or dislike of another—to enter into supplier selection.	63
7. Acceptance of trips, meals, or other free entertainment.	58
8. Seeking information about competitors by questioning suppliers.	42
9. Attempting to avoid a cancellation charge when the cancellation involves an order already being processed by the source.	40
10. Discrimination against a vendor whose salespeople try to deal with other company departments directly rather than go through purchasing.	35
11. To obtain a lower price or other concession, informing an existing supplier that the company may use a second source.	34
12. Solicitation of quotations from new sources, when a marked preference for existing suppliers is the norm, merely to fill a quota for bids.	23
13. Use of the company's buying power to obtain price or other concessions from a vendor.	22

SOURCE: William Rudelius and Rogene A. Buchholz, "Ethical Problems of Purchasing Managers," *Harvard Business Review,* Vol. 57, No. 2 (March–April 1979), p. 12.

The business lunch helps you to understand customers better.

reciprocity is a normal way of doing business, it must be used cautiously. Your products and services should be able to stand on their own merit.

Reciprocal buying has typically been a practice initiated by sellers, but many industrial purchasing managers have begun to use reciprocal arrangements. They usually take one of two forms. In *reverse reciprocity* buyers agree to sell scarce resources to sellers if in return sellers provide back scarce resources.[16] In *time reciprocity,* buyers emphasize their firm's past purchases from the seller to try to get scarce resources from the seller.[17]

Ethical Conduct Toward Your Company

Your relationships with your firm will also present ethical questions. You are on your own much of the time; no one is present to check on what you are doing, the hours you work, or the effort you expend. Furthermore, you often have discretionary control over expenditures for travel and entertainment. Therefore, it is up to you to see that your company receives a fair return on its investment in you. There is potential for ethical problems in personal use of company assets, filling out reports and expense accounts, participating in sales contests, allowing conflict-of-interest situations to develop, changing jobs, and moonlighting.

Personal use of company assets Often salespeople are permitted to use company assets such as automobiles and supplies; or equipment such as mobile telephones, pagers, or recorders. Some firms allow their salespeople to use

[16]See Monroe Bird, "Reverse Reciprocity: A New Twist to Industrial Buying Behavior," *Atlanta Economic Review,* Vol. 26 (1976), pp. 11–13.
[17]See Monroe Bird, "Time Reciprocity: A Possible Answer to Shortages," *Journal of Purchasing and Materials Management,* Vol. 10, No. 4 (November 1974), pp. 46–50.

these things just as if they were their own. Often, however, there are restrictions. For instance, salespeople may be restricted from taking vacations in company cars, or they may be forbidden to put company property to any personal use. Furthermore, because salespeople usually operate without close day-to-day supervision, they have ample opportunity to violate such policies and must take care to avoid temptations.

Filling out reports In filling out reports such as call reports, lost-business reports, and competitive activity reports, you will face ethical questions. Should you paint the real picture in your territory—even though this makes you look bad—or should you cover up to make yourself look good? An ethical report should be objective and honest, regardless of how it reflects on you. Without accurate information, your company will have difficulty correcting the problem. Furthermore, if you have worked hard and honestly, you should have nothing to hide.

Expense accounts Many ethical problems concern submitting expense accounts. Often these are caused by company policies that limit the amount that can be charged or the type of expenses that can be written off. For example, if your firm prohibits alcoholic beverages from being written off and you have a few drinks over dinner with a prospect, should you submit the total for dinner and drinks and indicate that the entire bill was for dinner—hiding the drinks in the total? Similarly, some firms have upper limits on certain types of expenses. Suppose your firm has a $75 per day limit on hotel rooms, and your room costs you $80. Should you pad your meals to make up for the extra $5? Salespeople juggling their expenses to try to comply with company policies may engage in unethical expense account reporting. Falsifying expense accounts can lead to serious problems. In addition to the ethical problems, discovery of this practice can mean dismissal and can hurt your ability to find other employment.

Another ethical issue concerns your use of company samples. Your ethics might be questioned should you pass out too many free samples to friends or relatives, if you give too many samples to customers for their personal use, or if you sell samples and claim that they were lost. Samples have a legitimate business purpose to demonstrate the product and to allow for trial prior to purchase. However, abuse of samples may cut into company sales and profits.

Sales contests Sales contests also offer the potential for some ethical problems. For instance, is it ethical to withhold orders until the start of a sales contest or to overload customers with merchandise simply to do well in a contest?

In some contests that are centered around a particular product, unethical behavior might consist of pushing large amounts of these products on customers, even though they do not need them. These strategies may win the contest, but they may not be in the best interest of the business and may cause hard feelings.

Conflict of interest You are in a conflict-of-interest situation any time you have interests that conflict with those of your company. For instance, suppose you work for ABC Computers, which sells computers and software, and on the side you start a firm to market software. When you discuss software with ABC's customers, you are subject to divided loyalty: should you suggest ABC software or the software of your side business? This sort of situation is not acceptable to most businesses and puts you in a compromised position.

Changing jobs When a sales representative changes jobs, a number of potential ethical questions come up. First, there is the question of how much notice to give the employer. The employer needs enough notice to be able to bring someone in to cover the territory so that customers continue to be serviced properly. On the other hand, you may have a commitment to begin your next selling job right away in order to cover your new territory properly.

If you go to work in the same area for a competing firm, should you try to take customers with you? Clearly, this is done; many of the ethical questions stem from *how* it is done. For instance, at one end of the spectrum you could merely announce you are leaving to go to work for a competitor. On the other end, you could talk against your former employers and their products. The second tactic would seem to pose some ethical questions. Finally, there is the question of what information you can take with you. In your status as an employee, you have had access to certain privileged information that you cannot be expected to forget. However, taking market research reports, customer files and confidential sales reports, and sharing them with your new employer would clearly be unethical. Many firms have handled these issues by having employees sign nondisclosure agreements or restrictive covenants restraining them from taking sales jobs that are directly competitive for a period of time.

Moonlighting Holding several jobs at once may raise some ethical questions if this keeps you from fulfilling your responsibilities to your employer. An outside interest that does not conflict with your job and takes only a few hours a week may cause no problems at all. If you are using time that should be devoted to your primary employer, however, moonlighting is ethically questionable.

Two related areas are carrying additional lines of merchandise and using company time to pursue other outside interests. Some manufacturers' representatives are permitted to carry noncompeting lines as long as they meet their obligations to the main line. A representative who carries men's slacks, for instance, may back up a line of sport shirts. There would be a conflict if the lines overlapped or if carrying another line caused you not to promote your original line sufficiently.

Using company time to pursue outside interests such as getting an MBA degree or a pilot's license, may raise ethical questions. Clearly, many companies sponsor additional education and even pay tuition to encourage salespeople to get MBA degrees; they may even allow courses to be attended on company time. On the other hand, some companies expect the outside classes to be taken at night rather than on company time. You should not take selling time to pursue these interests without your firm's knowledge and endorsement.

Ethical Conduct Toward Competition

When you deal with competitors, the best advice is the golden rule: "Do unto others as you would have them do unto you." You will in this way generate respect from your competitors as well as from your customers, and you may avoid unethical retaliation. Regarding your dealings with competitors, there are two areas of special concern: making untruthful statements and stealing shelf space.

Untruthful statements An ethical aspect of dealing with competitors is to make no untruthful statements about your competitor's offerings. Although such statements may bring a quick sale, they can backfire on you. Once customers find out you have lied to them, they will lose trust and respect for you, and your reputation will be damaged.

Stealing shelf space Shelf space in many retail stores is essential to making sales. Some salespeople have been known to expand their share of shelf space and decrease their competitor's share by placing competing products in the back or crowding them together. In addition to the ethical considerations of stealing shelf space, there is a strong probability of retaliation by competitors, and you may find your products pushed to the back of the shelf.

TABLE 17.4

SOME ETHICAL CONSIDERATIONS FOR SALESPEOPLE

---

1. You have invited a prospective customer out to lunch. Your firm does not permit more than one alcoholic drink per individual to be charged to the company's expense account at lunch. You and the customer have several drinks. You feel that you could hide the extra drinks in another part of the expense account and that you should be fully reimbursed for an expense you feel is truly part of doing business. What do you do?
2. You have a chance to win a large contract from the army that would mean a great deal to you and your company. The contract officer indicates that he would be positively influenced by a substantial "gift." What do you do?
3. A competitor is planning to announce a new product feature to a selected set of customers in his suite at a trade show. You feel that it would not be difficult to send a spy to learn what the new feature is. What do you do?
4. You firmly believe that the product you are selling is a high-quality item. However, at times you find yourself making a claim about the product that might be difficult to substantiate. You are quite sure the odds are slim that the customer would find out about your stretching the truth. What do you do?
5. You are a retail salesperson selling men's suits. A customer has just tried on a suit that obviously does not fit him. However, you feel that if you tell him it looks as though it was made for him, he would buy it. What do you do?

SOURCE: Several of these have been taken from Philip Kotler, *Marketing Management: Analysis Planning and Control,* second edition (Englewood Cliffs, N.J.: Prentice-Hall, 1972), p. 839.

The moral standards of salespeople vary just as do those of the rest of society. Most sales representatives are extremely ethical; others, unfortunately, are just the opposite. Although some sales representatives have done things they are not proud of, most of them try to maintain a set of values worthy of emulation. Table 17.4 presents a list of five difficult ethical considerations that many sales representatives face daily.[18] Before reading on, examine this list and take a stand on each consideration.

A CODE OF CONDUCT FOR THE SALESPERSON

In order to be ethical in your actions, you may wish to develop your own personal code of ethics. This code may differ, depending on the type of sales job you have, but you may find helpful as a starting point the code provided in Table 17.5. At the very least this code will make you aware of some of the activities that require careful managing if you are to maintain your ethics.

TABLE 17.5

GUIDELINES FOR ETHICAL BEHAVIOR

In order to act in an ethical manner, you should
- Avoid giving any gift, entertainment, bribe, or kickback that would unduly influence a customer or prospect.
- Avoid misrepresenting your company's offerings to your customers or prospects.
- Not use excessive pressure when dealing with prospects.
- Exercise great care in stressing reciprocity as a buying motive.
- Avoid disclosing any information that is proprietary to your company or your customers.
- Avoid using company assets for your own personal use unless this is expressly allowed.
- Make your reports and paperwork, including expense accounts, accurate and honest.
- Not engage in outside activities that would put you in a conflict-of-interest position.
- Avoid using your selling time to promote any outside interests.
- Avoid temptations to overload your customers or falsify your performance when participating in sales contests.
- Treat your firm fairly when changing jobs.
- Avoid speaking untruthfully or negatively about competitors.
- Always treat competitors the way you would want to be treated.

[18]For another interesting list of ethical questions, see Robert M. Mueier, "Test Your Integrity," _Success,_ Vol. 31, No. 8 (August 1984), pp. 31–33.

SUMMARY

Sales activity is regulated by federal, state, and local laws aimed at protecting competitive efforts and consumers' rights. Because this legal framework directly and indirectly affects the activities of salespeople, they should be aware and knowledgeable about the effects and consequences of the laws.

Government regulation of business activities has increased greatly since 1900. As an example, the Sherman Act (1890) states that "Every contract, combination in the form of trust or otherwise, or conspiracy, in restraint of trade or commerce . . ." is illegal. In contrast, the Robinson–Patman Act (1936) indicates that a person or company is guilty of price discrimination if the effects of such an act may be to substantially lessen competition or tend to create a monopoly in any line of commerce.

In addition, many other laws have been passed to provide further protection for the final consumer. These include the Federal Trade Commission (FTC) Act, federal consumer protection legislation, the Uniform Commercial Code (UCC), and state consumer protection legislation. It is important for the salesperson to be aware of certain types of activities that have become illegal.

A number of ethical questions for the salesperson were also discussed, and several ethical dilemmas were explored. You have ethical responsibilities toward your customers, your firm, and your competition; if you do not act in a professional, ethical manner, any short-term success will inevitably become long-term failure. With respect to your customers, you must be trustworthy, be judicious in the amount of pressure you apply, avoid misrepresentation, use discretion, avoid bribes, and use gifts and entertainment and business lunches carefully. Finally, you should exercise caution in dealing with accounts for which reciprocity is an issue. Concerning your company, you should be honest and open when using company assets, filling out reports and expense accounts, participating in sales contests, and changing jobs. You should also exercise caution if you moonlight, and you should avoid conflicts of interest. Finally, with respect to your competition, you should not make untruthful statements and or steal shelf space.

You, like your company, can survive and succeed only by maintaining standards above the legal must—must not and the ethical ought—ought not levels. The implication is that you must be a professional. Your conduct must be worthy of copying.

PROBLEMS

1. Outline a speech entitled, "The Legal Responsibilities of Salespeople."
2. How does federal legislation affect pricing practices by the salesperson's firm?
3. What aspects of the relationship of salespeople with their customers are affected by the Uniform Commercial Code?
4. Why is ethical behavior important for salespeople?
5. What are some of the ethical responsibilities salespeople have toward customers?

Objective: To gain increased insight regarding ethics and the law regarding selling

PART A Self-Analysis
Set forth in ought—ought not form your own code of personal ethics. Do the items of your code contrast with items of the code most businesspeople have adopted for themselves? If there are differences between the two sets of ethics, explain why you feel they exist.

PART B Salesperson Analysis
Make arrangements to interview a salesperson in your community. Try to determine the following.

1. What does the person know about the federal and state laws that govern selling behavior?
2. Does the salesperson feel that new laws should be passed to regulate selling? If so, what would these laws cover?
3. Does the salesperson feel that some of the existing laws governing salespeople should be eliminated? If so, which laws should be eliminated and why?
4. Does the salesperson feel that *other* salespeople are at times unethical? What does the person feel can be done about such practices if they occur?
5. Does the salesperson feel that customers are at times unethical? Have them explain.

Be very tactful when holding this interview, for many of these matters are quite delicate.

Case 17–1 The Singing Cow Dairy Company
The Singing Cow Dairy Company, located in Jollyville, Texas, was founded by Sam Fulcher, the owner of the Blue Ribbon Ranch. The company started as a family operation and sold a small line of dairy products to local retail stores. When Sam Fulcher died, his son, David, inherited the factory and decided to initiate an expansion program.

The Singing Cow Dairy products were well known within a 100-mile radius of Jollyville. The quality of the products and the reputation of the Fulcher family granted Singing Cow a stable market in that area. The same was not true, however, of the rest of the state, because Sam Fulcher had never believed in advertising; he relied solely on word-of-mouth communication to establish his demand.

David felt that his father's traditional business approach had limited the expansion of the firm. He believed that an intensive sales effort with retailers of major outlets in all large cities in Texas was necessary in order to gain their support and secure shelf space for the firm's products.

461

In order to accomplish this, David hired Thomas Achabal, an ambitious young man with a master's degree and five years of sales experience in the grocery business. Tom was given the responsibility of motivating the existing salespeople to pursue aggressively the major retail supermarket outlets in the state and secure their orders, as well as to obtain good shelf space for Singing Cow products. He was also told to hire additional salespersons to cover the rest of the Texas territory.

The Singing Cow products were priced slightly above average, and quantity discounts were granted. The product lines were available to any retailer in the state for the same price. The firm calculated a uniform markup for all their products, which allowed them to absorb freight and shipping charges regardless of the distance covered.

Approximately two months after he had started the new sales program, Tom Achabal received a long-distance call from one of his more abitious salespeople, Katherine Bentley. Katherine had been assigned the Lake Jackson territory and had already been successful in selling the firm's product line to several small retailers in the area.

Katherine was calling to obtain Mr. Achabal's permission to grant a special price reduction to a chain of food stores in that area. According to Ms. Bentley, the manager of the stores was willing to "deal" and to give Singing Cow products a very desirable shelf location, provided that he could have a special price on the products. Tom had been hoping to get a chance to obtain this support of a major retail chain in southeastern Texas, and the proposition seemed appealing. The discount would probably allow the chain to compete in price with the small retail stores in the area, but Achabal was more interested in the retail chain's support than in potential sales to small retailers. For all these reasons, he told Katherine to accept the proposition and grant the new customer a special discount of 15 percent.

Two weeks later, Tom Achabal met with David Fulcher to give him a first progress report on his activities. At that time, he was very proud to be able to report that the cooperation of a major food retail chain had been secured, and he explained the special conditions of the sale. He was very careful to mention, however, that the discount granted was a unique case, and a similar situation would not occur in the future. Fulcher was furious when he heard the story and fired Tom Achabal on the spot.

1. What was wrong with Achabal's decision?
2. Is it an unethical practice to allow large store chains to sell products at lower prices than the small competitors?

Case 17–2 The Great Electrical Conspiracy[19]

Flint Fletcherson was a senior salesperson for a large electrical firm. He had been with the company for ten years; before this he had been an honor engineering student at the University of Michigan. Flint had worked hard and was recognized as one of the company's "coming young men." He had sold for several of the firm's divisions but was currently selling their switch gear.

---

[19]This case is taken in part from "The Incredible Electrical Conspiracy," by Richard A. Smith, published in *Fortune*, Vol. 63, No. 4 (April 1961 and May 1961).

Flint was asked to attend a conference at which some very delicate matters would be discussed. After being sworn to secrecy, Flint was briefed by an aide to the sales manager's boss, Chuck Lewis. The conversation was as follows:

CHUCK: As you know, business has been very hard these last few months. Prices have fallen a great deal. If we had not decided to take rather bold action, the firm's profits would have dropped, and that $8000 bonus you received last year would have been in jeopardy.

FLINT: I am aware of the very tough competition we have faced. It seems that everyone wants too big a piece of the action.

CHUCK: Yes, this is correct. As a result we have contracted several of our competitiors and have asked them to meet with us in Portland next week. At that time we will try to reactivate a plan that gives us each a predetermined share of the market. As you may know, we have had this arrangement now for several years.

FLINT: I really did not know, Chuck; I had heard rumors like everyone else, but I really did not believe it.

CHUCK: When the plan is working, every ten days to two weeks a meeting is called to decide who gets the next order. Turns are decided by the ledger list, and the only decision that has to be made is the price the firm that is to "win" should submit.

FLINT: Isn't this illegal? What happens if you are caught?

CHUCK: First, you will never be caught, and second, it may be illegal but it certainly is not unethical. We certainly have never charged an unfairly high price for our product.

FLINT: Why are you telling me all this?

CHUCK: It should be obvious to you by now. We have decided to make you our representative to the weekly meetings where this actual price is set for the next contract. Of course, you will still be expected to handle your day-to-day sales activities, but you will receive a substantial salary adjustment at the end of the year. In addition, if you carry out this job effectively, I feel you will receive a promotion fairly quickly.

FLINT: How much of this is going on in the company now?

CHUCK: It is really difficult to say. It is not the type of thing we talk about regularly at staff meetings, but it certainly is quite pervasive in the industry.

FLINT: Well, I will have to think about it.

CHUCK: I understand; but whatever you decide, do not mention any of this to anyone.

FLINT: Okay.

1. Is the plan that has been discussed illegal? If so, under what statutes?
2. Is this plan unethical? Explain.
3. What should Flint do?

Career
Management

After you have studied this chapter, you should be able to

1. Develop a self-audit.
2. Specify the steps in securing your first selling position.
3. Identify career opportunities in selling and management.
4. Understand the importance of career planning.
5. Recognize the importance of continued growth.
6. Describe the activities that will help you to continue self-development.

Managing your career in selling consists of three principal activities: seeking your initial personal selling position, analyzing various career opportunities or career paths, and continuing your education to upgrade your skills and keep yourself well informed.

If these activities are planned and carefully managed rather than carried out haphazardly, the time spent on them can pay handsome dividends in success and satisfaction.

FINDING YOUR INITIAL PERSONAL SELLING POSITION

To find your first personal selling position, you may take the following steps: conduct a self-audit, prospect for positions, develop a resume, write a cover letter, fill out application forms, prepare for interviews, handle interviews, follow through, visit the company, and accept the offer. You should perform each of these activities carefully, with an eye toward marketing yourself to prospective companies.

Self-Audit

The first step in finding a position is to conduct a self-audit in order to determine what type of sales position you are seeking. As this book points out, sales positions vary widely; they have different types of products, different responsibilities, and different types of customers. An honest self-analysis will ensure that you apply for sales positions whose products you can believe in, whose daily routines you can enjoy, and whose customers you will feel comfortable with.

A self-audit also provides you with an opportunity to think about yourself, in terms of strengths and weaknesses. You can then respond more easily to interview questions during the job-hunting process.

Another good strategy is to have someone else evaluate you. Often you are not as objective about yourself as someone else might be. Thus, you may want to have a friend, teacher, parent, or someone else evaluate your strengths and weaknesses. They may be able to provide you with insight on career opportunities and strong points that you might overlook.

In conducting a self-audit, you determine your strengths and weaknesses, likes and dislikes, and other characteristics.

Strengths and weaknesses The first step is to determine your strengths and weaknesses. When looking for a position, you should concentrate on those that will capitalize on your strengths and for which your weaknesses will not be a detriment. It is important to remember that your strengths and weaknesses are always judged in relation to the particular position you are seeking. Thus, you may have the technical capability to sell copying machines, but you may lack the technical capability for selling computers.

The more you have thought about your background and strengths, the better you will be at selling yourself. Don't forget such experiences as part-time jobs, service to student organizations, or leadership positions; these often require contacting people and selling yourself. Be sure to consider courses you have taken to prepare yourself for a selling career. They are evidence of your commitment and genuine interest in preparing yourself. Although you should not oversell these activities, they do show that you have planned your career. It is important that you indicate how this background and experience will help you perform better in the position you are applying for.

Likes and dislikes Your likes and dislikes are another area of personal assessment. You can include here particular types of products or services you enjoy or are interested in. For example, if you are very interested in athletics, working for a sporting goods manufacturer might be interesting. Working for a firm whose products interest you will make you enthusiastic and will make working fun. You should also assess the types of people you enjoy and feel comfortable around. Some people feel very comfortable around executives, whereas others—because of their backgrounds, personalities, and interests— would feel much more comfortable selling equipment to farmers. The important thing is to try to capitalize on aspects of people and products in which you have a special interest and that will give you an advantage over others.

You should be careful not to restrict yourself too much. For instance, if you are interested in and have experience in the grocery business, you could work for a food broker, for a manufacturer, for an advertising agency with food or grocery accounts, and for other related firms. Similarly, if you are interested in hospitality, you might work for a travel agent, a hotel, an airline, a convention service, or a restaurant. Use your interest as a starting point, but be creative.

You will also have likes and dislikes about geographical locations, amount of travel, degree of supervision, and the amount of time you are willing to commit to your job. You should be honest with yourself about these things but not overly restrictive. If you get a position in which you dislike what you are doing, you will be unhappy and probably will not perform very well.

Questions for the self-audit Table 18.1 lists a number of questions you should ask yourself in assessing your capabilities and interests. Answer each question carefully. This information will be useful to you in thinking about your strengths and weaknesses and in planning your career.

Prospecting for Positions

Taking into account your strengths and weaknesses and your likes and dislikes, you should try to seek out sources of potential positions. Much like selling anything else, this is the prospecting stage. You may wish to develop a list of target companies that offer the type of sales positions and the career opportunities you are seeking. Then you can look for key contacts, references, employees, and people who know these companies, who can provide you with information, and who can help you make contacts.[1]

---

[1]Burton E. Tepman, *The Professional Job Search Program: How to Market Yourself* (New York: Wiley, 1983), p. 65.

TABLE 18.1

QUESTIONS YOU MAY ASK AS A GUIDE TO SELF-ASSESSMENT

1. What are your principal strong points?
2. What are your principal shortcomings?
3. What do you like best about yourself?
4. What do you like least about yourself?
5. Describe the most rewarding experience you have had in a job or in school.
6. Describe the least rewarding or most frustrating experience you have had.
7. In relation to other college students, rate yourself with respect to your

	ABOVE AVERAGE	AVERAGE	BELOW AVERAGE
Intelligence	_____	_____	_____
Verbal capabilities	_____	_____	_____
Breadth of interests	_____	_____	_____
Dependability	_____	_____	_____
Enthusiasm	_____	_____	_____
Ambition	_____	_____	_____

8. What are your career objectives? Where do you want to be five or ten years from now?
9. Write a paragraph describing your personality as you see it, and comment on how your perceptions of "you" compare with others' perceptions of you.
10. What have you done to prepare yourself for a sales position?
11. List the things you are really looking for in a position.
12. What don't you want in a position?

Some sources of opportunities include placement bureaus; newspapers; trade journals; friends, relatives, and acquaintances; professors; and former employers. Although this list is not exhaustive, it does give you some useful leads in identifying position opportunities.[2]

Placement bureaus Most universities and community colleges have placement bureaus where prospective employers interview prospective graduates. You should carefully consider the companies that come to your school's placement bureau and review posted sales positions to see whether any are attractive to you.

Newspapers The help-wanted section of the newspaper also lists sales positions. When examining these opportunities, try to judge whether they require experience. Even when ads say that experience is necessary, inexperienced applicants sometimes get the job. Experience in professional clubs, being an officer in fraternities or sororities, and work on a college newpaper can some-

[2]Among the several sources available to tell you about potential sales jobs are *Career Opportunity Index* (Fountain Valley, Calif. 1986) and *CPC Annual,* twenty-ninth edition (Bethlehem, Pa.: College Placement Council, Inc., 1985–1986).

The Help Wanted section can be a source of leads about sales jobs.

times be good substitutes for work experience if the applicant has other good qualities.

Trade journals If you are interested in a specific type of employment, you may wish to consult a trade journal for that industry. These might be available in your library, or you may have to borrow recent issues from someone in the industry. You might also consult the *Ayer Directory of Publications* to find the trade journals for the industry that interests you. It may even be a good investment to subscribe to a trade journal if you are rather certain you want employment in the industry. Many of these magazines contain a job listing section.

Friends, relatives, acquaintances Friends, relatives, or other acquaintances can also be good sources of opportunities. Often positions are not widely advertised, and your contacts can give you an inside advantage. You should let people know that you are looking for a position and what you are looking for.

Professors Prospective employers will often contact instructors to inform them of openings. If you are intersted in a specific type of sales position, let your instructors know so they can keep you in mind when opportunities become available.

Former employers If you have held part-time or summer positions, you should consult your former employers, who may have contacts or know of positions for which you would be qualified. If the opportunity is in a line of business where you have had previous experience, you may have an advantage over other candidates.

Resume

A resume is a valuable asset in your search for a position. You should carefully organize your resume, customize it as much as possible, and try to make it visually attractive. Your resume is like an advertisement for you. It is often the first thing prospective employers see, and if it does not catch their attention, you may not be considered further. Thus the purpose of a resume is to gain an employer's attention and get you an interview.[3]

Important headings for your resume are your name and address, objective, education, employment, activites, interests, and references. Figure 18.1 shows a sample resume.

Name and address When listing your address, provide your school address and a permanent address such as your parents' address, so that job recruiters will be able to find you. You should also include relevant telephone numbers.

Objectives Your career objective is another component of your resume. When seeking your first position, you will find this statement particularly difficult to formulate because you may be exploring several different types of sales positions. You have two options: placing the objective on the resume or including it in your cover letter. Putting it in your cover letter has the advantage of flexibility, since you can tailor your objective to reflect the specific job you are seeking. This is important, because an objective that sounds too vague or ambiguous may indicate a lack of career direction to prospective employers. Thus, if you put your objective on your resume, you might want to develop several objective statements to fit several different career options.

Your objective should be a concise statement of what you want to do and what you have to offer an employer: for example, "A position as a sales representative with a pharmaceutical house that will utilize my chemistry background and my ability to work on a self-directed basis in managing a sales territory."[4] Your objective should be centered on what you can do for the employer. The more you can customize the objective to the employer, the better. This may mean that you have to have several different versions of your resume.

Education When highlighting your education, you should stress your accomplishments and the courses you took to prepare you for the job you are seeking. List the names of the schools you have attended, degrees you hold, your major, special courses, and your awards.

---

[3]For a good discussion of developing a resume, see J. T. Biegeleisen, *Job Resumes* (New York: Grosset and Dunlap, 1982).

[4]See Ronald L. Krannich and William J. Banis, *High Impact Resumes and Letters* (Chesapeake, Va.: Progressive Concepts Incorporated, 1982), p. 6.

YOUR NAME

Campus Address
1101 Michigan Avenue #420
Arizona State University
Tempe, Arizona 85287
(602) 652-4762

Permanent Address
10 Secretariat
Grosse Pointe Woods, Michigan 48236
(313) 838-6002

Job Objective: A position as a sales representative with a computer company that will enable me to utilize my marketing and computer background.

Education: B.A. in Business Administration
Major: Marketing
Arizona State University, Tempe, AZ
Grade Point Average: 3.5 (4.0 index)

Job-related courses include:
Principles of Selling, Sales Management, Industrial Marketing, Interpersonal Communications, Speech, Nonverbal Communications, Computer programming courses in Basic, COBOL, and Fortran, Computer Information Systems.

Employment: ARIZONA STATE UNIVERSITY   1983–1986
Student employment in computer laboratory. Assisted other students in running programs.

NANTUCKET YACHT CLUB   Summers 1983–1986
Waiter. Worked with executive-type members; developed people skills.

Activities: Marketing Club, Secretary
Pi Sigma Epsilon: developed a sales plan for selling raffle tickets. Sold 52 tickets, first place in 1983 pledge class.

References: Available upon request

FIGURE 18.1 Sample resume.

Employment When describing your previous employment, be sure to list part-time and summer jobs and, where possible, show their relevance to the job you are seeking. For instance, if you had a part-time job as a waiter or waitress in a restaurant, you might indicate that you learned to work with people, handled customer complaints, and actively sold menu items. You should also list any usable work skills you acquired, such as typing or computer operation.

"*Your curriculum vitae is extremely detailed, isn't it? I don't quite know what to make of the fact that your third-grade teacher, Miss Hartley, made you stand in the corner for throwing an eraser although another kid did it.*"

"Drawing by Handelsman © 1986, The New Yorker."

When describing your work experience, even part-time jobs, use action verbs such as "organized, increased, administered, designed, directed, and initiated" if they are applicable.[5]

Activities and interests The activities listed on a resume are school activities, clubs, and outside activities that you have participated in. Wherever possible, you should try to relate these to the position you are seeking. When deciding which activities to list, you should consider how they will relate to your objective. Membership in a marketing club or professional sales fraternity such as Pi Sigma Epsilon can be related directly to sales positions. It is generally better to have held leadership positions in a few affiliations than to have joined a number of clubs without actively participating. When you list your activities, you should also describe any key accomplishments that are career-positive. If you were a member of a selling fraternity, for instance, you might

[5]See J. T. Biegeleisen, *Job Resumes* (New York: Grosset & Dunlap, 1982), p. 17.

have participated in an activity that might be stated, "developed sales plan for selling magazine advertising for the campus newspaper; sold over $5000 of space." These kinds of activities are valuable even if they are not full-time jobs.

Interests, an optional category, might include hobbies, sports, musical pursuits, and other pastimes. These should be related, if possible, to the position you are seeking. Your interests may also be a source of conversation in an interview. If interests are not related to the position you are seeking, they should be included only if space permits.

References As a general rule, the references line on your resume should state "References available upon request." Generally, references are not sought until an employer has screened the applicants to a few people. References should be typed on a separate sheet of paper, and each must be complete and accurate, including name, title, address, and telephone number. You should also contact references to make sure that it is appropriate to list them. It is also a good idea to send your references a resume so they can give a knowledgeable recommendation.

Cover Letter

Your resume is always accompanied by a one-page cover letter. This letter should be a typed original customized for the specific company you are applying to; it should not be a form letter. As with other paperwork generated in the employment-seeking process, your letter should be free of typographical or grammatical errors and poor English.

The first paragraph of your cover letter should explain why you are asking for an interview. The middle paragraphs should highlight your qualifications, and your closing paragraph should suggest possible arrangements for an interview.[6]

It is important that the cover letter get the reader's attention and highlight the key benefits you could offer an employer. Thus you would be wise to devote considerable time and effort to wording your cover letter properly.

Figure 18.2 gives several guidelines for developing an effective cover letter.

Application Form

Often you will be asked to fill out an application form before being interviewed. You should fill it out accurately and completely. In order to do this, it is useful to develop a list of previous jobs, your social security number, names and addresses of references, and other pertinent information. You should also be careful to fill out the forms neatly. The appearance of the form will affect the impact of the application. A form that is carelessly filled out and sloppy will hurt your evaluation. One sales manager indicated that she views the application as an example of the best paperwork the applicant will ever turn in. Thus, if the application is sloppy, incomplete, and contains

[6]See Adele Lewis, *How to Write a Better Resume* (Woodbury, N.Y.: Barron's Educational Series, 1977), pp. 6–8.

1. *Type* on good-quality *bond paper*.
2. Address to a *specific name* and *title*. If you are uncertain whom to address, look in library reference materials or call the company and ask the receptionist for an appropriate name and title. For openers, tell the receptionist: "I am sending some important papers to the head of the _____ Department. However, I'm not sure I have the correct name and address. Could you please tell me to whom I should address these documents?"
3. Writing style should be direct, powerful, and error-free. Edit to eliminate extraneous words and check grammar, spelling, and punctuation. In addition to stating your purpose, the letter tells the reader how well you communicate.
4. Use only one page. Do not overwhelm the resume with a lengthy cover letter or excessive repetition of the resume content.
5. Keep the letter short and to the point. Three paragraphs will suffice:
   Paragraph 1: State your interest and purpose.
   Paragraph 2: Highlight your enclosed resume by stressing what you will do for the employer.
   Paragraph 3: Request an interview and indicate that you will call for an appointment.
6. Use appropriate language. Repeat terms the employer uses. Avoid jargon and the passive voice. Use action verbs as well as the active voice. Don't try to be cute or too aggressive.
7. Always be positive by stressing your past accomplishments and skills as well as your future value.

FIGURE 18.2 Cover letter rules. SOURCE: Ronald L. Krannich and William J. Banis, *High Impact Resumes and Letters* (Manassas, Va.: Impact Publications, 1982), pp. 86–87.

grammatical mistakes, reports that she and the customer could expect from the applicant after hiring would probably be of the same poor quality.

Preparing for the Interview

In addition to the self-audit, you should also prepare for the interview. Proper interview preparation gives you several advantages. First, because you will not have to waste valuable time in the interview finding out general information, you will have extra time in which to sell yourself. Futhermore, by anticipating possible negative aspects of your background that may come up, you can prepare appropriate responses and avoid possible embarrassment.[7] Preparation for the interview includes researching the prospective employer, deciding which aspects of yourself to stress, formulating answers to prospective questions, and practicing the interview.

Research the prospective employer In order to prepare for the interview properly, you must know as much as you can about the firm interviewing you. The more you know about the company, the more confident you will

[7]See Tom Jackson, *Guerrilla Tactics in the Job Market* (Toronto: Bantam Books, 1978), p. 241.

be, and the more you can show the interviewer that you are interested. You can obtain information about companies, their policies, products, industry information, and more from the library. Reading the firm's annual reports and talking to people who work for the company or to its customers will furnish valuable information. Often in school you are assigned projects requiring you to find out about a company or an industry. This same sort of research will help you prepare for your interview.

The *College Placement Council Annual* is an excellent source of information on employers who traditionally seek entry-level college graduates. Volume 1 provides guidelines for seeking a job; Volume 2 lists administrative–business and other career options.[8] For recent information on the company, you can go to the library and use sources such as the *F & S Index of Corporations and Industries* or the *Business Periodicals Index*.

Decide what to stress Another step of interview preparation is deciding which aspects of yourself to stress. Although each interviewer and each company wants something special or unique, it is useful to know what interviewers look for in a prospective job applicant.

One study examined the personal traits that marketing and sales managers look for in applicants coming out of school. This study, outlined in Table 18.2, revealed several interesting findings. First, a very high rating is given to personal traits such as maturity, appearance, and cooperativeness. Second, outside activities, such as fraternities, hobbies, and sports, were given relatively low ratings. Third, personal selling skills were rated very high. Finally, many nonmarketing skills such as public speaking, writing, and management skills were rated very highly. This information can be useful to you in deciding which of your strong points to stress to recruiters. Although, all recruiters will not value the same traits, you can get some idea of the importance of various traits by examining the table.

Formulate answers to prospective questions It is important that you prepare answers to questions you are likely to be asked. This step ensures that you will have thought through some questions and will not be surprised or give inappropriate answers. If you have thought carefully about your answers you will also be more confident.

Table 18.3 provides a list of questions interviewers are likely to ask. You should prepare answers to each of these questions so that you will not be surprised in an interview. This list should be useful in practicing your skills as an interviewee. You may also wish to write out answers to these questions.

Practice being interviewed There are several ways to practice being interviewed. One method is to think through a typical interview, anticipating questions, developing answers for these questions, and thinking about questions you would ask. Another method is to have a friend interview you. Give the person a list of questions and role-play the interview as though the friend

[8]See *CPC Annual,* twenty-ninth edition (Bethlehem, Pa.: College Placement Council, Inc., 1985–1986).

TABLE 18.2

HIRING CRITERIA AS SEEN BY MANAGERS

RANK	CHARACTERISTIC[a]	VARIABLE	MEAN SCORE[b]
1	P	Maturity	3.68
2	M	Personal selling/sales management skills	3.67
3	P	Appearance	3.60
4	P	Cooperativeness	3.54
5	N	Communications/public speaking	3.45
6	P	Disposition	3.34
7	P	Punctuality	3.30
8	P	Mannerisms	3.28
9	M	General marketing skills	3.21
10	N	English/writing skills	3.14
11	N	Management skills	2.89
12	P	Extroversion	2.74
13	S	Marketing department reputation	2.60
14	M	Product development/management skills	2.59
15	N	Finance skills	2.55
16	M	Market research skills	2.51
17	M	Market logistics skills	2.49
18	N	Personnel management skills	2.48
19	O	Civic functions	2.48
20	N	Management science skills	2.47
21	M	Advertising/advertising management skills	2.45
22	M	Consumer/industrial buyer behavior skills	2.38
23	S	School reputation	2.38
24	M	Pricing skills	2.36
25	N	Accounting skills	2.36
26	S	Internship program	2.34
27	O	Social functions	2.30
28	S	Recruiting success with school	2.21
29	N	Internship training skills	2.19
30	O	Sports participation	2.10
31	M	Retailing/retail management skills	1.99
32	O	Home hobbies	1.99
33	O	Fraternal organizations	1.99
34	N	Social sciences/arts skills	1.93

[a]P, personal traits; M, marketing skills; N, nonmarketing skills; S, school reputation; O, outside activities.

[b]Based on a scale where 1 = no importance and 4 = very important.

SOURCE: Kenneth C. Schneider, "Personal Traits Most Important to Potential Employers," *Marketing News,* Vol. 12, No. 2 (January 23, 1978), p. 5. Reprinted from *Marketing News,* published by the American Marketing Association.

were the interviewer and you were being interviewed. Finally, you may tape-record the interview: either ask the questions yourself and then answer them, or have a friend ask the questions and then analyze your responses.[9]

The Interview
The interview is a crucial step in the employment-seeking process. Outlined in the following paragraphs are tips for the interview, kinds of interviews,

[9]See Caryl Ray Krannich, *Interview for Success* (Virginia Beach, Va. Impact Publications, 1982), p. 48.

TABLE 18.3
QUESTIONS FREQUENTLY ASKED IN INTERVIEWS

Following are some questions commonly asked in an employment interview. Keep in mind that the interviewer may be more interested in your *reaction* to some questions than in the actual answers you give.

1. What are your long-range career objectives?
2. What have you done to prepare yourself for a sales career?
3. Why did you choose a career in sales?
4. What do you consider to be your greatest strengths and weaknesses?
5. How would you describe yourself?
6. Why should I hire you?
7. In what ways do you think you can make a contribution to our company?
8. What percentage of your college expenses did you earn? How?
9. What two or three accomplishments have given you the most satisfaction? Why?
10. How do you feel about working overtime?
11. What college subjects did you like best? Least? Why?
12. Do you have plans for continued study? An advanced degree?
13. Do you think your grades are a good indication of your academic achievement?
14. What have you learned from participation in extracurricular activities?
15. How do you spend your spare time? What are your hobbies?
16. What have you done that shows initiative and willingness to work?
17. Why did you decide to seek a position with this company?
18. What do you know about our company?
19. Do you have a geographical preference? Why?
20. How much are you willing to travel?
21. What job have you liked best? Least? Why?
22. Which of your job supervisors have you liked most? Least? Why?
23. What do you see yourself doing five years from now?

SOURCE: Adapted from *Questions . . . The Key to the Interview* (Tempe, Ariz.: Career Services, Arizona State University, 1975).

patterns of interviews, key questions you are likely to be asked, and questions you can ask in the interview.

Tips for interviews Punctuality is important. If you arrive late, no matter how good your reason, you may damage your chances of getting a job. Thus, always try to arrive early for your interview. You can use the time before the interview begins for extra preparation and for reviewing key aspects of the company.

During the interview you should be aware of your nonverbal communication. Your posture should be such that you appear attentive and relaxed. Avoid fumbling with your hands, clenching your fists, or giving other signs of tension; you should also maintain good eye contact with the interviewer.

Your dress and appearance are important. You should dress conservatively to convey maturity and judgment to the interviewer. You may want to

The interview is an important part of the career hunting process.

review the dressing guidelines in Chapter 9. Good grooming is also important.

You should make every effort to remember the interviewer's name, although you should not use a first name unless invited to do so. Remembering the name shows you are paying attention, allows you to personalize your interview, and is essential if you are going to follow up with a letter.

Although the interviewer controls the questions in the interview, you control the answers. Thus, you must structure your answers to sell yourself and your ability to handle the position.[10] This involves taking your past experience and accomplishments and translating them into benefits for the prospective employer. You do this by showing how these attributes will help you be a better salesperson for the company.

Kinds of interviews There are three kinds of interviews: initial screening interviews, interviews with members of management, and interviews with salespeople.

The initial screening is frequently done at the firm's personnel office or at your school's placement bureau by people who talk with candidates and ask them to fill out application forms. The objectives of this interview are to determine whether you meet the general requirements, to furnish you with information you need for decision making, and to suggest what subsequent steps are appropriate.

Some firms may not use personnel staff members for this initial interviewing. One very successful department store uses only operating managers

[10]See, for example, John Bremner, "Words for Selling Yourself; Turn Misuse and Abuse into Deft Effective Sparkle," *Marketing Times,* Vol. 28 (March–April, 1981), pp. 40 – 43.

to do college recruiting, feeling that students want to talk with the people
who are actually running the business.

From your perspective, it is critically important to understand not only
that the firm is trying to make a sound hiring decision, but also that you are
making a vocational decision. First impressions count a great deal. Frequently, the first interview will take no more than fifteen to thirty minutes.
You should be neat and polite, but not shy. Managers who are considering
candidates for a sales position expect them to be well prepared, well
groomed, and enthusiastic.

Most firms will also want you to visit with several members of the company's management—usually the sales manager, assistants, and possibly the
director of marketing. These contacts are important because frequently more
than one person in the organization will be involved in deciding whether to
offer you a position. It may be that the sales manager is looking for a first-
rate career salesperson, whereas the marketing manager wants someone who
would stay in sales for a few years only and then move into product management or advertising. In addition, various members of the management team
will have different slants on company needs, and this diversity will help the
interviewee to understand the organizational dynamics of the firm.

No matter how hard management tries to give the prospective employee
a good understanding of the sales position, no one can do it as well as an
experienced sales representative. Many organizations will ask you to spend
two days visiting the firm. On the first day you will meet with the management, and the second day is spent traveling with a salesperson. This system
gives a good understanding of the position. Even though you do not accept
the position, the day that you spend working with a salesperson will usually
prove to be a very valuable experience.

Patterns of the interview Not all interviews follow the same pattern, but a
common format spends the first few minutes of the interview on greetings and
some general questions about background designed to put the interviewee at
ease. For instance, the interviewer might say,"I see from your resume that
you are a skier; where do you like to ski?"

The next portion of the interview often takes one of two forms. Sometimes the interviewer will give you a brief description of the company and
the position, and then ask you specific questions to see what kind of a match
there is between your qualifications and the position. Sometimes these items
are reversed, and the interviewer first asks you questions and then tells you
about the company. There is usually also a limited amount of time for you to
ask questions. The final portion of the interview usually consists of either a
thank-you or a statement of the next step in the interviewing process.

Key questions One question that is often asked is "Tell me about yourself."
If you have prepared and have taken an assessment of yourself, of the company, and of the job, you can really sell yourself rather than just providing
information that is available on your resume. "Try to formulate an answer to
this question *before* you go into the interview so that you can jump right into

it. It is actually a terrific opportunity to take charge of the interview and talk about your strengths."[11]

Another question that sometimes comes up is "Tell me about a weakness of yours." It is important to have thought about this so that you do not blurt out something that will hamper your ability to get a position. You want to show that you have thought about your weaknesses, but you do not want to lose a position offer because you present yourself in an unfavorable light.

There are four ways to discuss your weaknesses. You can discuss a negative that is not related to the position being considered. For instance, for a job selling men's clothing, you might indicate that you do not enjoy computer programming. You might also discuss a negative the interviewer already knows about, or you could discuss a negative that you have improved upon. If you have trouble with statistics, you might say "I don't particularly like statistics, but I have taken stat courses and feel much more comfortable with them now." Finally, you might discuss a negative that can also be a positive. You might say "I tend to be impatient with people who do not work hard. I tend to be a workaholic and enjoy getting things done, but I don't like to see people procrastinate."[12]

QUESTIONS YOU CAN ASK

- How did you get started with this company?
- What do you like most about your position?
- Can you give me an example of a successful person's career track in sales?
- What is the potential in this position?
- What advice would you give someone entering this field?
- Can you please describe your training program for me?

Specific questions that show you have researched the company are also useful, such as;

- I've read that you have just introduced a new product. What has the response been?

or

- *I've read that you have just acquired a new subsidiary. What effect is that having on this division?*

[11]See H. Anthony Medley, *Sweaty Palms: The Neglected Art of Being Interviewed* (Belmont, Calif.: Lifetime Learning Publications, 1978), p. 60.

[12]See Ronald L. Krannich and William J. Banis, *Moving out of Education: The Education Guide to Career Management and Change* (Chesapeake, Va.: Progressive Concepts, Inc., 1981) pp. 173–175.

Questions you can ask There are also a number of questions you can ask an interviewer during an interview. You should be careful not to ask sensitive or embarassing questions, but questions that show you have done your homework usually impress interviewers.

An important factor in asking questions is how you ask them. If you use a brash tone, you will tend to put the interviewer on the defensive. On the other hand, if you are sincere and ask the questions in a nonthreatening, inquisitive manner, they can help you.

At the conclusion of an interview you may want to summarize a few of your key credentials, express enthusiasm about working for the company, and express appreciation to the interviewer for his or her time.[13]

Interview Follow-up

If you are interested in the position, it is generally a good idea to write a follow-up letter after interviews, thanking interviewers for their time and indicating your continued interest in the position. It is a good idea to try to customize this letter by bringing up some point that was made during the interview. For example, you might say, "The training program you outlined and the career opportunities with your firm sound appealing. I was particularly impressed with the commitment your firm has to continuing education." This customizing will make your letter much more personal. Figure 18.3 gives an example of a thank-you letter.

Firm Visit

You should understand that if a firm thinks enough of you to invite you for a second interview, your chances of getting the position are quite good. The firm normally pays your expenses on the interview trip. In addition, the firm will give up several members of its management and sales teams for one or two days. The total cost amounts to a substantial investment on the part of the firm. For these reasons you should relax and ask the types of questions that will get at the points you consider to be important for sound decision making.

Generally, on a company visit, you will see a number of people—members of management, personnel, and other salespeople. You should be aware that you are constantly being evaluated, even when you go out to dinner or have lunch. Often the various people will compare notes, so you must be consistent in your objectives and statements. This does not mean that you cannot be natural and relaxed, but you must be aware that you are being evaluated.

Employment Offer

The final step in the process is the employment offer. You should expect to get several rejections for every offer you receive. Remember that from the perspective of employers this is a matching process—matching their needs

[13]See David Gootnick, "Selling Yourself in Interviews," *MBA Magazine* (October–November 1978), p. 37; or Nick DeBari, "Closing the Job Interview," *Sales and Marketing Management,* Vol. 133 (November 12, 1984), pp. 63–64.

1947 Grace Avenue
Springfield, Massachusetts 01281
November 17, 1981

James R. Quinn, Director
Personnel Department
Davis Enterprises
2290 Cambridge Street
Boston, Massachusetts 01181

Dear Mr. Quinn:

Thank you for the opportunity to interview yesterday for the Sales Trainee position. I enjoyed meeting you and learning more about Davis Enterprises. You have a fine staff and a sophisticated approach to marketing.

Your organization appears to be growing in a direction which parallels my interests and career goals. The interview with you and your staff confirmed my initial positive impressions of Davis Enterprises, and I want to reiterate my strong interest in working for you. My prior experience in operating office equipment plus my training in communication would enable me to progress steadily through your training program and become a productive member of your sales team.

Again, thank you for your consideration. If you need any additional information from me, please feel free to call.

Yours truly,

Gail S. Topper

Gail S. Topper

FIGURE 18.3 Example of a thank-you letter—after the interview. SOURCE: Ronald L. Krannich and William J. Banis, *High Impact Resumes and Letters* (Manassas, Va.: Impact Publications, 1982), p. 129.

with your qualifications. Regardless of how qualified you are, you may not meet their current needs. Thus, you should never take the rejection personally. Rejection does not mean that you are not qualified or that they do not like you; it only means that you do not meet their current needs.

Generally speaking, you should not accept an offer on the spot. You are better off taking some time to think the offer over and to weigh the decision. Accepting a job is an important decision, and you should make it carefully.

If you have more than one offer, you may want to compare them by evaluating the pluses and minuses of each offer. One offer may have a good location, lower starting salary, good fringe benefits, and good long-term potential; another might have a much higher starting salary but less long-term potential. When weighing the opportunities, you should consider your likes and dislikes and strengths and weaknesses. Potential for growth and career advancement are also important.

CAREER OPPORTUNITIES

An increasing number of companies provide a Y-shaped career track for the young person entering the sales force (Figure 18.4). Once you have finished your initial sales training and have demonstrated competence as a salesperson, you may pursue a rewarding, lifetime career as a salesperson; or you may aspire to progress into management. Definite opportunities exist along each path, and there are incentives for achieving excellence in both.

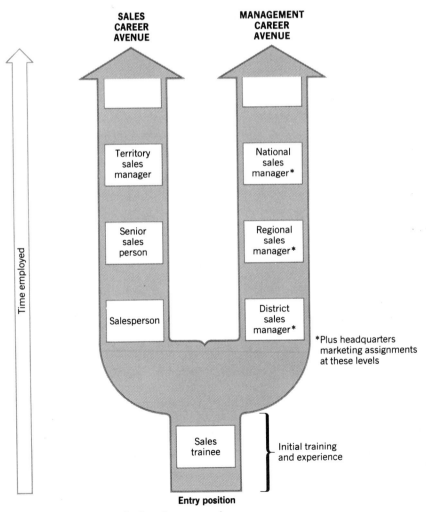

FIGURE 18.4 Career paths for sales personnel.

Career Avenues

There are many different types of opportunities in selling available to you; remember the many types of sales described in Chapter 1.[14]

Sales career avenue In most firms, there will be a greater number of openings along the sales career path than on the management path. One firm differentiates three positions in a sales career: a salesperson, senior salesperson, and territory sales manager. An individual may progress through all three steps while selling in the same territory. The differentiation occurs on the basis of competitive position, contribution to profit, amount and share of business in each category of account, and effectiveness in handling accounts. This company provides a higher salary base for each successive step of the sales career avenue as well as other special incentives.

As another example, 3M has installed a system for its sales force that allows outstanding salespeople to stay in the field as they move up through four different sales position levels, each with higher salaries and perks. The higher-level salespeople are expected to do more than sell. They are expected to train people, help in market research, field-test new products, or handle larger territories.[15]

Some companies provide advancement in the sales career avenue through transfer to a larger, more lucrative territory. One food processor categorizes territories by volume as A, B, and C. The salesperson in an A territory may earn double the average income of those in C territories. Other firms accomplish advancement by moving a salesperson to larger and more important accounts. In some situations, advancement comes in the form of increased responsibility for decisions in such matters as commitment of technical resources and pricing. Often, persons who advance to a higher point on the sales career avenue outearn the managers to whom they report. This creates no inequity in view of the salesperson's increased contribution to company well-being.

It is important to remember that with some firms, especially industrial firms, a career sales track is often a very attractive choice. Salespeople for these firms are usually very well paid and may earn substantially more than many managers in their firm. Often salespeople in these firms have no desire to get into management but are very content with their autonomy and earnings.

Management career avenue The opportunities are numerous and varied for those who aspire to move up the management career avenue. Initial advancement most often comes in the form of supervisory responsibility over other sales representatives. The position may be designated as district manager, branch manager, division manager, or field sales supervisor. To achieve success in such an assignment, you must be able to communicate your sales

---

[14]For further discussion of different types of sales, see Kenneth Haas, *Opportunities in Sales and Marketing* (Skokie, ILL.: VGM Career Horizons, 1982).

[15]"Dual Tracks for Low-Tech Employees, Too," *New York Times* (Sunday, November 16, 1986), p. 4F.

knowledge and skills to others in order to enlist their efforts. Depending on the organizational structure of the firm, such persons may, in addition to their "people" responsibilities, be responsible for market analysis, sales forecasting, and, in some cases the management of local inventories: a definite promotional ladder leads from this first-echelon post in field sales management to the position of national or general sales manager.

Less frequently, various parts of the regional marketing organization offer opportunities for promotion. Field sales experience is viewed by some companies as essential for advancement to product planning and management. Firms reason that a person needs such experience to understand products and product groups properly through the user's eyes. If this career avenue is followed, the initial assignment is likely to be as an assistant in a group handling one of the less important products or product groups of the company. The person is advanced by being offered positions with greater responsibility in the same group or, by moving to a more important product or product group.

Another movement on the management career avenue may be to national accounts management or into sales promotion, advertising, or merchandising. In all of these, the sales and marketing intelligence aspects of field selling have direct application. Sales representatives who show talent for quantitative and financial aspects of their work may move into sales analysis and forecasting. Here, field sales experience supplies a person with a feel for the data being analyzed, which is difficult to obtain in any other way.

Finally, a person may start out in selling and then advance into some other part of the enterprise. Experience gained in the field may be especially useful in research and development as well as in purchasing. In research and development, the salesperson's knowledge and experience with products in use complements the engineering and design expertise of research personnel. In purchasing, people with sales expertise have an appreciation for the sales representatives calling on them. They also have a sound basis for evaluating offerings.

Charting a Career Path

When you are looking at your career, it is wise to develop a plan. You should set objectives for yourself and develop an action plan for reaching your objective. Finally, you should evaluate your progress from time to time. When you look at positions, you should ask prospective employers what alternative career paths exist and ask yourself whether the company can offer you the type of career you are seeking. If, for instance, you are interested in a career as a professional salesperson, can the company offer you the type of sales position you are seeking and the financial rewards you desire from your career? On the other hand, if you seek a career in sales management, you must be in a company offering opportunites to advance into a management position. You must also plan your career so that you acquire the necessary experience to move into management.

If you do not plan your career and manage your progress, you may not be happy with the way it evolves. Being in the right place at the right time is not always possible unless you have carefully evaluated opportunities and career potential. Many salespeople or others drift from position to position or stay too long in one position because they have not set concrete goals or career plans for reaching these goals. Planning will help you to make better decisions at each step of your career.[16] Career planning is an important skill and one you should develop.[17]

CONTINUED GROWTH

After you have found your first position in selling, it is important that you continue to learn and to update your knowledge. There are a number of steps you can take to continue your professional growth and enhance your career, including a talent audit, sales training, continuing education, and professional development. Some of these activities will be provided by your firm, and some you will have to seek out on your own.

Talent Audit

The first specific step you should take in order to continue development is to conduct a talent audit, noting your strengths and weaknesses as specifically as possible.[18] If you are to find positive ways to keep up, you must come to grips with such question as: What are your weak areas of knowledge? What topics currently being discussed are foreign to you? What aspects of your position are undergoing rapid change? What do you need to know in order to maintain upward mobility in the firm?

Inasmuch as it is difficult to be objective about yourself, your personal judgments should be supplemented by other information. Appraisal by a superior may provide useful insights; close friends may contribute valuable ideas. Periodically, it may be worthwhile to obtain a comprehensive evaluation from a professional source such as an industrial psychologist.

Sales Training

One of the activities you can engage in is sales training. Your company will usually provide you with some sales training, although you can also obtain training from trade associations, universities, and other programs.

The content of sales training programs will differ considerably, yet there are still five basic areas that most programs should cover: products, markets, sales policies, selling techniques, and work patterns.

---

[16]For an interesting discussion of viewing your career as a life cycle over time, see Marvin A. Jolson, "The Salesman's Career Cycle," *Journal of Marketing*, Vol. 38, No. 3 (July 1974), pp. 39–46.

[17]There are a number of good books on career planning: Arthur G. Kirn, *Lifework Planning*, third edition (Hartford, Conn.: Arthur G. Kirn & Associates, 1974); Alan N. Schoonmaker, *Executive Career Strategy* (New York: American Management Associations, 1971).

[18]This section was adapted from W. J. E. Crissy and Donald W. Jackson, Jr., "The Executive and the Knowledge Dilemma," *Arizona Business* (June–July 1974), pp. 22–23. Reprinted with permission of *Arizona Business*, a monthly publication of The Center for Business Research, College of Business, Arizona State University, Tempe, Arizona 85287.

Product knowledge There is probably more emphasis on products than on any other aspect covered in most sales training programs. These sessions cover features of the product as well as its application to the customers' problems. In addition, these sessions frequently review the competition's product offering. This knowledge helps you to emphasize the aspects of your product that give it its greatest advantages.

Market knowledge Market knowledge is also important. New salespersons have to be taught how to identify potential customers and evaluate their future buying potential.

Sales policies As a salesperson, you must be aware of any company policies that affect you; these could range from the sales compensation plan to the firm's policy on cooperative advertising, shipping specifications, returns, and credit. If you are to be effective, you must understand the firm's policies that affect you directly and be able to explain them to customers.

Selling skills A major portion of the training session is often spent on selling skills. Most firms provide you with some classroom experience and then send you into the field for some firsthand experience. After several months of training you will be brought back for more intensive sales training. Regardless of the intitial sales training, most sales executives believe that it is important to provide salespeople with a way to update and review their selling skills periodically.

Effective work patterns Many sales training sessions will teach you how to use time more efficiently. This is particularly important for salespersons who work alone most of the time with little or no direct supervision. Topics such as routing, preparation of reports, call frequency, credit evaluation, and service responsibilities are discussed during these sessions.

Continuing Education

Given the likelihood of continued advancements in knowledge and the accelerated change in the physical and social environment, it is evident that education must be a continuing activity if you are to acquire new skills and be well informed. The third specific step to which you should allocate time and energy is a personal continuing education program. This may encompass, for example, planned reading, participation in formal courses, and exploration and use of cultural centers in the community.

Reading programs Reading programs may take many forms. Some firms carry out company-sponsored reading programs. These are usually conducted in conjunction with formal training or conferences. The company may also develop reading lists to aid you in the selection of reading material. A number of associations and universities also sponsor reading programs.

Any reading program has two key objectives. One is to remain current about changes in the internal and external business environments. Leading business and professional publications serve this purpose well. *The Wall*

Street Journal, Business Week, and *The Harvard Business Review,* for instance, enable you to keep abreast of many current developments.

The other objective is to acquire depth of knowledge in areas directly related to your position. The *Journal of Personal Selling and Sales Management* should be a key source of information on selling. In addition to articles, the journal also publishes book reviews and abstracts of current articles on selling and sales management. Books may also be useful. Many journals review books, a screening process that allows you to utilize your reading time in a way that will be most productive. Finally, you may also wish to improve your technical or product knowledge by reading brochures, technical reports, or other company literature. The more knowledge you have of these matters, the better prepared you will be.

Formal courses Formal courses may also be used to keep abreast of new trends. These may be credit courses leading to a degree, or noncredit seminars designed to enrich your selling skills. Many business schools provide such programs for salespeople. In addition, some business schools offer night credit programs leading to a Master of Business Administration degree.

Your firm may sponsor some seminars. Associations such as Sales Marketing Executives or the American Management Association also hold seminars.

Cultural development The tempo of business, the knowledge explosion, and the demands of business all combine to keep you from leading a well-rounded, full life. Time must be allocated to your personal life, to reading for enjoyment, to participating in the cultural life of the community, and to engaging in avocational and recreational pursuits. Far too many people immerse themselves in their work, this not only narrows their life but impairs the "people" skills they need for relating to others in business.

Professional Development

The fourth specific step is to map a program of professional development, interrelated with the previous activities, namely, talent audit, sales traning, and continuing education.

Personal affiliation with clubs and associations ranging from community service to industry, trade, and professional groups will help you develop professionally

Sometimes these affiliations have indirect career benefits by increasing your contacts or reputation, but some affiliations also offer direct on-the-job skills. For instance, you may wish to strengthen your speaking skills by joining a group such as Toastmasters. You can achieve more by limiting such memberships to those in which you can take an active, participative role; just joining has very limited development value. The payoff in terms of professional development is threefold. First, through active participation you develop your talents, in particular your interpersonal skills, tact, and poise. Second, you learn from the knowledge and skills displayed by others. Third, your affiliation enables you to know "who's who" and "what's what" in the community, local business, your own industry, and the appropriate professional groups.

Furthermore, you also have a great deal to give in such associations. Your people skills and communciation skills are valuable commodities to any organization. Thus your participation benefits both you and the organizations you serve.

In terms of your continued growth, you are faced with a definite dilemma. You are required to possess increased amounts of knowledge; yet on a relative basis you fall farther and farther behind. Faced with this dilemma, you may adjust positively by planning ways to increase your knowledge and then carrying out your plans, or you may adjust negatively by ignoring the available information or refusing to try to learn.

SUMMARY

Your future career in sales or management depends on your ability to market and sell yourself, and to manage your career. Career management consists of three important activities: finding your first selling position, analyzing various career opportunities, and continuing your education to keep yourself well informed.

In order to find your first selling position, you must first do a self-audit to determine your strengths and weaknesses, your likes and dislikes. Next you must go through the various aspects of the employment-seeking process to find a position: prospecting for various openings, developing a resume, writing cover letters to accompany your resume, filling out application blanks, preparing for interviews, and being interviewed. During the interview you should watch your nonverbal mannerisms, be prepared for key questions, and ask questions of the interviewer.

After the interview, you should follow up with a letter thanking the interviewer. You may also expect to be invited for a company visit if the employer is interested in you. Finally, you may receive several offers and you must weigh the advantages and disadvantages of each offer.

A number of career opportunities are available to you after you have held your initial position as a salesperson. One attractive opportunity in many firms is a sales career avenue, whereby you continue to grow and advance as a salesperson. Often the earnings and autonomy in these positions are substantial. Another career path goes into sales management or other marketing positions. The experience you have gained as a salesperson will be invaluable.

In order to manage your career, you should chart a path indicating your career objectives and your plan for reaching these objectives. You should also frequently evaluate your progress. Managing your career rather than just letting it evolve is a key to success.

Finally, you must continue to grow and acquire current knowledge. Here your first step is to take a talent audit to find out what information and training you need. Armed with this knowledge, you can then gain knowledge through sales training, continuing education, and professional development.

Sales training usually centers on product knowledge, market knowledge, sales policies, selling skills, and effective work patterns. Reading programs, formal courses, and attention to your cultural development are means of continuing your education. Your professional development may be enhanced by joining civic groups and professional associations.

PROBLEMS

1. Describe in your own words the benefits of the self-audit.
2. Which of the various sources of employment opportunities do you think would be most useful for you to find the type of position you are interested in?
3. What is the purpose of a resume? What items should be included in a resume? What items should be omitted?
4. Why is it important to research the prospective employer?
5. What characteristics do interviewers look for in applicants for selling positions?
6. Providing that the firm you are considering has an attractive sales career avenue, what are the advantages of following that avenue?
7. What content is appropriate to a training program for new salespeople?

EXERCISE 18

Objectives: To apply concepts of the self-audit

To illustrate the importance of formulating answers to prospective questions.

To develop a current resume and desired resume.

PART A Self-Audit
First, specify the type of sales position you are applying for. Remember that your qualifications are always judged in relation to the type of position you are applying for. Next, make a list of your strengths and weaknesses for this particular position. Then describe your weaknesses in terms that you could use in an interview.

PART B Formulate Answers to Prospective Questions
Take any ten of the questions in Table 18.3, apply them to the position you described in Part A, and develop a well-thought-out answer to each question.

PART C Resumes
Develop a current resume based on your current accomplishments and activities. Then devise a resume that you would like to be able to present when the time comes for real job seeking. By comparing the two, you may find some gaps. This offers you the opportunity to see what you have to do now to build your future resume during the remainder of your academic life.

Case 18-1 Henderson Electronics

Mike Scott, who is a senior at Southwest Texas University, has just completed a trip to Henderson Electronics. In the early spring of this year, Del Dowing, a sales manager for Henderson, interviewed Mike on the campus for a position in the firm's field sales operation. Mr. Dowing had been impressed with Mike during the interview and had invited him to Houston to spend two days visiting Henderson's home office.

While at Henderson's, Mike was treated extremely well. He had opportunities to talk with such people as the director of marketing, on down to a sales trainee who had been hired three weeks earlier for a position similar to the one Mike was considering. At the end of the second day, Mr. Dowing offered Mike a job as a junior salesperson at a base salary of $18,500. The second year his salary would be adjusted so that his base would be $16,000, but he would also have a 3 percent commission on sales, which should give him an income in the range of $31,000 to $34,000 for the second year.

Henderson Electronics manufactures and sells electrical conduit for buildings. The firm has a good reputation for selling high-quality products and for providing good service and technical support. Henderson's products are sold to two types of accounts. Approximately 35 percent of their sales are made to wholesalers who sell conduit to hardware and electrical supply outlets. The balance of their sales are direct to contractors who are bidding on large jobs. These contractors are particularly interested in obtaining Henderson's technical advice on what types of conduit they should use and on having a "competitive price."

Henderson salespeople are expected to handle most of the technical advice themselves. If they are bidding on a particularly large contract, or if they run into a problem they cannot deal with, they are encouraged to contact the home office for assistance. If necessary, Henderson can provide practically instantaneous technical backup for its sales representatives.

Over 80 percent of Henderson's sales force have graduated from a junior college or a four-year college or university. However, less than 30 percent of these individuals have a four-year technical degree. For this reason Henderson runs an extensive technical school for its new salespeople. At the end of the six-week program, the junior salespeople are expected to be able to deal with most of the technical problems they will run into.

After they complete the technical school, they spend six months assisting in a sales territory. This is an attempt to give the young people "on-the-job" training in both selling and solving technical conduit problems. After this six-month period is completed, they become full-fledged sales representatives and are given a territory of their own. In the beginning they can count on a little extra help from the sales manager in handling their accounts.

Henderson does not promise any new sales trainees a particular territory until they have completed the training program. However, most new salespersons are initially assigned to one of the smaller territories located in the Southwest. New salespeople will frequently have to spend several days on the road each week before being able to return to their home base. If they do well, they will be promoted by being assigned to a territory with a larger sales potential.

Mike Scott began his college career at Southwest Texas as a mechanical engineering student. After one year, he found himself on scholastic probation. He then transferred to the Business School, where his grades steadily improved. His grade-point average is now a B − and he has slightly over a B in his marketing classes. Mike told his academic advisor recently that "I really could have made it in engineering, but I guess I just was not interested enough in the subject to study."

Mike has been fairly active socially in college. He rushed a fraternity in his freshman year but could not become active because of his probationary status. Once he was restored to good standing, he never went back to the fraternity. He was elected vice-president of the ski club in his junior year, but was not elected president in his senior year. One of his friends stated, "It is too bad about Mike losing the election. Normally the vice-president is elevated to the presidency the next year. However, Mike tends to be a little too extroverted at times, and he gives people the feeling that he's trying to take over. I think that's what his problem was."

Mike has always been described as highly motivated. He has a definite interest in making money. When he was vice-president of the ski club, he managed the drive for new members, which brought in twice as much revenue as the club had ever had. Mike told his advisor, "I might enjoy working for myself some day. If this doesn't work out, I definitely want to get into a top-management position with the firm that I'm working for."

1. Does there seem to be a good match between Henderson and Mike?
2. What qualities does Mike have that would make him a valuable employee to Henderson? What qualities might cause him problems?
3. Would you recommend to Mike that he accept this job, assuming that he has also been offered a job as a bank trainee in the trust department of a Houston Bank?

Case 18-2 Victor Publishing Co.

Janice Spence is preparing for an interview with Victor Publishing Company. Victor is a small publishing firm located in Madison, Wisconsin. It specializes in texts for the college or university social science market.

Selling books to professors is a very unusual type of selling. First, professors are frequently given complimentary books with the hope that they will adopt them for their own classes. Very few books are ever sold directly to faculty members. In addition, the selling activity must be very low key. Professors must feel that they are deciding for themselves what they will use in their courses. As a result, textbook salespeople spend a great deal of their time just trying to make each account aware of what books the firm has to offer. In addition, salespeople try to point out the key points that make particular books different and better than any others.

Janice is just graduating from college and has always gotten along well with her professors, and so she is interested in the job that was recommended to her by her father who is a friend of the sales manager for Victor.

In preparing for her interview, Janice goes to the library and finds that
because Victor is so small and privately held, there is no information available on the company. In questioning several of her professors, she finds that
Victor is generally well respected in publishing and has some good titles.

1. What other sources of information should Janice consult?
2. Prepare a list of questions that Janice could ask in her interview to find
   out more about the position and the company.

Subject Index

Name/Author Index

Company/Organization